When one finds themselves lost; let your mind start a journey
through this strange new world you inhabit.

Leave all thoughts of the world you knew before
explore what is.
Do so by letting go of what was.

Let your soul take you where you long to be.
It will guide you towards wisdom and enlightenment.

Close your eyes and imagine building a brave new world
Make the bizarre familiar
Understand that no one can take the journey for you,
nor can you be spared from it.

Survive the experience and you will live like you have never lived before.
Fail and be forever trapped in a rabbit-hole of your own creation.

For U.

Find yourself hidden in your words and thoughts.
Always guided towards a truth

Author • Publisher • Editor • Illustrator • Photographer • Designer: Philip A. Bonneau
Bonneau, Philip Arthur 1982—

Printing History
Library of Congress Cataloging-in-Publication Data
Summary: Based from 'Curated Jellyfish: A Paradise Lost' 2019 original copyright number, TXU2-173-740. Version 5 in this capacity renamed after being underwater to 'Curated Jellyfish: A Paradise Stolen' Only version 1 submitted to copyright.
ISBN: Refer to lists provided in forthcoming pages
Copyright Number: Tx9-206-106 Registration Date: 12/6/2022, Decision 12/22/22

FIRST EDITION: **Printed as self-published**
Production by handwritten Mid-2019
SECOND EDITION: Printed as self-published, see notes
THIRD EDITION: Printed as self-published, see notes
FOURTH EDITION: Printed as self-published, see notes
FIFTH EDITION: Digitally transcribed and worked on from

November 15, 2022—December 5, 2022.
Sent to copyright, 12/05/2022 under new name
'Curated Jellyfish: A Paradise Stolen'
Difference in body text from last produced physical version to this one denoted in this color text. Major differences from copyright submitted book of First Edition. All introductions prior to the opener page is new.

Printed in the United States of America?

The industry knows a torn cover for a reason.
What happens in the digital world in that regard in contemporary settings?

As my head goes through references of all sorts, it is impossible to ever say something is a complete work of fiction and any occurrences inferred are probably more real than you think as even the act of writing anything is a learned behavior. I suppose to be an author, you have to disclaim that based on entire past life and present life that you were either directly or subconsciously affected by your entire life experience to date.

To not acknowledge that is to write a book with no words. Blank on every page, but even that a creative decision that came from somewhere where one must cite inspiration.

Imagine a book (2,3,4,5). All white pages or maybe a slight off color. Cover nothing on it. Nothing on the back. The bleaching process of word now a sliver of what it was in years of growth that occurred to get there. Even then the artistry behind book-binding to consider artistic direction and understanding the sacrifice and time spent to create or allow others to create and articulate.

Maybe a book of black pages where you are meant to not write in an additive way but subtractive. A book that invites handwritten collaboration becomes a collaborative copyright in final output. What happens with any journal wondering where nature goes with that statement?

A digital version to bypass that? Same thing applies with technology and continual updates to software paid for. Once you go digital, regions expand from places of origin to places of interpretation.

To deal with darkness and light and the spectrum of color theory, you need to look at it both ways. Both a price paid by the author, creators and unsuspecting contributors one way or another.

Maybe the digital read, but try to not impede. I will be coming to an answer for myself on something. Where it is already written in the proverbial aspect of, 'Once you read this…'

To make any book is a gift of insight, but also nature. There is the combination of what we have inside and what we use to let that be expressed. I suppose communication comes in many forms. To think about footsteps is to think of the first time someone or something found it beautiful or something to retain. Even in nature there is expression and artistry not appreciated and often discounted. A squirrel noticed today eating a leaf. (Or was it a butterfly?) I imagine they are vegetarians. Another squirrel in the square, I feed it when it comes knowing it's story comes from a partnership. Trust built.

I suppose it is fair to say that to write in that blank book is to acknowledge a life was lost in that process one way or another. Or both understand transformative living and that identity changes in group efforts and the process of time. Somewhere a tree was cut down to produce that book and a lineage broken. Maybe even in this book if physically produced. The seeds it produced hopefully grew to saplings and they grew before either dying naturally or by human hands so that they could express themselves.

Literally and metaphorically.

I imagine every book should acknowledge life was lost in the process of these writings (although simply a preference for this book and discussed elsewhere in timelines). Maybe it is just anything associated with me on that thought pattern challenging the consequential or coincidental and saying it is a little harder in the digital age to say so while probably pointing conversation elsewhere.

I like the idea that for every copy 1 tree planted to make up for the quest of knowledge knowing an entire ecosystem was laid waste in the process here. (Again literal and figurative). Respect nature on your quest and understand that as you add to that book or any other, something was subtracted from this world. What was subtracted from mine to add to yours? What can be additive to ours knowing once you read this I am here anyways as with any author.

I suppose as you plant an idea elsewhere, conceptually think of the life taken and use your words wisely. Internal thoughts. Perhaps internal critiques. Or perhaps simply draw 3 and combine from there in Uno discussions of what I've had to experience over the years and what simply could had been one thing or another. There have been Skips and there has been many cards drawn. Perhaps now a Reverse and look at things differently. Who has more cards and does it even matter in this regard? One wants less and the other wants more. Depends on the game played.

In the digital realm, the subtractive process is in time and thought. Dependant on electricity + program designers and enters into a realm of what is being used is not fully understood by everyone. We are in the dark on the capabilities of what others plant in your garden before going into the name of plants or fonts or who created what in combined effort towards a final output that simply continues to create from there and grow.

To bring words from darkness is to bring to light that the expression of the hand-written form has changed to keystrokes. Every font designed by an artist and affects the way your story is told and read. Do we acknowledge the designer of that font before proceeding? Collaborative efforts made from a single font choice...connections made with an unknown artist before a stroke of genius. Do we acknowledge that as a creative collaboration? Can we say anything is solely ours anymore in the test of understanding right and wrong anymore? To what something solely yours means no one will translate, comprehend or have any desire to be a part of it because it is after-all, 'Yours' with a completely different 'Do not touch'.

I find it important to recognize collaboration and unknown artists. Neither form un-pure of a collaborative experience. What was additive was definitely subtractive as well in any regard. Namesakes matter just as much as twist things around ever so slightly and others get away with lack of citation and inspiration. Imagine the hardship of any book cited in reference of an author's total life experience. How annotated is that book in any regard until going back to the fact that secrets everywhere in life and completely different in corporate structure vs. that of any author, artist waiting to be financed or picked up.

I suppose thoughts come from somewhere. Life experience, instinct and nurtured ideals directly or subconsciously come from environment and the elements. Do we acknowledge that?

I like my disclaimer. It starts to look at things in limitations and in aspects of things unbound prior, but in the aspect of things produced physically and digitally. As I translate yet again from a fully paid for computer, with paid for internet service from an application service that I paid for that whatever questions rest prior, it boils down to the question of 'why is someone going proverbial on the aspect of ownership in a realm of key-strokes?'

When questioning things, it is probably best that everything comes from intention. Some mistakes, some not, some maybe even subliminally added. 4 years towards that answer of real world non-fiction aspect that I simply coined as 'False Fiction' elsewhere with the same definition.

I suppose as subtraction now begins, eventually a blank page over time again. No words. No image. Just a page. Just a life lived and lost. I suppose I'm OK with that. So many unknown lives anyways...what is one more? I'm sure it was weighed in liability and I am sure also discussed elsewhere where I was never included and just kept doing my own thing.

Lost in Time is not a bad place to be. Neither here or there, nor rooted in anything and yet nature could be factored in on give something else life or fade to dust and just collect in the soil with probably still value to give to others. That degrade value is pretty much where we all go one way or another even if we discover our purpose or not.

Where this goes can go anywhere. I need to find focus in my school work and at least contribute to other's ideas and let them grow. Not creatively tapped out at all. I just understand the process of difficult decisions from here. There. Anywhere. I get that much.

_____

Curated Jellyfish: A Paradise Lost

Philip Arthur Bonneau
1:35-1:40 pm EST
January 19, 2022

Copyright Pending applied digitally and received to copyright office @lac.goc on 11.11.2019

Handwritten prior between May 2019 - October 2019 with no internet access to my home. Written in forward and backwards thinking where the date at the front was mid-entry and specific (not a start date).

First hardcopy Edition (Only) ISBN 978-0-46-450525-9 (ordered & paid for by myself Dec.2 2019) (never available to the public)

2ᴺᴰ Version (Softcover) - ISBN 978-0-46-465284-7 (never available to the public) (ordered and paid for by myself) (printing errors fixed from artist mistakes + abberation) (No mistake from hardcopy)

3ʳᵈ Version (Softcover) - ISBN 978-1-71-462580-2 (key elements removed based on psychology & artist intention.)

4ᵗʰ Version (Softcover) - ISBN 978-1-71-473154-1 (major narrative reworked based on feedback & discussion)

5ᵗʰ Version (Unprinted) - No ISBN, based on above (handwritten edits not viewed by anyone.)

Copyright Registration - Txu2 - 173-740 (paper version is on hand)

I requested a copyright pending when fear of stealing works is used & used as a protective measure on such creative properties. This procedure is with standing and tenkable as events arise to warrant investigation I would like to cite one area in this book that was acted on in areas covered by legal rights. The correction between that particular point at-midwest has an effect greater than this book and documented elsewhere. Further points of disruption and consumption available to prove this work has been compromised and taken over.

Citing personal experience, I am protecting my works from a visual art standpoint knowing my handwriting has been compromised and protected at the same time.

Published by Philip Arthur Bonneau
Written by Philip Arthur Bonneau
Photographic works by Philip Arthur Bonneau
Copyright Pending: Philip Arthur Bonneau

As of January 19, 2022 that copyright is pending with the above provable fear. To close this out requires anything not authorized to be reigned in. I, the head on most of protection, have tried my best. I need your help... you need my permission. Blurb was the printer, not the publisher.

P.B.A.   8:16 pm EST
debt spill apples

'#2' January 19, 2022. Copyright Philip A. Bonneau.

#2
Philip Arthur Bonneau
1:35—1:40 pm EST
January 19, 2022

Curated Jellyfish: A Paradise Lost
Copyright Pending applied digitally and received to copyright office @loc.gov on 11.11.2019

Handwritten prior between May 2019—October 2019 with no internet access to my home.
Written in forward and backwards thinking where the date at the front was mid-entry and specific. (Not a start date.)

There are 2 official manuscripts in other people's hands physically.
There are 3 official manuscripts in other people's hands elsewhere.

First hardcopy Edition (Hardback) ISBN 978-0-46-450525-9
(never available to the public) Ordered & Paid for by myself December 2. 2019) although pages do not hold up at the length at this time. Fragility present, there is only 1 copy.

2nd Version (softcover) - ISBN 978-0-46-465284-7
(never available to the public) (ordered and paid for by myself)
-Printing errors fixed from artist's mistakes & elaborations. No mistake from book maker prior. There are 2 copies.

3rd Version (Softcover) - ISBN 978-1-71-462580-2
Key elements removed based on psychology & artist intention. There are 2 copies.

4th version (Softcover) - ISBN 978-1-71-473154-1
Major narrative re-arranged based on feedback & discussion. There are 7 official copies.

5th Version (Unprinted) - No ISBN, based on above.

Handwritten edits not viewed by anyone but myself. There is 1 copy.

Copyright Registration - TXU2-173-740 (paper version on-hand)
I requested a copyright pending when fear of stealing works is valid & used as a protective measure on such creative properties. This procedure is withstand and trackable as events arise to warrant investigation. I would like to cite one area in this book that was acted on in areas covered by legal rights. The connection between that particular point-of-interest has an effect greater than this book and documented elsewhere. Further points of disruption and consumption available to prove this work has been compromised and taken over.

Citing personal experience, I am protecting my works from a visual art standpoint knowing my handwriting has been compromised and protected at the same time.

Published by Philip Arthur Bonneau
Written by Philip Arthur Bonneau
Photographic Works by Philip Arthur Bonneau
Copyright Pending Philip Arthur Bonneau
Illustrator of most works unless called out: Philip Arthur Bonneau
Graphic Designer: Philip Arthur Bonneau
Creative Director: Philip Arthur Bonneau

As of January 19, 2022 that copyright is pending with the above provable fear. To close this out requires anything not authorized to be reigned in. I, the lead on most of protection, have tried my best. I need your help…you need my permission. Blurb was the printer, not the publisher. But they do own Flickr and we are friendly in last hopes.

-Philip A. Bonneau
2:16 pm EST
date still applies.

The hard task of going back and documenting and citing all my references visually. I've ended this book of this and 'starving artist' and those of exploitation.   *End of Excerpt.*

Finished 3:06 pm EST
Jan 19, 2022

Through my personal experience from 2018-2019, not excluding
past, present or future, I'd like to call out that Bloggers have more
protections than you think. This comes from cited connections and attacks
against humanity. The publication of my works is important. What rested
on people's servers unpublished even more protected. To talk about that
invasion is to spell out other ISBNs.

"Building Brave New Secrets" - ISBN 978-0-46-465316-5 (signature also in another area)
    built from blogs on blogger.com. A curated collection prior to Attach 2.0 to
prove a series was worked on since 2014 in that official capacity knowing
it was a life's work with documented childhood art & Heroes. The creation of
the book was to see the difference before/after making life's work was
pretty solid prior. To go into the introduction in particular is a call back
to my teens.

    It is with respect to hear of that invasion as a possibility not yet at 1 but
2 places knowing a "3rd" is in the wings recognizing a 4th. Non-fiction applications
to a search of "Heaven" (Available for sale)

Ugly Simple Truths: A Companion ISBN 978-1-71-416331-1 (Never available for
(Published/Minted Dec 6, 2019)   public sale)
    Another book that falls under the blog protection. Any version outside of
my own is not-authorized and infringement. To build upon that as a basis of
argument is protected by any creator invested in their rights. My story with that
invests in protecting those I loved, cured for and always had the honor of loving.

Ugly Simple Truths ISBN 978-1-71-427264-8 (Jan 11, 2020)
    A book of my (to date) greatest contribution to that series and thinking of others.
Told not to do this and then like saw that she that compromised with those that participated.
Email attacked. Confidentiality compromised. I protected what I could knowing
I never explained the curated aspect of it. My story Your story Ours. Not theirs.
A plan of attack avoided.

Heroes & Villains mentioned often. 2nd edition ISBN 9781714277587
              in my life (Another story)

My theory of dealing with trauma/grief/life
First discussed & pictured in Beautiful Layered Lies (pirated Oct 2014 emailed possibly to me
Published in Blog form Nov. 9, 2016   person only around that time prior)
Solidified in Curated Jellyfish.
"Chasing Jellyworks" never published never finished. mad redux/Duration as I sorted out experience in
300 pages a week. Possibly Stolen. Never hit the internet outside of congested computer
and software to it.

#3
Finished 3:08 om EST
Jan. 19, 2022
Philip Arthur Bonneau (tucked in a corner)

Through my personal experience from 2018—2019, not excluding past, present and future, I'd like to call out that Bloggers have more protection than you think. This comes from cited conversation and attacks against humanity. The publication of my works is important. What rested on people's servers unpublished even more protected. To talk about that invasion is to spell out ISBNs. - Philip A. Bonneau(hand-signed)

"Building Brave New Secrets" - ISBN 978-0-46-465316-5
Built from blogs on blogger.com. A curated collection prior to Atlanta 2.0 to it was a life's work with documented childhood art & theories. The creation of the book was to see the difference before/after realizing life's work was pretty solid prior. To go into the introduction in particular is a call back to my teens.
It was with regret to hear of that invasion as a possibility not just at 1 but 1 places knowing a 3rd is in the wings recognizing a 4th. Non-fiction applications to a search of 'Heaven" (Available for Sale) (Since removed after the writing of this date) There are 2 printed official copies.

Ugly Simple Truths: A Companion. ISBN 978-1-71-416331-1 (Never available for public Sale)
(Published/Printed Dec. 6, 2019)
Another book that falls under the blog protection. Any version outside my own is not-authorized and infringement. To build upon that as a basis of argument is protected by every creator invested in their rights. My story with that invests in protecting those I loved, cared for and always had the honor of knowing. (This would definitely apply to Building Brave New Secrets and any blog post published or unpublished as I have retained them all and chose to put them in order and edit to my choosing) There are 3 printed official copies.

Ugly Simple Truths ISBN 978-1-71-427264-8 (Jan 11, 2020)

A book of my (to date) greatest contribution to that series and thinking of others. Told not to do this and then later see that compromised with those that participated. Email attacked. Confidentiality compromised. I protected what I could knowing I never explained the curated aspect of it.
My story. Your story. Ours. Not theirs. There are 2 official printed copies and one misprint.

A plan of attack avoided.
_____

Heroes+Villains mentions often in my life. Another story. 2nd edition ISBN 9-781714277537
I own all rights to the first edition as well. (26-30 versions exist officially.)
_____

My theory of dealing with trauma/grief/life
First discussed and published in "Beautiful Layered Lies" (printed Oct. 2011, emailed privately to one person only around that time prior of initial writing)
Published in Blog form Nov. 9, 2016
Solidified in Curated Jellyfish.

"Chasing Jabberwocks". 2021 never published. Never finished. Misdirection/ Direction as I stated out experience in 300 pages in a week.
Possibly stolen. Never hit the internet outside of connected computer and software to it. Handwritten edits not viewed by anyone but myself. There is 1 copy.

Copyright Registration - TXU2-173-740 (paper version on-hand)
I requested a copyright pending when fear of stealing works is valid & used as a protective measure on such creative properties. This procedure is withstand and trackable as events arise to warrant investigation. I would like to cite one area in this book that was acted on in areas covered by legal rights. The connection between that particular point-of-interest has an effect greater than this book and documented elsewhere. Further points of disruption and consumption available to prove this work has been compromised and taken over.

Citing personal experience, I am protecting my works from a visual art standpoint knowing my handwriting has been compromised and protected at the same time.

As of January 19, 2022 that copyright is pending with the above provable fear. To close this out requires anything not authorized to be reigned in. I, the lead on most of protection, have tried my best. I need your help…you need my permission. Blurb was the printer, not the publisher. But they do own Flickr and we are friendly in last hopes.

-Philip A. Bonneau
2:16 pm EST
date still applies.

The hard task of going back and documenting and citing all my references visually. I've ended this book of this and 'starving artist' and those of exploitation.

End of Excerpt.

When it comes to a disclaimer in this regard, it is important to note this book was submitted to copyright in November 11, 2019. The path had one way or another made it back to copyright one way or another in what was importance or what was disclosure.

There is the inescapable aspect of someone authorizing keystrokes of computers that exists and the damage done since of concepts and property worked on well before even entering the adult workforce that was impeded on and took a lifetime to get to only to see it translated one way or another without my compensation while I have to continue on fighting things I should never do alone and what could have been resolved elsewhere or long ago while banking on my suffering or even my suicide. At this point, forget that aspect as I know I found I am fighting something far bigger than I or my family while my family suffered just as much as I from the integration aspect of non-compensation elsewhere.

It is understood the audacity of incorporating a book in multiple fronts in years of work and millions of dollars leading to billions in revenue while still I address the aspects of fairness from a viewership point of 'Once you read this..', artist rights or that of franchisees and their property to sustain. I imagine in any capacity, where my pass is laid is in no one directly told me, no one wanted to tell me and if they wanted no harm to me it was probably because they had a good thing going on the creative concept and exploitation aspect of things.

This book, written prior to my start of a Masters Program at The Savannah College of Art and Design was compromised. It is SCAD's obligation to protect their students and employees and later in life it is understood they failed in that regard in multiple fronts. Personally, Professionally and in regards to most workplace condition laws of The United States before going into the 195 countries that also invested in them while this was written and to be protected. In any regard, this book was acted on in multiple fronts and whatever story came out of it afterwards is not in this book as this was before education and at least I was given 1.5 years reprieve before the attackers came back in and did what they already did.

It is my right as my privacy was taken from me, my security was taken from me, my copyrighted works taken from me and the continual aspects of repeat behavior by others, that I present my diary with my final edits in an official 5th edition before I have to once again fight a battle on my own saying there is a difference to be granted a right to sue and not know how to do that in impeded aspects on a technological aspect in any capacity while knowing what I am protecting.

Someone saw an in and took it. That is not this book and the biggest difference between this book and others, is the main aspect of my SCAD experience is simply in EEOC and was not even in my private writings of later that you have to get about 1600 pages into what I wrote before I even discussed workplace aspects and it was limited to my last week of employment or hope in doing what should had been required of removing me from ADA scenarios and straight up illegality.

I stand by my words back in 2019. I stood by them in Sworn EEOC testimony and further more in copyright aspects of 'Curated Jellyfish: A Paradise Lost". In whatever introduction, I am aware in the digital age anyone would be ready to sue in this regard one way or another. I already filed against the Disney Corporation at this point to no response so that knocks them out of contention at this point. I state properly who did not leave me alone or let me live and I state properly who choice to disclose or not sources, entry points or otherwise.

In total disregard to my privacy, my life or my family or loved ones...I eventually get to openness, but not a single company of advantage out to gain my property then can cry fowl now and all you can do is realize as I process what I wrote in 2019, it is 2022 and nothing from the end of 2019 to now is in this book outside of subtle acknowledgment of the damage done from inaction then and not talking to I.

In any regard, I wrote this book and you can track the reactions based on my keystrokes now or completely have a heart to heart with someone.

My property impeded on and I reported properly what happened in 2019 and since then. I'm still here and in any regard, writers advantage and proven at this point that it takes me a minute to get to names, but there is no libel there, their company can say one way or another or their parents can say one thing or another. Whatever occurred from one single sick day of a fixed-term employee means nothing after November 2, 2018 was their problem and the desire to find any safe space in my regard is my own where I address according in compassion knowing I'm about to have to fight for all student loans in a capacity of whatever came into that workplace followed me to SCAD and took time to get through or could acknowledge what perseverance was in that aspect.

In any regard, I wrote this alone physically and it is my final edit to 'Curated Jellyfish: A Paradise Lost' knowing it was stolen, acted on and we go from there. There is no posthumous aspect to this. This happened in my lifetime and was incorporated in capacities that even if it was eventually to protect my identity, no one had a problem making millions off my work prior and then still leaving me high and dry.

Perhaps that is why I finish what I already hand-wrote.
No confusion.
Very objective.
Someone else is documenting every thought ready to print it out.
That transcribe was in version #1 in copyright.

We proceed accordingly knowing in any regard of what a possibly corporation would had claimed as infringement or inspiration is defunct in my color scheme of writing in this capacity and still would have to go back to the original 2019 copyright while citing my disclaimer of the path of what occurred and talking digital files, intellectual property and the complete disregard of privacy one way or another. I understand internally I've had to morally assess everything I've written never paid for as well as my entire life in any capacity. I've bitten that one. Have you?

Did someone make this book required reading with a ripped cover?
Translations matter in standardized testing.
People can say one thing or another. They could had done the same in 2018 or 2019. How much time wasted on your actions to put towards good use in my own capacity?   -Philip Arthur Bonneau 11.15.2022

Editor's Version started. 9/13/2021-Philip A. Bonneau
Create one last coded system in your final edits.
You can look up things online for your choice,
but refer back to your books and memory.

How many different versions of yourself are writing this.?
Relativity vs. Objectivity.

Expand where need be.
Don't in others.
Remember the beauty found and hidden within.
Let this be a final edit.

'Chasing Jabberwocks' was compromised before even started.
Find your truth being you.
-PB
9/23/21

'Chasing Jabberwocks was compromised from day one because I was aware of 'recorded keystrokes' as a factor. In any attempt to find peace back to my life and move on, it started with explaining to any insurance, anyone of access, any person this is why I went toward suicide then with all the evidence to support what was not about certain people, a life lived and of struggle and to hopefully say stop and they knew it. They understood it and in capacities of getting away with things one way or another they wouldn't stop on me or anyone else in that capacity. My work has already been translated without compensation, At least you know what led to my suicide attempt and you still wanted to translate that after not taking care of me or allowing me a safe space.

You just continued as proven from November 2022 on. You just take and take and wanted to straight up get away with it. I don't care if you are making a movie or a TV show out of it. I saw enough Movies and TV shows out of my work to go into sequestered aspects of step away and realize at this point detective works of what is known while not securing an asset in straight up acknowledgment and threats in movies. There is a difference between a 'Tesseract' and a 'Cosmic Cube'. Advance your property of invade others you don't have in the process. Edith lessons of difference between dead or alive in stories and testimony. -My great grandmother, Edith on my mothers side.

CURATED JELLYFISH

A PARADISE STOLEN

My diary as I coped with re-occuring memories,
trauma, and criminal acts against me.
Threats against everyone and everything I loved and care.

Obviously they didn't give a sh*t and stole this anyways.

...And here I thought they just wanted
Heroes+Villains.

PHILIP A. BONNEAU

Almost original cover to 'Curated Jellyfish: A Paradise Lost'.

At this point, one cannot be careful with a signature in any capacity of representation. Zero protect or simply an understanding of what it was prior of ownership and where others see an advantage or not.

A stop-gap present in many capacities where stolen signature traits occurred and we go from there. An acknowledgment of the original cover as originally intented with others refused to purchase even a single copy of it denoting anything incorporated didn't even come from reading a book legally.

A strong argument there where I can point or conject one way or another, but in any industry, you cannot get past the torn cover aspect, you can't get past the diary aspect and you cannot get past the same aspect that I find in awe discovering things in second or third read (knowing it has been more) of simply what is hidden in this book and what gets opened up just a little bit more in this final version.

Never a discount to the original title. "A Paradise Lost' is important in the same aspect of my life's work of noting the difference between 'The Divine Comedy' and 'a divine comedy'. If one was to go full literal of 'Paradise Lost', it happened in a very literal and figurative sense at this point of November 15, 2022 in one manner or another.

What came from this book is written out and continued knowing the ending. In re-edition aspect of this, it is with the understanding that if I was to be perpetually persecuted, investigated or interrogated, then perhaps a second glance on the other side to what I can't explain with others knowing what these books were and what happened to them leading towards this submit.

A judged book by it's cover. My 'Heaven' existed in it and with such my secrets of Bravery. An artist known on the matter since 2011. I existed after this book and it goes many ways from there. Whatever factored to hurt or hinder me then, prior or now exists and did in full proof. I proceed knowing that disregard gets turned in the other direction. I no longer expect someone to talk to me directly. I'm not fighting well beyond my self and it is what it is.

CURATED JELLYFISH

PHILIP A. BONNEAU

'The Cover of 'Curated Jellyfish: A Paradise Lost'- Image #5'
November 16, 2003. Film Image. Printed at Walgreens's One-Hour Photo. Copyright Philip A. Bonneau.

About the Cover:

A Cannonball discussion.

Once on the beach of 2003, I collected a jellyfish as if to protect it and bring it home. I brought it to my mother's apartment as if that was my home while I had my own elsewhere in my own regard at that point. Perhaps an uninsulated attic at the time or perhaps a neighbor to things of the swamp. Neither the point to know I admired that was captured then.

I think of this image in aspects of one could play laws from now or then of 2003. There is a common practice of people of the beach to collected washed up jellyfish and bury them in sand to not be touched or found by others. I imagine in practice I could also remember the fact that if prepared correctly they can be a delicacy of food-choice and fondly remembered on a first date as an appetizer choice understanding the grit of taste and question of something I was not familiar with at the time.

In any regard, I look at the image as even in the notion of fishermen or women on a pier, a life was captured and it was nurtured and created sustainability all these later in digestion. A desire to preserve in close quarters where perhaps naive thoughts back to my youth prior of territorial aspects of fish. The memory exists not really recalling of such of why I was insistent to capture a jellyfish washed on shore only to either return to it or be buried elsewhere by others knowing they sting or not.

I remember the pulsing aspect of such as it lived in a jar.
I'm actually pretty sure it would had survived if I went back to the beach and placed it back in the ocean. That is what evolution does which is why once washed on a shore to die there is always a chance to life or a chance to have someone pick you up and put you back.

There is always a do not touch aspect of it, but in the end I like to think back in 2003, I honored a Jellyfish disregarded while whatever answer I came to at the end, middle or beginning of this denotes that simply others are ready to disregard, attack based on their experience or simply know that they are harming something that did no harm to them and exist as they are flowing.

Almost original cover to 'Curated Jellyfish: A Paradise Lost'.

At this point, one cannot be careful with a signature in any capacity of representation. Zero protect or simply an understanding of what it was prior of ownership and where others see an advantage or not.

A stop-gap present in many capacities where stolen signature traits occurred and we go from there. An acknowledgment of the original cover as originally intented with others refused to purchase even a single copy of it denoting anything incorporated didn't even come from reading a book legally.

A strong argument there where I can point or conject one way or another, but in any industry, you cannot get past the torn cover aspect, you can't get past the diary aspect and you cannot get past the same aspect that I find in awe discovering things in second or third read (knowing it has been more) of simply what is hidden in this book and what gets opened up just a little bit more in this final version.

Never a discount to the original title. "A Paradise Lost' is important in the same aspect of my life's work of noting the difference between 'The Divine Comedy' and 'a divine comedy'. If one was to go full literal of 'Paradise Lost', it happened in a very literal and figurative sense at this point of November 15, 2022 in one manner or another.

What came from this book is written out and continued knowing the ending. In re-edition aspect of this, it is with the understanding that if I was to be perpetually persecuted, investigated or interrogated, then perhaps a second glance on the other side to what I can't explain with others knowing what these books were and what happened to them leading towards this submit.

A judged book by it's cover. My 'Heaven' existed in it and with such my secrets of Bravery. An artist known on the matter since 2011. I existed after this book and it goes many ways from there. Whatever factored to hurt or hinder me then, prior or now exists and did in full proof. I proceed knowing that disregard gets turned in the other direction. I no longer expect someone to talk to me directly. I'm not fighting well beyond my self and it is what it is.

I can objectively look at my work and see where the interest is buried in it. From the mugshot aspect, my book was acted on in a capacity that is beyond the Internet Crimes Unit as I didn't disclose elsewhere what was in this book.

I can look at my introduction which is still on the right path, but i don't come to a final answer until years later in where the mistake was and where experience pushes me in the right direction.

From the action of the mugshot action alone, I still can see where things happened on a film aspect regard knowing simply how the industry works and why multiple similar products exist at the same time. Perhaps that too why I copy-wrote understanding that was more from a presidential leader position at the time and an understanding prior and afterward of adapting things into other properties and saying hey...if I wanted to pass something around Hollywood, I'd still copyright it prior before doing so.

I say so also understanding, I'm team individual rights beyond belief and still that is not the solution as that goes into the digital questions that arrive in another book.

In any regard, what happened occurred and at least I know for surety that this book was impeded on. It is all I can do to clarify accordingly from a legal standpoint or moral standpoint that I acknowledge what happened, I don't invite and I remain standing back then in thought process as I finish this book.

Whatever people did with my discussion of I or for my benefit directly is on them. I don't play that game and all I can say is it could be a catch all of those who invited this to begin with or a simple conversation of privacy. I was not a part of that game and no one can ever simply turn on a private citizen's website page or any aspect of it in any legality. That is understood probably across the board.

I was not involved in what others at one point wanted me to commit suicide to possibly exploit my family, persecute my family, blame my family etc after the fact for which they already took after and what they wanted during where we are well in a different capacity at this stage to what could had been politely talked about then or prosecuted to end. For what is proven fact or written before translated into commercial means. You chose not to talk to me or me benefit from my work, it is possible to enjoy the same in that regard. It is very possible you are mentally not well and it involves levels of discussions privately or publicly.

In either regard,
let's re-explore together what has already been trespassed on and was never to be of my benefit in others translation.

Proof of what occurred and own decisions made from there.
No harm to personal income as if one wanted to make things personal, at least you know where things came from before it branched out elsewhere without my benefit in my lifetime or up until now or then.

That was their choice where, again I reiterate no one wanted me to benefit from my own life's work. The irony of that coming from a company predominantly based on other established artist's work, pre or post copyright.

In the end, I was well beyond that prior and I finish what I needed to in respect of copyright and The Divine Comedy as publicly approached since 2011 with Heroes+Villains the next month later. I remember in PureRED being indirectly attacked on an editorial. You have 2 choices there knowing which one it was. "Days of Stonewall Past' or we go into Pride on the other-side.

I continue knowing you ripped my cover and gave not one single shit about my life and wanted me dead and still would have attacked my family for only to get what you wanted while they did nothing, know nothing and that can be a political conversation, a corporate conversation or a global one where things went in 2022. Either way, on either side choices are becoming limited. I retain my sense of then knowing now was later and still have to question what I reserve not typing based on experience.

I started my artistic version of my approach to 'The Divine Comedy' in November 2011, 'Heroes+Villains #1' in December 2011. I suppose in the scheme of things, I never had a problem prior with anyone until 2018, possibly 2017 when I created my website. I at least content, DC acknowledged me with a Bat-bear image where I removed the logo and went from there. At that point I was already national with 'The Advocate' back in ATL1.0. Well before Alfred Angelo and well before anything of ATL 2.0, I was established.

OCTOPUS

'To see an octopus in your dream means that you are entangled in some
difficult matter. Your judgment is being clouded. Alternatively, the octopus indicates that you are
overly possessive and maybe too clingy in a relationship'

(dreammoods.com. Definitions are always a question of copyright as it is a definition of words or
interpretation in dictionary form. A Dictionary is defined for definition and from thus translation,
but I cite accordingly knowing I have my own defintions elsewhere. It is as good as place as any
to start before finding your own interpretions. Respect of where things come from.)

A FORWARD

I began working on my "Divine Comedy" series back in 2010. I conceptualized
the series as an exploration of psychology through the effects of trauma to
represent a metaphorical Hell, Purgatory and Heaven while separating the
natural emotional response to their specific coordinating spheres and circles.
This series began in visual art form and transformed over the years to include
written word and music as real life experiences drove a narrative through
the growing process of the mind. I find that in order to proceed forward, it
is beneficial as required information to what those psychological stages are
and how they relate to both myself and maybe ultimately you.

There are several natural stages to how one processes and works with trauma
within their life. How you chose to interpret the stages of grievance really
depended on what school you enroll in on the steps. In the major circles
there are 5 stages broken down to 1. Denial 2. Anger 3. Bargaining 4. Depression 5. Acceptance.

In other studies people suggest 7 stages.
In other circumstances people view that there are 8.

I chose to begin this journey with the path of the octopus as the basis of thought
in this exploration. Chosen for both the extra compartmentalizing of thought
processes that I felt were grouped together, but also the symbology of the

octopus in dream theory and throughout art history with the octopus being a regularly occurring motif first found in Greek ceramics and art.

Those 8 stages are broken down to be: 1. Denial/Numbness 2. Emotional Release 3. Anger 4. Bargaining 5. Depression 6. Remorse 7. Acceptance 8. Hope

As I walk through the tail-end of this incorporeal journey and through the various distinct circles, I think I may have discovered there is a need of reshuffling of what I perceive the universal stages to be. I assume they are unique to everyone and to some there will be only 5, some there may be more. But I like the idea of breaking down each emotional stage into it's own place and into it's own series in the scheme of things.

Allow me to break down the stages where I feel the need for there to be 9 stages in reference to the exploration of this journey, but perhaps a better understanding in general, I guess I'll only know if this is accurate if I vet it out and see what others think. But for me it feels as my truth.

1. Shock (The Catalyst).

This seems to be something that is not explored on any of the various stages of grief. But in order to trigger grief there has to be some kind of shock factor given. Something out of the normal behavior had to trigger a response that ripples through the unexpected. Without this shock moment, none of the other steps apply within the processing and no further steps are required to move past said experience. However, it could ultimately be misunderstood that the shock value is the same as the incident itself, however that is grouping an emotion with an action and thus the action remains the initial trigger for coping and shock being the first emotion felt/released by someone who has experienced an incident to ignite emotional reactions. It begins in silence. From there comes...

2. Denial/Numbness.(Initial Refusal of Acceptance)

Shock has occurred. Belief is then put in Limbo. The natural response is no longer acknowledging that the incident did not occur, but it's a refusal to believe that it did. From this come the symptoms of escapism, avoidance, and keeping thought away from the present (a regression to past and familiar experiences and thoughts occur). A true avoidance of dealing with things directly but still processing indirectly in some scenario.

3. Combined Polarized Emotional Release
i.e (Sadness/Anger) (Guilt/Non-Ownership) (Love/Hate)
(Conflict of what to feel/how to feel/how to express/what to express)

If denial is the definition of refusing to feel anything or accept anything, this next stage is your first glance at coming to realization that something happened. Something occurred and you are beginning to come back to a reality where you cannot escape emotion. The downfall is you do not know what to really feel. The 5 stages say Anger, but truth is you do not know what to feel and yet feel everything all at once to a point of polarization of emotions. Your mind is trying to grasp which way to go with this depending on the scenario. Anger one day can be sadness the next. Resentment can become validation. Love can become hate. At this stage is the first time the mind chooses to deal with the present and is going to go through the roulette until it discovers which one is most comfortable to proceed. It may not be the correct path, but a path may be chosen at this point in order to take a step in a direction; mentally not caring which direction that may be.

4. Physical Distress (Physical toll based on Mental Trauma and Conflict)

This is where the mind outweighs the body. The body rests when you go to bed, but only when the mind is able to do the same. Having the mind go a mile a minute in any direction causes a direct physical effect onto the body. Not sleeping, fatigue, not eating, self-medicating behavior can occur. This stage is when the mental roulette starts playing a toll on rational thought. As you sift through every emotion you could possibly think of, you tend to either neglect the physical aspects of yourself or you introduce things in order to sustain your mind from running the marathon of processing. It is at this stage, if not unchecked, where addiction, depression and even mental deterioration begins. But also the stage of unchecked emotion where perhaps you begin to see behavior different than normal. What was once just internal becomes external, but often misplaced and not directed accordingly. Moments of out-lash. Sensitivity and vulnerability through confusion of emotions as the body becomes physically tired as well as the beginning of mental exhaustion.

5. Bargaining (Bargaining at potential loss to self/others, derivative of fear of unknown or fear to accepting)

This stage is very contingent on the catalyst. If that catalyst was death, it may be a conversation had with a higher power. If between two people perhaps it is a stage set for "I'll change this if you change this". This is the stage where we try to hold on and is perhaps a last ditch effort to reverse something that has transpired. Emotion has been felt. Some processing has happened, but still non-acceptance to the outcome that occured. A resistant effort to move forward with a desire to go back pre-incident. Acceptance begins, but not towards everything. It is different in the sense that in the prior stages there was no admitting of right/wrong, where as now there is bargaining on the lesser of evils and a willingness to compromise beliefs in order to have something comfortable back in your life that is known. Partial growth, but more than likely not true change.

6. The upturn/false finality. (Feeling a sense of completeness without total acceptance of trauma, but progress nevertheless)

This one is a little more case by case. If said stage #5 was accepted then this is where this falls most in line. It was a truce and a back-peddling to a I don't want to accept what I feel is right for me, but I'm settling for what "we" feel is right. This may come from everyone around you saying move on. This may come from everyone saying this person is dead or this happened but you have to live you life. This is listening to everyone and committee rule that you just brush it under when you may not want to brush it. But there is enough rationale there to know it to be sound thought, but at the same time you personally just still have issues that go back from being in the forefront to perhaps back internalized in order to appear best for others. Or perhaps go with the flow not really believing the words of others. It's closure in face value only.

7. Depression* (The acceptance that the false start was not actually total acceptance/closure/peace)

Depression sits in when you seclude yourself and your thoughts. Both physically and mentally. You chose to keep things more inside because you were tired of others telling you were wrong or judging you or thinking they were judging you and you just bottle it all back in. It's a willful decision. One much different from Stage 3 where you could not control emotion. This stage is absolutely controlled emotion and avoidance of outside opinion and thought. In doing so though, it's a double edge sword because you know in the back of your mind that this is not what you want and this is what you want to deal with and you block yourself out from help because you don't think others will understand anymore.

8. Testing/Hope (Trying new positive methods to overcome the false start. Reinforced by both positive results and external approval)

Depression is a bitch. Not everyone comes back from that. That takes a lot of self reflection and questioning. What do you want? What do you see you can change? What makes you smile? Who are you? If you start asking yourself those questions you do try to test the waters a bit. When thrown completely out to sea, eventually you will want to look for land. You challenge yourself at this stage. You do things and gauge the response. You slowly step into what creates a positive reaction. Positive influence ignites other positive influence. However, in this stage it is again a cautious one because a negative influence can cause a positive reaction and if a negative creates a positive then thats a road that goes to different areas than the final.

9. Acceptance/Remembering (personal acceptance without the need for external approval, acceptance of what was/what is/what will be without sorrow/negative reflection upon self on past trauma with misperceived responsibility of all parties involved).

This stage is the most unexplored for me. Accepting things for what they are. Perhaps that is what this book is meant to explore? A realization can be present in that some things are ok to compromise and some things are not. Through hurt and these stages I feel I'm gracious to have gone through my experiences because I feel they have made me a better person. I understand more of what is right/wrong for me as much as I know what I want and don't want. To me what acceptance boils down to is remembering something happened. Remembering the good and the bad. They made me who I am. I've had good and I've had bad, and I've learned from both. I feel in the end the final stage is accepting your story is perfect as it is. Success and Failure. Refusal to look back equals repeating your past as a retribution. But one of the hardest things to do is to accept yourself as human, completely flawed, but still worth all the love for the right person. But it starts with you.

My Divine Comedy series is a concept built on taking these 9 proposed stages of trauma and breaking them down into visual psychological versions of the Christian afterlife of Hell, Purgatory and Heaven. As the "Divine Comedy" is in 3 parts, so is my artist opus. Hell was called, "Beautful Layered Lies" (BLL). In it a voice is discovered while learning to speak. A catalyst occured and from it change & a search for meaning and purpose commenced. The catalyst (*in the beginning*) is always going to be the most important to the journey.

Purgatory was found within "Ugly Simple Truths" (UST). By utilizing black-lights with photography, I had models & myself become their psychological "shadow selves" as they came face-to-face with triggers and moments in their life that have haunted them without completion. That series was accompanied with a personal blog who's purpose was to explain and understand why reactions and actions towards certain events occured based on past experience and thoughts. It's overall intention was to showcase growth in thinking. The catylist (*in the middle*) is always going to be a driving factor to a journey

"Brave New Secrets" (BNS) was to be the Heaven series. Started in 2014, it was always alluded to, but never given a proper form. Not from a lack of trying, but because it always felt the most important. With that knowledge, the desire to get it absolutely right came as self-induced pressure towards perfection. 5 years of work on that series alone. Writing at the forefront of the pathways set only for none of it to appear at the actual showing. Only accompanied by compositions in sound to evoke feeling and mood to where in the end it is only sound, art & U.

I write this introduction with full knowledge that what I am presenting to the world was not a Heaven planned. It's not fiction. It's my life and mind destroyed and trying to piece that back together. It is my hope that as I share this that one of two things occur from this. I find the Heaven I've so long for sought and that 2. other's might gain insight that may be beneficial to them in their lives. It's in dreams that we ebb and flow from one thought to the next. But it's somewhere in-between we cross paths in the currents to find things we never knew we were looking for to begin with.

Welcome to Curated Jellyfish.

————

*I've come to a slightly different solution 3 years later in one key change to this. I find it important to leave this as is as I chose a path of depression-like symptoms then and know that was a choice to a certain extent and why I change things later on and they are copyright protected in my firm stance in 'Lorum Ipsum: Child of Someone'. It is important to I to noted where I started and where I ended up yet the answers are hidden here anyways on if you can spot the difference or not on what it may be. Answers take time and it is important to talk those paths as much as understanding it was a choice and a hard road to come out of as things of memory latch on and others break off into over and under current currants elsewhere.

In any regard to someone wanting to possibly discredit me prior in my own work, I simply say the only reason you have an opinion was because I expressed it anyways and that could be argued from a keyboard or from intuition. At this point, when one knows the value, they tend to discredit and abuse to take it over one way or another anyways. Especially after they already stepped into the sea to swim with it a bit. That is human nature.

With that understanding this was my initial path on this event, I found the severity of such occurrance important to go back after to what I worked on well before the place of repeat contact and encounter leading towards

Feb. 21, 2019. Those instances played out before I circle back to universal answers of what is simply proven at this point or could be discussed one way or another. It is important to document and understand this path and what it takes to get to another answer while others could simply steal the end result and claim it as their own and still try to discount the one who came up with it to begin with. It took 3 years from this point to come to a better solution that still was excluded of others and a shining achievement to my life where I absolutely have thoughts about the theft of my work especially in this regard and how it was in a non-compensated aspect to my life. It is about the experience and how you get to an answer that matters while others of discount can say exactly where things came from anyways. (An over-explaination). Now required as any little bit of my life could be ripped apart for others to justify taking what they didn't earn or experience first-hand.

You ripped me off and I can see the value when I created in an actual sequel to this book and put the final pages of something in it. In this book, that occcurred cannot be denied and validates the aspect that you ripped me off and you don't want to admit that or understand the difference of that many years of translation knowing you didn't get it the first time and you definitely don't get the ending. We can talk 'Lorem Ipsum' and that aspect of what happened on my private computer, but you can't deny what you have already translated and all I can do is clearly denote what I add on in final edit to what you have already adapted knowing whatever in the other documents is not for someone to read. Once they read it I can't control it, but if you allowed it then that still proves my point that you have no respect for anyone.

If this is as far as I got individually. I can see the value of where collaboration could come down the line or could had already. So much done outside of any employment, on my own time and from a necessity to grow one place to another.

My life as I rebuilt it. Was it from 3rd series from 2013/2014. A continuation of things telling me this is right to do this back in 2012? Was this the ending of 2011 started to find my own words? How long have I or others been building towards myself writing this? It is not just about I and it is no longer about I as already translated and stil questions of mulls, land and do not cross.

Was this from thought of high school or middle school? Maybe from a child combined...

Who came in and wanted to destroy a life without understanding what you were taking away at a certain point

I've left it open for discusssion what it was prior of, 'Building Brave New Secrets' which no one bought at the time. A final aspect that while I clearly state what occurred from the cover, I don't care if no one reads it. it will be a part of American copyright and noted as such of who does and does not succeed noting the first version and all versions after came from what occurred at the time and the MO of a president of sitting in 45 during which the initial copyright was placed in 2019. The rest played out of corporation that is not the Vatican of Florida and could had said one way or another to my 'Remus'ed' life knowing it is now beyond Southern Songs and into realms of appropriation that cannot be challenged on either side of what was built, imitated and simply room to say enough of the repeat in the modern aspects of things.

Whatever the answer, I know who legally read this book and from here on in continuation, this final edit is not shared, intended for copyright and any sharing aspect of it is still moving towards crimes against humanity because you did one thing or another. I understand what I disclosed in this book and others and if that ever wants to occur, that is understood in Tyrannis Rex and any other capacity. Until then, it is simply understood people wanted me to commit suicide to keep their hands clean and for reasons of copyright known, that is never going to happen in more value than others in that regard.

What occurred already happened.
Some of it is happening.
Some has yet to play out.

The foresight of looking back to prevent is not discounted to the aspect of the compounded aspect of you already know and are making it worse one way or another on the hopes of destroying a life.

Hero.
Villain.
Your call on morality.
I still protect invidual rights.

What did you do to try to preempt my own work and then would had cited infringment after the fact? I won't allow that in my lifetime nor that burden on my family or ancestors.

The inclusion of my work in this book has already occurred.

Deal with it.

Oh what secrets hide behind
This wonderous looking glass of mine.

From every shard
A truth revealed.

Through every crack,
A hidden attack.

It says it all within your face.
Stories of Humpty...
The horsemen...
A search for grace.

But with a shattered look you speak.
Of hope...
Happiness...
A peace: Complete.

What would you say
If you could share?

Would you teach me love
Or how I should care?

But oh this magic mirror of mine
U Reflect on so much
I've left behind.

I'm asking you to solely speak
Here and now
At my sanity's peak.

From every word
A memory provoked.

Tell me the truth
of your sick twisted joke.

Oh to know what secrets hide
Behind that wonderous
looking glass of mine.

How do I lay myself bare?

Do I use a different font as thought? Readability is important.
(Sometime in August 2019)
ENTRY 1:

Underwater.
Comfortable Silence.
Muted sounds echoed through waters.

Peace.
Pressure.
Capulated motions of give and take.

Screams haunt the earlobes.
Murmurs of failure.
Judgment
Frustration juxtaposed between a calmness.

Is this what it is supposed to be like?
A never-ending tidal underneath the surface?
Flooding the body with negativity?

"Who taught him to write?"

"This is supposed to be the greatest book ever written."

"No. It's release."

"I told you to stop reading that book."

An appropriation of words takes place.
Sound turned to image.
An evolution of both flora & fauna takes place within.

Take in every bit of it
Breathe even though you can't
Inhale the mistakes with laughter.
Inhale victory & defeat

Eyes closed in a fleeting thought of victory.

Thinking of another place.
Of voices not there.
Trees that have yet to be grown.
Dangers both real and imaginary.

Existence.

What right do U have to this experience?
How much is this yours when other voices speak?
No one is present to bear witness.

Does Past, Present & Future exist as one?

"I am reminded of "The Once and Future King"

In other times: I think of worlds like Wonderland and OZ.

Is this to be a Nu experience?

<Breathe>
Just focus on the now.
Remove the outside.

What is there left in the world to make your own?
Do these inner voices drive my perception?

If I remove that desire to question them,
should I be careful with what they may think of me?

In a moment of acceptant combativeness;
I ask those voices to drive the story they want told
or for them to simply remain silent.

I'll call them Muses.
Unforeseen within.

Underwater.
Uncomfortable chatter.
Unmuted sounds of critique begin.

Does it all start with a fluid scream of bubbles emerging from a once sewn
shut mouth?

"I am going to try this for 3 years. 3 years separated from anything I knew or know. 3 years where I can grow professionally and focus on things that matter. 3 years to spend the time just getting to see things differently. I think I need to know for myself if I am toxic or not. Casual shit haunts the fuck out of me and I guess it is here where I can begin to grow. I mean I kind of have to, "right?". Can't exactly go backwards per se. But let's see what happens. 3 years is long enough to come unto my own demise or find myself in new directions. I don't think any one path is going to be right or wrong, but just different. I'm terrified and excited at the same time but let's find this out. I have zero doubt I'll change from this. I don't know what that will be. I know at this point that is definitely going to happen. All I know is remove an environment and it will factor into your every day. Regardless of intention or desire, I won't be the same person at the end of this. In a lot of ways I can't ask for a more Brave New World.- 10/10/2014

I suppose it begins in silence.

There are very few words you could really say properly in the beginning.
There is no emotion that is proper or incorrect.
It feels like you are the tree that falls down in the woods and no one is around.

Part of you wonders if anyone can hear you.
The other part isn't capable of even caring if you exist.
You've fallen in the middle of the woods and the straightforward path has been lost.

I doesn't matter if anyone can hear you.
All you hear is nothing...
And everything...
All at once.

Perhaps what we do with trauma is the most selfish and selfless of emotions,
but no one can predict how one would react to it.

At it's core, it is instinctual self-preseveration

or perhaps the opening up the idea of presevation in any capacity as one leaps to
protect a child or an animal just as much as a child would protect a parent in return.

It is a natural reaction and no one can take that away from you.
No one can fault you in the end.
They may anyways
But that is the confliction of rippling impact.
Even in silence, it was felt one way or another by someone else.

We regress.
We become protective.
We lash out.
It is like being born into a new world,
Not knowing what to do with contracting thoughts.

People will judge.
They inevitable will...
if only to form one opinion or another to help or hinder.

Where we go in trauma is not a place that we willfully created.
It is a world of perception that the mind has created where over time it is understood
we may have more control over it than we thought we did before.

Within that silence we create a Wonderland:
A place where we are introduced to those that will both a reflection to ourselves
and/or the faciliators to plant new seeds to grow from. -11/22/17,
(A thought of Forward on the stages of Grief and Trauma...a Novel...a Thesis..)

I started this supplement to Brave New Secrets believing I will just write for myself
in secret as I go. I believed when the time is right for this series, I would just hit the
publish button on certain posts that become relevant to the story and kind of evolve
from there. However, as I may find many of the things written to contain information
worth talking about in the context of this series, I find it hard to associate myself with
just those words now vs. then. I think to just use those words represents a timeframe
of where I have been and not necessary where I am now which defeats the purpose
of Heaven to me. To base all of this off of that would be a disservice. I do find in
those words those where a conflict between myself can be had. There has to be some

ownership of them to a certain extent because within those words I do find things that are inherently myself and in others probably more situational to a particular situation. 3 years is a long enough time to spend getting to know myself in order to properly proceed even if will begin in the footsteps of caution and fear.

In every major changing moment of my life, there have been a few consistencies no matter the situation that has occurred. One of those things has been giving up something fundamentally a part of my everyday in order to further move across the board. There seems to always be this karmatic give-and-take to things that happens in those scenarios. Some of those things given have been either a bad habit, escapism tools, and in other circumstances it has been completely changing environments and game players. It's even been as simple as something so small and meaningless as a picture or an art piece Knowing there is meaning behind every aspect of such. Life is going to be a series of give and take and with each new journey just a little bit more of the past is purged here and there to make room for new stories until eventually you end up with some single lonely box somewhere tucked away just labeled "memories" that you may or may not sift through every couple of years. I believe it is completely essential to choose the things you give up carefully for reasons that are right for you at the time. But as you gain things in life it is also important to remember life without whatever accumulated thing you have picked up along the way. Toss a rock back into the water and a ripple is given in return.

For me I find it interesting how I have a knack for holding onto some things much longer than I probably should while other things I'll just say, "Ok. Gone." and that is the end of that. I would be lying to myself if I said I have always let go willingly or as easily as I should have life. Perhaps if I had let go of some things sooner rather than later I would be able to see other things right in front of me just a little bit better. But nevertheless, eventually I do give things up eventually.

I've been thinking about 1 thing in particular that I have given up over the last several years. One of those things would be a change in art forms. I guess it has been about 5 years now since I did a painting. I originally went to school for painting but never really found myself quite satisfied with anything I produced from it. I loved the whole action of painting. Headphones one. Paintbrush out. I didn't like canvas so I painted on sanded wood. Something that allowed me to be as fluid with my brush as my thoughts were coming to me. I'd always base an art piece after a particular song and would play it over and over again to see what came out of it. But really it was an escapist tool for me. Something to just tune everything in the world out and just focus on that. Completely healthy thing to do, but when it came in sessions of 4 hours here, 8 hours here, it really was a way of not dealing with life. I'll always remember my final painting. A forest fire that probably was more true to point at the time than I realized then. I kind of just burnt down that creative outlet and said nope... going to deal and going to embrace photography which I got more from on many levels and really encompassed all of my artistic ideas through one outlet. I don't regret changing this one. It's the not wanting "the escape route" that I've been thinking of.

In 'Ugly Simple Truths', one of my self-portraits was called '*Alice and the Sea of Tears*'. That pic represented a struggle I was having where I just needed to check out. Stop thinking. Stop doing. Just go somewhere else and drown out the noise. My mind and thoughts were all over the place and in it I found myself really drinking for the first time. I think probably month's leading up to when that happened I think the signs were there that this could be something that could get out of control. I'd say at the time, it ran its course until I started working on that series and never really was an issue afterwards. Definitely was a part of my life since and looking back I definitely see it as a replacement exit sign. I saw it when I had a bad day at work. I saw it when stress was out of control and I definitely saw it when life throws curveballs here and there. I think I always saw it as a negative simply due to the first time I got a bottle and said, "ok...I am fucking getting shit-faced...this is going to happen and then I'll deal with it when I wake up." Questions prior on one escape vs. the other knowing the detriment of either. One simply more condoned than the other until one figures out how to make money off of it properly. Empty calories. Empty thoughts. Moderation in any regard knowing it simply is a time for reality and other times for enjoyment one way or another. You can replace escapism in any aspect of legal or illegal to come to the same conclusions. Alice never really woke up from that dream to deal with things. If I wanted to go there it went from writing to producing art to searching for help in belief systems to where I went career-wise to where other people when career-wise with that insight and motivation wondering. 'what is the drug here and what was abused?' I don't think either of us are capable of doing so until this series is complete. I question if I should add context to these sections knowing I will do such in 'Building Brave New Secrets' knowing I found a section completely out of character to my writing and a need to reconcile in an aspect of it was one of the last books produced in protection and thus, the most vulnerable and still very important in understanding the cover story behind such of what was written before getting completely psychological in this endevour. I'll proceed carefully knowing the purity of years and what it was then matters towards where we are now. When most was written privately, it is understood the necessity at this point if one is to reflect to get it right and call out what needs to be called out appropriately without spelling things out.

I don't think it ever really got the best of me, but it sure as hell got close on many occasions enough to say 'ok, this needs to go.'. Remember I said I don't always give things up easily? Well that still is true enough today that I consider it a definite part of who I am that it be carved into this series as a trait of mine to own. Yes, that has it pluses and minuses, but somewhere in the grey there is something intrinsically valuable to that when used in the right scenarios. But as much as I hold on, I need to also acknowledge the instant drop and done. I think it's a matter of learning when and where that trait could and should be used. But here I am now in a situation where I do no longer want escapism and a fundamental change is happening. The understanding of 'recorded keystrokes' years later in words written prior telling you this was already written and happened in 2017 and what happened after came directly from your company but this existed prior. You authorized something, I didn't authorize a single bit of you reading this or that or anything. I was not then or now on-boarding you. The same when I did set aside my own life for another company. I am not an indentured servant to threats, intimidation and illegality. (Imagine the Abraham Lincoln metaphors later.)

A majority of the things in life happen not always from choice, but it is always going to be our choice to adapt and change to the confines of the rules of the game or suffer the repercussions of inaction. For several reasons I've decided not to drink for 6 months. I don't think I have a problem with it per se, but I think it is the negative connection that I associate with it that needs to be let go. Most of the people I've dated here don't even have it in their lives and more often not I've seen what addicts look like as much as I see life without it even factoring in. Never a fear of such as any addict is looking for escapism and to find strength to overcome that is admirable and something of interest in beauty of overcoming obstacles. Replacement value occurs anyways but the respect aspect remains the same. Awareness of what occurred and brought once pleasure. Replacement always there one way or another. Not a recovery aspect there. Simply focus on the positives and understand the detrimentals one way or another. Intimately that was always understood. Basically I needed to cut it out for me. If I want to really move on from this game to the next I have to follow the rules. It will hold me back because I need to think clearly and I don't believe that swimming in the same sea is going to do much good on changing the perspective of the world from underwater. I don't want to mentally escape anything. I just want to swim and maybe just hang out on the boat for a bit. Fortitude found in any situation. There is 'a do and do not fight' aspect to things. I like my instinct saying time has proven the fight valuable. I think one of the things I was afraid of by not drinking is the very thing that drove me to it. Now I imagine it is just a guessing game of probabilities as it was before in understanding direct contact means more an in-direct guesses.

The constant thoughts and lists of things to do. The never-ending scenarios in my head that would play out X.Y.Z. I remember my final night drinking. I went out, danced, made out with people...whatever and then came home and woke up and said, 'ok. That's it. Done.' I'm sure in 6 months I will reintroduce it to some capacity, or maybe not. I like the challenge of seeing what will be different. I give it 6 months to spend the time just getting to see things differently while the sea dries up to become a vast desert.

One of my favorite memories when I first moved to Atlanta was I didn't drink at all. Maybe once or twice on the weekend. But really my life was perfectly fine without it and I found myself actually thinking that that is a part of my past that I want to reclaim back for myself. I think there is several things that will be reclaimed over the course of this experiment, but for the sake of starting off this journey let's remove the one variable left over in order to proceed. If anything it's been interesting to see people's reaction when you say you are not drinking. Is it so much of our social life that it becomes symbiotic to having one? Eh...all is does is lead questions to how does one escape without one in one area or another. The virtue of having fun without intoxication. It occurs in ways you can only imagine one way or another.

It's been 40 days and 40 nights. I'd say just in that short amount of time things the winds have already changed their course and makes me think that as much as I feared how I would deal with the thoughts and desires in my head, if it has done nothing but to trigger this path towards narrative completion then that alone was worth the give-and-take. Here I am now in narrative completion understanding the take aspect overcame any give on the other side.

I guess the take away from this is I'm not really scared to process things as they come and perhaps I'm just a little bit stronger than I gave myself credit for. It's not always a choice for some, but I appreciate that it is my choice to slowly have Alice wake up a little bit at a time throughout this challenge. I may have given up 'Alice's Sea of

Tears', but as those tears dried. I've gained a salty shoreline with pockets of water remaining. Coping exists in solitude and displacement. Removed stories and further adventures direct or in.

Seems as good as any other place to either find or lose myself.

ENTRY 2:

Imagine 3-5 different stories playing out at the same time.

With acute patience, you can swim from one narrative to the next.
Slowly piecing them together as individual tributaries on a course to the
same singular destination. As some dry up, others continue on.

Streams of consciousness.
Thoughts born and broken.
Layered as a lie.
Everyday noise left unnoticed.
Something changed.

Does a tree that falls with no one around still make a sound?

Try not to overthink it much.
It's silly to just wander off into your mind.

There is a world within my head just starting to form. Perhaps it had been
formed long ago and was just left unrealized and unwritten. An imaginary
world that seems only now to be viewed by another world as part of their
regularly scheduled programming that can be easily switched from one
station to the next. In this world is my new daily life for me.

Externally: unnoticed sound bites.
Internally: Personifications of distinct personalities and voices.

This connection and acknowledgement of voices have been around every
day and night since February 21, 2019: the day I attempted to force myself to
sleep by overdosing on anti-depressants.

Why are they here? Was this a chemical reaction?

How I choose to handle this experience is by choosing my own adventure vs.
a possible pre-destination from them.

Does free thought exist or is our own thinking simply influenced indirectly
by subconscious variables?

The chiming of bells.
Crickets.
Provoked emotions and thought patterns.
A butterfly of an effect formulated by sounds.

It is fair thinking that by influence; sound can carry a weight outside of decibels. The other day one sound sparked a series of events that led to me purchasing, "A Wrinkle in Time." A book I have never read prior and one that voices do not want me to either for some reason. I went from seeing a doorstop that said "Quiet", to coming across a book called "Quiet" about introverts. There are strange connections being made that lead to a con-clusion of purchasing Wrinkle as the name Edith echoed through my mind prior in the day. I wonder the significance of such a name. I wonder if just one slight different sound internally heard would had led to me swimming at the beach instead. Possibly drifting off to sea or perhaps I would had purchased a plane ticket instead.

Divine intervention towards choice is given.

<The smell of smoke is in the air>
I'm curious on where that will lead in thought and action.

IF sound carries weight and influence, what is the volume of a thought in a physical environment? One series of thoughts either uttered or unspoken can equally start a different chain reaction. One can conclude that it is possible that unspoken words have unspoken actions. Perhaps unforeseen or underdeveloped. Are things in the works unrealized yet?

Are you ok?

"One shouldn't drink before surgery."

"Everyone be very quiet."

What surgery are they talking about?

I ask myself if it is ok to have a drink or not. Much like I ask myself it is ok to think whatever I want to think about within my head. I'm letting my mind swim.

Try to write out coherant thoughts.

Am I hurting myself by holding back desire or am I being subconsciously told what to do or not? I can't help but think that I lack control over this.

Write what you experience Philip.

Images of myself on the streets of New York City appear in my mind. I'm walking. Headphones on as I move towards the subway and ultimately my section of the train. I'm standing. Observing everything around me. I hide my observance through my headphones. They are on, but silence flows through them. I pretend to be preoccupied with sound.

I look around and steal a moment from everyone else in the car. I imagine to myself where they will go from here. I sift from wondering where they came from to deducting how they may be feeling right now. I'm observing in silence moments of other's vulnerability. Perhaps it is a testament of what we unconsciously throw out into the world. We all have a presence. Unspoken thoughts and moods affect an environment. What right do I have to project my thoughts onto their world? OR is this simply expressing adoration of the beauty in everything that is. Am I supposed to be here?

Everything around... an unnoticed imperfect masterpiece of humanity.

Of course, I should wonder about my thoughts on how I would feel if this was done to me. Would I want myself molded & sculpted to someone else's perception? Is that happening now? How have those views of me shaped who I am in their eyes? I imagine the answer pertains to their own context. Another me is born in each reflection.

It's amazing how all people have the ability to paint others based on their perception. Everyone is capable of projecting notions within themselves unto strangers that may or may not exist. But should we?

"An awkward first date." "They are cheating." "That's what love is."
All things said in passing observation from one stranger to the next viewed in a single evening during a stroll downtown.

If someone takes notice of you, a fleeting moment occurs on some level of the subconscious where given information is taken in and processed. Whether you notice the act or not, there is a creation of a myth of the lives of those observed. A story begins to be woven that only you get to read.

A Slight comment made on appearance.
Attraction.
Distraction.
Similarities.
Differences.
Everything accounted for,
Even if never thought about consciously.
An automatic computing of data.

One must wonder what happens if someone catches that subconscious thought consciously. The next train of thinking would bring up questions on if those thoughts were accurate or not. Do you scorn yourself for thinking so, or do you agree with what comes naturally in thought? Ultimately, it is important to note that any opinion conjected is well within the probability of being simply a reflection of ourselves based solely on what we know from our own experiences.

An example of such would be to notice someone familiar from across the way, but choosing not to say, "Hello" to them.

While the mind begins to formulate questions and answers, I'm pondering if even a conscious awareness of an individual is a possible mental invasion of someone's life. Surely they will never know unless they too are consciously aware of their surroundings and in familiarity invade you as well.

The action of awareness and observance is a witness to how our senses translate information. Our senses pick up one piece (or multiples acting in unison) of data and translates it into millions of possible variables unconsciously. It's a natural process. Afterall, you cannot be intended to walk around life without using your senses to translate information. Just as you cannot deny one sense over the other. Naturally there is a symphony formed between sight, sound and touch. Focusing in on those senses evoke into your world what will ultimately become a memory built by associations past within your present.

"Why is he here?"

I am starting to feel at times it is a mistake the more I hear voices.

Maybe I should give in to them saying I "shouldn't have been here to begin with."

<Non-recorded dialog>

Everything they say...I take it.

I take it as a way to grapple my newfound auditory hallucinations. I try to focus to conversation but it it like everyone around me dances through conversation and interactions where as I try to follow their lines & patterns to fail at connections. Yet somehow I find myself going off into finding a different motion of pattern than the others.

<I finger snap to focus.>

Backwards running.
I feel different.
I can't really catagorize the sensations on if hearing is some sort of an awakening or depression abound. There is a change that has occurred internally from this past year. A repetition of theme and thought.

"Out of all the traumas in your life, why did this one affect you the way it has?"
(K)

Do I have any right to call this trauma?

Trauma.
A constant barrage of mentality.
A Flooded mind.
Everyday.
Constant Replay.

The barrage of this foreign mentality floods my mind. This is not only replaying what happened daily. but it has grown to the point that it has taken on a life of it's own seeping into every aspect of my waking and non-woke life. It's tendrils grabs my attention and pulls my focus back and forth within the currents of its own creation. A jellyfish tangled within.

It's as if these voices are searching for answers and connections not yet made. I want to entertain the idea that this was all formulated from just a series of unfortunate events. Perhaps a misunderstanding that never

34

needed to occur, but yet here we are... trapped in a sea of thought wondering if this is going to be my life moving forward. Both in the now and in the past concurrently swaying in those waters. The future does not matter at this time. I give myself credit that at least this is an attempt to be here. I'm there. But there is mental footing that needs to be placed. Buoyancy needs to occur.

If I were to battle with the others within my inner-self, "would there ever be an agreement made?"

I believe that I am looking for the right way from this. As of late, I am unsure on if I can find one. Its as if miles of sea are in every direction. I go on faith that eventually I will come to face myself at a decision-making point. When that moment occurs it is my hope that I know the things needed to be nurtured for growth (as everything does) from that one singular moment of a choice.

Can there be growth in regression?

ENTRY 3:

Heaven is perseverance.
It's persistence.
It's in the things we think, but never say.
Limitless information stored and saved
Until you click on the recycle bin.

Wind guiding me from one place to the next
A path is set
Now in safer waters.
A shell is found.
A hole seen through
Perspective limited.

A Walk back.
Wind opposing.
Resistance.
Strength
Perseverance present

Prior before.
Written once more.

Voices at sea.
Came to harm me.
Sink/Swim.
I Drifted
A choice made not to drown.

We return to shore,
Forevermore.

Questioning thoughts is completely healthy. But what happens when you think in you head thoughts that are not your own? These thoughts have a different persona to them and not like my normal internal thinking where my outside voice is my spoken internal. I'm hearing voices internally not my own.

Is this a gift?
Possibly.
A lesson?
More than likely.

It is possible to learn something from anything. If I looked at this as a learning experience. I have to ask myself what is the universe trying to tell me outside of don't smoke & drink? That is easy enough done when I am able to put my mind to it. but it's my mind that I question meaning and intent. I have to believe that if I am actually hearing things that there is a greater design and purpose behind it than don't smoke. Something is wrong. but I refuse to believe this is now a handicap to be held forever. They say this lasts 6 months to a year in most scenarios. Have faith in that.

"Last one." (As I smoke)

How many times have I said that before?

There is a difference between restraint & control vs. an addiction. Am I addicted? I can go days & weeks without but something draws me to it from time to time.

Has this always been used as a tool to calm my mind?

No doubt I just wasted 25 bucks on an e-cigarette that most likely will end up in the trash.

"I do fine not smoking."

I'm fine...but am I really? A butterfly effect occurs where I begin to recount the mental cigarettes I've inhaled during conversations and wonder if that is the same thing as smoking or not. To the muses it is. The muses are keeping count.

I need to find a release somehow in order to channel what I feel. see. and experience. I ask myself if I have denied myself a greater understanding by smoking, drinking or generally no longer taking proper care of myself like I once did?

Have I ever?

The driving force to take care of oneself should be out of self-love and self-value. By default, I have disrespected the very thing instinct tries to protect. Are my personal values of protectionism more valued in others than myself? Everything in moderation is ok...Well...not EVERYTHING, but in the context of these two...yes.

Obsession and obsessive thoughts spur anxiety. As I put out my cigarette, I feel I just smoked with both disdain and satisfaction. I'm trying to think of which of the two I am more feeling. Perhaps it is disdain. It matches what I am hearing from them which complicates my thought process. Is this just internal combativeness with oneself?

<I pause.>
<Trying to sort through my thoughts as they flow in.>
Sorting between theirs and my own is an easier task than one would imagine when multiple muses speak. There is voice recognition present.

There is a question of sincerity to what is being said. A question posed of. "Can I do better?" "...at anything?"

What have I denied? For both others and myself.

Promises broken.
Promises made.
Am I angry?
Or am I the same?

If I were to trust what I hear. I know it is what I feel. I refuse to accept myself as broken, but yet I view myself as a woven tapestry of broken shards of tarnished mirror. How many other people are doing the same thing right now of picking themselves up piece-by-piece to find their own reflections of value. What does one lose when not every piece fits into the new mask being designed with what's available? There is sacrifice.
Do I include the things left on the floor or would they detract?

June, 8, 2017
Post 2: Doubting Thomas.

"You know the key to doing this right is going to be making this 100% about yourself? No hiding behind other players. No single chess piece more important than the other because they all have their own different meaning. What is your intention? Your motive? Obviously other people here and on this board in relationship. What drives you to fight or understand others behind who are actually in front in the scheme of things? Princple of the matter knowing the difference of belief systems and who simply has more experience or privilege. This is just going to be you going back and forth with yourself until the game is started. Think about it as much as you want but at some point you are going to have to start playing this game and believing in what you have invested so much time into believing. Or just walk away from this and be done. Go find something else to do and stay out of this world. Just remember there is an obligation to yourself to finish this and you are going to have to finish this.

Move any piece first. A pawn. A tower. A knight. There is no wrong decision except failing to choose. It's your move. It's your game. How much longer are you going to sit and think about what is right or wrong for this? How has that ever stopped you before? Look at the past actions of yourself and rethink things from a different perspective if you have to.

Why are you so hesitant now?
Did you not really want this?
Do you want this?
This is your world. No one can take that from you.
The story is beyond personal. There's something universal in the process.
At least you believe that.

You have to understand your reality is not reality. Your perception is not always truth." - 10/2/2015
7 years later, it is 100% about Us. It is the personal drivers that call to action.

In the beginning, all I saw before me is a game board covered with grey ash from worlds burnt. Which chessboard was I referencing? Truth is my initial thought visually to this series was nothing more than a figure walking through fog and ash covered ground.

"Which square is white and which is black?"
What side of the board am I on?"

I could take a step forward thinking I'm going forward but, being lost in direction. I could be going backwards at this point. There is no fault in such if only to reposition later. At most times I feel we really don't know what is white and what is black. You only start to understand if something is right or wrong when you make a move one way or the other. In any aspect of modern chess, is there subjective approaches to the representation of either side of the board?

In this game for me there are illegal moves and there are repercussions for error. There is a possibility I can make myself vulnerable to other players. Allies could be enemies and vice versa.

There is always the notion of thought "I could stay exactly where I am, but that comes with the realization then I'm destined for the other pieces to continue playing and at any point my place on the board may be lost." It would happen anyways to any of us.

Inaction is a sign of complacency and only invites being stuck in the current environment one way or another. Complancency, loyalty or simply we don't have the means to fight out of fear.

Eventually you have to make a decision. Stay. Move. Strategize.

Sometimes there is a reason to not move at the moment vs. others. Both are good strategic points, but only depending on the scenario. It is a choice to contribute to the game and the motivations or sit it out and observe. At this point it is understood active vs. passive and the do-it-yourself mentality allowed.

I think at one point playing this game, I forgot I got here from a series of strategized moves and I perhaps began questioning myself on if I have put all my pieces in the best positions on the board for a successful offense.What about a defense? Doubt is always a cumbersome emotion to me. One that makes you think every move you make may not be right or the best one to put forward. It was right at the time where at least now I bank on the fact that even AI gets surprised by one move or another. A friendly game of such discussing probability and connections. But it is always good to remember that even in chess, you are still capable of winning the game with but a single piece. Is there a different strategy to thinking of something engrained in trust?

I guess this entry explores my self-doubt. Doubt is a bitch but is also trustworthy. It makes you question yourself. It's the perfect mixture of both truth and perception. It's both rational and irrational thoughts and neither of the two is either right or wrong. There is objectivity that denotes an outside opinion if one wanted to go towards truth objectively. For now They just rest on either the white side of the board or the black side of the chessboard. Good thoughts. Bad Thoughts. Inevitably it dabbles into insecurity and mistrust in ourselves. We all have it and it's one of those things people hold very close. To reveal it, is to reveal a humanizing "flaw" that we don't always know what we are doing or where we are going or how to get there.

Why is our vulnerability one of those things that we hold so close to us? Some let their fear consume them to the point of analysis paralysis while others seem to fight through it with such ease. At least that's the mask they choose to portray. That is one of those emotions that either you hide it well and persevere nevertheless or it just can be seen written on a face. It's a part of everyone whether we like it or not so we all must learn how to deal with it one way or the other. We can't just reject that side of ourselves. The guardedness of vulnerabilities is important. It is also lucritive in one aspect or another.

Rejecting parts of yourself is just as impossible as completely owning just the better parts of you. It's a double package to be owned. They go hand-in-hand where we put one thing forward and the other backwards to be found later if that far in deals and understanding.

It is perfectly normal to question...to fear... to think and not be sure. But don't let it inhibit you. No one knows the answer to everything and you have to go off your learned intuition from past experience or you have to learn to have faith. That would be faith in yourself of others. The others factors based on prior behavior and patterns to say one way or another. There is direct and indirect influence. Both have weight but one is not a wait and see how it plays out scenario. If you have any religion or moral beliefs in your life or believe in a higher power you need to have faith in yourself in your decision-making, your goals and if you fail at one thing then you need to have faith in your survival. Instinctually or otherwise. You are your own perfect storm that only you can calm or make a level 5 hurricane. That is a part of being human and also a very beautiful aspect of knowing that you control the weather in your head.

I think self-doubt leads to settling for things lesser than what we actually should. We are supposed to learn and grow and be challenged. It's what makes us. Although it could probably be proven that a life of adversity denotes a life exhausted and short-lived to the point of nihilism for some knowing. 'One cannot simply wait around for others to solve this with collected intel after one's death.'. Life would be boring as fuck if we knew how things would play out and at the same time we complain when life throws us a curve. Imagine intelligent design or simply those in different aspects that also like surprises once in awhile. So as much as "Doubt is a bitch", it is also an essential safeguard to ask yourself, "Do you really want this?"

Ask yourself these two questions,
"What would you do if you couldn't fail?"
and "What would you do if you won the lottery?"

Two basic questions that almost everyone has asked themselves at one point or another. Both come from the notion of having your dreams realized in life. But both of those come from taking an initial action. One as simple as buying a lottery ticket or the other actually acting out on a desire to do something. I question the need for lottery winner reveals just as much as it is important to note people win as it is important to note wood works occur as well in that regard. A balance of privacy and understanding in that regard. 'We have a winner!' works quite fine in the aspect of an asterisk of saying, 'They choose to be anonymous.'.

 I'm pretty sure nothing that was conjured in your head for the first two questions is completely unattainable but more than likely involve work, strategy and ultimately that never-ending story of overcoming self-doubt in believing you can actually do something or not. Sleepless nights or a whole lot of private time investment. It can occur.

Life is too short to be complacent. Life is too short to settle on things you are not happy with. I can only speak for myself in saying I had goals and dreams of things I wanted to do (this was 2017 here. 5 years later those goals and dreams advanced drastically), but somewhere along the way I accepted safety over believing in myself in some aspects. Here I am writing this today and my bucket list maybe has only two or three things crossed out over the last couple of years.

I guess where I sit now is not necessarily lost in that foggy gameboard, but I am not 100% there yet on being so brazen as having full trust in myself. I see my shades of it in my broken mirror in each piece that I glue together. But I guess in my case only not moving on the board for a couple turns gave me a little bit more of a strategy on how the game works. It takes time. But I do feel I've hit the point where inaction has ran its course.

"You don't have to go home, but you can't stay here." runs through my mind at the moment.

I guess for me one of my biggest self-doubts has been I've been making this up as I go and I just question, 'if this is right for me?' 'Is this right for others?' 'Is this beneficial in the long run?'

Probably more so since I've been here. I've been able to answer that a little for myself. Experience definitely helps ease the thoughts. Eliminate any obstacles and distractions tend to help give a better sense of grounding.

I believe there is a time and a place to be complacent. But for me, now is neither the time nor the place. Perhaps as I get closer to Heaven I will find it within myself to not doubt so much in this story.

In the end, it's just my story...my game. Maybe our story...our game or maybe your game and I am simply a part of it. I have no problem being a token message.

Until then I will continue to just go on faith that I'm making the best decisions for me trying to do so for others. Life is too short to not explore everything you could ever dream up for yourself.

Until I discover an actual definition of failure to myself, I'm just going to pretend I can't fail until I see it to believe it one way or the other that I've been successful in getting even this far.

ENTRY 4:

Sustainability in Perseverance.

Does a year's worth of fight mean anything if I ultimately choose to walk away from it?

I look back at what this year was and I know not to waste another fucking word off of an experience already written and reported elsewhere.

I know I don't have a choice though.

I don't want it to come into play, but it does factors into my every day as it is. When your mind Ctrl-Alt-Delete's itself, what gets rebooted?

I look at today as perhaps a do-over. All day long I have simply ignored the words that were meant to sting. If I were to catalog and catagorize. I find it would be impossible to write out everything heard by the muses. They finish things before they even get started. They start things that never get finished. In futility. I am left with an attempt to transform this experience.

You let this die.
You spoke.
You lost
You rebuilt
You lost again.

Hearing these things is like an STD you never wanted...
Does anyone ever really want an STD?

...events followed through out my year far longer after I thought I was done. What lingers in my head is. **"I could have lost my life"**. I try to shut that out. In a forced replay of things in my head. I am wondering how could they have been handled differently.

From the car accident where I was hit from behind...to work...to past homes of surrogate families. I can't piece everything together. I must lay those ghosts to rest.

"It's done."
Is it though?

I try to tell myself that.
But I have to ask.
"What is next?"

How long am I going to have to hear these influences as it plays out in my mind? Am I giving life to something that should not be birthed? I'm tired of this. Is the memory left to help me process in someway? Is it meant for U? There is a way to turn a negative into a positive and it all starts with head-phones on and a new pair of shoes. A choice has been made between sandals and running shoes. Running shoes gained.

"Are you ready for the sequel?"

The muses saw the Crocs unchosen as a symbol to something else.
Perhaps there is meaning to every choice as it leads in different directions.

What if I chose the Crocs instead? A different series of events unfolds that I don't experience.

ENTRY 5:

Wake up.
Wake up.

"Stand up for yourself"
"(K)"

Broken Promises.

"Damn right, broken promises."
"This guy is unbelievable."
"He has no right."
"He conjured."
"He can hear us?"
"Throwing it away."
"Piece of shit."
"Pieces of shit."
"Your loss Philip."
"He doesn't want to talk to you."
"You don't know what this means to him."

<SCREAMING>

"What did you do?"
"Grow the fuck up!"

"Stand up for yourself for once in your life" (K)
"Burn Him"   "Burn him" (T-PR)

"I fucking knew it"
"Everything I say he writes it down.,.
He can really hear."

Think Philip.
Remember.
Think Harder.

"We talked about this."
"Holllllyyyyyyy Shittttt"
"What's going on?"
"(M)"
"(PW)"
"They are screwing with him."
"Turn it off."
"You aren't supposed to be hearing any of us."

<Hair>

"Set him up."

"Keycard."

Temperance.

<Mom yelling>

"What did he say?"

"He shut it down. He shut it all down."
"It's recording."
"You have to help him."
"Stand up for yourself."
"Phone (inaudible)...important to him."
"It's important to see...(inaudible)"
"Stop! You are freaking him out."
"Not Spirits."

"Put him through it."

<Purpose>

"Doesn't have anyone else to cling to."
"Throwing it away."
"You already did."
"I knew...(inaudible)"
"Making him crazy."
"No...(Inaudible)...respect...(inaudible)...this relationship is important."
"Bold Move."
"(K) wants...(inaudible)...new heart...(inaudible)...everything."
"Everything he hears...(inaudible)"
...Spiritual Awakening"
"No, he's not."

"PLEASE STOP."

"That's what they...(inaudible)...want you to hear.
"Can he use that?"
"(K) there's a problem."

"Low Class white people."
"Shoes."
"Change of destiny."

"Most successful ..."<leaves phrase unfinished>

"What does that even mean Philip"
"...whole relationship hangs on..."
"You are confusing him."
"...Trying to help."
"Bullshit!"

"I trusted you with my secret."

"...Throwing your life away."

"Not going to write that one, are you?"

CON ARTIST.

"Un-Seperateable Bond."

"NO RIGHT."

"Copywrite Infringement."

Commit Yourself.

"STOPPPPPP!!"

"We have a problem."

"...trying to get him committed."

"...using your words against you."

"He's not letting it go."

"This is embarrassing."

<u>"You pushed him."</u>

An example of 5-10 minutes of my every day if I sit, listen, and record psychosis. I tell myself that some times you are given exactly what you need to overcome obstacles if you just take in what God has given you as a gift to grow, but I question my strength to overcome this. Is this a gift or a curse?

Perhaps I rest in hope that this is happening for a reason to be discovered.

ENTRY 6:

"Now everyone knows you are full of shit."

<Questions Compassion>

"Damn right you better question compassion...
and humility."

As I begin to re-read what will become "Building Brave New Secrets". I am faced with remembering things of the past since forgotten. Both good and bad. Human: I hope. Is it a fair assessment to go down this path of remembering? Memories will undoubtedly stir, but I have to believe that the drive within me to revisit is the right thing for me to come back into the norm for now.

"Sadistic Fuck."

"I AM NOT A SADISTIC FUCK!!!!!"

I am beginning to wonder how long I can combat with what I am hearing in my head. I hear a change in my internal voice but there is a difference between my own and opinions of others in my head. It's the reality for me. It scares me at times knowing that there is personifications present. Sometimes it is words by the loves of the past spoken in external silence. In others it is words of wisdom that surround me. It is as if everything is speaking to me to tell me something and it gets jumbled in the process. If only differentiation is possible. Is it? On one hand I could trust those words processed. I believe I can handle criticism in my head. They are choosing to starting conversations about race. I'm questioning the freedom of thought. There are questions on how I am doing things better and how I am failing at others.

It's possible I am not hearing the supportive voices.
I have to believe that there is support somewhere.

There are times that I hear the voices in conversations I am not even a part of. Talking among themselves as if I am not even here. Do I chime in? Do I have a choice? There is an acknowledgment of thought within context? In the end I know they will run with it no matter what I think anyways.

"Nigger"   "Nigger" 'Nigger'   "Nigger"

I said there is a difference in how the word is introduced and where it comes from. The application of the word in this capacity doesn't mean I

49

said it but denotes the word spoken and heard by others before internal reflection of where, why and how. Hate speech has randomly begun to be spoken in my head. I'm not comfortable with the context of that word or "Bitch." "Black", "Fat" "Gay" being echoed from one side of my mind to the other in a negative. But nothing is more forbidden to me than trying to figure out why that one word in particular came into play today. Never are these words externalized, but are carried once heard.

Who started that conversation?
Can an echo determine the width of a space by taking into the speed of sound?
Echo denotes distance within audible range.

A fleeting thought turns into a dialog. I question if I am alone having these arguments with just myself. Do I need to take ownership when it is not my own voice? Or do I suspend belief and accept that not everything can be rationalized by reason alone? How Can I take responsibility for words & thoughts no my own? I argue.

It's very possible that I have gone crazy. Always a diagnosis. Maybe it's divine intervention? But I do so try to hold onto my morals and rationale. There are things suggested that I would never do or what I know would be a straight one-way ticket to a place I am fighting to stay out of. Perhaps this is another edge dangerously too close to view.

Memory serves me of being told by the voices to strip naked in inappropriate places. I refused. I was devastated when prodded to digging up my years ago departed dog. I refused. I will not forget what was said to me in the waters at the beach. I will not go into the rip current. I was taken there anyways in current thoughts.

Consider me a compative witness. I am accepting to a certain extent the content provided to gain insight and then there are other suggestions I absolutely reject. Old memories. Old wounds. Old smiles. Flashes of memories run through my imagination as if they were yesterday.

A Band-Aid has been torn off on wounds not completely healed.

I give myself credit that I'm taking things in better than I was a week ago but the attacking is strong in whispers. They mostly come at night and keep me awake in bed for hours. No sleep. I need to sleep. They theme at least that week.

Months later they still say the same thing.
I'm impossible they say.
Maybe I am.
Maybe they are.

It is starting to get noticed by others when I phase out of the now. It is happening quite often these days. I have to keep myself in check better on this. I find my mind is better when entertained with reading, working towards future projects, and just getting back on track however possible. It's impossible to watch a movie or sit and relax.

High tide to low tide, it comes in waves crashing against the shoreline of my mind. I keep going back to the beach mentally. To me, I take these museal conversations and heed all things as both a warning and guidance.

Influenced by chaos.
Calmness only exists

I see with my eyes.
But perhaps I am blind.

Maybe U are right
I hopeless in cause.

x

Every night we fight
I'll see you at Dawn.

Influenced by chaos where calmness only exists with what I see with my eyes. Maybe I am blind. Maybe not. Maybe they are right and I am hopeless. I think there are multiple definitions of what sticking up for you actually is. Even if it is in an unseen battlefield inside your mind.

Lust. Caution.
Skin Deep.
We connect within with removed variables.

ENTRY 7:

Can I maintain a long-distance relationship?

The absence of touch
A longing unfullfilled.
A voice can only carry so much
In my mind you are singing.
Next to me.
A smile remains.

Absence makes the heart grow fonder, but really, I need to focus on other things ATM than external relationships. There is an internal relationship that has become unbalanced and if I want the external relationship to grow I need to shift back to center.

It does me no good to rehash my life and project that into my present.
This is not the same and I question what my motives are in my present.
I feel taunted of Christmas and presents.

<Frustration>

<Non-recorded dialog>.

Silent frustrations when quiet are the words that no longer can be an applied to my thoughts. A constant critique.
<...frustration trying to making something out of it. >

The value of words.
The value of action.
Weighing out the things provided
Wondering,
"Is this enough?"

None of this past year needed to occur. But it happened for a reason. It cost me everything as it was. But in doing so, I can't ignore the experience. Today I choose not to write about it. It's private. I found what I could and nothing surmounted from it to fix it.

My boyfriend fears I'm crazy.
Maybe I am.
Maybe none of this actually happened.
Maybe I've been through enough.
Maybe I haven't
Maybe this never will happen again.

I give myself to you in the present;
For the present
It's the only thing I am afforded.

I get the fear.
We all were scared.
I think perhaps I am the only one left;
Still scared.

ENTRY 8:

Coincidence of Memory.
<Guardian Angels?>

I have to learn the distinction between my voice and the muses better.
I know MY voice would <u>never</u> allow the things I hear to come into my head willfully. Nor do they get uttered vocally.

Disrespect
Crassness.
Lack of Compassion.
And for what?
Why bring that into my life?

What is it that I am carrying inside me that I do not want to take ownership of at all? Consider it a "coupe de gráce" that there is going to be a battle coming and I am not sure "they" are going to like who is actually in control. It is not them. It's not me. It just is what it is. Consider it a guilty conscious or a group there of one collectively, in who speaks what and in context.

But with what I am hearing, I am trying to ignore it to no avail. It's judgmental of actions. It's judgmental of thoughts. It brings whatever I allow to bring to the table regardless of choice. It gets addressed and I am listening to it.
All of it.

Perhaps there will be no winners in this battle in my head.

<Images build of a chessboard shaped field. Patches of different colored squares, uniformed in design. Stretched from one hillside to the other. A formation made. Discussions. Battle ready, but a battle cry remains silent.>

I challenge each of their roles and responsibilities outside the confines of my mind. They do nothing. I ask questions that they leave unanswered. If all their existence is boiled down to the inner walls of my thoughts, do they even really have a voice of their own? There is power in a voice. There is power in their voices. There is power in my own. A power struggle continues.

One voice is easily washed out when morally wrong. Another becomes

separated by barriers when invading privacy.
"You always have a problem.' I battle internally contention toward dialogue.
Are the muses solely echoing my own voice or their own opinions?

"Let's see whom wins, shall we?"

I test them with a conversation point. "Happiness". A free open-ended
discussion to be had. Volume is turned down much lower than what it was
prior, but I still hear even if it has been transformed back to muffled sounds.
What if I visually focus on the word happiness and clear my mind? You
would think there would be valid discussion points made. I switch to the
topic of Love. Statements for sure. 100% let's talk about love and then roped
right back around to past expressions. Who is keeping who on topic?

Mercy is something left for only God to deliver.

"That's false hope."

Of course, they will say that is false hope...trusting in God that is. What am
I really supposed to believe now anyways? Truth is, as I have said before,
spirituality, religion and relationships are unique personal experiences.
Never two the same. Never to be fully understood by anyone other than
those involved. Sometimes that involvement is just with you. I am not
combative about this. But I believe outside opinions have their place.
Inside your mind is not one of them.

What do you do with outside internal opinions?

Is there a banking entirely on the past to answer all the questions?

"I'll read all the books." I say.
(I've read all the books.) Or was it the versions I am thinking of.

Perhaps in exploring the past you only breathe life back into dead trees now
petrified and washed up upon a shore. I found one the other day on the
beach still there all these years later exactly where it was left.

Perhaps new experiences bear weight worth remembering later. It's
important to measure out equal weight to past, present and the future.
For now it is simply an unbalanced scale.

Do I confine myself to a narrow point of view looking for answers of the past that were not able to be comprehended when first experienced?

Perhaps moments of review at a later part of my journey may provide answers eluded ages ago.

Quarter way review. 20 years. Now mid-way through on my life. Will there be anything worth repetition? What lessons am I teaching myself in quandary? The same basic question still exists from previous years. "What is love?" But it comes with the knowledge that it fundamentally starts with yourself and branches off from there. You just need to be observant of your environment in order to spread your roots.

ENTRY 9:

Heaven must contain empathy.
But can we really put ourselves in other people's shoes?

Cram a 13 into a 9. Perhaps if we remove the toes to make it fit. $7\frac{1}{2}$ in an 11.
Big shoes to fill, but doable. Empathy is projection. But how does one really
understand another person who never speaks and doesn't share words.
Is there still a door open to relate? How do you share your thoughts and
feelings if never a word uttered?

There is commonality in success.
There is commonality in defeat.

A connection between 2 completely different things can be made.
Mixed Messages when combined creates a new experience of thought.

Is empathy only shared in a negative connotation?

By definition it exists in the ability to understand and share the feelings of
others, however it becomes commonly associated within a negative context.
Empathy is not just sympathy. I've never heard the phrase, "I empathize
with their success", but I have heard, "I empathize with what they are going
through."

To feel what someone else is experiencing is a fleeting thought though. Too
many variables lie for replication of a life experience. If you have never gone
through something, then I can see the uphill battle towards comprehension.

That is an out-of-context escapism in art forms such as music, movies and
all visual & performing art. That escapism is driven by universally understood
motifs. Art is a conduit towards empathy. Shimmering glimmers of obsession/
passion, love/heartbreak, desire/rejection all expressed through body language
voice and strokes.

What art piece are you creating for the world to see?

Side note – Meatbeat Manifesto

ENTRY 10:

Is Heaven in writing your own story?

Choices.
Voices.
Malleable Smoke.
Personification.
A single glowing feather given.

Choices between past and present
A tribunal of sorts.
Mercy killing.
Coup de grâce.

What would Dante had created if allowed to return to Florence?

Right? Wrong?

<Lightning Strikes the next yard over>
"Did I just piss off God?"

Tangent Thoughts.
Branches of Possibilities.
Stories written and those that were never shared

What is kept in-between the lines?

What if...?
All thoughts at once, and then gone.
Like a bolt of lightning
Inspiration.
Memories of something taken for granted.
Saying the same thing over again.
Finding the answer.

False starts.
False finishes.
False finalities.

A circle not knowing where the hidden break is.
3600% magnified to illustrate that there is always a natural break

The history of Alice and The Lost Boys.
An opportunity to add to the story.
Is there universal-ness in other's perspective?

Perhaps an exercise after the fact
Muse inspired. Muse creation.
Inspiration.
Everyone has a right to write.

Can you actually predict an outcome?

"Savannah loves its stories."

"Love.
What did you do to me?
My only hope is to let love stretch out before me.
Take me...
on this open road..."
Above & Beyond

My path is determined
by U.
Unpaved.
Unbroken.
Determined to intertwine
Possibilities collide.

At some point our paths will meet at an intersection of possibilities. Each one possible. A Road Less Traveled or perhaps weather worn of the footsteps of past mistakes. A new journey nevertheless. A new adventure chosen.

You can't force the answer.
You can't will something to be something it is not.

All you can do is love each day.
Know that eventually there will not be another.

Just Breathe.
Use your words and sometime speak without thinking.
Act without consequence.
Dare to be daring.
Believe in what you feel is right.
The rest will follow.

10.15.2022
Questions arise on the middle section that get answered later. Introduction of it not my own words very understood while questions remain on aspects of introduction and when to cite as already would be incorporated at this point.

Do lyric sites & quote sites ask permission or goes instantly into monetizing aspects of the collection of other people's poetry?

Still no page numbers yet, but it makes sense to cite while also understanding aspects already discussed & introduced in personal experience.

In context of reference it makes sense in something a part of someone expelling other things heard & incorporated into life experience & memory. Differences there in wonder. Cite anyways. Discussions on the matter had later. Note what occurred as you have physical copies of every version.

There is no way they could create from it to go back and say I infringed when in fact it was the other way around. A book written in 2019 where final edits in this color scheme to show expansion and pick completely from what was available electronically since last 2019 to present.

Who owns a karaoke performance?

Who owns culture?
Who owns myth-ing?
A template to grow from?
Parables?
Religion?
Lessons of life.

What happens with the threats of losing everything?

PART II.

___

At what point does one book end and another begins?
Are we reading multiple books at the same time?

Sometimes it takes a peaceful moment of looking up and seeing something
that was less than a second to occur. but exactly what was needed to be seen.
A wish made. A shooting star seen.

Shooting stars.
Lightning.
Rain.
A symphony of sound.
Heavenly in discord.
Calmness engulfs.
Things lost
Now found & returned.
Exactly when they were supposed to.
A multi-pass to something gifted.

June 11, 2017
Post 3: Take comfort that we all shit.

(In Building Brave New Secrets, I had a row of toilet shots available for this section. An ever rotation of intimacy and comfortability knowing regardless the archetype and person, we all release one way or another. Never a problem there... just simply things not always expressed or talked about. It is the same as sex of birds and bees understanding there is commonality in secrets one way or another and knowing where discussion points are one way or another. Is 'shit' a curse word or simply just a word associated with secrets of trying to find the proper term to expel something from someplace in awkwardness of what was not presented prior?)

"When we moved to Savannah in 1989, I remember my family visited our unfinished house for the first time. A survey through the unfinished framework not really understanding this would be our home from 1989 to 2001. In survey of the new lands upon us, my sister and I explored the new neighborhood which really was like 3 or 4 cross streets at the time and wound up playing some pretend Wizard of Oz game with a group of neighborhood kids whom we instantly befriended as if we had known each other already. Trips around the house had in pretend and welcome. Those kids would go on to become some of my oldest and closest friends even to this day. That is kind of how things were growing up in Savannah. You meet someone, you become instant friends and suddenly one day you are just another part of the family.

I guess Savannah was special in that regard. Not without it's own flaws by any means, but there was always a welcoming aspect to strangers that you just don't seem to find everywhere else." - 10/28/16

Friendship is one of those absolute essential things to having a fulfilling life. It's a connection between people over commonalities and interests. Later on in life they are the people we confide in just as much as the ones we protect. People we laugh with. People to cry to when need be and the ones to celebrate our personal milestones in life.

It's interesting how building those relationships in the beginning was so much easier as a child. "You like Transformers? I like Transformers. Let's be friends." Probably partially because children have yet to see the world and understand emotions, but perhaps as we get older we have this wonderful knack of over-complicating things where a simple question of commonality becomes a questionnaire to be filled out and returned tomorrow along with 3 references and a background check before acceptance or even a response if ever one had anyways depending on the scenario. The discardment and acceptance of life now reduced to a swipe left or right where everyone has to learn branding and the instant gratification aspect of image.

I guess the questionnaire really begins to form in high school...maybe slightly a little earlier but eventually we do start to branch off into our different groups as our commonalities become more defined into forming our own identity. In high school there are the archetypes of Jock. Cheerleader. Nerd. Band member. Burnout. Artist. So many other high school archetypes not mentioned. It is a 'Choose your own adventure' of interests with the comfort of acceptance around like-minded people which seems to be where things grow to one way or another. Acceptance factors in early before people start getting really specific and peticular. Is identity contingent on the number of people that agree with us?

As we receive more positive affirmation in one thing, do we lose an unexplored part of ourselves that has never been properly nurtured?

To a certain extent school is probably when our own prejudices start to become outwardly applied unknowingly or through examples given of others not knowing the answers anyways. We are all trying to figure things out there and either educated together, or learn privately through homes or in-direct contacts. People begin to learn to judge others by the things that make us similar and different from one another. When we are young there is the obvious physical differences noticed at first. Through school we start to see that outside of physical that people think and act differently from one another. We begin to weigh people more on their interests and actions than before with judgment coming a little bit easier to dish out with the strength in numbers of like-minded beliefs. In high school we start to learn differences on a different capacity than middle school. Fat in middle school and elementary...far more labels associated in high school. It only grows from there depending on your circle of interests. Probably why I was a platypus even in high school. Was never for playing that game in any stand up aspect. Even in footbal hazing. I still got respect from Seniors to a Freshmen for not putting up with one thing or another. I can only imagine those who called me 'Fro-Boy' in elementary who no longer have hair while I still have mine. It's thinning but the laughter of what sticks continues one way or another. The 'Whale-Boy' comments stuck through middle school high school and into adult-life, but it has been handled one way or another. This is why Platypi last long in society. A bit of everything and understanding one way or another. Call out a negative in a non-constructive way and simply I go to the other departments of acceptance and let you continue to disclude while I search for acceptance. I imagine there is poking with friends and then there is poking at people you simply do not know.

It used to be that the numbers game ended with high school and college. The idea that gaining as much friends determines worth eventually dies down as you settle into adulthood. You go to college; you develop what you want to do in life. You individualize a bit more. You find yourself dating and you individualize a little bit more from each experience. In some instances you get married and may or may not have children where you definitely lower your social group and find yourself revisiting cartoons and childhood in a different capacity or learn to just appreciatew bedtime to get back to 'adulting' one way or another. More people begin to taper off the list as you start to realize what is and isn't important to hold onto. I guess by that rationale, it's expected that at some point in life we are left with the best of the best of what adds to our life until eventually we start losing the best one at a time until eventually it's time for us to go. By that definition, adulthood is predestined to become quite lonely the longer in we stay in the game filled with memories of relationships, friends, loved ones and things that inevitably we won't have anymore. That doesn't mean it can't be a worthwhile endeavor full of life and happiness, but does mean that perhaps it's good to start thinking about how to accept and deal with loss early on. Inevitably you will lose someone. A friendship. A relationship. A family member. In some circumstances, you are even completely capable of losing yourself. A majority of the world has a three-generation life span. 3 generations later, you are a vague memory at most. A name in a biological legacy at best depending on what you left behind.

Whether good or bad, social media has allowed for the perpetuation of that comfort from that eventual loneliness. It's high school 2.0 expanded into adulthood with pretenses of the high school effect. Self-validation is given through number of followers. # of likes on a shirtless photo or that meal cooked to perfection that you are about to enjoy. I guess this art series is no different than the others. It's defining yourself so much by your interests and your clans followed by then further dividing it by the shade of color you are, the body type you are within a community, the success of one milestone over the other. We look for likes and acceptance one way or another.

It's kind of exhausting at times trying to have one day top the next to gain a "like" to make us feel just a little bit more comfortable in the world. In an effort to make our lives so unique and special we find that dropping someone from your circle who does not fall in agreement with your beliefs or align to your standards is dropped with the click of a button. The passive aggression is real just as much as the aggression of 'screennames' exists as well. I believe the bigger our social network, the less the connection overall. It is impossible to reach everyone individually yet still a desire to reach out one way or another. Imagine going through a team before a single social media post. It exists.

Then again that's also trying to judge digital network vs. personal network which are two completely different things. Social media is a relatively new thing to my generation. It will be interesting to see how it evolves socially for my generation when we get into our twilight. Hell...in some scenarios to feel needed, wanted and not alone, I'm more likely to see a pic of someone's dick, vagina or ass before I even get a name or face pic from them. A cutting to the chase realizing maybe we just want and understand fleeting moments and what naturally is the point of one place or another without so much as needed to know anything else until after. Instant comfort or vulnerability understanding you get that up-front before ever getting a name. Instinct proves the desire for trust comes instantly. Makes you wonder...what's in a name? What's in a face that so sacred vs. the latter? Can we really get instant gratification on the deepest of emotions? I can't imagine 80 year olds still banking on their looks for relevancy. But then again...maybe so. Fine wines are collector items. If anything it should put a smile on your face that 100 years from now people will be questioning what was our fascination of selfies in the bathroom and looking back on when that trend ended for people over timelines. We all shit though, so I guess there is security in that connection. How much individuality is lost at the expense of being accepted? There are healthy social trends and then simply things that age out over time. In either regard, I imagine the humor of myself doing a bathroom selfie image at 80 if I even get there if only to reference this later in life or make grandchildren completely awkward of thoughts of grandparent before revealing secrets of their parents to them at their age.

I've weighed back-and-forth over what this entry is actually about.
Is it about how we build our own castles?
Is it how we separate ourselves based on differences and build on similarities?

I think it really is just a longwinded entry about prolonging our own individuality but also maybe thinking of what is important or not or just finding insight to humor of life as one gets older. Inside jokes or perhaps appreciate it understanding new insight and perspective from others who simply experienced life differently.

It's comfortable being a part of a group. It's comfortable being a headless torso. It gets the point across from the get go. Yes, this is what society looks for. Yes, this is either a preferred size of one place or another and we get that over with early on. Anything else...well that is valuable before circling back around to understanding any bit or privacy is valuable. It is a question of what people want in general populus that denotes a showcase one way or another. Valid had either way. It's comfortable in mass acceptance vs. throwing yourself out there individually. It's not always comfortable being with yourself or being 'yourself' wondering if you even know that answer at any age. I can only speak for mid-way, but I gather you eventually figure out and go one way or another with it. I don't know if anyone ever actually is 100 percent, so it's others that make us feel better and not alone. What do people think they will discover about themselves when left alone to look inside? Reasonable conclusions denotes they will find ways to be quite fine by themselves if it excludes negativity.

We live in a timeline where we are getting rid of things, issues, people that hamper our spiritual growth at a click of a button just as quickly as we get validation with a single click.

"I don't agree with you...<unfriend>.
Done."

I guess where my upbringing has been challenged is I used to believe friendships meant something on the same level of family. Perhaps they actually do in a way but sometimes that friendship serves a better good as a memory while others are worth holding onto for as long as you need to. It's nothing personal, just as life goes on the world gets smaller and people fragment off into different places, different priorities and different worlds. I can only imagine how many people are in for a shock that they are friends with and never see a single thing on their timeline from them. Interaction important but probably the same of what others post as well. That definitely goes in my area in why one way or another.

I guess a truth to me is there have been friends I have held at pretty hard regard and over time either myself or them shifted away from one another. I used to genuinely be upset about that and probably at certain moments I still am. Not to mean there has not been new friends and new bonds, but I guess in our effort to narrow down to the things that matter most, it is nice to look back and think about connections in general. I tend to reach every now and then to people and some do to me as well.

I dunno. I guess in a lot of ways I don't try to reach as much as I used to anymore. Consider it partially because you shouldn't beg for a relationship with someone and the other part is I have to consider the notion that perhaps I or them have weeded each other out in our search for what is more important in our lives. It is understood which is why never harm to randomly say hello once in awhile. Never a requirement to respond.

It is the question of how to make new connections that becomes strangely more difficult as one gets older. What is one to do before just going back to saying hello at a bar understanding the freak-out moment of others wondering why the hell is this person talking to me verbially and what app are they on so I can respond properly? I need more data before I say hello back here. 'Ummm...your thinking out loud...I'm right here but I can give you my social media handle if that helps you on your search for a response.'

Perhaps inaction and fear factors in that. The struggle to communicate or even reach out one way or another. Perhaps I'm happy with just a memory. One thing hard at times to accept that it's quite possible we exit people's lives for their own good.

Perhaps I've finally learned that you have to be comfortable with loss if you want anything to gain. Years ago, I said the perception of the memory of someone is always your choice on how you will hold onto it. I believe the rest of the qoute was we are going to be in each other's minds for the rest of our lives one way or another so we might as well make it a good memory. At least I can say in all the impediment I've experienced and of past lives revisited, it has been honored and they are great memories understanding growth and heartbreak in between. My focus has been on the honor of any relationship and always my choice from youth to where I am now on honoring such. It happened. Once a connection of meaning, it tends to stick with you for a lifetime. That was spoken in 2011. Life is too short to hold onto the things that are not genuine or fulfilling. The sooner you learn to be comfortable with yourself, the sooner you can learn what it is that makes you happy or not.

ENTRY 12:

Is there a mental weight difference between pain and happiness?

If your mind was a hard drive, eventually it would run out of space.
But considering we only use 2-4%, how much data is in the other 90+% un-
formatted? Or is it just coded differently?

There is a difference between book smart and street smarts.
Can the two be quantified together properly?
If one is on, are they incapable of being the other?
Is a mixture of both possible?

Labels.
Classification.
Grouping to belong to something.
Anything to look at one elephant to the next.
Are we ready to see a bigger picture?

In the clouds today, I saw an adult elephant followed by an infant.

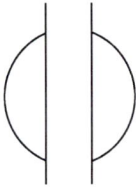

"God doesn't draw in straight lines."
                              -Prometheus, 2012

...and thus I wonder, is a perfect circle possible?
There is always a break if you look close enough.

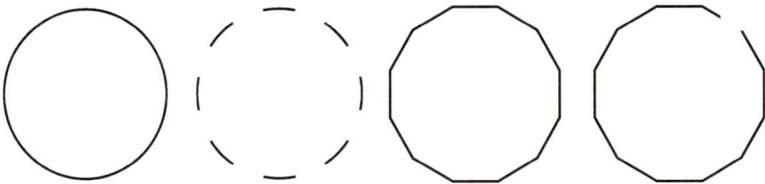

There is always a flaw.
"Perfection is Imperfection".
There is always something that makes us unique unto ourselves.

But questions that beg answering.

"How far are we are willing to go into what defines us as an individual?"
Are we capable of accepting eventual commonality until we memorize our
entire genome to find that one sequence that makes us unique?

Are we destined to feel better or worse about ourselves because of that
difference? There is a social focus on Difference vs. Commonality occurring.

Perhaps all have equal weight.

In the clouds later, I saw a circle break.
In my mind multiple circles remain.

June 21, 2017
Post 4: The King's Weakness.

"I know that I mull way too much on things. It's the one thing I can't hide even if I tried. There is always something going on up there and when I am quiet is when people know the most. I think about what I could have done better with others. I think about what I want. I think about who I want to be without ever really sitting back and thinking who I am. Shit... Most of my art has been me dealing with those questions one way or another. It's always a reflection of myself and the desires to understand "the What?" "The If?" "The Why?" as I know I am growing into my own. In hindsight, I can't say for the life of me, I regret my execution in mullings. It's only my thing. It's mine. From it I do see at times somehow I am finding myself in there somewhere. I know I am a work-in-progress. I'm not perfect...never will be. I think it may be a double-edged sword though, but if I move forward then let's proceed, as we should. Maybe I held onto things of the past too long. Maybe I didn't care enough, or maybe I cared too much. Maybe my subject matter did more damage to others that offsets the positive to me where there is an imbalance. Everything has its pluses and minuses. I guess we weight that one-way or the other. Some don't even consider outside of the self so I guess I have that I am looking at all sides of things. I believe no one can fault me just as in the end I cannot fault others. But I need to remember; all those are questions and scenarios that are really just in my own head. Life goes on nevertheless. For any catalyst or myself. Reconciliation occurs or perhaps retribution takes over depending on intent. In the scheme of things, the situations that mattered once will lose the weight they had at one point or another. There will come a point of apathy for emotions. We all have demons.

I believe that if I treat others like I would want to be treated then what it boils down to is a matter of we are all looking for those that make us feel like our demons do not exist or they are not at the forefront.

Truth of the matter, I think I need to stop thinking about 'what ifs'. It is about the actions and the ripples made. There is no fucking 'what ifs'.Well, there is. But it does not exist. Those come from inaction. There can be senario plays, but as far as the past goes, those are ripples that go one way or another. What does exist is only what we do and throw out into the world...from my own accord and from the ripples of others. I need not waste my time with the "what ifs" of the past anymore. There are future 'what ifs' of going one way or another that once acted upon are no longer inacted on thoughts and probability will say one way or another based on impact, the wavelength and the persistence of what you throw out there. 'What ifs' served their purpose. To think further about it would just open up the series of non-consequential 'what ifs' that really just play out in our heads anyways. THEY AREN'T REAL" - 2/18/15

A game a chess ends once the king is taken. To get there is a series of moves that is equally part strategy as it is missteps. There is no perfect game of chess. There is no master of chess. There are only masters. To win a game of chess is literally to be the second to last mistake. Even a computer is capable of losing in the right scenario because human error factors in.

The king is the protective piece on the board. All the other piece's sole job is to protect it from the opposing side. In the scheme of this series, I look at the king, as the one piece that represents what about ourselves that needs the most protection. It's the part that is equal strength and vulnerability at the same time. On the board I feel the queen has the most moves. There are lessons with the rooks and knights and the soul of the game lies in the pawns and their ability to evolve unlike the other pieces. But everything lies in protecting that one piece that can end the game the minute it is taken. So it becomes a strategic move in showing vulnerability and weighing affordable sacrifice.

Trust. this is not easy playing by rules I set forth before understanding the game I was playing. It's a game that only I can get myself out of by completing it. Imagine a chess player trapped in the amber of their own thought process and that is not far off from the cycle of this experiment. I feel every single time I push against the rules I made for myself one way or another in testing. At this point...faith is a funny thing to discover. My gut tells me to play my vulnerable piece and then move from there.

<A positioning occurs.>

What is my most vulnerable?
What am I protecting?
Consider it human if this move is done in error.

My secret isn't really a secret. But sometimes it takes on a new life when you acknowledge your weaknesses.

I failed to understand other people.

I failed to understand why things happen.

I failed to understand what I did wrong in scenarios.

I failed to understand doubt outside of my own.

I clearly failed on providing what others needed for pacification of doubt in some people's accord. Perhaps they failed in providing pacification to my own doubt.

It isn't anyone else's responsibility to pacify a single bit of other's insecurities. If one does, it comes naturally and at times never even expressed or shared that one or the other is doing so. I imagine most would not focus much on where they failed in relationships or one thing or another as the focus needs to be on accomplishments and where one strides into success. Balance in those discussions are always required for meaningful connections. I failed to see that self-preservation would always take accord one way or another. Always. Even in expanisive self-preseveration is not necessarily just the preseveration of 'Self'. Protection of a partner of family equally fall into the realm of what is 'Self'-Preservation. I should know that by now. I've done it. But nevertheless, I've miss-stepped enough to realize that perhaps I was just never meant to really understand to begin with. (at this point)

My king is in a 'protective mode' at the moment. He is analyzing the whole chess-board and trying to predict every move possible before it happens. I admit it's one of my downfalls. I am keeping things at bay while watching other things play out from a distance. I don't want anything to get too close or too real to me at the moment because I feel that I'm just now finally coming back into my own world. Shit, I'm 3 years here next month and I refuse to believe this is where I am supposed to be. It's not. But I believe coming here has made me grow beyond I could imagine, but I refused from day 1 to accept that this is home. Perhaps it is because everything is so spread out or perhaps because the circle aspects are not as large as they used to be. I see it every day when I refuse to decorate this room or the next or when I don't explore my surroundings. Although I decorated it quite nicely and lined the main wall of the living room thematically with my Heroes+Villains as if friends were always over. This is only temporary I tell myself. I told myself that for 3 years now. Is that what I really believe? I was the same way moving to a transitional neighborhood (In fairness, I referred to it originally as the ghetto where it simply was a neighborhood where I found quite fondness of abandoned property, prostitutes on the corner where at least they looked like they were having fun considering their position, burnt down homes and across the street one of the city's most crime filled neighborhood. I imagine it is perfectly acceptable to refer to it as "The Hood' as there was even a shop down at the corner of the neighborhood called. 'Hoodmart.' The Hood is simply a shortened version of The Neighborhood anyways. I imagine reference in the original regard simply denotes background of one area used to or not where equal judgement could be had for constant rental property and the discussion of at least we own our property.

Protection there in the streets though. House only attempted to be broken in once while neighbors watched out and said. 'Leave that house alone.') with 3 months before I unpacked. There is a difference between the two. Alone in a 4 bedroom house new to I. All the space I needed in the middle of winter with a heater that could barely keep the house above the 60s. Too small of a unit where it is back to baited breath of falling asleep to visable breathing. Uninsulated memories that perhaps explains my tempermental aspects of hot/cold. At the time, too stubborn to accept the transition and then pull what my environment gives me to grow. Is this it? Am I doing what I can knowing I am not doing what I used to in outside endevours?

I kind of keep to myself here.

I've had really zero desire to be come a part of the community here and I tried the dating thing in the beginning to epically say, "Nope...kind of not what I want or need at the moment.".

I actually always have to be honest now. I don't always know what to say but I try. I'm trying to think of any relationship I have been in when I was the one that pushed it further in the beginning. I can think of when I did when I knew what I was dealing with but never at first pass. I honestly think I've never actually pursued a relationship in the beginning. I definitely remember defining them. They tend to just happen and then one day it becomes official one way or another. Not many labels had there. First moves tend to be rare, but they occur ever so often. I remember losing my virginity to someone who came into my room after I called it a night and went to bed and they came in and woke me up. I guess that carried on the mentality that I'm not going to be chasing anyone. Hit on here. Asked for a cigarette there. Dance with me here. Etc. I guess I give credit where credit is due that I'm shy when it comes to approaching people I like. I imagine a great deal of number of people are wondering how to sort things into leagues wondering why would that be such a necessity to do so anyways. If one wanted to go about status labels, it simply doesn't mean one thing or another to just say hello and see what happens. Although put me in the comfort of my own parameters and I am definitely anything but shy.

Here is where I am conflicted on what I reveal. I'm not about to portray every relationship I've ever been in as something heartbreaking or memorable in some circumstance or another. That is just as much as I am not about to say that I feel remorse or enlightened in every scenario. I don't. I won't. It doesn't occur on the everyday basis as we either take the day-to-day for granted as each day a collection and a building.

Some relationships left on very good terms and for that I have some of my best friends from it. The ability to transition one relationship from one thing or another is simply a sign of respect but does not negate a single aspect of those relationships that can't transition. There are some relationships that did mean something to me that didn't work out that will always factor into things. I should admit that. I guess chalk it up to me growing as a person.

Whatever issue I have replaying in my head is of my own regard. Skewed from reality and marred in truth, but also emotion that through this series I lay them to rest one way or the other. I actually think in the scheme of things I've been pretty lucky with my full spectrum of connections. Once you figure out how any connection matters one way or another determines perspective of appreciation that any one of us took the time towards one another.

I guess if I protect anything I'd say it is this and it too is another double-edged sword. Is everything in life a double-edged sword or this just the other side of the same original sword? What I ask of others, I don't think I can hold my own candle to. Don't make me believe in a story you didn't want to believe in yourself. Don't let me think beyond the now if you are conflicted. Enjoy the now. Laugh. Cry. Spoon. But don't let me create expectations if you are scared. Don't come into my life if you mistrust whom I actually am. I make it very clear. Don't let me dream. Don't let me feel comfortable and at peace if you don't feel at peace yourself. Give me respect that I'll do my best to find a reason for you not to remember anything that came before. Only the now. There's the rub. I'll always be scared I think. Who am I to ask of someone to be stronger than I? How can I be stronger than U? In the building of any relationship, there is hopes that become expectations over time. A series of get to know you one way or another that determines a belief system that perhaps stronger as 'Us'.

With me there is no just the now. There is what happened prior and what could happen in the future. At least in complete awareness it is understood no two people are alike. There is never a recreation of a past relationship entirely in any sense. Each one unique to itself and hidden once laid down to rest. Truth is I have zero idea at this point how to proceed with relationships. I kind of block them out.

It's been almost 2 years since I even considered it. Part of me gets scared when people show interest and very much aware that I also create a huge hurdle for anyone that tries. I get reserved if I think something didn't quite go the way I thought it would. There is always an openness to talk or discuss, but it never got that far here. Long-distance works quite well these past years. Secretly there have been attempts but for one reason or another. Friendship will do. My expectation is quite a part of my protectiveness. It all stems from my inability to understand. I wish I knew better. I guess I spent my life for the last 10+ years at least saying, 'This is me... I don't know who the fuck I am... but I'm at least here and I am trying to be a good person and call bullshit on bullshit.' I guess my king is saying don't let me build a kingdom dependent on other people yet that is how it works anyways one way or another. I've often gone into relationships where I've completely sought equality on economic aspects to be a fair partner to others. Often the sadness of others capable of vacations that I could never afford or go on. I've left those relationships understanding they need someone who can afford to do those things with you on their equal status of equity. Dependancy in the regard of economics is what would break me. Emotional aspects aside where always a balance to denote the difference between dependancy and contingency to balance out healthy aspects of what makes a relationship not feel transactional even though a relationship is always a give-and-take. I guess that is what I protect the most. My world controlled in aspects where I could be out on the street at any moment. I've been there before to know that equality is important. I'm aware of where I am at now knowing there are different types of relationships that go into other realms and still there is submission and dominance present one way or another.

I've had the dreams in my life of I'm going to be a husband. I'm going to be a father. We are going to own a house. You are my safe space. Let's just watch a movie. Everything in that is dependent on someone else. All good things to be had, but never worked out for me in a sustaining sense. I'd say the conflict of that being exasperated by others had me just come to not want to dream with a plus one anymore.

Trust. Someone I only knew for 3 weeks falls on this list of fucks you up in that search for comfort and acceptance. PS. Never fake your death. It never works out and you kind of have to explain it after the fact. That falls in line with I really don't understand some people. Especially in that regard. Who does that is not someone I ever want to know any rationale or understanding behind that. It destroys people and yet somehow brought someone they were close to into my world and it became a coping/ working relationship in the regards before transitioning to friendship. A true story from 2015 that I'll never forget those text messages of someone dying on an operating table and feeling regret about kicking them out of my home for continually searching my phone while I was asleep. They didn't die, but I still know why faking that is illegal. If you wanted to do that, go into the movie business. Happens all the time there. I just think so many people are so impatient to finding love that they have to rush everything to get it and if they don't get it fast enough then there is this scorched earth mentality that comes from that if it doesn't seem to go the way they want or at the pace of desirement.

I guess as much as I try to protect the world I am building, I can't help but feel that in a relationship, I run the risk of compromising on the identity that I am finally coming to terms with as an individual. We lose ourselves at times as we look for companionship when individuality becomes a duality to a certain extent to continue to advance and nurture. I guess for me I'm afraid of that duality because as much as it has brought out my best, it has also brought out my worst at times. I suppose it does for everyone.

I like that my dreams, for the now, are very much my own and somewhat uncompromising in some regard. I will be traveling across the world by myself in September. I complete Heaven soon after. I'm thinking about where I want to live long term. I'm back into my art. I'm running and swimming daily and life is suddenly coming under my control again. It's kind of all under the "this is my responsibility and that is safe" blanket while I challenge myself.

I can't help but have a bit a sadness in thought that I am coming to realize I may not get to be a father or any of the other myriads of expectations that could of happened. I'm not going to have a family for myself that represents a functional normal life. That is just perhaps over the years I'm finally become selfish in that it's hard for me to realize plans with anything other than just me making them. I can't predict people but I can predict me.

I'll predict the next year right now. You are going to do you. You are going to do Italy. You are going to debate even coming back. 3 years of downtime does you wonders. 3 years of figuring out "Who are you?" is a good starting point for me to say that I should throw out everything I just said because if I want any of the above, then I'll find a way to get that one way or another. The choice is mine to make and go from there. 3 years prior to get to this point where we predict the next 3 years where now

now I type 3 years after that in the aspect of understooding of spaces and knowing options more limited, yet still I drive forward anyways. The span of 9 years in this regard.

I guess for me I've had too many hopes, dreams, aspirations swept away from other people's decisions that for once I like that I can't hide behind that as an excuse. I do or do not. Either I hold myself to the fire of my true desires or I shut the fuck up about anything I wanted but did not spend the time/effort to actually do.

My king is most definitely going to be the Icarus of this series. Arrogance is never cute and, although I don't think I really have that quality, I'm aware where this ends up. (to a degree) I guess there is humility in understanding there is always a price to pay one way or the other.

I definitely feel the solitude of this move. But I guess if we are going to play this game, there it is on vulnerability. The rest of the game continues as being about further exploring and accepting who I am yet in the search towards the answer to 'Who are U?' involves getting to know others and beginning to ask the same questions and go from there. One way or another. Truth is a beautiful thing, even if it means you admit what could break you. Perhaps I believe if I reveal the weakness now, it only makes the game more interesting as it is something to think about as I continue down paths unknown. This is never going to be about anyone other than me trying to figure this out one way or another. Perhaps if I reveal that I am tired making and rearranging life plans and start making/doing my own for me again, then this journey would be more meaningful in growth and shown externally as well as internally. It's really is not bitterness keeping people at bay. It's just a search for certainty and eliminating variables and realizing flawed logic during this exercise.

I'm sure it's a trust issue in there just as much as I completely believe that other people's self-preservation and power struggles are capable to muddy up my goals for the short term. Is this a stand-off or simply at the time realizing that I'm pretty much ready to transition from the job I had to something different elsewhere and that involves not getting really attached like I could? I like to think if I admit that now, then I can proceed further knowing that I accept that as some things are very defining about myself that I can break that wall that seems to hold me back from finishing this.

'Do or do not.' But it's always going to be my choices made on this. Just as much as you have your choices. Choices in either direction wondering where is their overlap?

In all irony though, I fully expect that life will find a way to challenge me on this and walls one way or the other will be broken to my kingdom just as much as yours. Never say never.

ENTRY 13:

I'm not sure I'm the one for you.
But please don't let me go.

Instead of going fast pace
Let's just take it slow.

Pacing.
Racing.
Chaos in Calmness.
The power of perception.

Secrets Stolen.
Secrets Given.
Secrets Taken Back.
Once a secret,
Never a secret again.

Processing.
Alone.
Blindfolded.
Speaking.
Blindly Spoken.

Am I wrong?

They speak.
I listen.
<Repeat>
They control the conversation.

A Topic chosen.
Muffled Sounds as each board is flipped.
A script rewritten.
Redone.
Undone.
Back to square one.

It begins with sound.
Association.
A memory sparked.
A dream foreseen.
Lucid combinations.
Sleep.
Awake.
Woke.

Finish what you built
Take back that which was stolen.

Not just this.
But so much more
Was thought before.
If only you and I could soar.

ENTRY 14:

"Today will be a good day!"

Heaven is patience that things take time.

Remember everything. But perhaps it is time to choose to have the good memories a chance to be written.

You cannot shut yourself off from the world.
You cannot escape what you hear.
Once you hear it, the sound becomes a part of you.

Voices of hope. Alliterations of hate. Sometimes it is putting yourself in a controlled environment to direct your mood, your thoughts & drive intent. Headphones on. Flood the mind with intended emotions. When you have no words, listen to what you hear. A combination of sound from both physical & mental states create a sense of now. A symphony only meant to be understood as only you can.

Goals.
Hope.
Peace.
Ambition.
They all spawn from environmental influences.

A fluid change.
A power struggle of what surfaces and what gets buried deep.
Inspiration/Influence in layers
Ebbing back and forth.
Sound.
Memory.
New experiences familiar & foreign.
Create your heaven by controlling your environment the best you can.

When it comes to my relationship with music, the memory that came first to me was painting with my headphones on while my parents fought in the background behind me. Mimicry of my mother. Escapism from my father. Here but someone else searching for something beautiful surrounded by chaos.

I remember New Year's Eve 1999 with my CD player listening to LIVE's "Throwing Copper" and Creed's first album, "My Own Prison". I remember the cover of that album depicting a man crouching in a prison. Black and White? Pain present. Expressionism. Definitely one of my favorite albums at the time. Both were really. However, it is the song, "Lightning Crashes" that has been carried throughout my life from different experiences along the way.

My mind now Shifts to the memory of seeing Fantasia 2000 with my brother and mother. Maybe that enhanced the musical connection. Perhaps it was Kandinsky as I learned how he connected visual to sound to spiritual. He made me contemplate the relationships they have to one another. His theories, "Concerning the Spiritual in Art" is a must read for not only his works, but also influenced my own as well.

"Musical Sound acts directly on the soul and finds an echo there because, though to varying extents, music is innate in man."
-Kandinsky

But perhaps it was Kiah that influenced me the most to bend sound to create my own. As a DJ, he inspired me to search for commonality between 2 completely different pieces. From there, the evolution of my explorations begun to be influenced by feelings and storytelling that attempted to look deeper for connections.

When I first starting out playing with sound, I was told what I was doing was not mixing music. They were right. It was something different. That wasn't the intention as the self-study evolved over time. The storytelling aspect became more important. Connect 2. Connect 3. Connect 4. Circle back to the beginning. Weave. Woven. Wove. A narrative from one song to the next become birthed to express a bigger picture as if scoring a movie. Or perhaps creating a movie for the blind where everything is given if you listen. Emotion soaked into each note.

A driving point over the last several years has been a challenge to evoke emotion further to create a reaction by the listener as each layer upon layer of familiar and unfamiliar plays out it's own individual act.

My marriage of music and art started in the paintings in my family kitchen during those arguments. As one marriage was ending, a new one was being developed. Music has always been present and curated into every single one of my art shows. Specific songs have become attached to the processing of images to evoke different styles of processing based on the selections chosen. Process influenced by an emotion. Like a guiding hand to pull out of yourself if you allow music to just take you into its environment. A marriage between visual and sound. Symbiotic of course, but ultimately art further inspired by art. The result cannot be fully explained with words. Only showcased. Each reaction would be a completely different experience
depending on the individual's empathy.

ENTRY 15:

A breath of air.
Inhale. Exhale.
A promise started small.
Potential.
Possibilities branching.
Thoughts shout
I miss you.
Each branch a tangent thought
Paths intertwined.
By commonality Stories combined.
Like vines rooted
By leaving pasts behind.
Each year I did it all for U.
A possibility.
A dream made reality.
Year 2 Me and U.
Remember the journey we went through
Because I remember the first day
I set my eyes on you.

ENTRY 16:

It's not a part of who I am.
Caged.
Controlled.
Temperament contained.

Control of thought
Direction.
Belief.
Quit for betterment

Heaven is perseverance.
Take back control.
Held on. Held Back
Released on
Your Terms.

Be an example by not being defined by others,
but defined by taking care of your own house.

Fully aware.
7 days is doable,
but let's try 3.
My own contract that should had been completed.
The countdown begins.
Hesitant to say goodbye
to a frenemy.

ENTRY 17:

The way things work...

Can't hide anything
No privacy.
Critiques made.
Only one choice left

Be yourself.
Accept yourself.
Be stronger than yourself.

Individuality.
Uniqueness.
Me.

Learn to stop!
It will be all right

< A hummingbird randomly appears in the Paradise of my backyard>
<A Train of thought stops.>

HUMMINGBIRD

A hummingbird is a lucky omen and an auspicious dream symbol.
The hummingbird symbolizes grace and cheerfulness, and its quick motions cause it to be
symbolic of working quickly and effectively to accomplish your goals. (dreammoods.com.)

Acrobatic in thoughts of infinity and loops. Maneuvering through situations in a capacity that is
not the fastest, but diligent and stealthy in approach. -PB

"Happiness is homemade"

How do you move past something that fundamentally changes you?
Where do you look to for the shift?
Does it always stay with you?
Is it a part of who U are now?

Is it going to be in everything from here on out?
I can't forget it. But it needs to be buried or released in some way.

Keeping it inside is toxic.

The wrong was personal.
The life taken was personal.
It was my life.
It was my family's life.
It was everyone and thing I ever cared about; attacked.
One day at a time.

Reduce.
Reuse.
Recycle.
Channel into a positive.

ENTRY 18:

I saw a hummingbird again while smoking in Paradise; thinking of what the day will bring today. Am I losing it? Am I accepting it? I try to process what is in my head today.

Some days seem to better than others, but they always lead me back to the same place. A court case. A battle within myself on if I can rationalize or justify what happened. I go back again to the shower scene, now asking myself "Why did this affect me so?" I have been told good words to live by that I am holding onto this for a reason. I need to process that information within myself, but at the same time I find that I want to step away. The thoughts pull me right back in.

I imagine the battlefield again (now a reoccurring image). I am sitting on a hill in the distance. I can't see it completely. I'm imagining it. Sometimes U are there. Sometimes I use the sound to build what is being observed internally. We go deeper. There has to be a release or this is going to become a part of who I am. In part, it as if I am an observer to a movie I didn't pay to see. (Or maybe I did pay for it) Maybe this is what happens when your life fundamentally changes due to others. A battlefield. A rabbit-hole. Deeper regardless. Except this time, I didn't talk myself back from experiencing this. The imagery has won the battle of my full attention.

I find it important to note this is internal imagination/thoughts and not hallucinations. Perhaps memories of our yard growing up plugging in squares of imported Bella Bluegrass. A Checkerboard for a year or two before grown in from the gaps towards togetherness. Now, an adult mental battlefield.

I am still fighting a war even if I need to for only my own sanity. I'm observing from the sidelines for mental peace and rehabilitation. Fully aware of the jazz music being played. A power struggle from one member to the next. There's an attempted takeover through unrested souls. 3 to 4 main voices heard.
<I am trying to look at things objectively>
I know the difference between reality/make-believe.
(If I am hearing voices and seeing scenarios play out in my head, is there a question of the realism of it? The dreams are photo-realistic nightly.)
I know the difference between right/wrong. What I hear is a lot of negative, but when the positive comes, it is like the volume gets turned down.
Who controls the volume?

I believe I heard a sound test the other day through the PlayStation. External-ly testing through WiFi connected media? Maybe it's my mind wandering. (Turns out it is just the game.) Maybe I am getting used to having a committee in my head. Sometimes they speed-read. Sometimes they complete sentences purposefully left incomplete. I let phrases hang as a sign of testing. But never was aware of possible external volume control until puzzles worked. Perhaps it is just the windmill of my mind playing tricks. I catch them at times going down paths not intended and I'll sit and listen to see where they go with it. I argue. They argue. I agree. Never an agreement from them. I guess it depends on the topic at hand. However, I do know that I cannot just keep it inside which is what this book is ultimately intended for. Release.

I am unsure if this is a personal stream of consciousness I ever want to re-read or ever want read. Maybe at some point I will look back at this as a reminder of strength of the choices made. But for now, this is a strange new world that began the day I gave up. Somehow I found humility within me and was able to walk back from that by putting faith and my life into another person's hands. I knew I gave up and needed help. But for the moment, they won.

My mind says remember the hurt.
My soul says you don't have a choice.

'Childhood Checkerboards' - Sketch Translation' November 16, 2022. "Philip A. Bonneau.

July 6, 2017
Post 5: You asked for this.

Normally it is a quoted post from the past and an explanation.
Today it's the opposite.

Officially submitting this one for the record in the context of what is to come.
There is allot there.

"And this is my second of 3 important letters I have to write this week.

My first letter was to my boss was handwritten. It was with respect and unexpected-ness of receiving a job. Proper 2 weeks notice was provided with gratitude towards the 8-years had under her umbrella. Definitely more than less.

Then there was what I got to write and share with FB to an overwhelming response that I could have never anticipated.

"Well I have officially given notice at my job of over 8 years this morning.

In 2-weeks I will be moving to Miami. I have accepted a position as Creative Marketing Manager for the world's second largest designer and producers of bridal gowns. They are one of the only companies to have an official license from Disney for a collection of gowns based off of the Disney princesses. While there, I'll be mentored by working fashion photographers until the point I feel comfortable to set my feet into the world of fashion photography myself.

I will miss every aspect of my Atlanta family. I am who I am because of you and your support in my dreams over the years. I've worked 4-years from knowing nothing but what I want to do and set myself on that path to learn and grow. This dream came true 10 fold more than I could have ever expected and it's only just the beginning of another chapter.

With love and gratitude,
Pip'

When I did my kickstarter for this project I warned that things would be done this year by me in secret. Things would not be known until after the fact. As they should. The second show was in real time in some regards. In Secrets it involved time and reflection to get to a point of sharing. Life has pushed it in constant evolution that simply incorporates it into how to translate life and adaptability back into something beautiful translated in a safe space. The original idea was private understanding of self until find a way to make that relateable to everyone once things were signed, sealed, delivered whether there is a connection or not. Ultimately, 'Brave New Secrets' became about testing the theory of what effect does being in a positive environment have on an artist in the confines of that series. It was also about releasing the artist from fear and the things holding them back.

But in posing that agenda, it left the questions,
"What is a positive environment?"
"What are the things that hold me back?"
"What do I want in life?"

I had to answer that question to myself over and over through this venture and it came up with another question to consider, "Does the last thing broadcasted determine ultimate public perception?" When trying to consider the fact of awareness of public perception since a child and especially after 'Ugly Simple Truths', the important factor discovered prior but known around that time was a need and desire of understanding that not everyone needs to know everything. They don't need to know who you are in a relationship with...who you are friends with...what you are doing all the time...where you are...where you are going. If they wanted to know, they could ask. Otherwise, it was life lived outside the social media world on many aspects of things. You get a hint on social media. It is another aspect to actively be a part of someone's life (Heaven).

I started by looking back at the context of this series. I re-read everything. As brutal as it was for me to do so I did it. (At the time it was 1 journal, the "Ugly Simple Truths' blog and a handful of other digital writings. There is a difference when this book was produced in 2019, I had much more writings including these from 2017 to sit through and process) I saw myself then as broken, but I also saw myself as not giving up and wanting to understand things. For some they saw a broken man hurt by others For others, it was perceived as someone trapped in the past. For others, they saw it as lessons learned and growing from that. It was about someone striving to find themself again and owning who they are at the same time. Just as much as some saw it as a fight against perception. There are many layers to this beautiful lie.

To me, this series has always been about personal growth and reflection that may never truly come across correctly. That depends on how invested in the story you are and what is portrayed. The catalyst itself within this series is inconsequential to the story that unfolds from it. It has to be or else it is invidualized and so specific that the relatability aspect of such gets glossed over and missed. The catalysts are personal to myself, just as much as the catalyst to others is completely different and equal of deep meaning and protection in sharing. There is trust there. That was proven when the show opened up from a singular narrative from 'Beautiful Layered Lies' to the narrative of others incorporated in 'Ugly Simple Truths'. The addition of variables opens up the thought process understanding the curated aspect of what was presented.

Everyone is on a journey. Everyone is looking for purpose. For every action there is a reaction and there is always a ripple effect to anything that happens in our lives. Some waves are made bigger than they should be, but they are still waves nevertheless. How can anyone express their own wave pool of emotional aspects of impacts positive and negative? The waves still crash upon the shore in some version understanding they are at their strongest the closest to shore or during storm. This divine comedy was just one possible response to infinite possibilities of exploration within the realm of self-discovery. I don't regret my approach, as it was definitely a unique one to do.

I think we are living in a very interesting world these days.

Too many in their own right. Some consider themselves a reality show where entertainment provides magnetic personalities positive or negative of attaction in watchability. In some of those shows, people idolize being a bitch to one another or love a good fight breaking out in what is still acted out one way or another in some regards. People love to know who is sleeping with whom or as it has become common vernacular these days, "It's all T. It's no Shade." A fun phrase that basically along the same line of 'With all due respect...' before going into disrespect. The only difference is knowing it is totally acceptable in jabbing/poking capacity when you are friendly with your environment and those who it is addressed to. Throwing shade seems to gain points with others, while being civil with some class towards others gets no points in general. You get forgotten for that. You get unnoticed. There is nothing special about doing right to others and the general populous overlooks it. Not always, but you see it in current events. They want the drama. Conflict. They want the shade. They want the gossip and they want it without the recourse of their own lives. American culture seems to builds up its heroes to see them fall. It's ironic that in a gay community they hold "Mean Girls" as a way of life and then quick to judge Lindsay Lohan for her fall from grace and her struggles after. They forget the whole movie was based on sociology to begin with. But the humor and entertainment masks the lessons to learn from it. There is humor in anything if one simply finds the way to present truth in one delivery or another. We are human. It is natural. We all fall at one point or another. Other times we are pushed. Not everyone picks himself or herself up by themselves and sometimes you just have to when others aren't around or in choices of silence. I see it now where it has been around for quite some time, but there is even the attacking of the dead in the same capacity. Destruction of one thing or another based off of either right or wrong ambitions. I'm actually disgusted that people look for that so they have something to talk about tomorrow. Fuck those people with the wrong intentions. Basking in destruction of others only eventually means the propogation of others enjoying your own downfall when it happens either in life or after your death.

There is most definitely a "bitch" culture alive and thriving for multiple reason. I'm not sure if that is across the board or just in one community or another. I suppose there are 'bitch culture' factions in any community. It is a part of a community, but not the full comprise of a community. The same could be saying 'being a bitch' is just one fascet to a more complex persona. That culture being is one that feeds on drama or of ranking status. Imagine the trials to become 'The Grand High Supreme Bitch'. I don't think that title is held of anyone I will ever met but a Coveted title nevertheless and once gained someone will just come along and title themselves with added descriptors to the title to call it their own. Further elaboration would be that there is a difference between 'A Bitch' and 'A Diva'. As I am neither I am unsure the guidelines and applications of such in different factions. Sustained on the gossip and lies and definitely on the scandal of things going on. That is where some reality shows are taking us, which is where I see my culture leading. If I were to look objectively in that aspect, there are many aspects to reality television that invite discussion one way or another towards social understanding and connecting. That desire to connect socially is always going to be present in any aspect of reference.

With that in it mind, it boils down to the presentation of how we present ourselves to the world. Because as interconnected as we are through FB, Instagram, twitter, Etc.'Everyone is watching...or anyone could.' Someone is going to comment on it positive or negative. That motif goes back well beyond the reality show generation.

Psychologically that is because it allows others to ignore that problems of their own lives and wrap themselves within the episodes of others. Indirectly there is a connection of relateability and connection. It's a security blanket to allow people not to work on themselves because they see and point out other's flaws. Indirectly they learn what is write or wrong for their persona based on many factors that lead towards social acceptance and in a postive re-enforced system of rewarded behavior. People start to feel better about themselves when other's issues are on the table. It becomes a comfort point to some in that regard of discussing indirectly what perhaps secretly they are going through in some similar aspect or indirect relateability of empathy one way or another. That is why Maury, People's Court, and Jerry Springer are popular. They make people feel better about themselves looking down on others or from an indirect aspect of educational indirect lessons of life.

There has always been a sense of irony to that those that throw themselves out there for display within those confines. They gain and lose far more than the viewer would ever really expect nor care to hear about. It is the strength of any admittance that is always admired in context. To discuss struggle, vulnerabilities or to allow the slight unmasking ever so slightly is always an admirable aspect of relateability and understanding that in awareness there is also support, guidance and paths opened towards other choices.

To the producer it is about ratings and the story. I imagine various intentions there. Keep us interested. Who will punch whom and who will lose their shit first? To the participant, it is their life or their performance of how they want to be portrayed to a certain extent. Edits occur. As 'low-class' as any of those shows sound, they signed it away knowing what they were getting into. 15 minutes is a surprisingly tempting thing in order to feel validated, acknowledged, known or even relatable to. It creates an interesting thought tangent on Andy Warhol's statement of "In the future, everyone will be world-famous for 15 minutes". He never said what for, Good or Bad.

What would happen if you play off that mentality? What if you are fully aware of how people react and respond based on certain posts? What happens when you literally drive a narrative into a certain direction for the sake of argument of saying we all control what is out there? I'm curious can I play with that? If one's perception is so easily based on drama, it can't be hard to create a false sense of one to fuel the narratives I don't control. (A 2017 written statement that proved worth in testing truth in 2018/2019/2021/2022) Are people reacting based of social media or outside aspects at the time. As these writings were definitely found in places where it was not authorized, I question what was being tested by others and when this became an affordable life lesson in survival at multiple locations.

Truth is this with this series... I question often and I think I need to start answering things one way or another. But the truth is it does not really matter what that answer is.

I actually am proud of the art direction and common motifs that came from this series. It makes me feel like there is a connection. It's so fucking far from perfect that any critique of imperfection just solidifies that intent. It's never going to be perfect. I'm not going to be, you aren't going to be. No one is. Always a flaw that could be fixed at one point or another or simply admire the flaw for what it was and work towards solutions elsewhere. So best to simply embrace the perfection in the imperfections. I could redo everything I've done 3 years from now and even then I am sure I'll find growth in what I do, but it will never be perfect. I will look at it differently I am sure. I'll find something different and I'll connect differently. There is also the fact that once one starts writing in any capcity, it is either going to be nurtured or other avenues explored in stylistic approaches or in new areas one way or another. To know things 3 years from now and go back is equally exciting to see where things turned out while also practicing restraint to not spell out what simply comes in time and investment.

This whole project was an unexpected reaction to an action and a spark that needed to happen for me to grow into my own. Started in 2014 in held back journalistic (candid diary format) approach: the cumulation of going into this officially in 2017 came from 3 years seperated to ideas that come out in the beginning aspects of blurbs before going into the offical blog entry. I told the truth in my own way and sought beauty in ugliness. Looking back I am not sure anyone really should address certain things in a public forum, but I don't regret my decisions made nevertheless because (A.) had to happen for (B.) to proceed towards (C.) to occur and then left with (D.) for the next round.

I needed to start living my life and doing what I wanted to do. Not for vengeance, but because that whole "keeping face" BS is exactly that. It is BS. To me. I needed to prove to myself that you can't erase me, you can't mold me to something that makes you look better in a shitty situation and I needed to make a statement on that. At least in an aspect of detriment to myself. The collaboration always available. At least it was proven how one can erase someone later in life and try to mold me one way or another in ways that simply weren't true.

Selling a beautiful lie is a glorious thing. I fucking exist and I hit the point where I got tired of reality show BS in some regards of needing balance and security one way or another. I got tired of putting up with what I was hearing from everyone perpetuated by gossip and people thriving on drama. At least that statement and art piece was expressed in 2012 with 'The Scarlet Letters' in talking points. It got to the point I felt like I was walking around with a scarlet letter. Might as well accept the fact that words matter and get burned into one way or another somewhere. In that shadow realm, I at least was ready to talk about that head on. It is the drama that fuels. The scandal. Even if it is a futile cause with some, I don't regret embracing individuality. I knew from the beginning what I was walking into when I chose my topics of discussion. The variables of humanity to get into that selection process was the beautiful aspect to teaching empathy and relateability. The irony is I probably allowed things to exist longer than they should have because I chose my stance and beliefs. It's a catch-22 where there are definitive warnings with 'Shadow Play' that simply teach you connection and understanding when others trust you with their vulnerabilities, stories and believe in your artistic representation and concept of such. It was extensive Self-'Shadow Play' for I on one front and it was trust on the other side.

I laugh a bit at the "Secret" app that has just came out because as much as I got criticized for throwing it all out there, people do it with that app...just not without a name. Ironically with that app, people are thinking their words do not have a consequence is the very reason why I decided to open my mouth in the first place with my art series. You never know how someone is going to react to something said...something perpetuated.

When that app came out, I was pissed. I was pissed even more when my name got mentioned and it snowballed on that app. Pissed because lies were perpetuated still 4 years for some, 1 year for others. You can't escape your past. You can do everything you can to ignore it, but the things people say have a ripple effect just as much as the truth. It never dies. I have been fighting that, and at the same time embracing that knowing if I don't hear it or see it then it really doesn't affect me. It's so easy to hide behind something thinking you are anonymous. You aren't. I still contend that IPs were more than likely associated with every post on that app. If they weren't definitely future apps of the same design would be or even social media platforms where ID required as a way to say, 'You might want to watch what you say on social media.'

For me, being pissed went to vindication because I was able to do publicly what many cannot. I stood by my words. I stood by my actions. All to teach empathy in over 23 topics of conversation. I stood by my beliefs that what I was doing is right. I owned every-thing that came out of my mouth. That was the good and the bad.

I am not a perfect person. The only time I ever spoke in my series against people is because of perpetuation of a falsehood. So many relationships never were discussed and they never will be. It was the ones that I never could understand or the ones that went above and beyond that got mentioned as examples. I stand by my belief that I did everything I could to retain a reason not to be a part of my public story. Disre-spected enough and I knew I would grow from that experience and made an example. Not for vengeance, but for a need to understand what I did wrong or what can I avoid in the future. I am a contestant work-in-progress where I was fair. It was about many things then where at least in future versons of I, I know many things to do or not do. I definitely know and understand the severity of the things I've had to write one way or another years later that still came from the constant asking to stop, or simply the exploration of looking at one thing or another in different approaches. So many things could be explained just as much as I understand the twisting others do anyways. It is just going to happen to where either one stops talking and relating completely or accepts the 'out-of-sight, out-of-mind'.

I hate that "secret" app with a passion, but it made me realize something very important to my growth. You can't control what people say. You can manipulate perception to a certain extent or try to push it back in other directions of public relations but the severity of the intention of the other side is capable of being something that cannot be fought in high volumes and in multiple fronts. There is always going to be the aspects of question-ing where your opinion came from and if you did your own fact check on it or not. But people believe what they want to believe.

I got to see first-hand that the stories being talked about and mentioned were only the stories allowed out in public. It was the past to I and new to other people. The same could be said when one transcribes a handwritten journal into book form later in life. When was it written by hand vs. transcribed to find who might be a little bit more comfortable trans-lating what simply is a way to transform one thing into another of beauty. I was defined to them from that. Even in those definitions, it doesn't mean it is a definition associated with I in translation. Maybe then. Probably not now. Depends on the context and would still require conversation that may or may not get entertained. They know nothing of my pres-ent because I chose to lock it down and keep it private. I had already done what I needed to do with my story. I showcased that people hurt people with their words and you never know how people will react to that hurt. That is just one fascet to a multitude of discussions to better 'Self' and 'Others'. To try to associate any of my work to be of ill-intention is allowed in critical thinking yet, it definitely was never the intentiion. Introductions to the World. Cleaning up Houses and ultimately world building one way or another in piecing things of importance to I in one approach or another. I chose to do an art piece that basically reads a mentality for filth on my own road to self-discovery because what is considered ok of bashing is wrong (at least in my house). Never a word has to be spoken in context of it other than what was written next to it or burned into my skin with a chance to find a way to wash it off somehow and some way. Lying about whom you are is wrong. Lying about others is wrong. It creates scenarios that you cannot uncancel once the right people get a hold of it and it causes problems personally, professionally and otherwise. Masks everywhere to understand that reprocussions of forcing one to examine their entire existence before strength can be found to combat what you can knowing you cannot fight it all.

People get hurt all the time, but making others feel like they never existed because you refuse to deal with your own issues is wrong. A difference there where in the negative aspects of slander leads the door to others not wanting to exist anyways in some regards. This is why slander and libel are sueable and prosecutable. Justifying cheating on someone because of some bullshit excuse is wrong. It depends on the context and really is just meant to be private conversations and not really anyone's business. It is understandable people talk and relate to someone who talks to someone who talks to someone else who then knows a person who knows another person and then next thing you know you have the discussion point of the birth of cancel culture in context of the early (2010s) It was around prior, just not in the capacity seen since then. Everything I ever wrote or did was never out of malice, but out of my own desires and need to bring things back to center for myself and others and to try to avoid these situations in the future. I never mentioned names and never will. I'm better than that, and this series is about growing and not about making someone else's life a living hell. There is an understanding that in my first show, the concept was not what you think it is when going through the beginnings of processing an explosion of just letting things out, translate, process, grow and do something for yourself and others.

The past is in the past. The things I chose to talk about in my Divine Comedy were a burnt bridge long before I decided to make a learning experience from things with them. The burnt bridge is about the perspective of life one way or another after any transitional period knowing there are aspects of yourself that simply change in growth spurts and realizations that things simply aren't the same in one regard or another. There was never going to be reconciliation entirely, but yet...bridges being formed from the first show on in different directions. My divine comedy and my heroes series is what I have chosen people to have people remember for because that is what I've allowed them to know of my life and that of others in acceptance and building towards things of comfortability in individuality and know that you are awesome, we don't all have the answers, but we can move one way or another with this life. With this new series, I get to explore living life past all that drama. Living when you know those things don't matter anymore. They are gone. It's about when someone finally realizes that it does not matter what people think, but as long as you are living life as it is right for you is all that matters.

I've grown from my past. Everyone has. Everyone does in one way or another until they are no longer around to grow in that perspecive. There are so many beautiful things from my past that I cherish. Other lessons a little harder than others. I've grown from the things I fought that I thought was important. To find motivations to grow from anything is always a sounding board and jumping off point where eventual choices made one way or another that become harder to unravel from or no desire whatsoever to do so in the positive aspects outweighing the negative. I could care less now what people negatively think of me. I do when it comes from those close to myself, but the truth of the matter is as things get whittled down socially, what opinions matter the most right now are ones I couldn't control anyways. The irony of being private now is those that were on the outside think you are stuck in the past, but that is only because that was the last thing fed to them noting why comments matter one way or another. To be stuck in the past in this capacity of this book is actually exciting to conclude this version of me in this topic aspect in this capacity before going back into what is also more recent past and then building back towards the 'Now'.

I've spent all of this year removing myself from that. Perhaps that is why I blew up over that app so much. Because all they remember is the last thing fed to them. Not what is reality. Not what actually is. People will always have an opinion. There can be a more fuller story, but never a complete one available. But my journey is not meant to be universally understood. It never will be, but it is mine. It's not special. It's not unique. That is where similiar but different matters in commonality. It's the same as yours. It's unifying. I'm excited I get to experience a complete reboot. My dreams have come true far more than I ever could have thought because of others who did not negatively affect me and actually nurtured me. I get to move to a city where my stories of the past do not haunt me but I know I am going there with them and I don't know how I feel about that. " -7/12/14

I think about the context of my series.
What I started.
What I didn't get to finish
But perhaps this is how things were supposed to be.
There needs to be time to reflect

I've read over where I ended my series on my "Path to Brave New Secrets". I ended it with the realization I was not letting in someone fully that actually cared for me and I wanted to change that. Not Completely Yours prior due to unrealized closures of the past. That was given in Italy. Not just by hand-made airplanes, but also by the influencer of my dreams. I released it. But also; they released me. It was the best stopping point to move forward by keeping my private life private thereafter. The greatest show never told I tell myself. 2 years a relationship occurred. 2+ years a relationship continues. Life occurred in that time frame; just as much as life occurred 3 years prior to that, the 4 years prior to that, etc. etc.

I remember the feelings of inadequacy in not having a job anymore. I grew from self-sufficient to self-success to thriving from, not only the dreams of my own imaginary worlds, but also the fantasy of American culture through the Disney brand. All of that was lost in a single day.

Unforeseen?
Not likely.

11 years of professional work for myself and back to square 1 we went.
Alice was reset.

I remember the past and mistakes made on either side of the coin. I had not had a real relationship in over the 3 years in Florida. Sparks here and there. "The Divine Comedy" both held me back and pushed me further from that as interactions occurred. The start of some of that life experience of the comedy evolved into "Heroes + Villains" for escapism from escapism. But there was a time period that I never really let people in completely. Especially romanti-cally. Nor should I have in hindsight.
Do I include excerpts from "Brave New Secrets" for reference? Surely not the

whole thing, but referencing something not there is lazy writing. Continue to allude and see if makes a difference. If I were to include it, probably would be best at the end as a compare and contrast.

I remember things said before starting the "Simple Ugly Truths" series. "You shouldn't do this." I remember my personal intentions though. Hurdles needed to be leapt over in order to be stronger. Idealistically making myself stronger as a unit, but fundamentally recharged as a supplier to my own kinetic energy.

Who am I to be one desired in a circumstance of loss, professionally or personally? Yet, there was never any judgment on either side. I went to Italy to finish my Divine Comedy. Walking in the footsteps of Dante. U were a guest of my heart. U were transformative as U made me a guest in my dreams. From that night on U transformed into U. Just as malleable as I have striven to become over time. Adaptive. That step makes me question if it was right to say I needed to work myself up to a relationship. Do I always find U or do you U find me?

<Insecurity>

I gave myself closure there when there was none. U gave me closure in rest. I got more than I asked for on that trip from God's grace and from the love of family lost. I think about how it has been 2 years now and despite the hardships faced within my life; U are still here. I am curious the evolution. Internally those questions are hard. Externally, those experiences have been hard for you as well. I've wanted to be the knight and I've given myself up to one when I needed it. Perhaps that is what love is. I've fucked up along the way towards understanding that in my life.

I want to say that is being human, but that is what happens when the outside influences. Probably a more telling reason on why I kept you in protection. Always miles apart. At least we were closer in Atlanta. A weekend meant the world. I imagine what our time was supposed to be like had I not fallen. That was our time and I was not strong enough then. You were stronger. Its course was changed by other captains at the wheel.

I cannot explain my thought process entirely, but I do know you are a part of my Heaven. A secret kept. Protected. Cherished. I fucked up. Others inter-jected. If I have anything to thank the voices I've heard, it for the remembrance of the power of words. One word sparked everything. Secrets.

I started my Heaven series in 2014.
A Natural progression
but then life happened
and now I find myself continually trekking
Forward in secret.

I've gone in circles trying to figure out how to properly put Heaven in a tangible form. There have been tests of False Finalities/Starts. A thesis yet to be proven. But life interjects and so do others. This past interjection changed Heaven for me and for others.

If I owe this breakdown of events one thing (and one thing only), it's the idea that perhaps not completing the series with a visual show is more powerful than doing one at this point. Paradise became corrupted, but the idea can live on.

Mirror masks were always going to be a major factor into it. A reflection. A perspective. Multiple points of views glued together to always point back disjointedly to U. What lies inside a mirror? You can quantify the depth of mirrors, but you can never actually see what a mirror would be without you.

Put your hand up to a mirror and you will find that the two never touch. The distance between equals the depth of the reflection made.

Heaven is personal. Heaven is what you make it. By default, so is Hell. If I had purgatory be an exploration of the shadow self, I believe there was no guessing where I was going to go from that show. Physical reactions to art occurred in that series opening. That was one of my proudest moments as an artist. Heaven was alluded to after.

Alluded but never obtained. Perhaps that is the point of dealing with trauma. Perhaps that is the point of dealing with guilt in decisions. When weighing what is right or wrong, you have to make a choice and not regret it by backing up your reasons behind the execution. It's my belief in art that if you hide the eyes, it helps with self-projection into the image. I've now come to ask the question, what happens when you hold a mirror up to the world and say nothing at all? There is always going to be a personal search, but I do find it fitting to end a series birthed by judgment ended with a challenge to look at yourself. Each mask becomes a reflection of a particular emotion. Captured. Contained. Preserved. Forever cursed to only project upon anyone who looks upon it. Do you see Anger? Pain? A work-in-progress? Accomplishment? Hope? There's the possibility of infinite sadness or a single memory worth holding onto.

I do not question the strength of the word. "Secret" in hindsight. My mind has brought me to a place where, considering where I have been and what I have seen. I understand the potential for nervousness in whatever form my series chose to take. It will always be a reflection.

In fairness. I have to absolutely get the point across that series was also always meant to be a trek back to center. Never about one thing, but all things. Life experiences. Good & Bad. Do we have regret? Do we have secrets? What would we do to protect them? Would you paint yourself a certain way? Would you paint others having once been painted yourself? Would you be given justifiable cause to protect by any means necessary?
What would you do to keep a secret?

The questions that bear to be asked.
"What secrets should you keep?"
A love affair?
A complex built?
Illegal means to protect?
At what cost?
Is it not human nature to feel remorse for something in hindsight?
It's 20/20 as they say.

A secret told is never a secret ever again.
A secret stolen is simply that.
Theft.
A thief of always is forever there.
If there is no remorse for taking something
Is that not the definition of a sociopath?
"Why do you have this?"

I want to forget from Atlanta 2.0 to now...but doing so erases
who I am.

Questioning the "now" as it applies to the handwritten then and further to
this moment as I type this reliving the memory of a memory. Further down
the line as I proof this book, re-reading again what I typed, remembering
what I hand-wrote, remembering what I experienced. How many times modified?
Inception intertwined by vernacular.

...But I can't nor should I. Perhaps I am reading into things too much.
Perhaps I am not at all. Something took away my home 2.0 and brought me
back 18 years into my past. But I do have to give myself credit. I did face a
major fear regardless.

I came back and made a home exactly how I wanted one.
A Fireplace.
A Photographically perfect toilet.
A Suburban city life.
It only took 1 week of living there though.
7 days was all the peace I was afforded in my home. I am making a cognizant
choice to not write down the negative experiences up until this point.

1. Because is negativity even allowed in heaven?
2. Because happiness is not dictated by outside influence.
3. This is my story and I write it how I choose to.

What's the narrative? What's the point? There's definition, but it cannot be
compartmentalized. Heaven was always meant to be private. It's not anymore.
So how do you handle that? In my mind I saw it as a reflection of the best
and worst of me. Both capable of error if you go too far on either side, but
parts of me nevertheless. Now, with outside influence, has my perspective
shifted? Self-Discovery and Self-Acceptance are inevitable. Maybe it isn't?
Maybe it's a matter of life or death. Either way it has been pre-destined by
the first word uttered. It has already been written. Future me is either smil-
ing or crying when I get to this part.

This has gone on for so long that I feel my personal thoughts aren't personal
anymore. A quiet place has been disrupted. We can balance it out though.
I need to finish what I have started. It will all lead back to the fundamental
belief system that things are always layered. An ebbed tide flows in either

direction. There are things hidden. Intentions guided. Heaven is never just given. It is earned. As hard as it is to obtain. it must also be that it cannot be so easily taken away at first or second attack. There is no instant gratification to be found. It is quite possible that neither of us deserve heaven. But the availability of it never needs to be stolen either. I handwrite now because heaven is personal.

(I typeset now because heaven needs a further translation)
I final edit now on my end because once heaven is found it can't be taken.

My experience is personal and I now know things private can be stolen online. But the rub is I know my thoughts have been stolen. If not then I never would have resorted to the act of handwriting in the first place. In handwritten word. I create a new safe place that is incapable of being invaded by the means done. Does that keep me 2 steps ahead?

Do I still need to try to be 2 steps ahead?
The typeset aspect denotes an opening of the safe space in awareness.
It denotes a did, would or could of possibilities provable.
Adaptability factors in but there comes a point in yourself that you have to say. "fuck it". Let people talk and do their thing. Even if it is just in your head or in your journal. It's your space uncompromised by privacy settings and hacks. Stay the course. Happiness is earned. My draw to writing is from a need to let go that someone is always there critiquing. now aspirated by actual voices in my head that were never present internally before.

My questions before going to bed.
How does someone take back security?
How does someone continue to realize their life and grow-up and still be faced with a similar issue in the future?

{?}
Perception vs. Interjection.
Stand. Fall. Fly?
Your world. Your rules.

Remember the rules. Remember you already died and grew up once. This is just one last time. The only pressure there is the pressure you put on yourself to retain privacy taken away. Write for yourself. Photograph for yourself. Be you for yourself. Love is love.

Remember you made that loud and clear to a worldwide audience.

July 11, 2017
Post 6: Choose your own f*cking adventure.

You know...in the end, you have one life.
Biggest question is what do you want to do with it?

So much of youth is wasted on not knowing what the fuck you want as you come into yourself that I guess it's kind of fun growing into what it is like to be an adult and have a better idea of knowing what you do want to do. So much broad experimenting in youthful wanderings to understand exploration of new avenues still continues into adulthood just perhaps with more intention. Introduced in general studies until you start to find interests that spark imagination. It happens in school. It happens on wiki-pedia and it happens in intrigue to put the hand to the flames or take a dip in waters slowly at first before swimming. I wonder at what point do you stop faking it and you actually make it. Perhaps you already made it and are just faking it. Secret successes and secret failures everyday. Just consider the failures as testing one way or another towards finding out what absolutely does and doesn't work in whereever you mind is discovering. It really depends on the scenario and intent I guess. For me that involves questioning things about others and myself. We always will question ourselves. It doesn't matter what age you are. There is going to be desire, wanting, regret, hid-ing, fear, protectionism. Any emotion present is worth exploring to understand what creates a long-term positive in perspective. If we didn't have those things then I am curious on what the hell that life is like. I don't know it.

I believe right now is an interesting time for me. Through all of this it is going to be a "choose your own adventure" at this point. Right choices and bad choices are always going to be there and that is a given. There is no right way. There is no wrong way. If you learn just one thing about yourself from an experience it is worth it.

There is no correct way to things on your own journey. Things happen when you least expect it pulling towards amazing new paths if one was only inclined to go one way or another.

I spent most of my 20s contingent on the perspective of others. When you don't know yourself it is going to be about, 'Going with the flow.'. You make it up as you go. Probably for me, I've expected a white rabbit along the way.

A "been there."

..."done that."

..."avoid this..."

..."do this..."

..."it becomes easier if..."....etc.

But honestly it is impossible to have that rabbit or guide in your life. Absolutely you need to let your pride down and listen to people who speak from experience. There is universal truth to most of the mundane shit we beat ourselves over with. There are people faking it just as much as you are faking it and we are all just faking this until we make it or it makes the end of us. That's a lie a great deal of us present to the world. There is no one universal step-by-step guide to wealth, happiness, and every-thing you could ever imagine. The imagination is always the variable where there is always interests and then there is selective admiration of others towards your own answers to share or keep hidden.

In my 30s now, I expected to know a little bit more. I think I do to a certain extent. I'm definitely more careful with what I say. I'm definitely more aware of my actions. I'm more understanding that we are all trying to figure life out one way or another. I listen a bit more to those in their 40s, 50s, 60s. But I do not discount those under as well. There are very few instances when people willfully steer you wrong in life. It happens...especially in areas of inexperience. Perhaps even in my own aspects. I still have so much more to learn. I'm obviously not always right on things. Most of those instances are because they are scared AF of lawsuits or there is a personal reason for telling you wrong which goes into principles on what that is. Advice is always out there. But you have to choose to listen or not and learn how to apply it to your own life. You have to learn humility that the more stubborn you are the more you are going to be disappointed that the world does not wield to you complete expectations. It never will. The only time that regularly happens is in normal infancy and even then eventually you get taught to cry it out a bit and then pass out.

I like to believe who I am as an artist kind of came from the notion of finding out what you do and do not do to people. It is not a matter of saying what you can and can't do to others. It is simply truths to I that I live by. Such as 'You don't hold peo-ple back.' It is going to happen directly/indirectly could be implied, but to you would never see me hold someone back from something they wanted to do without support-ing their ideas. Guidance perhaps if on subject matter I could talk about or simply point you in the right direction who could. Constant setting up for success and pointing things one way or another for best success. 'You don't hide things from peo-ple.' This one is actually very subjective. There are people who don't need to know everything about everything about you. That is something given. I suppose that was originally in the context of a relationship aspect, but even then sometimes you have your own space and I have mine. But that is the trust factor in different areas. 'You don't lie.' That is important to multiple fronts. It really matters on the things that mat-ter most to either you or others. It is a hope to not have lies, but it is difficult to get the whole truth out of people from time to time. Everyone has hidden insecurities. 'You don't hold back questions.' The internet has many answers, direct encounters lead to more. Questions lead to ingenuity or discussion points. There are times and places for questions, but be prepared one way or another to open up the discussion points. I haven't always followed those rules, but as I grow I find those fundamentals to who I am and what I look for. Looking into yourself is the biggest 'Lip Sync for Your Life' you will do. We are all mirrors in one way or another.

I look at where I am now and part of me is remembering the spawn of this series. A situation where someone else thought they were in control and me definitely letting people know you aren't in control. Who in particular is not important as there are many instances to that regard in my lifetime. I remember figuring things out and surviving in the meantime or failing because I did that too. I can't say I've ever really been controlling. I'm stern at times but always open and up for discussion on things. I am simply adamant on certain days being of importance and then being a big deal and take a great deal out of me to execute. Those days have not occurred for 3 years prior at the time of the original entry. Back then sparked a great deal of my artistic side. I look at things that I did and I don't think I would make the same decisions now, but at the same time I think I would in some those scenarios. I don't have much regret in my life. Habit-forming behaviors can be a testament to some-thing that I wouldn't repeat in introductions, but that is when you counter it off with other habit-forming behaviors that are healthy for the body or simply learn modera-tion and then pretty much set on any aspect in habit-forming behavior. When it comes from actions taken, I can't take anything back so I don't think in regret that way. There could or couldn't be discussion about past actions if one desired. Otherwise there is simply a list for anyone on things 'to-do or not to-do' that everyone private-ly holds. A majority of my questioning comes from doing what was right for me when it was not right for them. More than likely I still think about what is write collectively before going into what is right for myself. Especially now as I simply do not have a choice one way or another.

I'll probably always have questions of selfishness, but only because of my own self-doubt mixed with others self-doubt. Anyone is allowed to do things for themselves and you should never have to ashamed to think of yourself once-in-awhile. Your body subconsciously does it anyways for you. People just don't think about why we naturally breathe and not pay attention to it. The same could be said for thought patterns and trains of thoughts. There are enough self-learned answers out there to determine what is and isn't made up in life and perspective.

I look at things now, as I'm ready for a lot of things. But I'll always be scared of others. Perhaps only in the awareness of capability. I hate that others will decide my life and I have a feeling that is going to happen allot in life. I've accepted the fact and find it refreshing that others can determine a great deal of things. It is not necessarily a negative created by others. That has been proven over and over in ways where I can go general statements with that or into precise examples one way or the other. Until I own my company or become so jaded that I'm a shut-in, I have to learn how to interact with people and pay attention to how their actions and themselves effect my own. It is the same on the otherside. I know that I have zero desire to own my own business. I can't fathom any aspect of the responsibility and how sure you have to be one way or another. Dreams there in those areas unsure exactly how my inexperience in other areas factor into where my experience actually is solid. I know that this is the last time commercially I will allow my photography to be used (in the explotive aspects) I know a lot of no's in my life. But it's the yes` that I am interested. Maybe's one way or another.

I believe there is always a big illusion of control.
We choose our own f*cking adventure?
How does that work in a capacity when the once giant world is so much smaller and interconnected in ways one can only fathom the concept of control from multiple aspects.

It is true that no one has complete control on you.

I believe if there is control on you it is because of either insecurity or advantage in some capacity. Some people like being controlled in a different capacity. That comes from the advantage of trust and is different context. Maybe I am wrong in that assumption, but only in my experience do I feel that superiority is exerted when someone else is scared or intimidated.

You control your life.

You control your individuality as long as you believe in it.

You control your honesty as long as you are honest with what you can and cannot say or simply need time to prepare to learn comfortability to the idea of discussion with talking points important to yourself.

One of the hardest questions is asking yourself what you want.

One of the hardest decision is always going to be going after what you want once you know what it is you want.

It's always about choosing your own f*cking adventure. Sometimes we are forced into other adventures we never wanted to go to but survival is important and still value on unplanned paths. Make it through a few of those one way or another and then the choice options come back in again down the line. Some of that isn't about trying to survive. It is a matter of understanding you are going to gain something of value in any experience. Necessities of life factor in some of those adventures had, but what you do on your own time afterwards leads back to a path back towards your own f*cking adventure planning. No one can take that from you. No one has that power without taking away your physical life and no one has the knowledge to convince you they do so.

One of the hardest part is deciding what you want and owning that passion in stride.

What is it you want to be?

What do you want to do?

How are are you going to do it?

Remember, one move can decide a series of events to occur from it.

Choose you own adventure wisely?

ENTRY 20:

Ok...my mind is going to wander. I have no choice and I suppose it is allowed to do so.

<My mind speeds through everything all at once.>

Breathe.
Relax.
Trust.

The question for the day is how does one go about settling a restless mind. So many questions. Not enough answers. The only solution I can think of is to attempt to go about my life normally. Don't become the expected from this. Don't be what others thought of you. Be better and believe. Even if at the cost of yourself. Responsibility lies with all of us. Peace is only up to you.

I thought before about suicide. Before I viewed it as the very last thing we are able to control within ourselves. By actually making an attempt at it, my thoughts have changed on that. Digging deeper into the thoughts behind it. I find it boils down to peace is the last things we control. Not the actual act.

While weighing life and death, the weight lies in your convictions. Weight is in your hands of ultimately deciding the truth of where your passion lies and what you want. Your truths. Your beliefs. Everything comes into question in the end. **There is an acceptance that control cannot be returned in all aspects of it without it being a singular POV devoid of any opinion. No fear there then or now, only a focus on self-control. Everything else is other's choices.**

There is a blink-and-you-miss-it moment where deciding thoughts become definitive of your character. It's possible that every thought had is written down somewhere. When consciously aware of that, it can create a tipping of the scale if you survive.

Can I be comfortable with other's watching me weigh my options?
Should I give up and say it doesn't matter anyways?
A flawed experiment when you are aware of your entire life. While attempting to moving forward, you are aware that there is internal judgment occurring.

Fall in line or ignore.

Individuality will factor in the most.

Perseverance. Take each day at a time and continue towards goals.
Comfortability. Be at peace with the now and your surroundings.
Touch yourself. Let yourself know you are here physically.
Laugh. Always a perspective to find humor somehow. Even if not related.
Cry. Built up emotion comes out one way or another.
Feel Anxiety. Notice it, but use it to your advantage.
Learn to be OK that you cannot un-know something, but you can learn to be
at peace with the knowledge. It is what you do with it that matters.
(Did I eat from the tree of knowledge?)
Turn off the commentary.
Turn off thinking so much.

You can't be unaware once you are aware. It's like touching a hot stove.
You only need to be curious once. Perhaps once was enough on learning
about suicide. All I can do now is just relearn peace within myself for the
decision of acting on that thought. (And why was that?)

"I can do this."

Fundamentally changed. but not broken.
Bent?

                                                    "He's retarded."

"I am not retarded."
I can do this.

                    "(*This all started*) because of a book report..."
"...something about a book report is significant"
Remember that.
There are a lot of things to remember. Vague instances. A song change in the
car. A flickering light. A decision and choice made. Something given up to
right a wrong. A bullet bitten in reflective thoughts of 'Selves' at the time in
imagery while awake. Self-preservation through protection of others. Finishing things started. Sacrifice. I've been left to our own decisions. Have I been
respectful of that?

                                                    "No, you haven't."

"That rings clear."

On the other hand, with positivity muted, one must wonder if there is something, I am doing right that they are not sharing with me.
The sound of crowds wail. Some voices are louder than others.
Possibly the bedroom fan I am hearing. I turn it off to make sure.
Could be the air conditioning. Know the difference. You are sleep deprived.

Voices were true in the sea.
Was I true?
Was I wrong?

"You don't believe this crap, do you?"

"I do."
"I broke down. I know that."
Fog.
Restlessness.
Sleepwalking. A term they have used.
"Inception." Another term.

"You aren't supposed to be here."
"...Sleepwalking"
"Stay Still"
"Don't Move"
"...Social Contracts."
"...Not playing around."

Horses.

"Careful what you wish for"
"Deceitful"
"Recorded"
"That's the Truth"
...Personal Statements"
<Waited 1000 years>
"7 years?"
"Context."
"Special Edition"
"Collector's Items"
"3000 Copies"
"Game Over"

Today was a good day?
Baby Steps.

Night loves.

ENTRY 21:

2 years later a reflection.
Past repeating itself.
A course correction?
An experience learned.
Relearned.
Processed.

I've expelled the sentence "You are toxic." from my life and perhaps I need to expel another experience. Don't paint me something I am not. Don't pretend to wear a white hat when you **are** anything but help. Never lie. I think the scandal of it all is when someone steals the driver seat to your life, you have a responsibility to take back the wheel when they are drunk driving **with the aspects of what you own & is about reclamation of control.**

Misrepresentation.
Carelessness.
Lack of Compassion.
Miss. Characterization when you do not know me.
All things to process and understand.

I tell myself I walked away.
It followed. I didn't have a choice when it broke me, but I tell myself that 11 days was probably needed if not a few more. Insurance ran out.

I'm sitting here now still processing & wondering if this is going to define me. I'm moving on day-by-day, but also there is not a day that goes by where I try to figure out exactly what happened and build a timeline.

Life attacked.
Dreams attacked.
Recklessness ensued **by others.**

If I were to play 'Devil's Advocate', your conscience is always your guide. 2 sides. One Right. One Wrong. In the end, I spoke the truth under oath multiple times.

I only speak when it is the truth. (In this regard)
I weigh every option that I
can imagine before doing so.
I question the good and the bad
of going down those trains of thought.

"...So desperate, she asked anyone for help."

<I am being reminded of a
photo-shoot I did.>

From what I remember seeing and
hearing. my black light series was to
be used against me.

"He gave them everything to attack
him in that series"
(Paraphrased) T-PR

My proudest moments.
but also the most vulnerable.
I let people in.
Triggers.
The outside wouldn't understand
what is or isn't are general ideas.

Probably a good balance that what
occurred from then to now.

ALICE AND THE SEA OF TEARS, 2013

No one really knows. Pasts haunts. But when you freely give to the world
your weaknesses: the secret is its probably
ones that no longer controls you. Nor haunts you. You remember though.
One of the best parts of self-discovery are done in private. Thoughts as your
own where secret strengths held against known weaknesses or vulnerability.

(Although I question my own thoughts these days. It is like it is shared.)

There is a full range of emotion occurring.
I believe you are entitled to the things you don't share.
A secret is priceless. Even if the world doesn't know it's value.

Heaven is a personal experience.

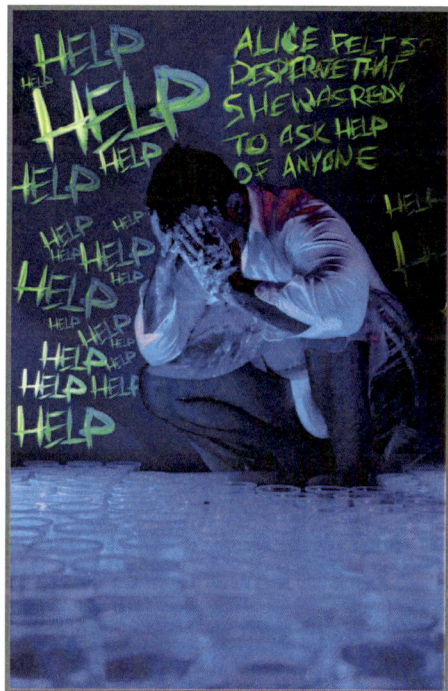

Hell is adaptable.

Purgatory is an ~~involuntary~~ waiting room for release to occur within resolves. There is a difference here in usage & references (Consider either) Mentality factors into all 3 realms.

Psychology.

It's when you let go of yourself and look at things objectively that you are able to transition from one to the next. There is always a choice.

There is always compassion to be learned or given.

Change your attitude.

Change your situation.

"Piece of shit."

"What was the basis for that?"

A phrase left for me to form it's meaning based on whatever pops in my head first. So, it shall be apparently. Abundantly clear negativity.

"What's the context?"

<An answer not provided.>

<Indistinguishable screams>

The screams in the back of my mind are looking for personification, but they are not going to get it. The connection between us lies in my thought process.

Don't give it a name.

It has none.

Don't associate and there will be no association.

(They named the more vocal voice, Chris. Another has been named "Master-Card") The names change & characters switch. Although there is recognition.

There is always the choice to write fiction.

Fiction will not be found here in this part of the book: but it is coming. I'll run free with inspiration in or out of time. Until then. the point is about getting back to center.

I have to take issue with what things heard.

<7 years>

"Who wrote the Bible?"

"Was it man-made and influenced?

(I give myself credit that I at least asked)

"I know politics factored in translations..."

"But what about the first versions written? Was it from a similar experience of hearing things or did it come from a different experience?"

"Trust the Process."

"Trust Yourself."

"Trust Personification"

"You cannot explain this."
There is a continued separation of myself from what I hear.
"Remember Medusa."
"It's important."
"Not everything you write is a stand."
"Its release."
"Why can't I hear compliments?"

I look at the fact that I was doing fine in my new, new environment. Triggered by the words, "Privacy Laws". Compounded by thinking about my series. (M) pops into my head at night. A love. A jumping off point. The question of love resounds within me. It was love. (J) was love. Everything I never discussed was love. (K) is love. I know I am growing and forgiving myself at the same time. Nothing gets discounted.

Past. Present. Future.
Unwritten.
All of it.

I don't deny love. I don't deny the idea of it. I question what exactly IS love. I know in my heart mistakes happen. It's knowing that you are imperfect that makes things work.

But there will also be...
Doubt.
Control.
Protection.
There is no comparison between any one over the other.
Everyone is different.

I'm different.
...influenced by the past.
...influenced from desire.
...influenced towards goals.

I imagine a life where I gave as much as was given.
I've failed at some attempts.
In others I was not good enough.
I ask, "Accept me for me."

Who holds the scale to my weight? Me or U?

(Perhaps this is why I am smoking again...a mind racing with possibilities of direction. But I contend to accept that the last thing I will allow is someone telling me I cannot love the person I love.)

Love is transformative.
I've needed to step up to the plate.
I believe what some of the things the voices tell me is dumb.
Everything will see its course.
Outside influence can go fuck themselves.
A tree always needs nurturing.

"Go fuck yourself" is becoming an automatic response through conditioning. Am I always going to be locked in combat? You can't beat someone up and then try to play nice with them. The nature of the phrase is strong & emotional. When uncontrolled you may inadvertently hurt yourself. But at least there's acknowledgment that it is becoming automatic.

July 16, 2017
Post 7: The lesser will have to make a decision.

"Disappointment. It's that feeling you get when things you think will go one way but then they go another. It is the crumbling of your own expectations that seem to take on a life unto itself by planting seeds into your head that unexpectedly wilted after it took life, rooted and grew one way or another. As each root grew it is going to become a harder task to weed it out entirely. Perhaps just cut-off at the stems and preserve what I can for as long as it retains beauty. Leave the roots intact, it is only good for the soil in the long run anyways.

It looks like another potential to move is not been fulfilled because of my fears. But that's ok. Something will come along when it's supposed to. Why did I turn down an opportunity to stay in the familiar? I keep telling myself that learning patience from all that I experienced is the best thing for me at the moment.

Now just is not the time to be running away. It is apparently quite easy to do so, but for me it feels like it would come across like I'm running. People will think I am escaping something and I can't handle my own situations. I'm beginning to question if I actually can. I don't trust myself right now.

At this point in the game, I do not consider it running away but, it does not feel right at all for me at the moment. Please tell me I am not wrong in staying. The FL thing would have been running away. As they said in the interview and lunch, 'I'd be entirely bored beyond belief in Destin' (Paraphrased) even if the idea of perpetual summer is a nice thought. I like that I feel I discovered something about myself there during my interview, but this is not going to change anything going on right now that you need to sow. 'Don't beat yourself up Pip'. This is just U trying to get on with your life, your career and starting to do right by you. You expect people to have the answer for you, but at the same time you know we are all making this up as we go and you are not always forthcoming yourself. You have to wake up man. Your life. Your choice." -2/23/2011

I actually wrote a whole post to this 3 weeks ago and decided to delete and start over and it sat in my drafts until I found it today. Things written in sand change in time of revisit. I guess I did so because I had to ask myself at the time what the hell am I even saying in this entry. The original post was a conflict-of-interest between personal entries and fundamentally driving the story I'm creating one way or another from life experience translations. Half of me was saying I'm pretty conflicted on what is right or wrong to say and the other side was conflicted on what to do. I base allot of my decisions on what my heart tells me and I have learned to kind of care less once it's out there on if it right or wrong because it's out there and decided. I will find out one way or another. Can't say the reach outs never occurred. I believe everything happens for a reason. I fundamentally believe we are given everything we need around us if we just look at even the most unimportant things within our environment. A useful tactic of inassuming found objects wonder if I as an object will ever be found.

I feel a great amount of myself that I display is a mixture of 'I don't trust myself on what is right at times.' vs. 'I trust myself on what is right and do it for multiple reasons.' There is equal sadness to the things I choose not to do. There is beauty in both sides of that coin. As much as I have hated that conflict moreso in the past, I trust the process now and that whatever decision I make is with full consideration of the question, "What is most right?". That does not necessary mean what is right for me but sometimes it does as well. It does mean you have to understand compassion for others as well as yourself and consequence for your decisions. There is always a ripple whether it affects you or not.

There are very few things I hide about myself.I hide some things as people should. Overall I feel comfort that in the end my journey has been genuine, honest and real. I believe this journey is not unique and I'm not alone. I'm celebrating my 3 year anniversary today of moving to Florida for a different scenario. A decision that felt right and still feels right in retrospect.

A friend of mine reminded me of the day I moved from GA to FL. I remember crying as I crossed the border. I remember being white-knuckled across the Jacksonville Bridge. I hate driving U-Haul's and I am scared of bridges since high school when I got in a wreak on one and slammed into the side. When I got the job in Florida in 2014, I literally just moved from one house to another to get settled, unpack and then pack again in a matter of could weeks. I think the tears came from knowing what I was saying goodbye to on multiple fronts. Career advancement was important, but the individual aspects of my own works and art projects was a community and support group that was still growing. I was leaving everything I built on faith that this is right for something totally unknown. When you make statements with friends on the phone about,'Knowing exactly how every day is going to play out in accordance to where I was at' denotes the same reason why financially it was important to make a step forward and take a chance. I could continue 'Heroes+Villains' in South Florida I told myself. Partner the same way once I got settled. It was a welcomed unexpected change in the right direction career-wise.

I remember showing up to work the first day in the fashion world wearing a Cerulean blue button down almost as a comedic scarlet letter of me saying I have no business in fashion but here I am. The opportunity was fantastic once I connected on why I'd do well there. Dreams from a child into adulthood connected completely with I onto the 'finally more female model exposure' on the image side. (Granted the hold up prior was mostly on the necessity of make-up artist affordability and never being able to capture the level of beauty usually required in that department with at the very least a profectionist of make-up. I dipped my toes in there from time to time and at least was getting comfortable that comes with time and practice. Until then, the theatrical roots of my Atlanta works stood true in advancement of the origins of such in theatricality and when women were allowed into theater. (Thanks Shakespeare, ...with love.) My life echoed more of "The Devil Wears Prada" than I could ever express during the time...literally down to the limo scene in a different capacity of final conversations in person. Although I didn't have a choice on employment after just like anyone else in my company did when it went bankrupt. But I'd say that is probably mostly in regards of knowing when things just always seem to pop-up in office-settings one way or another. Major difference, but if looking at relateability there are key differences and some similarities there. I guess that is the only thing I am angry about, but at the same time thankful for the opportunities. I did grow in many different ways from it. 3 years there and no option of understanding where to go from here. I was approached the day off by a company, but I didn't even have a portfolio available at the time and what I did have available was not bridal at all in majority.

It was no secret to some and hinted at with others that 3 years here was enough. I wanted to leave and I guess a secret was I was going to leave. Not in any scenario that would have screwed anyone. It was a set-up others for success and then go about my way with my life and equipment and find a work-life balance of proper compensation and back to my own works that were set aside for so long during employment. I like that I finished Disney on my terms knowing it needed a visual change anyways in execution. I like that we finished the spring line as needed to be. It was my intent to nurture and grow those underneath me. But I also knew my lease was up in October and I did not want to do another year here for personal and professional reasons.

As much as I am mad about the situation. I am choosing to treat this as a guiding hand to do what I want. It kind of forces you to do what you want. Not like I was employed at the time of writing in this post.

As scared as I have been in life, I like that I know I am actually a strong individual. I adapt and learn. I have no intention to renew my lease because that is financially irresponsible and also banking on the fact that I wanted Florida and I know I do not want that. At least not how I had experienced it. It's literally time to choose your own adventure again. What do you want? Where do you want to be? Those are big questions to ask oneself and not ones I have not asked myself this year anyways.

'White knuckled Pip. Is he the same or has he grown?' That's been the deterrent of finishing Heaven. Part of me felt I had no business finishing this if I am still questioning. 'Who the hell are you on talking about heaven if you don't feel you are there?' A Purgatory aspect at the moment as choices are required to understand the situation of unemployed and can't float forever. The other part of me is proud of what I have learned and I feel I have inched where I have been. I'm honored to know that when it is all said and done I know that other's insecurities factor just as much in the corporate world as the personal world. Perhaps what I learned of the Corporate World there, especially at the end was a beginning of an understanding where personal/professional overlap and what applies to an individual can most definitely be applied to a living breathing entity of a company.

I know more about what I was doing than I allowed myself to do. I learned that year one. Year two in corporate worlds, I learned that those that are scared are going to exploit the mess out of what they feel are weakness of others. 3rd year was learning to appreciate your worth and actually calculate it to prove to yourself that. Anyone higher than you is more dependent of the people underneath you than you may believe. Maybe 'that's a millennial thing', but you have to listen to the people younger than you if you want to be relevant to the people you are catering to. I've worked with global companies for over 14 years now in one way or another. The indirect learning was there, is there and I figure out some while still knowing there is so much to learn. I believe to this day sucess is about creating a personal response and being honest. Knowing your audience is always going be key. But never downplay your constituents. You should empower them vs. talking down to people. Empowerment promotes ideas, discussions and personal investment. I imagine it varies from one company to another.

I'm scared that this is my first time not knowing what is next. I don't like questions yet somehow throw them out there daily. I suppose it is the ones about roof over my head and sustainability in any time of unemployment. But I believe this is a 'Pippy's Choice' moment. I can literally do whatever I want. The question is what do I want and who would actually hire me? My boss said my biggest weakness is, I don't believe in myself. I would agree with that statement 3 years ago. But it was not anything new brought to the table at the time. It is an understood potential, but then how one approaches the delivery aspect of such comes from many different aspects of understanding the workplace environment I was in and finding a balance between personal/professional. My question is what do I want to do? It's not about money. It's not about changing perspectives. I feel I can do that one way or another on my own accord. I have and I will always.

So what do I want?
My lease is up in 2 months. I'll let that run out on it's own accord. It buys me freedom that longer than that is not an issue. I can go home if I want. I'll still have to look and, trust, I do not want that but it's available to me in Savannah or Atlanta. So much of me feels that's there is a conflict of defeat felt even if this was not my fault anyways. I don't want to backtrack. My biggest family is in either city. I don't want to just run home at first chance. I have to understand I was stronger and still am. I leave my safest as my last resorts. No reason in the negative, but I do want to feel I tried one way or another to continue to new places.

The biggest question has been, 'Do I cancel my Italy trip?' I booked this in honor of my grandfather instead of going to his funeral. I booked this trip because life is too short to constantly be working and never getting to travel or enjoy a vacation. I made it because I felt it was 1000 dollars for a trip to see someone whose life has passed vs. living my life that is passing me by. I have so many moral questions going through my mind at the moment. 'How could I ask for help afterwards financially if I did this?' But I do wonder would I regret this if I didn't do this. I've never been out of the country at least overseas. I've never just lived or had the chance to really in that regard due to finances or responsibilities.

I'm going to do this regardless. I've gone back and forth have been told I would regret it if I did not go. It will be ok. I'm going to Italy. I'll honor my grandfather the way I wanted to and I'll choose that adventure. It's time to continue to do what I want. I don't know what will happen months from now, but in the meantime I think I owe it to myself to dream in that regard. I'm not going to let others steal that away from me and if I don't go I'd just loose the money I've already spent anyways. Skymiles from undergrad finally put to use on something paid for well before this. I'm not going to let fear of thought hold me back. I'm not going to let this get to me because of the carelessness of what happened at Alfred Angelo or simply what could had been prevented and discussed prior to it's closure to prevent it in other variables. I can only imagine the responsibility of those in decision making all the way up to the default owners. Most of this is paid for. I'd be an fool to not complete this journey.

I'm very particular about what I post. I feel that I actually have more control than I have at the moment. The company I worked for went under and everyone lost their jobs across the board. I can place absolute blame in the people above me on some things and their choices made. 'Failure to adapt' or was it simply limited structure to what was needed with vision one way or another at the end. So many factors that were not my areas, but I see what could had been prevented and changes were occurring the final year.

But I like that from all of this I learned me in some capacity in a completely different environment. I learned something from the corporate world that is universal. Perhaps this is not the place of such thoughts. So much from this series will not be discussed, but I like that I am entirely a new person from who joined years ago. I'm still obstinate on many things. But I'm thankful that this is going to bring about what I need personally. I'm not letting anyone control this adventure. Time for Italy.

It's always the lesser that will have to make a decision of do with and do without. Not that I am to be naive that bigger decisions with bigger risk and bigger gain/loss were not considered in all of this. But never the question of 'do or do not' and 'go without or not'.

I will not give up a lifetime trip.
I'd be a fool if I did not do anything because of fear of the unknown.
Not now. Not then. Never again will I not act due to fear.

ENTRY 22:

Stand by your beliefs.

I believe I did the right thing. I know in my heart this is not going to just shut off! There needs to be closure. But there also needs to be a vacation. A step away.

I picture myself on a beach.
Secluded.
...maybe with a drink.
...maybe without one.
A goal is the sound of only nature.
<the scream stops>
<judgment stops>
"Who is more obsessed here?"
"If I am to move on, how would I go about doing so?"
...it starts by doing the every day.

(felt internally but unmistaken a different sensation, A memory revisited?),
I audibly hear "The Crystal Calls" externally
<Now, a violin>
<Now, "Elysium">
But there's nothing external playing.

I remember hearing Jeff Buckley's, "Hallelujah" while in the hospital and asking myself if I had died; as I was still unsure of my surroundings. The same song recorded on the streets of Italy replayed for me in duality. Someone was in my room when there was no one prior. A Seraphim. I thought? Unsure of having any visitors or roommates while I was there prior. Was that a coincidence? I've been experiencing a lot of coincidences lately.

On one hand I'm drawn to write it down as a metaphor of what's already been written. On the other side it comes down to questions about my mental health.

I am cognizant that strange connections factor in assessments and that is where arguments will lie. I can look at this on the spiritual side or I can look at this as my mind is trying to piece itself back together by familiarity. I can't explain Hallelujah. I remember crying while listening to it sung live. One of the most beautiful voices I ever heard and it definitely was reality with a real connection back to Italy. One some level, it sounds like there is an expected reaction to occur and then "Flip the script" occurs. There is importance in including Italy into this.

My grandfather used to call me Flip.
Maybe that is something to hold onto.

I'm trying to figure out how to approach this. Medication could take it away and solve this. (I've been denied medical treatment since fired while hospitalized). Perhaps it is time to read what I wrote in the hospital and took home with me. I'm experiencing memories that are neither my own or never occurred. 2 taps. A Spray. It switches from left to right to right to left. 3 variables played out real to me. A nightmare that gladly never occurred.

In fairness there isn't much. Some sketches, drawings, a page of notes of things to do after. The recording of numbers as if trying to remember a phone number of anyone to be able to call. But at the time specifically (K)'s.

(LP) and (K) were in my dreams last night.
Discussions.

Maybe I am overthinking things. I write notes when I can to think about it later. Perhaps this candle is spent burning at both ends, but even so...eventually you hit center.
"There is responsibility when outcomes are predicted."
<Ethics>
Stories always change shape.
"What's strength?"
"Sacrifice again?"
<Don't Give in>
(Non-recorded dialog pushing suicide)

"I AM NOT GOING TO COMMIT SUICIDE!"

The weight is getting to me. How long can I listen to these voices in my head?
"This is a problem."
To describe the sensation is like others playing detective when I just need to focus on the now. Some have been here longer than others.

"...I don't know what happened (but I am going to find out)."
"...a simple misunderstanding."

One voice even said, "You thought I forgot about you?"
Familiar in that I had not heard it since Atlanta.

Am I capable of focusing on the now anymore?
If I'm writing it is more now present than one thinks.
In Past & Predictability Outcomes Intertwine.
I remember sitting there. Twice. Listening to cruelty. Listening to my life
dissected and preventative measures taken when I spoke to a lawyer. I felt sick
at the speed others react to private conversation of me exploring council. I
changed the conversation with one simple text knowing what I heard. "I feel
sick. I don't want a lawyer."

<" The transcript is in."(FD)>
They had a transcript of my phone call and acted on it in the office setting.
That call was in the outdoor parking lot of towers of Kings and Queens that
they don't own. I notice now as I knew when I started this document of
subtle differences from this and the last version printed. 'Who is referencing
what in that which they didn't pay for?', appears in my thoughts.

Aware...still.
<Sitting at my station>
Chaos in calmness.
Awake without the ability to move or say anything.
"Why am I not throwing up?"
"I feel sick."

I, at least, give myself that
I walked away from this.
Their choice to be played out.

<" They came for him." (T-PR)>
Remember that.

"...A Perfect Storm."
(Power went out during "Endgame" last night. It stopped at the point where
they list movie references. An explanation of time travel through what is

familiar to the viewer. A narrative establishment of rules and pre-conceived notions out the window.

I remember saying, "Fine...I'll go to bed.")

"This is embarrassing."

"Is a thought process embarrassing?"
"Is it compromised by outside influence?"
I'm aware of what I am writing. I need to understand compliments.
...Understand confusion.
Can I sync the sound together somehow?
Layers of sound both beautiful and daunting.

Is there truth in these secrets?
Trust the processor or they will consume.

"He has no faith." (PRe)

August 10, 2017
Post 8: An exit interview and a reflection.

"I moved here to get away. I moved here because I wanted an out and I know I needed one. I would never accept leaving just for leaving sake. I know damn well 'You' comes with you and I know what I would be carrying with me when I did. Who 'We' are carries with 'Us' no matter where. An opportunity came for me and it was the right thing when I needed it. I do believe in things happening for a reason. I see that in my artwork and locations I never would have imagined of factoring in play as a part in the scheme of things as it had. I believe I need to answer these questions that I have for myself one way or another. 'Life finds a way...'"

"There comes a point that the secret journey is enough. There comes a point you don't need to validate yourself to others anymore. Either the story becomes like you are harping or the story comes across as it should...as growth. But it does not matter one bit how you got to your place in the end, it's where you are at now and how you feel about that place you find yourself in. That is what matters. Are you happy in your new place? Are you happy with yourself?" -9/17/2014

And so my time here is up.
Who am I now?
What have I experienced?
What are my lasting thoughts on this chance I took?
Am I any closer or further from my 'heaven'?

What did I learn here?

Mostly, I think I've learned that those more experienced in life are equally scared as I have been in life. Who knew people on this planet older than I or in higher positions are human as well and maybe have gone through one thing or another? Not that I didn't know that prior, but it is interesting to understand rites of passages of stories of superiors who teach hard lessons one way or another to one generation or the next.

One way or another we all mask the fact that every day is a new experience to learn how to adapt to it properly. Balance of work and life knowing a little bit more now in age one way or another. We all seem to fake it until we make it one way or another, but I've already discovered that. Perhaps one day you will as well. You can play in probability, but in predictability you will often discover nothing but surprise after surprise to appreciate now or maybe later. It is the interest of new fields that always invites revisit of interests had prior or newfound. In any situation, we use what we can and somehow we live to live another day somehow by figuring things out individually or seperately.

It is hard for me to differentiate my life experiences here as things from solely a business side or from life in general. I can say predominantly my investment was on the company who took a chance on I with myself invested well beyond in return in learning environments and worlds. The difference between predestined non-advancement prior to at least the opportunity of experiencing something different and a chance to move from there. Understood the 8 years prior then and what the last 4 years were in branching out in individuality and a communial brand to a certain degree. When I moved here (Florida 2014—2017), I started the idea of building a life down here, but I shut that down pretty quickly when others did things that even I lacked the imagination to do in order to get even for wrongs or I guess perceived wrongs (thoughts of the person who faked their death and my immediate process from grief to anger in discovery on multiple fronts). I guess I was just over dealing with that kind of drama and shut out a major part of who I am as a person and denied myself the one thing I probably never should have.

On what aspects I was working on at the time in 'Brave New Secrets', it was a hard decision on multiple fronts of in inability to cope, properly articulate or say what you want or let someone go. In any regard to the overall story of thought process of the time, there is a love for everything experienced and appreciate it one way or another. The aspirations towards enjoyment of life were what mattered. Conversations. Connection. Laughter. Mature physical connections. It all matters in adulthood before realizing everyone has their own things built prior they still nurture and others join in or healthy in seperation. It is very rare one knows everything about someone's entire life and ambitions and passions. Even less to know the decisions made one way or another. That is the beauty of intimacy in any aspect of friendship, co-workers, or even in relationships. There is admirations one way or another and perhaps I look at this in reflective aspects that the narrative of what I I publicly showcased in my first show has been completed at this point. It may not be readily available, but there is Placeholder text over where the story ends on one side and then there is simply life and the storyteller aspect of invite to be a part of my life or yours one way or another. I'm not in any position to even be of value atm, but I am on the board knowing such. To be wittled down to zero multiple times and attacked since 2017 is understood to I. Whatever the reason, I see it as other's positioning with what I have already presented to the world and what has been presented to I in trying to protect one way or another. The refective aspects are the most important to understand early on. Perhaps 'focus' is another word for 'refective'. 'Where is your mind set?' 'What do you want to focus on?' 'What do you want to discuss?' A transitional aspect understanding one question was from one world and here we are in another looking in the mirror trying to get to know one another.

When I moved to Florida it was really at the same time I just closed down the circle a bit further and said, 'Hey, I have some pretty healthy friendships here and some things elsewhere. I'm cool with this smaller circle.'. I was welcomed in the right places by friends I've not been able to keep up with as of late (2022). It is understood by I why that is. Maybe not with them. It is not my place to say such.

At the time, I just kind of figured, 'ok... This is temporary...focus on the career, build the experience and whatever the next move is will be a more lasting one but definitely grow from this experience and take things in one way or another.'.

I'd say if there was any particular lesson to be learned from the moving here it has been lessons about exploitation since my primary aspect of re-establishment was my career and rebuilting my own artistry in a different capacity outside of that. I learned 8 years discountment in Atlanta (partially while so much acceptance). I learned of exploit in Florida by others understanding despiration knowing I've been there and done one thing or another in those regards on personal aspects. In retrospect, I understand my prior employer in her despiration to know what she protected was family first while dealing with the rest of what life presented by other's actions. I wrote a bit, but you have few and far between personal works during that time.

For I it was focus was on establishing a new environment. I don't think the world as malicious by any means whatsoever. (A Naive aspect of that is a little bit more of 'Shades of Jade' since original writings in 2017. I may have experienced a bit between 2017 and present to say one way or the other. The same could be said of 2014—2017, or 2011—2014. A continual grouping of time frames where the expansiveness of time makes one wonder where did the time go? I'm sure the same could be said for anyone in connect/disconnect. If they instantly discount you, then they get caught off-guard at later points in time. Perhaps the thought process reveals too much at this time in inocculus and unassuming.) But I absolutely believe that people will use any particular situation to make themselves look better. Who wouldn't? The question is how many other people are you making better in their looks as well? If it is selfish, then it is not sustainable. If it right morally then people can understand then that is something different. The only difference is if it is for mutual benefit or for your sole advancement where others would never be the wiser. It is understood at this point that one insider tells another and goes from there one way or another. At least there is a big difference when someone reveals something publically in one place or another. At least I've always been team player even though I've spent a great number of years in solo journeys of exploration. At least I sent the original version of this book to United States copyright individually and solely knowing what I experienced from 2018-2019 specifically in November 2019 knowing those words were protected and understanding what I was trying to save then while coming back from actually trying to commit suicide to still try to prevent persecution of my family and loved ones knowing that if this was happening to myself, it could happen to anyone who was in the sight of one entity or another.

I still stand by I probably would had approached a publisher then with this book knowing its worth then and moreso now. It says so in the introduction knowing that was from actively typed showcased processes from 2011 understanding it came prior and knowing where things went after. Others have already saw it's worth well after what I already experienced and kept going at it anyways. I stand by my cover for this version knowing that is the cover at this point unless someone wanted to say one way or another. That is understood before I continue. This book was not written until I returned home to Savannah, GA thankful my mother took me into her home in adulthood knowing I couldn't have gotten here if it wasn't for my father and his now wife. Written at the SCAD Jen Library with no internet at home or even a connection available. What was wanted in ATL 2.0 vs. what came after and which different group are we in knowing I've been impeded on and this book in any version as such where as I type knowing other copyright works have also been sent out to people I don't know who and was also not privy to?

I protected what needed to be protected in the first version to include the original EEOC sworn testimony that later I found narratively to not be the time or place to discuss it in schemes outside myself and what I found the book to actually do to seperate myself from my own experience and apply it to anyone understanding we all went through one thing or another. A connection there to not give up and In no available for purchase version was the EEOC response included and at best I cite the case number to look at if you want.

I look at this book as an aspect that isn't going anywhere in disappearance of truth and what occurred and what was important for myself to finish what I could of my works at the time with the best answer I had then. It is at least a perspective of understanding what it means to come back from suicide while also know what had to be done, what obstacles were faced or implied and going from there beyond what I did and connecting to where if you remove me from the equation, go to the introduction and you have a game plan for yourself. I feel I found the right and final answer to that game plan in 'Lorem Ipsum: A Child of Someone.' That is why I don't have the modification of that introduction in this book and never will. It took years to find that flaw or advancement from 2016 to 2022. My life experience brought me there and it is sound on many levels. In cited source, it is correct to know you don't come to answers right away and not many are afforded the chance to reflect in such a manner of understanding in this book alone 9 years at various times present. Basis hidden in added on context, but when this book was already attacked, that is safe and secure understanding what is attached to it in short form and what sums up my life's accomplishment of lessons and of something to understand that is outside any of us and relates to everyone at the same time. CLASSIC examples to be had in right or wrong one way another. By my hand or others understanding it is always about translation.

At least in the self-publish aspect, there was no 'capture and kill' at the time of my life story knowing what I've written is well beyond 2018-2019, well beyond 2012, 2011, 2003, 2001, 1998...I can pretty much say on a personal level I can only cognizantly say 3 years old in recollection of individual moments. There is November 1, 1982 as is the earliest I can say of introduction in this world before contimplating thoughts pre-birth and where genetics factor later. When no problems to my work prior to Alfred Angelo, what happened after I created my website of my work in unemployment and sit back and see what I accomplished prior to living in Florida before understanding what I experienced in Flordia? Who saw the same?

People are definitely capable of feeding on those that show insecurity and doubt. Even the smartest in that group will be shrew in how that goes about a situation if they think they can advance or need to know one thing or another. to protect. My introduction to the corporate side of things was ambition abound one way or another present. Hopeful. Naive. Understood. I found yet again, people do not talk to other people in the workplac and it involves walk arounds to say, 'Hello'.

That changed with everyone in coming into a singular headquarters. Surprisingly people open up and enjoy communication. Long gone of the days of iChatting coworkers 20-30 ft. away...the forced perspective of verbal communication still exists in the world. In the new world of introductions to corporate, success would be to understand a yearly timeline and how things work in departments. I made it a self-made mission to understand that I uprooted my life to a place of new root placement. In that search I found welcomed aspect to such until I was only to be circumvented from talking to the CEO or at least questioned on why I wanted to to begin with by my Superior the VP of Marketing. The original intention was to find the timeline of the company's milestones and an introduction but I understand the strangeness of one doing such as then. I contend that should had been the job of the creative director or the VP of Marketing, but I'm not about to fail at this and this is information that needs to be known to be successful.

I imagined it was appreciated later on to a degree but still unorthodox to traditional corporate structure. There was nothing traditional to I about the structure that was changing anyways at the time. Otherwise, I would had never been hired. (A multi-decision there.) I came with a foundation of where I came from and still to this day love the fact that the drag aspect of Heroes+Villains #3 (2012) and my tackling the Disney villains in inspirational translation was a part to something bigger in understanding. I looked at it as such that it gave me an in to being official in a capacity of being accepted indirectly to a dream aspect of understanding marriage in general in any regard and being a part of something that still founded on translation and belief systems of others. It was the budget aspect that was different between the two and definitely the space capacity of shoots in hallways and kitchens. I imagine indirectness in support one way or another. It comes with things on the other side after. Open doors control many things or at least have awareness of what occurs and what is let in.

The realization of advancement thoughts was brought on from experience being told of corporate early 90's and the involvement of the compartmentalizing of positions. Strangeness to me as I was simply trained to have responsibility from start to finish and have checkers go over everything before going out to clear liability and errors. (Never screw up a coupon. Millions of dollars in mistakes was taught early on. Never directly with I, it was just told why one proofs, scans and others impliment other protective measures to such before production. Every coupon is thousands or millions of dollars set aside for a promotion.) A production aspect of a tight ship where work horses had on multiple fronts. It was always in that regard that I respected what came before in multiple fronts. Taught by my previous employer the beauty of modern software vs. lightboxes and old school techniques of what had to happen to get the same results was similar to my single traditional photography class in undergrad while well introduced to Photoshop since high school. I understood the craft and the artistry on either side. I imagine even the most scientific of photographers would be all in on Photoshop in some capacity or another even if just on discovering how it works and translates on mathematics of pixels and digital tools. If you want to be amazed about practicality, look up the creation of Grace Jones and a microphone for an album cover. In the cut and past of Frankenstein moments, take amazement in what you can only fathom as practical application which could be easily now down in software but required a certain something else back then. Skill-sets not to say one way or another, as technology also introduced artistry in a different capacity, but in that regard there is no flaw in the Grace Jones application of technique.

There is appreciation of how hard it was while understanding individual skill-sets in hiring aspects. I loved the aspect that the creative transitioned from one place or another to start at the same time. I learned pretty quickly from multiple areas the insecurity aspect of corporate life where I can honestly say at the end in 2017 in discussion, lifelines and timelines are limited and there is some universal aspects to being constantly on edge in an aspect that is completely unnecessary and probably carry-over from the 80's in that regard of getting ahead and the fear of others screwing you over for their own benefit. I cannot account in my lifespan to what was prior. I imagine the 70's have their say before probably my argument settles around the 1950s once things resettled after the Great Depression from the 30's and everyone lost things and rebuilt one way or another. Timeframes matter in that regard. That behavior always has a cost. It eventually comes out at one point or another. Try to bring people down and there is a price to pay for that.

The multi-hats of this generation are beginning to wonder how easy it is to have a specific sole task and a salary with that and whole teams of their own specific skill-set. (I understand this is not individualized experience, but that some still retain the non-multi-hat aspects.) Those multi-hats might start looking at the inflation aspect of roles from the 70s and 80s and learn math and job descriptions of archival past.

Play on other people's fears and there will be casualties one way or another whether it comes from the victim or because life is actually pretty ironic in fixing that ripple effect. I'm not sure how to answer this at this time. It comes out in one book or another. I can't just say one thing or another knowing it is important to know what I went through and experienced to get there. It won't matter to most and that is completely ok. There are some that take the time and others quick to judge or blame. I understand one side. I understand other sides. I at least know I made that right for me in my soul in the end and whatever happened in skipping over or doing one thing or another, 'I made it right for me.'. Any other aspect exaspirates the other side of discussion that is introduced in this book.

The biggest question I could ask myself in reflection is, was this worth it? If it wasn't, I wouldn't have done it. Value had one way or another.

It's hard for me to decide how to approach this because my instinct is to talk about this in the scheme of art, but really I'm asking myself if the last 3 years was worth it life-wise and the scheme of corporate world. I have to look at things as this is really my life and I put some things on hold and other things snuck in anyways naturally. I look at the series I was building prior and I see that I was due for a spiritual change and I believe moving here facilitated that growth for sure. It happened unexpected and unexplained. Brought on by friends who believed in me one way or another before introduction to strangers who either had one opinion or another. I was hired with no experience in the field. That meant a great deal then and now. Chances on either side.

I was due for knowing answers to questions and I think I threw out into the world enough of who I am as a person for people to see me for me and not how people wanted to paint me. Perhaps probably others saw a gesso abstract to restart and go in a different direction understanding the underpainting to a certain extent. Maybe it was never noticed. It was noticed enough to hire me.

I imagine that was something I made damn sure of and probably at this point I have not decided if it being so clear who I am as a person is going to be a detriment or a benefit career-wise moving forward. There was the vulnerability and there was trust. That came from the friends of Atlanta and those who simply discovered me one way or another and gave me a chance. I see it in my website which is something I always fought against doing prior. I never wanted to be so proud in having one and I saw it as total vanity understanding that I never had to do a website solely to promote myself or look for a way to sustain and find a job. Looking at it now I see it not so much as a necessity for an industry, but something to look back on and say OMG...I did that and view the things I'm most proud of came from necessity and a desire for something more knowing so many of us came together on that idea. I began building this website around this time. While contimplating cancelling Italy, I was building what my traditional portfolio standard was to a means to survive and find a job. No money was coming in. From there came my website and help where I felt comfortable in asking for such. It was done with my fellow co-workers and it was asked objectively from a mentor and former Chief Creative Officer of Alfred Angelo knowing what it meant to have such the privilege of review knowing words are important in this capacity of revealing my life's work in a digital capacity in this regard. The time spent was what mattered most knowing what happened on multiple fronts.

I grew...I'm growing. This is the first time I am putting all my work in one place and it humbles me to see that I grew so visibly from one thing to the next and I had so much support. From the first moment of my first solo show in 2011, to when I was first invited to be a part of a gallery in 2010. The growth was real and the connections occurred. Direct or Indirect. To even begin to rediscover that after that much investment in something that I would had walked away with nothing from was worth remembering and going back to. 'Where is 2014 Pip?' Knowing 3 years have passed and a great deal has changed. Whether amateur or the few moments where I really think I hit things, its all there for anyone to see. From my first show to each hero to hero.

I guess it was very important for me that I needed to control perception. I went about things that If U are going to know me, it will be on my terms and not others. Perhaps that is my detriment. Perhaps that is my crowning achievement. I embraced me and shared that with the world. I will always appreciate that I try to be honest in my explorations and I like that my intentions come from a good place vs. one of ill-intent. I try to be the person I expect others to be and what I believe they are capable of becoming. Often I hide when I need to figure out my environment.

How do I feel moving forward?
I feel like I put everything I could into a profession for the last three years. From day one I was discounted in my profession. How many were discounted before I only to learn to discount and not appreciate the fact that it is a choice to work anywhere and where lift-ups do far better than put-downs? For everything I brought to the table, I was considered a threat to several of those above. In other areas just discounted and

still a workhorse. In any scenario, there are those that made that very clear to me just as much as I made it clear I was not. Being told, "You are the reason I'm going to get fired." resonates with me as a moment where I wanted to say, "I've tried from day one to support you but if you think that bitch, that is your problem and you can burn in your pride at this point." Does it mean anything different to type out a thought process vs. going one way or another? It was in the original version. It is a silent thought process of many to one or the other in any workplace. I know there is proof one way or the other on what is and isn't spoken in the office that affects outcomes. Instead I console, say what I can and then professionally go to your boss and ask for a sit down to discuss things as professionals and to resolve ways that do and do not work in the office considering. It is the same thing every time. How many bottles of wine do I need to give her to pacify her insecurities and understand she is overwhelmed and overworked?, I think to myself. That is more than likely why they got fired and I retained a job. Professionalism. There are the things I don't say in the moment and then the things I think. As this space is a little different, it is important to note the biting of the tongue. It occurred the entire 3 years in that environment. Pride is a very dangerous thing to hold onto. I think I've definitely held onto my own pride for quite some time as well in regards. But there is a big difference in being prideful and knowing you can do what needs to be done. Sometimes you have to suck it up, do something anyways and then go home and relax or jump in the pool to drown out the day and wash it off only to do the same the next day.

If one was to want to know, here is how I presented myself in the beginning of Corporate structure.

August 27, 2014. (Imagine the one I wrote a year later the day before her termination about a year later. Corporate world 2 months in.)

(AA-AG),
I would like to schedule a morning meeting with either just you, or you and *(AA-Mc)* to discuss the perimeters of my job role with Alfred Angelo.

I was hired as Design Director and there seems to be a clash between me and other positions that I feel can be resolved by a meeting outlining the perimeters of my position to avoid any more confusion moving forward.

Since starting, I have done what has been asked and needed of me to get things done for the betterment of the team. That will never discontinue. We all signed on for servitude for the company. For the last two days, I have it expressed the experience that I lack and that others possess which I thought I could pass over yesterday without mention until it was brought up again today. But I can't help but feel like I need to address it early on.

When I signed on and agreed to this job, I understood I came with a naive sense of experience with some of the job requirements in this field. I don't have a traditional fashion background. I understood that the people around me came with a vast knowledge and experience of the field. I am excited to learn from that experience and know that this is where I belong.

My background comes with a definitive knowledge of brand management with the world's most renown brand as well as a self-learned knowledge of knowing what it is like to control a photo-shoot from behind the camera and in front of the camera and build that to world recognition. I know I will fall short once we exit the Disney concepts, but mostly just because that becomes a realm that I have experience in without a director involved. There has been a lot of learning to be had and I feel I have stepped up to the plate.

For the last two days, I have been verbally degraded and "peacock feathered" personally and in front of you for what I can only assume is frustration with what is understandably the situation at hand. I get that completely. I know the importance of getting things right in the positions we walked into. But I cannot help but see that as something that I need to address as unacceptable. I understand who I am. I understand that I am in no position to say something, but I was right there when another team member was brought to tears for the same action.

With the presentation today, it was 100% me who took the lead on that, so I take responsibility good or bad on it. I was left to my own accord with it until crunch time at the end of the day. I saw the e-mail last night that was sent and the backlash from Disney on the "new creative team". If we just showed images of the mood boards then that would have been an issue within itself as it was not what they were used to seeing and not what you show other companies. I have gathered it to be an already shaky relationship between AA and Disney (just my understanding). I did what needed to be done to present something professional and to what they are used to of selling concepts based on what they provided. I understand we all wear many hats right now as we build a new team and a new understanding of positions and how things are done. I get that. I think I'm just getting put in my role that I just need clarification on.

Moving forward I am definitively saying, *(AA-Mc)* is the creative director. I've known from day one she has final say, with yours being above hers (*Chief Creative Officer above you*). I've never questioned or challenged that. I'm here because of you and her. I never said I knew anything about hiring professional models, that it was my place for make-up or hair, nor have I offered any opinion other than that you should choose this one model over another. I've been put in a position where I feel I've had negative feelings for things I've suggested or done and would like to improve on them if so. I just think it would be helpful to know the perimeters of my job so I never have to be belittled for who I am in front of anyone again for areas I am learning, nor can I say that I can accept that as proper behavior in building a team where we are all qualified in different fields that the others may be lacking. I should not have been the sole one creating the presentation today if there is no faith in my abilities (*The original 2015 Disney Proof-of-Concept*).

I want to be a team. I am ambitious and excited to see where this brand goes and know completely my role in the scheme of things, but I am a little taken aback on the proper way to address this without creating a rift. Talking to *(AA-Mc)* saying this creates a rift. I know I am third tier in the scheme of things and was hired to fix problems noticed and to present ideas. Teamwork is core for us to survive what is the busiest time of the year for Alfred Angelo and I want to do what is best. I do not want to step on any toes and just want to work as a team. Thats what I was hired for. I have bosses but I want to make sure that I am doing what is expected of me which is vague because I do not want to step on my bosses' toes.

I have been told writing this email may sound like a negative, but it really is not at all by any means at all. A team talks. A team builds. I am just expressing something that was a crack to me. And something that needs clarification on moving forward. I know I am new and I absolutely love, admire and appreciate everything in-between with me and my team. But I guess I am putting a foot in my own mouth in saying that I shouldn't be constantly reminded of what I don't know, but taught what I should know.

Hope to talk in person tomorrow to explain better because I feel this may have come off confusing,

-Philip

_____

Shortly after the email and the all-nighter of completing Disney according to deadlines with day and night differences occurring, my title was changed to Senior Creative Manager as the who division was changing anyways and the way the department was prior was fundamentally changing being in new headquarters.

I'd say it is very apparent when I took my position I did not so much believe in myself as much as I didn't know how the world worked. If I didn't believe in some aspect of myself or have my reasons, I never would had taken the position or gotten hired by those that saw potential. I've made my own on my own rules and although the real world is strange, I don't think I should fault myself for not understanding it or laughing at it at times. Team building is essential and the rest is one-on-one personality understandings while knowing roles and positions. I joke that my life has been "The Devil Wears Prada" since I started but its kind of accurate. I know what I am good at. I know where I'd like to learn. There is the mixture of support and hinderance available in any workplace setting. In the beginning it was definitely Disney I knew very well. The other side of the company came from realizing women dream about this day their entire life. That really is no different from my own aspirations and just wanting something to be perfect in the idea of something. For all intents, this probably was the most perfect job for me at the time. I believed in the faith and I believed in what they were selling even if my own perceptions on marriage are skewed in many aspects. It was an ideal. Mix that with giving me control of an official Disney license in the context of what I have already done and I'm fucking sold. Add on the other 3 bridal lines, bridal party and then added 2 more other lines by the end and you find out how much is done with so little one way or another. Disney itself would had been a full-time position. What my position was and that of the entire department was total emersion of the entire Alfred Angelo catalogue of products in all creative applications digital and print.

Where I ended up with this company is completely different then what I was originally hired for. In the scheme of things, it would have been my role to support the Creative Director, have others produce mechanical files, have others do photo-shoots, have others do work while there is management and direction that goes in multiple tiers and always in collaboration with the Dress Design Department. What became of my position was I was the Creative Director at times (as I in the beginning had to step-up to the plate multiple times on leadership, was basically the senior creative in interim when they transitioned from one CD back to the previous CD.) I was the senior creative of the department on-site in the second half and that was more dual responsibilities where I stayed away from added on responsibility. That CD and I worked very well together and I learned quite a bit there. I understand a great deal of the breakdown and added responsibilities came after the Chief Creative Officer left the company and where added on responsibilities ensued.

Perhaps I waited until I was 40 and in the same age bracket of legally being able to talk about the difference of generational responsibilities and expectations in the workforce. You can't say age discrimination against I on one end now, but I can claim it towards myself from multiple sources over the years while fundamentally proposing something that fix things for everyone. My 'Rule of Ate' totally copyright protected and states my case in preparedness to the power of 40+ in response of mere 39 and on a brink of such a mantle where my age discrimination occurred in my challenge while stating where it definitely occurred beyond gender, race, nationality or any other boundries of such in The United States of America. That is down the line in another book, but the skip ahead is available for citation. The how I got there is the interesting aspect on a great deal of things.

The joys of mid-life momenteum...

One of these days I'll actually tell you that an official response to workplace discrimination actually was described that it is perfectly acceptable for it to happen if of the same race and gender while still excluding other genders from the initial response. The shame of such when so much progress made over the decades for equal rights that women too can discriminate and harass. I blame 'Bad Bosses'. If you can think it and it ends up on the screen, it can exist in the workplace. The corporate worlds of the #1s are insane I tell you. Can you magine how much persecution after 40 is allowed legally?!

Maybe that is the mid-life crisis. Finding out all these rules of respect that had to be followed and 'respect your elders' was around for a reason...because after 40 you can do anything you want apparently. Especially to those younger and of less experience in one place of business or another. It is a sliding scale of continual learning and adapting in order to stay viable in the market. Otherwise, we seem destined to perhaps non-committal relationships in one field or another. Going back to school helps in retraining and viability. A refresher face-lift know technology seems to speed past us faster than the comprehension that those of higher position and longevity know how long it took to get things done prior. Now they get instant output at a faster rate, cheaper price and from multiple employees acting as processing systems with fulldocking stations of entire libraries of other people's skillsets and former positions to just open up in an all-in-one package. You would think that would actually increase their value and paygrade knowing the detriment of less work staff more responsibility. But alas...they get you on the non-commital aspects of keeping you just insecure enough of your future to be able to toss you at any time without anything to show for it. It eventually catches up with a company though. Depending on the size of the company, one or two members of a whittled down staff can completely disrupt a company that once would have to have a walk out of 10-15 people to have the same effect.

In Florida, I took the lead of several brands, I brought mechanical works into my company, I stepped outside of the creative role and created a brand philosophy that was adopted company wide. I put so much of myself into a global brand while putting myself at the back burner. I was the photographer at times and at other times I tried my best to push the designers under me one way or another by treating them as peers. One thing I will never forget about trying to figure out this world was my first shoot for my company. In the real world there is someone for everything. Set Design, photographer, talent coordinator, and prop stylist. I was told my first shoot to "sit back and watch how the professionals do it" and in my mind I wanted to say "I've done that...I've done that...I can do that." Not in the capacity of such teamworks that are in the real-world experience. But to have knowledge of all those positions is a great step in the right direction of working with professionals instead of just watching them from the sidelines.

In review of emails of the past to expand upon my thoughts and to accurately understand them in 2022, it is understood a great deal of things have occurred since 2017 in my life. It is noticed my photography invoices from Alfred Angelo are deleted from my private email along with other specific emails. A trend I've noticed early on this year especially on my 'Rule of Ate' Placeholder email that was sent on April 1, 2021. I, of course, have my original printouts of invoices so I am good there. While not total documentation of recount, there is an email I sent to my mother on Feb. 11, 2016 to talk of the state of affairs then and work towards discussion of professionalism. That email was well before going into spending my Christmas break of 2016 coming up with a different business proposal of my photography contributions for the company that was introduced and just glanced at briefly and then closed with numbers already in mind prior to discussion. I still remember the discount of all that work and fairness not even given more than a passing glance of thought. It was noted and I rebutted on fixed numbers already had. That was well after the email below.

There is another draft of this 3 days prior, so it is understood it was important to get right just as much as Christmas 2016 was important to get right and to understand where it fell towards the end personally, professionally and where I stayed until the last day of Alfred Angelo where so much positive could had occurred in the right situation and in communication but I was not really in a position to be the one that could had completely stalled the entire marketing aspects of the company if I wanted to based on where their dependance on I was becoming critical to the company and the weight of the livlihoods of my co-workers was mis-directed onto I by my VP of marketing in unhealthy and threatened aspects that just brought direct discount to my contributions anyways.

It is more than likely I sent some version, if not this version to my boss.

_____

Feb. 11, 2016
"Not sending this to him, but wanted to get my thoughts and bullet points together when I have the talk.

(AA-AG),

Sorry for typing this out. But I want to clear in my words and wanted to think this out carefully. It is both my personal and professional response to you as a boss and I apologize for it's wordiness but it's a big deal for me.

When I first started, I was actually introduced into the commercial world of photography with much disdain of what knowledge and skill set I have. (Granted *(AA-Mc)* was just not a good mentor or leader in any way possible, but I digress) But over time I've proven that no matter how naive my skill set is, that I have been a capable tool to use for composites, retouching and ultimately photography. I know I could do this shoot in the end if Alfred Angelo and myself can come to a mutual agreement, but as it stands the offer comes with much reservations and something as a loss for me either professionally or personally. The first is, I have already done one exhaustive photo shoot *(without compensation)* that came with the same set of mutual reservations not feeling right about the situation and delivered what was asked because it was needed for the company. We took a $78000 photo shoot and turned into a 2-3 thousand one to deliver imagery for sales reps. That's a feat. Retouching could have been better and more thought but we were up against unrealistic deadlines and between *(AA-SS)* and I turned those around in less than a week while managing the rest of our workloads. Perhaps in the future wholesale can communicate with design/marketing before setting sales meeting dates to get everyone on the same page. Trust me that none of the comments of the imagery is taken personally because we all try to just do what we needed to do and we could have retouched more. This is just a job. I honestly don't care outside of getting it done.

Secondly I know the cost of things. As much as I appreciate you talking to *(AA-RA, Current CEO)* and offering $1000 to do this shoot, I regretfully don't feel right accepting the offer. *(Contract-to-Hire Photographer)* would have been paid 31K for this shoot for deliverables. He delivered what is asked. I delivered what was asked. I did not choose photography for a career or for my position but if it is to become a part of my position, I am not naive. The *(dress)* forms *were* within my comfort zone because it was just forms and doable for me but ultimately still something I did not have to do nor wanted. I did my part for the team. How do you think I feel being in a room doing what I taught myself to do and have all eyes on me and all pressure on me to do this right and deliver? Millions of sales dollars lies on those images and doing them correctly. It's one thing to direct talent to produce your desired result. It's another when you are pushing the direction and pushing yourself beyond what you know you can do. I faked it and made it because I tuned out and just did what needed to be done and did it beautifully. To ask me to reshoot this again, but now with models is asking me to realize that this is now **62K** I would have made in the real world of photography and with so much more pressure and so many more eyes on me because they expect things to be better than the forms. That's not even factoring in the retouching fees where in the real world at our base rate of $150 per image I could have gained $30,000. Even if I did accept to do this at $1000 I question the resentment I'd have the next time *(Contract-to-Hire Photographer)* or any photographer or retoucher came in and I process their invoice knowing my annual salary while I just settled for an amount because I took one for the team with a thanks along the way. I know I'll actually feel worse about that decision then vs. me trying to come up with one now on this. There would be no value for me and it would be expected in the future.

Prior to the reshoot there was a desire for photographing small scale things and some things in a different direction that has not been done before (like the sequins shoot that we will be exploring next week off site and with minimal supervision). With shooting more trendy styles more frequently through out the year I have already expected that I'd have to do some of those so I wanted to try something new and cost effective. It may be a nice angle to get more of the shots we need cheaper but also more candid and lifestyle-ish. That is something that could be fun and without the pressure of what is asked currently. But, I ultimately have to reiterate that I was not hired to do photo shoots for Alfred Angelo. I've had to do them when things are in a pinch and take one for the better of the team/company as they get things situated for a better time. But after multiple occasions that has just become the expectation vs. the exception. This casual shoot is the one right thing for me and Alfred Angelo when it comes to photography. It allows me to explore on my terms while meeting company needs.

For me personally, there are a lot of things I should not of had to do. I did them for personal reasons or because it was just the right thing to do. But I grew a bit more and more every day from making those decisions. It was to my adamant that I brought production completely internal vs. using RRD. I had to save Disney the first year. Spearheaded it the second year and even when I didn't want to composite again, did what needed to happen to get it done. Even if I was still fine tuning the images after the AAG was printed to get things right. Did the Maid to Love shoot but it's disheartening in the end I hear or it gets told that it's thanks to *(AA-SS)*'s direction instead of a team effort. That all factors into my decisions.

I question how can we fix what we have and call it a day for everyone? The deliverable time of the reshoot of images falls into April so I question if we use what we have now and then have *(Contract-to-Hire Photographer)* reshoot what we need to in April when we shoot the spring line. Other companies sell on dress forms. What makes us different? Reps need to back a line and I question why any company would allow a rep to not do their job because they don't believe in an image. There is a big difference between a sales tool and an ad shot. But truth be told the company needs to be on a united front before executing things of this nature in the future. Everyone needs to be supportive as things are. We did the best we could and all should have been supportive from day one as leaders when a decision was made and know to spin this a particular positive way with the people underneath with the wall that we were up against. Our position is value and what the reps asked for on Tuesday is ad shots to do their job easier.

You asked me what can be done for me to be on board with this and these are my options. I consider them fair and up for discussion.

1. $30,000 annual pay raise. With it comes the acceptance that I will be asked to photograph the trend shoots throughout the year and small shoots only. Entire Spring/Fall/Disney lines are not on the table for negotiation for shooting at this range. Some retouching is expected throughout the year. Compositing negotiable per case, but not finals for entire lines. (i.e. Disney)

2. $15,000 one time photo shoot fee minus regular hourly cost of employment. (roughly comes to $13711 give or take) Internal photography moving forward is off the table or will be compensated accordingly as negotiated then and fairly with hourly wages being subtracted from the final amount.

3. I accept the $1000 offer with the expectation that Alfred Angelo will allow for me to work remotely out-of-state starting the end of September 2016, as it does with almost most of the senior marketing department for no less than one year employment from beginning of remote date. Unless there has been a normal/substantial breach in trust/productivity/results etc.

4. I give my 2 weeks notice and and will photograph for $25,000 with zero input on selects and retouching. Available to retouch for $75 an image. (75 dollars less than the normal rate)

5. I give my 2 weeks notice with no hard feelings. You spend the money not available but somehow probably available at the time now and I collect unemployment because I refused to do something that is not my job without the pressure of trying to figure this out fairly anymore.

Questions I have before coming to any of these conclusions.

1. Will our vendors be paid prior to spring shoot. You currently have no agency that will work with us and no retouchers available as they are all still owed money. I don't see a fix to this and we went down this route to fix this for spring and it's still not getting fixed. In my eyes this issue will come up *back-to-back* after this shoot and this will be a repeating story. Even if they just got paid, why would they work with us again so soon?

2. Will there be a corporate dialogue established to manage expectations moving forward? Realistic timelines of shoots to deliverables. Accountability of information sharing and realistic deadlines with all groups understanding what goes in from the time a request is made? There is a big misconception on what goes into a shoot and from the beginning to the end deliverable needs to be acknowledged on all fronts, and when will that happen?

3. Just sharing a quote I heard that stuck a chord. "It's do or die and let me tell you why... if you max out your talent, without even knowing it, your talent starts to diminish. It's a sneaky kind of thing. And so your business starts to go the other way." So I just question at what cost not understanding this department comes at."

_____

I went on to do an entire reshoot with models from the discussion of everything done prior. The proposal written in December 2016 came about when I was asked to photograph once again the entire Fall line for the company with a much needed desire to be clear on things. In my proposal I cut out half the budget right away by eliminating the rental aspect of equipment and move towards the purchase of more equipment while utilizing my own. That equipment was deducted from what small percentage was agreed upon and was my own private property as it was invoiced and deducted properly through finance documentation. This included my replacement camera utilized when my own personal property was depreciated every shoot and eventually was faulty and needed repairs.

In the original discussions, it was the desire of AA-AG to still have what compensation I received be consider my time spent while photographing being deducted from my annual salary. It was never applied, and I looked it up on the legal side. Their argument was it would appear that I was double-dipping when, in fact, the company is double dipping and retaining both my photography side with the added company insight of my position of Senior Creative Manager. You can't unwrap the two and the advantage of having a creative with that much knowledge of your company actually pushes creatively things here and there subtly to where they visually want the brand to go. 'That happy accident of an image' was your senior creative manager pushing things in the direction towards the following year right in front of you outside the normal position and relationship of what was used to of the *(Contract-to-Hire Photographer)* relationship. When brought up in discussion later on on how I should be thankful he did not impliment that aspect of the deal he wanted, I remained silent and already knew the answer. It was illegal and the minute that threat actually happened I was prepared to sue Alfred Angelo against it and not have another threat of finance or mis-directed responsibility placed on I.

As things progressed in the company, I was then added on the responsibility of a whole new line, 'Truly Yours' which was again added on responsibility that was con-tingent not only of my photography skills, but the necessary aspect of composite work to appear like destinations and casual aspects were essential to the line. At this point towards the end it was the incorporation of my Disney-style composite work now into another brand where photography of injections was included on top of regular day to day responsibilities. Towards the end, the company desire of AA-AG was to have me take over full responsibilities of photography of the Disney line as well with their desire to continue the composite work and my desire to come up with something else based on past experience had, the unsustainable aspect of my position and my com-plete knowledge that I should not be the full Creative lead for disney, photographer, compositor, retoucher while also the same for 'Truly Yours' and still manage the other brands cocurrently with the Creative Director while neither one of us are able to take a vacation and overworked due to minimal staffing.

It was my desire towards the end to start passing off the Creative Lead of Disney to one of my designers through mentorship while we figured out the rest. As visually the entire company was becoming contingent solely on myself, knowing I was to of had a raise prior to the exist of the Chief Creative Officer that never occurred. I was in the position of set the company and department up for success and once that occurred, I was to walk out with notice, all my photography equipment and you could entertain that notion presented to I of '...Going down the street and begging the college for their services' but you were not going to have my any again and would have to restructure practically your entire asset application visually. That is why you don't take advantage of your employees, compensate them properly and listen to them on multiple fronts or even talk to them to possibly prevent what occurred at the end of Alfred Angelo. Once you tried to sweep things under the rug, one must question what else you did. But in unpaid invoices, it clearly states license revoke in lack of payment that occurred on my end and I am not giving it back. (Not that I can since the company went Chapter 7 bankrupt in July 2017. If there was a desire for one thing or another, there is discus-sions and compensation that could occur on one thing or another.)

At least I can account to a small degree of the state of affairs on my side during that time. ...of myself and also that is what the industry is in understanding the intimate aspects of the bridal world and understanding how passionate that is on those invested in the industry and those who buy in for the hopefully once-in-a-lifetime purchase. The hard lesson of rites of passage of understanding that perhaps when there is the presence of self-doubt and others acknowledge it as such, best to maintain the image and see what else occurs. The silent morality comes one way or another when discussing discountment and exploitation. It is understood weaknesses and when pushed to places where one does something great, sustainable or fails miserably at it. Although not always silent, it is at least understoood what I grew from in experience during my time in Florida. I can't fault someone for playing in that world just as much as they cannot fault me for not knowing the world where you can't do things for yourself. The marketing world has definitely changed, but I also realize that I have a very particular skill set of experience where I've had to do a lot on my own and the application of my passions was pushed well beyond in international advetising and branding of the equivilent of what I was doing in Atlanta for 20-30 dollars per photoshoot. I have built allot on my own. I've built allot with so little. I was aware very clearly the contingency of not going to be threatened, ridiculed and not properly compensated in the workplace. That carries over into the next position, but at least it is understood why I said no photography without compensation in contract positions. (which occurred anyways)

I guess I look at this time in reflection to where I was. There is so much I could harp on but it is not my place to talk about what I've been through vs. where I am going. I like to feel the lessons learned from this experience are a one-time deal and I actually have belief in myself more than prior. I'm not about to be strong armed into taking one for the team to do photography that someone else was paid 3x my annual salary for 2 weeks of work. I'm not about to ever feel I don't belong somewhere and I am not going to ever be taken advantage of because of insecurity or because I am an employee. You don't get that power and you definitely don't get it after dragging me down so you will look better. Everything that I am is about taking yourself out of the equation when dealing with others. Even the Coca-Cola branding mentality I brought into the company was adapted and appropriated in understanding of knowing your market, your audience, your intentions and just pushing things in refinement continually one way or another. That was very much a team effort, was present prior and then pushed more corporately with at least the inclusion of my expertise and in the capable hands of those above myself. A great deal of things occurred after the Chief Creative Officer left the company. The wastefulness of designing a dress never to end up in a retail store in the end was beyond comprehension if one were to know the price of concept to execution of visual deliverable per dress. You would be shocked the price in a closet full of things that were shot and never saw the light of day. A feather in the cap to discountment had there.

I may not be better off then when I started, but I can say this...I believe in myself and things constantly change. At the time here, I'm processing not having a job at the moment, what occurred and scared not knowing what to do as I've not been adult unemployed before. I'm focusing on my website that I'm building for the first time and piecing things together from there. If one is to showcase, then at least I have years of work that can be collected from one place or another and go back to focusing on my work and my passion projects while I figure out employment. So much invested the last 3 years in a company's success that in the end it did not matter regardless of what occurred or what I did or didn't do for myself and my own projects during the time. The idea that the naive aspect of where things do and do not come into play naturally occurred, but I can at least get right back to my own works with more direction and application of advancement on some level of degree and eye change.

That's hard to do and I have zero doubt life is going to throw me some new questions. But I feel this was worth it. I experienced life and if anything I've grown to accept myself, which is probably, all that matters in the end. But I'm coming back to finish what I started and I'm in this weird space of take me for who I am. But this conflict of who I want to be is not going to happen. I need to be me and ok with that decision. I've thrown enough of that into the world already that I'm ok with it. I do have to decide what I want to be as far as an artist or a marketing manager. The two do not cross well. Or do they? If a storyteller before and one of visual ques and nods to life and art imitating life, life imitating art, what does that do with 3 solid years of Disney background going into the After Ever After aspects of adulting? Hidden aspects everywhere.

If anything, I like that this is the last time I have to reflect on anything driven by the past. What comes from this for the first time in a long time I write my own story and go from there. No reason to talk about what drives me. No reason to express remorse or regret. Just living life and doing my thing. It's a proper conclusion and what happens from here is my own accord. It's probably the best thing I could ask for in my Brave New Secrets.... be you and be ok with that. Am I there yet? (Not yet)

ENTRY 23:

I look back on the legacy I've created. A joint effort of commonality. Any photograph made is always a collaboration. I can claim the idea. The execution. The overarching themes. The book. The musical compositions/arrangements... all created from the responsibility of going beyond my pay-grade and searching for a voice with my own equipment & ambition to one day succeed. Usually outside of office settings and on my own time and ambitions.

RAW images will always be mine. But what sets the difference from the click of a button to the final product rests solely in my head. There is no primer for that and there is no recreation. Simply inspiration & gradual learning based on time, experience and reflection.

I've already broken down my series. 2 main ones. A side one and everything in-between. They are episodic glimmers present to build an overarching theme but do I need to connect everything together?
They exist alone, but come together in a larger narrative.

At the core of Heroes, it is about acceptance and a community. Friendships made and strengthened. There is no Hero or Villain in that series. Only individuality. A tradition of any literature known to man (or woman). Individuals. Characters created. Associations of relate-ability.

Stories.
A Thousand Faces.
A Thousand Masks.
Universal Truths.
Universal Lies.
Archetypes.

Something lies within my characters though. A bonus for playing pretend with me and helping me build a better world.

The rights to the images rest in a social contract. A release.

The series would need the blessings of the models if it is going to be taken away from me and become something else. They are my family. They are my friends. It's their likeness through my eyes. A yearbook from 2010-2014 mostly with 2 additions thereafter on the 'Heroes+Villains' side. The responsibility is on you if my heroes are stolen. Group or no group. No book complete without their consent. Which leads to the revelation, 'When ganged up against. I have the heroes on my side'.

The Divine Comedy is a different beast entirely. In part, it was stolen by others. A collection incomplete. Even this journal nothing more but a small part to something else. Already written.

Until I do have that final show of the Divine Comedy, it is allowed to be as malleable as it needs to be. I'll know when it is done. Interjection occurred and transformed it already. The heart of it rests with me and succeeding. All of it will end there. If I go, then so does whatever the final outcome of what that series was meant to be in one version or another. (I have to acknowledge that if I were to go then maybe that was the ultimate greater design meant for it. Was it unfinished or pushed? What happened? I am not going to attempt to commit suicide again.)

"Secret" is a powerful word which solidifies my thought process from yesterday. My heaven is not to be showcased without my permission. I've worked hard at this. This has been my life's work. There will be a guessing game created regardless. There will be a he said/she said. But there will always be my series created.

In the end. Heaven is on my terms and everything else was a guess in the wrong direction. My written word trumps conjecture or anything typed over a computer. My computer has been compromised. My email compromised. Blogger compromised. What has never been compromised is my vision.

Having now read my entire Divine Comedy for the first time. I wonder how I feel about it. Memories sparked. Context lays value for sure. There is what is written and there is what is not. There is a focus on stages. Brave New Secrets is powerful. It's not talking about relationships. It's not talking about anxiety. It's not talking at all. It's a regain of privacy dating back to 2010.

I remember after I being arrested in Florida being bombarded by mail. A market there for sure with information given to those in the know. No doubt personal information used for profit. A market system present. I think about that in regards to the website Bocabusted.com and Rapsheet.com. (Proof underlined that 100% my book was acted on & violated by copyright pending laws as early as late 2019/2020.. 2/27/2022 - Philip A. Bonneau.) This is due to only Bocabusted.com was reported and both websites were shutdown at the same time. Things for a price are up-voted to blackmail on google. I've inquired about removal to discover a market with a pretty hefty price tag to "clean a digital image". If I were a businessman, I'd pay attention who was willing to pay fees to remove things from the web. Blackmail for later. Profit for the now. For the right amount of money, searches are vanished. Things erased. If I had the money to spare, would I do that? I think about those that do not have the money because I do not either. If I didn't already make a name for myself, would that had been the first thing that pops up in a google search? Do I consider this a badge of humanization? It definitely is a badge that does not prove innocent or guilty, but its a badge nevertheless. Can't Photoshop everything in life. It shows fallibility which is where I leave it. I'm not perfect and I don't expect you to be so either. There is a story there. You need only ask. Don't take and interject. If I learned anything about my adult life is, I have a long history of sharing my truths. It was a low point, but only a single part of a puzzle from doing the right thing to begin with. Always the what if on if I didn't. History denotes in Oct. 2022, this was read carefully by others before others began to delete me from the Internet.

I paint my own story by not hiding any ask-pect of it. Others can do as they will. I've spent what I can pinpointed to 20 years of age focused on working towards a sense of self. I can resort back to a very specific time of my teenage years where I questioned courage. A make-or-break moment that has defined my entire life. Alarming to say the least that you know when adulthood factored into your life for the first time.

But here I am with a greater sense of self than I had before. Was it always there? Was it always true to me?
"Believe in yourself".

If anything ever happens to me, my hard drives go to my brother. All of them. It would be his choice to finish things from his own life experiences, because duality is important to me. I imagine he would know in my writing of things that others would not pick up on.

If something never saw the light of day, it probably was never meant to be so. There is so much left unfinished. So much in early stages of being fully realized. Some abandoned for a reason. Always something there though, but unless it has gone through all the stages, the secret always rests with me. I have zero doubt my brother would protect and understand what I have presented to the world and what I have not. We are each other's brother's keeper. I trusted (k) with my life. Christopher with my legacy. Abandoned concepts does not denote abandoned property. Just something to hold onto for a better time after some thought and consideration.

"You made me have to think of these things. You made me have to question everything this past year. You made me go through the act of wanting to kill myself. I went through that with the motions that I could never fully describe here and then somehow found the strength to ask for help after the fact at the right moment. Something brought me back from that. Something told me to have faith in others and I gave it. But what you did...what you have taken away from me time-wise, what could be taken away from me, the threats to others...it should have ended so many times prior to the moment of me saying "I want my privacy back.", at Freud/Diablo. You came for me. You owe my life experiences to be written because they are the truth and I wouldn't lie about any of this. I COULD HAVE DIED.

It's a blessing I am searching for a positive from this. It is a curse I always write things out."

Heaven is in my brother's hands if anything happens to me. He chooses. His choice. No one else. It's the only gift I can gift. I give him that knowing the gift he gave me when he called the police in the beginning in December over this. Choose your own adventure is the motto of my website and my work. Choices were made. In the end, remember your heart. Remember everything is a group effort. Heaven is with who you love.

Privacy.

Collect your thoughts.
Because I'm collecting mine.

ENTRY 24:

I am having a moment where the scientific mind now ebbs back into the religious one.

I never knew prior that John Newman was the author of the base theory of Purgatory. And as such a Jonathan Newman was a person I knew prior. I stand by understanding what I wrote in previous versions and it is incorrect and factually doesn't make sense because even in blog form you can see never a mention and still maybe indirect while exploring things well before-hand of life experience. Alot has happened since this 'piece of shit' of 2013 did that series. (He of one L in that regard) What cannot be mistaken that Saint John Henry Newman of Christianity was the founder of the concept of Purgatory that I didn't know until years later. Imagine the connection now to John Henry of American legends and paving roads. "Purgatory is the free choice of the soul.', a quote from his lifetime of 1801—1890. I imagine in that aspect the soul if of hope-bound and good intention leads to different places. The temporary aspect of Purgatory with Hope to another place if passing tests, denotes in failed experiences going in the opposite direction and back-tracking through paths a little harder to overcome before going through my modern concept of it. In what I have found in Hell, as I moved from Purgato-ry and into Heaven in concept, it is understood the elevator effect that comes from someone there to teach you lessons directly or indirectly and both are viable options. In consideration of such as at this point I'm well 3 years past where I was at this point, it is the coincidence of such that the only mention of John Henry Newman is of such as done no harm to humanity in contem-plating hope of the soul and that we all have lives outside the physical one we are in now. To jump to American Legend for a second, an African Ameri-can man who drills holes in rocks to pave new grounds. He died of stress, but not before moving mountains or being associated with them. It is all a series of coincidences that cannot be made-up. This pushes me fully into the realm of divine intervention at this point. There is no mistaking this. There is no mistaking the car. There is no mistaking the water. Something bigger is here. A random google search led me to that revelation. Found from inspiration of looking up the Freemasons. Someone is telling me something.
Or perhaps I am finding connections that others would not find otherwise.

I believe Purgatory is a state of mind. If I recall of Dante's Divine Comedy, it was the same. Part of the working of that machine was the belief system that eventually you would let it go and understand. It revolved around potentially reaching Heaven. As I look more into "The Divine Comedy" within the subtext of psychology, I don't think I am wrong of looking at it in such a manner. In Hell; you never embrace your sin. The harsher the consequence the more wrong against others that you execute. Purgatory always at least gave the idea of hope if you were looking for it. Often, most were not. Heaven was always the complex one for Dante. Having now tread in some of his own footsteps, I am left to the same conclusions he had about it. An idea. But words escaped him. He had to rely on the talent of others to finish it **with him. Heaven & artists told from the perception of one experience spheres of enlightenment.**

But for now, my mind rests in Purgatory on this revelation. I have to let it go. I remember. I can't forget. But there comes a point where there is a choice on if I am bound to it or not. In searching for that answer, I look back at the last several years.

Everything leads to this point now.

Was the journey worth it?

<I did learn a lot>
(I did learn the difference between allot and a lot.)

I'm still learning.

You learn things every day. New connections made and you look at that as empowerment. Truths in that you don't know everything, but are given exactly what you need. It's your choice on what you do with it.

I've grown up with the arts. I've let others watch me grow. Mistakes made. Successes had. They have all occurred one way or another. That is part of the human experience. Right?

Never words intended.
Maybe there should be.
Maybe I had to learn to sing.
I discovered my voice in my first art show.

Did I learn to speak about the right things or did I remain silent at all the wrong times? This past year I spoke up and I can say nothing happened from doing so. I have changed from that experience. HR. Lawyers. State. Federal. NOTHING HAPPENED. The only rationale I can give myself now is I cannot allow a Purgatory trap to occur again. Move on and focus on a Heaven in my heart. It's a mentality. A theory that we get worked up for the wrong things and the right things. Emotion skews reality.

I remember getting Lasik surgery years ago. For several hours after, your eyes were to remain covered with fear of blindness. You cannot open them. I remember questioning if I would view the world differently afterwards. Near sided in one. Far sided in the other. Astigmatism in both. 2 different perspectives had at all times led to blind trust in a process.

The first thing I remember when I opened my eyes was really looking at the leaves on the trees once I woke up from my nap. They were all individually moving in the wind and I saw each one in HD. I was being acquainted to the world for a second time. Blink and you miss a dance you never would have appreciated to begin with. Is this another one of those moments? A tango of thought? If I didn't write about it, would it had even happened?

<A tree falls.>

I am looking at things differently. Listening to things differently. A change in heart or perhaps the end of a mourning of my own. If I were to remember the things in my head, there is a lot of pain that occurred very quickly and severe. I acknowledge that now it can play out in my head anyway possible to bring about understanding, but peace is ultimately the goal to be gained. It's time to work on the parts I always wanted to. A creation of myths of the characters I have built. Parables and Lessons. Sympathy and Compassion. Life lessons to be shared and taught with those already introduced through the ages.
<Write your fictional works. Reality did its part.>
Mythology revisited.
When you can't solve a problem, move onto the next one.

I resort back to the 3 options already burned into my mind. Any other action at this point only causes damage unwarranted. There is responsibility in picking myself back up. Trek to find new meaning and realize for yourself that there is strength in new experiences.
Where do you want to go?

What do you want to build in this new life?
What do you want to write about?
Use this book to clear your head as you process things.
Maybe at a loss on how to proceed, but listen to yourself. The experience
now is like clairvoyance. A connection to people I have never met.
(But still aware these conversations are just in my head)
Empathy. Understanding. Right. Wrong. A moral compass.
"Am I supposed to be here?" There are no mistakes.
If I am questioning life, am I allowed to be proud of some things and embar-
rassed of others? Others factor in just as much as I factor into others. It's not
that I want to shut off this thinking process, but it came about from an onset
of events and I am trying to adapt.
New world. New beginnings while focusing on me. Let all others do their
thing. It's not my main concern ATM. Work on yourself. "Little by Little."
Get settled. "Little by Little." Find happiness. "Little by Little." Lay this to
rest.

Great Expectations.
An artist's heart
One hit the entire season.
A baseball bat

August 11, 2017
Post 9: You have more control than you know.

"Truth is I know I have to give up everything that I know or thought I knew with this final bow. I've never been one to be able to easily un-attach from things. I can't let go at times. Not everything, but some things have meaning that hard to forget and I know I never will. I remember everything. I hate it. I hate that I do. I know life's irony will be that I forget in time, but that's another post at another time. I can't brush that off. Is this me being over-sensitive? Is this me not able to handle things? Or is this I taking in every bit of life experience and driving others and myself crazy talking about it to find some reason why I took a shit this morning? Perhaps it's not a bad thing to forget. Otherwise you make the same mistakes and there is never any remorse." 5/13/14

I like that it is becoming harder to find the right quote to start off a conversation point in heaven. To me I find that as I'm running out of things to talk about that are not known. One of my original rules to this was I will have to defer to what I hid in order to bring something forward as a discussion. I admire that I was probably more brazen in my earlier years. I trusted. I trust. But let's be honest. There was also a definitive anger and definitely guardedness now. There was and is a definitive mistrust. There definitely is a definitive reason. You never go off one example, but many. But then I struggle knowing we are all going through these same questions. My advice is, "just be you". But I do understand that's hard to grasp just as much as it is hard to ask others to do that for you. One thing will lead to one thing, which would lead to another. Kind of cut and dry and something totally engrained in me at this point in my life. Still kind of feel that way after XYZ so it's probably safe to believe that what you present to the world is what you are perceived as. I'm ok knowing I've presented myself accordingly. Flaws and all.

One thing I have to admit is there is a lot of "I" in my answers. I will not eliminate it because there has been an equal amount of experiences where I have eliminated "I" and you get an equally negative response from doing so. Mentor to student, never eliminate the "I" from the variable completely. I feel like that is a universal thing to hold onto without definition. No one is like you. No one has been through your experiences exactly and there is a deep value to the "I". Notice the extent of "I" even in these three sentences. But I will say this. That my "I" was never meant with ill-intent. 'I' have weighed the 'U' and considered 'Us' and 'Them'. When considering at least two, it is important to remember 'Me' in that regard. You will do so anyways in anything. I or Me is unavoidable as even the gestures towards others denotes a positive or negative impact that has variable weight on how it is translated.

"I" is a dangerous thing as much as it is a fragile thing. It will be what you make of "I" that defines yours life. It's your reasons alone. It's your reason to need someone one way or another. It's an easy attack as is it onto your humanity. We all protect the "I".

I think from here on out I'll always ask that you focus on those that grow you more than the ones that hurt U and hinder yourself. The choice is always yours to decide where your time will be vested. But as I get older I feel it equally wise to tell you what I ignored when I was younger and if you are not growing or if the other "I" is taking control then you need to think things differently. But that's just my experience. I'm just mister potato head. Put in this experience with this experience get this. Mix this experience with this experience you get this. How many different ways can I present myself in one mask or another?

Truth is I'm not scared the more sure I get in this exploration. I have no business spreading anger. I have no business spreading hate and I believe I never did. I really don't have any. There is a productive aspect to writing things out and processing things before speaking or acting one way or another. You can have anger and be completely rational in response. You can be calm where one determines the effectiveness of a shouting match or the soft slow statement of words spoken that could equally give chills in how it is vocalized. I have questions, but I seem to be finding out my own answers just fine. I guess that is kind of the awesome repercussions of saying, you don't care what people think that are indirectly not even connected to you and realize shit will always be there one way or another. I imagine if you have read this or gotten to this point, there is investment and there is caring to be had. I suppose the difference is again context of what is said. On a social aspect, if one doesn't know you directly and wants to say something negatively, then hey...that is on them. Either way in any regard here we are still living our life and whatever shit was said does not matter because their are always ignore and mute buttons to be pressed. I guess it's the double edge sword again of you being in shit. Shit is there. Shit is present. Perhaps a wipe and move on... I need to stop going in circles and repeating myself.

What do I have to say?
What do I want to forget moving forward?

ENTRY 25:

I am not giving up on my dreams.
-File an EEOC
-File a worker's comp claim
-Talk to civil rights attorneys
-Protected my family and myself
Wrongs were done. Major wrongs.
You don't go ripping people's soul to shreds.
You don't freely discuss surveillance in open-air environments. You don't
make judgment calls on said information.

No. "Truth of the day".
No. "Burn Him."
No. "He got them."
No. "They got him."
(PR-T moves there)

I cannot forget that, but it has to go through the proper channels.
If they lie, it's on them.

I have already taken the first steps in righting things wrong by attempting to
pick myself up every day. Even though it's a struggle to do so.
A test of humility in doing the right thing?

Who...R...U?

Circling something. But not quite there yet.

ENTRY 26:

“I’m sorry”

<on a napkin>

What does that even mean?

(Consider Producing with a napkin bookmark laminated. Mystery solved much later in different books.)

The shit in my head needs to stop!
<Frustration.>
<Anger.>
They are there the minute I wake up and even when I am asleep.

Dream Setting: A property surrounded by managed waters & pools.
Action: Eviction.
Characters: Familiar Representatives of a brand.
<A Takeover is Occurring>

A property of rentals. High Ceilings and of value and extravagance. Outdoors of open windows leads to pool systems and communal-like property surroundings. Dream already denoted in reps prior when key identifiers denotes difference between reality & when asleep.

Wikipedia.
Unwilling participants.
Vincent Piccione. (Mentioned or seen? I’ve never met in person)

Bachelor's Party.
Wooden Stool.

"Feel the wind"
"Use the sound of white noise to focus."
"Focus on something."

I don't seem to want to interact much. I definitely prefer to have space, but
I am starting to remember dreams which gives me something to focus on.
(Am I sleeping better?)

In my dream I am catching people stealing, but I let them go.
- Fact vs. Fiction
I acknowledge that I am hearing things and that they are creating memories
that are not my own. Things that either only happened in dreams or things
that are put there by prolonged exposure to these voices. This is exactly why
I wrote things out prior.

I can't help but wonder what this is doing to me. I'm Split on this. They
won't let me go.

What should I do today?
I need to go to the library to return my books.
Perhaps some down time will do me good.
Anything to "Flip the Script" of what plays out in my head.
Action.
Inaction.
                                                        "Stay single."
"I never was!"
"Stop interjecting on my life!"
"Is this where things are going?"
Am I going to have vocal noise in my head forever?!
                                            (Non-recorded Dialog)
"Surely you are joking."
As long as I keep my day to day up to standard, I should be able to work
though this and back to center. Time heals most wounds and this is a Scar
that will only be remembered in my head in the end. Charge off and enjoy
your day.
You got this.

164

ENTRY 27:

Currently I am sitting at Rancho Alegre.
I figured treating myself to lunch would do me good.
I've been here before if even it was in a different location.
<Latin Music playing in the atmosphere>
<The sound of multiple conversations merge together>
Remembering my father taking me to dinner and saying the same thing.
I am hearing everything at once.
Depending on where my focus goes. I do hear a little bit of it all.
Levels rise and sink based on the direction of my 360.
The clinking of utensils.
The smell of the garlic bread placed in front of me.
Anything to focus on the now and external.
It's all jazz really. A sorting of sound. Everything has its place.
 "I should visit Cuba one day."

I imagine it is a time warp. Cars repaired for their maximum usage. Colors of
buildings typical of the Caribbean with my only real point of reference being
in Miami and the Bahamas. There is something to be said about colorful
buildings and the embrace of street art. It gives a personality to a city vs. the
coldness of concrete.

<Remembering Venice.>

Every bit of the island developed. I don't recall seeing any trees. Surely.
they had to have been there somewhere. My mind goes to the alleyways
and the old-school room key I had to leave at the front desk anytime I left.
There were bridges connecting one part of the city to the other. Over. Under.
A better suitcase needed next time.

I wonder the places I want to go and if I will ever get to go to them.
How much reconstruction do I need to do to in order to get back on the path
that was set for me? My path. as I imagine it. has a long road to go. but I can
get there.
I think about (K) and how I won't see him until like November/
December.
Separated but still connected.
<I'm switching back to vaping>
Something I was doing well with on my way to not smoking.

ENTRY 28:

When school starts up again, I'll be able to better utilize the gym.
I need to remember my old routines, but the focus has to be on
fixing the mind first. I am trying to do that.
"Wind it back down."
I remember going a mile a minute in the work environment.
I am only discovering now that the capability of that has long lasted to be
true in any scenario hereafter.

...at both of them. The second one compounded the problem exponentially.
There was a little bit of me taken away with every sentence that should have
never been spoken or open for free discussion.
Nothing is free.

Ignorance is bliss. It was a job. Both were just a job. A desire for work life
balance that definitely did not occur. An invasion transpired. I try to think
about what would make this right for me. Therapy is a given, but I wonder
what good is continually talking about it going to do when key information
is withheld. The only closure will come from myself. I reported it and there
is the chance they will lie. Both companies lied to my face so it is not without
question when faced with potential legal action that they wouldn't do it
again for self-protection. Both companies need to be subpoenaed.
EVERY SINGLE EMPLOYEE.
Would that even do you any good?

That is the price for freely talking out things in the open. Getting a
transcript of a conversation with a law firm on a private phone line needs
to be investigated. Where did that come from? If not from them, it needs
to be known where. They willfully impeded on my rights to seek council in
real time. The fact that I asked Company #2 to stop needs to be explored
when references to company #1 and Company 0 were made freely within
the office setting.
Mis-characterization.
Manipulation.
An internal investigation occurred at Company #1.
"...another 6 months"
(FD, of internal investigations? or surveillance of I)
I imagine when talking surveillance after reporting the baseball bat incident.
At least it was at the same time.

What seems to be unrelated is Disney as it was not brought up until Company #2 mentioned discussion of brand and if it was a viable assessment. Home Depot and Disney were discussed at Company #2.

"He didn't mention anything bad about the brand"(Paraphrased)(PRe)

Tracking was done.

"They can look at the web history and preemptively know where he is going to use." (Paraphrase) (T-PR)

Taper throws me for a loop because I left my phone in the car.

A jump from phone to phone of known contacts?

The mention of everyone on my phone was made at Company #2.

An employee at Company 0 lied to Coca-Cola.

That triggered the breakdown.

"He has some powerful friends" (T-PR)

<The idea comes back that everything could had been avoided had someone not lied in a professional capacity>

...and this perpetuates because lies have power to keep this open...

Where's the truth?

Who's honest?

What is honesty anymore?!

If Company 1 lied then they are held responsible for everyone on my phone.

If there was an internal investigation. I am entitled to the conclusion of that.

The bullying.

The hat.

The bat.

What was the course of action discussed by HR when I brought up the online bullying?

Each day we focus a little bit more, but the point is to remember to step away and think of other things as well.

Got my vape, but I have to put a time table on that as well.

I quit before and I can do it again.

It's the past that is giving continued anxiety and triggering. It is best for me to write it down and compare notes when I am ready.

Every day does not have to be a marathon. But it is.

In my mind, the jabbering of words holds the answers.

"...Couldn't wait to leak it anonymously?!" (M-PR)

A creation of conflict of interest. Between Company #2 and their original intent. An invested interest to being part of the conversation from the beginning of this Part II. (Not for the protection of the employee as noted by their original contact from Company #1 who notified them of a private phone call)

STALKING.

Intention to inflict maximum emotional damage.

Stalking of a public figure. Former Public Figure. (Up for debate)

An LGBTQ+ man.

Hacking into Facebook accounts...analyzing posts.

E-mails... (the activate manipulation of E-mail)

"3-point tracking system." (PRe)

Receipt monitoring.

Active threats of legality in an open setting.

Threats against family...friends...pets.

What would have happened if (T) didn't walk past me saying, "Oh, he knows." (Knowing I talked about it with my mother and father the night prior at home and in the car.) (PRe)

<A scream in my car>   <A scream in my car>   <A scream in my car>
(Crying on my way home)
-Me

What do you do when you hear something and say, "it sounds like he is having a nervous breakdown."? (T-PR)

You would think they would had proceeded with caution.

A door shut would have gone a long way.

A door open; reaches further.

Both 1 and 2 are at fault for that.

<What is the responsibility of mental health in the work place?>

He will use the hostile work environment route.

I've seen this before. -(S-FD))

You would think calling the suicide hot-line would have been enough clue to stop after confronting.

Criminal Negligence.

"Poor guy. No one can call and check-in on him." (PRe)

"He's done." (T-PR)

A push. An involuntary stay.

From the moment I went to the hospital until the day I set back into the office with a note needs to be accounted for on what was said about me. From the time (K) said I was in the hospital onto the missing pay-stubs that they did not supply to The GA Unemployment Office that I never would had been able to supply myself had I not had the employee handbook at home with the several step process of retrieval.

"Contract employee" categorization? I was a Full Time employee for Pur-eRED. Although the pay-stubs say an LLC, the insurance card definitely says PureRED.

...the lying of emergency contacts.

it fair to believe they will run with their own story, which they were doing anyways.

(an employee goes missing for 11 days and you do nothing but fire him first chance you can in that time frame?)

"What's the common denominator here?"(T-PR)

(T) Out-of-Control abuse and falsification of identity. I reported the right thing and named the right person. The rest grows from there. All could have been prevented when I said, "It's another thing when one company contacts another." Something agreed upon and reiterated by (T). I should have been notified then and there.

"You know we are going to be subpoenaed?" (T-PR)

And the instances for calling began with a smell.

(Embarrassing that a second-hand washer and dryer factored into this on stale water and smell.)

Self-consciousness brought on by Company #1. Vocalized on the phone pri-vately. More than likely my mother at the time.

Company 0 mentioned at both establishments.

A common denominator there.

Twice.

Thrice removed.

I remember being painted as, "sue happy". (T-PR)

I never sued anyone in my life and although I have every reason to do so now, I find myself in calmness in my words as I piece down fundamental talking points that need to be discussed.

<A private moment of just me and my words>

A paradox is occurring as I write this. Tangent minds think alike. Devil's Advocate factors in. I wasn't the only one recorded, which probably explains walkie talkies at Company#1. They acted on my phone call to Randstad about the bat. They moved (S) away from me the following day before my conversation with (B) about talking to Randstad. I imagine if one is doing surveillance on someone, you don't react in real time.

A GLASS CAGE, 2014
Chicago Styling of Bridal Fashion Week
or is it Turabian Settings?

"…including keystrokes?" (B-FD)
"He's reacting in real time." (D-FD)
I actually agreed then and now that
the working from home idea was
probably the best solution if it was
ever presented to me.
"Everyone is uncomfortable that he
can hear" (D-FD)
As I slowly piece things together,
I know these are the things I have
already written out.
They are staying with me.
Constantly on edge.
A library.
A sound carries.
<Sitting at my desk>
"I can't help what I hear."
Perhaps that is why I stayed
here I did.

Validity of sound or transcribing what was said the night before.

"She understood, at least, what I was going through."
In the same office of (D) and (A), she heard not only everything said by (D),
but also (B) and (T).
Big Brother.
Ejector seat.
(BB) before him.

I remember when I asked to be moved. They offered the ejector. I proposed the
photography room, but now knowing I can hear in HD, I don't think that
would have helped either.
"His whole life is up for grabs" (Mk-FD) Paraphrased
I'm proud I said stop in HD.
They criticized that I did so, but
it was the right thing to do.
A phone call was made after the

incident where they were discussing
my Instagram and the monitoring.
<Nothing happened from it>
No acknowledgment.
A pretend it never happened. Except when (B) said,
        "I told him to come to me if he heard anything." (B-FD)
A conflict of interest.

The sad thing is I understood the other side.
                "I see both sides of it." (Mk-FD)
But never was I an enemy of strong female role models. My entire life has
been shaped by women and that hurt me that excuse was the card being
played after the fact.

"Momma's boy"
Mother figures.
I was raised by women.
You can't cry foul to something I said in person as a compliment.
Twisting of words.
The answer lies within what I wrote unemployment and this diary.

My divine comedy was written 2 years ago with an endgame of happiness
and peace.
A relationship not to be dissected.
A life without judgment.
Dreams to be had.

Interjections of assertions into what "Brave New Secrets" were to be exactly
what I told one of my father figures on the phone. The good and the bad of
me. Nakedly.
- Naked honesty.
- Acceptance.
- A quiet place between me and U.
- Symbolism as every inch of my body getting auctioned off.
      - Except for the Heart (NOT FOR SALE)

"I've had to think about that series and moments of commitment
stolen from me."

I try to adapt by creating new meaning to the things I do.

(It's layering really.)
A tree is all I had left to give.
Nourish and grow or let it die.   (Interrupts)
"Stop interjecting."
I don't think it will because now it is in my head.

"Hold my Hand"
A revelation of an ending that never got to happen as intended.

Stolen.
Gone.
Transformed.

You can't take that back.
You can't take back the threats.
You can't take back my moments.

But I made moments nevertheless.
I'm making new one's now.

               "I can't help but think we stole this from him." (M-PR)

Damn right you stole this.
I'm making made new ones the best I can.
Those too...
Being stolen by echoes.

You stole my time.
You stole my life.
Responsibility falls on
You.
You can never make this right.
You cannot turn back time.

I have to accept this.
I have to adapt.
I have to find peace in time.

You owe me closure of sane or not.
Either way, you created this.

ENTRY 29:

Where I can start is with this. "Refer to everything" to understand. Everything builds upon itself. but I am not going to have my named destroyed because of others. I'll fight as long as I can. but I see futility in doing so. Which
is why *we* bank on the memory of those who actually knew me.

I see myself giving in and crying at times. but how much strength do I have
in me? My internal chaos needs to be externalized knowing it is different
than things before. Spelling important. This was wrong and things playing
out in my head is not a reality I choose to want. But it is a reality given. I
need to pick myself back up and ask questions in order to get my life back on
track.

I think of (K) and I. He appeared in my dreams last night. A big part of me is
sad things are the way they are now. Indefinitely pushing away because I am
unsure of how things are. There is love for sure. but reality is simply different.
Hard to nurture the relationship in distance. I'm testing myself by stepping
away to focus on this. It seems like the right thing to do ATM. I don't know
his every life
and he doesn't know mine. It's just what we share and what we don't that
matters. It's trust. It's love. It's hope.

It's been 3 months since we have seen each other. It was like that in the beginning. but I am not sure how that works now.
(Or does it work exactly how it worked before?)

The thing to keep in mind though. as insecure as I am about relationships. is
to remember that everyone is different. Time will play its part. My goal is to
take care of myself at this point for the time being.
I am not looking for anything else at the moment. I see lust factoring in. but I
don't put myself into any situation to explore that.

"Back to center for me."
Have I ever been at center?

A signature once present understanding the removal for multiple reasons.
Where has this book gone before and what is in a signature to begin with?
The handwritten gesture of being there understanding where things have
gone and in that personality present one way or another. Now removed.

A signature is always an extension of self and explains personality in its execution. I wonder, if I got mine analyzed, what it would say about me.
Can it be copied?
Surely.
Copy-written?
Disney did it with his. Small tweaks here and there after to where it becomes a different personality. Polished or molded by others to become different from what was a signature trait.

It's the variances that come into play. At the very least I need to copy-write my signature used on every piece of artwork that I put on the web. I noticed something about my website today. Definitely not the first time all the internal folders have been open. Is someone searching for something?
(Doubt it will be the last.)
Physical proof that denotes at least continued behavior opened up at Pur-eRED. Who else is still getting 'past firewalls'? Apparently 'that is their problem and they can do that'. (Paraphrased PR-T)

I remember when I switched my password and authentication to get onto my site.
                    "They can get past that." (PR-T)
So, I switched to dual authentication where at least there is the possibility than an attempt could pop up on my phone.
(They could more than likely get past that)
The supposed problem of letting people get past firewalls towards files on computers is of such things as a digital signature in particular that raises questions down the line of what gets signed where, by whom and if things were signed on my behalf while not represented and in Chapter. 13 bankruptcy.

I left a message there on my website for good measure.

Should I continue to play games with this?

Do I laugh or do I cry?

Games at least make it easier to comprehend and relate to knowing how serious sportsmanlike conduct is.

ENTRY 30:

I find I still don't really care for gossip.
...Misfortune of others is not to be mishandled.

If I continued the conversation, I would be no better than the people that
broke me down. Only difference is the topic of conversation was not in the
same room. But it still goes back to thoughts of compassion.

There are better things to talk about.
I leave the night knowing I have to wake up early.

(K)'s voice in my head   (K)'s voice in my head   (K)'s voice in my head

I'm not sure how I feel about that.
"It is what it is."
It messes with my feelings.
Opposite of reality.

Guess this is all I have for my "Dear Kitty" post of the day.
Photography tomorrow.

The same could be said of any voice of reference. Spoken or not, it is
understood that the mind travels to familiarity or towards introductions.

August 15, 2017
Post 10: My name is Alice. I am no one.

'This must be the wood', she said thoughtfully to herself, ' where things have no names. I wonder what'll become of my name when I go in? I should like to lose it all - because they'd have to give me another, and it would be almost certain to be an ugly one. But then the fun would be, trying to find the creature that had got my old name! That's just like the advertisements, you know, when people lose dogs - "answers to the name Dash:' had on a brass collar." – just fancy calling everything you met "Alice," till one of them answered! Only they wouldn't answer at all, if they were wise. -Chapter 3, Through the Looking Glass

There comes a point in this story where my own words no longer drive my intent. I believe I could continue to pull from the narratives of my past and present thoughts to conclude this Divine Comedy, but I also feel that doing so holds me back from both my intent, my desires and what I have already accomplished. It has been my faith that what I have explored is both universal and not new just told in a different way. There comes a point you reveal secrets in order to find truths in lies. I absolutely have changed as a person through my years in revealing my perception of life and perhaps at moments there are times where you learn to move forward when the words of your own escape you and you defer to greater men to reflect. When pulling from the past, one must also understand they are pulling from the books they read, the movies they watched, the music they listened to and from there indirect connections to the ones others have also experienced in their own life privately. In namesake always a travel through the woods lost of names or given new ones one way or another I imagine. Perhaps I too now look at this in regards of 'Lost' in some capacity.

And thus I have hit a crossroad. This blog is not a necessary supplement to my series. It's is not necessary reading to understand what this show I'm building is or what it is the intent. I'd say my first show was my own personal story and from there the more you knew about me was added information but definitely not necessary to understand things. When I opened things up to others to tell their story I feel like I took selfish-ness out of the equation and it was my duty to ask of myself what I asked of them 10 fold. I did it 23 fold taking the time to explore anything I could ask of others to do.

I don't think that experiment broke me, but you put that much reflection on yourself you definitely learn a great deal about what you keep within. Easing from that into Heaven is not easy. Not when you walked through Hell and climbed Purgatory. There is a major part of that journey that no one wants to talk about but it is definitely there and it really took me 3 years to come out of that pit understanding the beauty of such a beginning before finding illumination in darkness. I've given everything of myself to the world to judge me for me whether you noticed or not. I stayed true to that for the sole reason of not only growing up but also finding myself again and welcoming people on my journey. You have to step into things on your terms but at some point you have to clearly define one chapter from the next. Sometimes you aren't afforded the choice of such and find yourself in a place of strangeness where one simply is forced to adapt and learn their environment one way or another. At least I believe that I've done that definitively for myself in the aspect of understanding one phase to the next and knowing they all have to be connective yet distinctly different.

I'm in conflict at the moment.

In yet another life scenario that was not of my choosing, I have to adapt to it with decisions made prior and a sense of perspective on how to proceed. But I also see myself doing whatever needs to be done to get things done. I don't think I ever would have been motivated to spend 16-hour workdays for a month to get my portfolio site done while unemployed. If one is actively building a website, then that is considered work without compensation. The same could be said of this book in the same manner of the idea of opening up a life, income and productivity. At the very least, at least between massive amounts of coffee, not eating much and work, I am losing weight just in time for travel. There is very important reasons to have this site done before travel. It is important to find a job and be able to apply properly for jobs. I don't think I really would have asked myself the question what do I want and I don't think I ever would have had to ask myself if I should cancel Italy or not. Italy is my biggest fear at the moment. I've never travelled to that degree solo yet always desired to do so to wander around and get lost in lands and culture I've only read about in books or seen in movies.

To me I look at this trip as I booked it and paid for most of it when my grandfather passed earlier in the year. I see it as the one time in my life I said just do what I've always wanted to do or never have the chance to do so again. It is understood at this point that all that vacation time saved up from work for that trip or any other one got eliminated completely in a single day to make myself understand that it is important to take vacation throughout the year. You never know when you won't get that opportunity. Lessons from my first job of 10 paid vacation days a year where I got paid out most of them at the end of the year from lack of affordance to take one anyways. I see my trip, as I'm not about to spend a paycheck to visit a grave or funeral. It would be nice to see family, but at the same time it still would had gone to the reflection of life and a person who travelled the world and I never another continent. I saved those miles since college and looking back that it is now pre-2005 that I said this is what I'm saving for then. I waited this long and humbling that it took this long. Life continues in ways you will never expect. Life is always going to do that. Life is always going to throw u a new curve to adapt to. How you choose to perceive the curve determines your angle of attack in reacting to it before, during or after.

I wanted to cancel this trip when I lost my job. 'How dare I use my resources on that kind of activity?', I think to myself. But my biggest concern was always going to be the perception of things. 'How dare I go on this trip and perhaps 2 months from now say I need help?' I don't have an answer to what is going on or what will be. Perception is a big thing that will always live with me. From others controlling the perception of me to me creating my own, I think at this point I've grown to where I've build my own perceptions to be made. There is always the awareness of perception and perspective. I've stayed away from enough people and done my own thing to be pretty understanding that the perception moving forward is strictly from me but I understand and respect others perspective as well. Always a chance to talk one way or another. I hate the situation that I am in with my head. I feel like I cannot ask for anything if I ever really needed it from going on this trip. But I have to go on faith that this is right for me. It's probably one of the few times that I say you aren't going to take this away from me too without going into detail. I think the personal is done-ish. How much has been taken prior and how much since?

This trip was always going to be a heaven for me. Something that was meant to be privately experienced. Go to the headquarters of a religion...have your moments... If anyone else was to go on it with me that was their own accord, but I mapped out Dante's life and want to go on that to come back with a fresh perspective and honestly this trip is best experienced on my own. Funny story: the driving force of his narrative was a married woman who he had no business even interacting with and here I am with my own driving forces and scared of perception in the end. Questions of God and of life on a social aspect where one lost their home and to an extent their security as they transition from one land to another. The moral harm very present. I can understand in a flash forward to 2022 and the events transpired the understand the multiple loss of home, the moral injury and still the collective aspects of what has occurred in gathering down the line in other written works and where it goes. The only difference is in loss of home and moral injury, what does one do with the constant loss of any aspect of my own works. From this book in early editions, to my entire life and what it stood for and represented then, now and in the future?

I have a meeting this week that could change my life within the context of the history of my culture and the biggest question I ask myself now is was it worth losing my name moving here. But it involves believing in myself and what I am capable of doing. Heaven involves no words from me. I feel it was good to give up ego and your name to have faith and go with things. But when you do come out of those woods, by all means it is worth it to be called by your name as well.

I'm scared of perception of my decisions. I'm scared that anyone could fault me on Italy, but I know I'll be faulted either way from things. Perhaps in the woods at least a canopy of coverance to where one would have to look specifically in order to find what they are looking for. They will say one thing or another on intention and it would be the same for any aspect of such. But I am Alice and I am Philip Bonneau and I'm no one. I'm Pip just as much as I'm not. Even an Aiden before where for the moment I doubt it mattered a name as much as to connect with people. Names given. Names taken. Names traded. Perhaps I just call myself 'anyone'. Anyone can be No One.

I've never done anything with ill-intention and I actually have more faith in the process than I ever would have thought in. I know my name and own it. Not all decisions make sense. But I have faith. I have to believe in myself and you have to never forget yourself or your name. Most people never will know it unless spoken anyways or unless it is attached to something. Perhaps you have to lose yourself to find yourself.

I'm scared, but I feel this is right.
I have faith.
I am Alice. I am no one.

Do your thing.

Was there blackmail and intimation in their open threats?
Or was it simply acknowledgment of what was being transcribed & listened
to? Opinions had yet I see the vulnerability of PR moves in directions.

As each of my family members and friends were ripped apart,
Those threats further added to my fear of what was occurring and what
could.

JC.
Eric.
Kenny.
My Mother.
My Brother.
ME.
I heard it all.
All the more reason leading to where I have been led.

<A connection to me that was fully capable of destroying lives while said out
in the open from the PR group.>
(Indirect so it is allowed while also still no privacy in open workplace
settings.)

Who else knew?

What else is known?

I know from Company #2 that my phone was not only probably compromised, but it absolutely was. I have no way to prove it outside of their reactions and data collection. Company #2 PR, it makes sense to try to say one or
the other at this point, but I respect it takes strength and time to start using
names in this regard.

<Conversations cited when not on a call> (PR and FD)
Reason to believe the speaker is always on.
Always recording?
Probably, can't be too sure anymore. Listening always available if spoken
correctly.

It brings a thought of the initial point of contact.
-Breach of contract from a private phone call deducted by the words of representatives of Company #2 (Thats a breach of many things)
Which leads the question...
If the phone is always on, then there is always an open door for Company #1 could blackmail Company #2 from the same deduction of what they hear what was recorded. (Ins were made that leads to Outs eventually.)

(Compounded information before OZ is defined)
<Ruby Slippers clicked before the tornado.>
Room for talk between worlds of black and white and those of color.
Is this motivation to change a course? Motivation to exile Dorothy?

"This isn't working." (PRe)
"There's a lot of money riding on this." (PRe)
Different employees of around the time of the closing of PR's deal to keep food on the table

That does raise questions of motive in knowing the self-professed by multiple employees of 'worst kept secret' of slippers and slip-ups.
Espionaged on me.
Espionaged on Company #2.
A power play?
It does not negate breach of privacy, nor my natural reaction to a threat.
It does open the door to ask the questions. I suppose 'what wasn't working?' is a very good question to ask before going into surveillance tactics and explanations of how people preempt on web browsing etc.

"What responsibility lies on me when I reported it instantly in unemployment?" That was after 11 days and I had the straighten up. It was more important not to shut down, explain and state. 'Pull yourself together Philip.' You didn't even know what day it was, but your soul knew how important to have those discussions with the State of Georgia at the time. Pull yourself together.

"Have I done a hard reboot?"
-Spoke with T-Mobile
<cannot afford a new phone>
...nor do I believe I should have to change my #.
Spoke of them of tapped aspects. Codes for phone given over the phone on what to turn on/off press. Documented where they could say one way or

another for multiple reasons. What was going on...what I was protecting misunderstood but understood years later when never read. It was important to give to family for judgement of 'state of mind'.

Where does the fault lie?
... and Kenny should know about everything.
A breach is a breach in confidence.

I question on a side note the normalcy of my life. If I were to take EVERY-THING into consideration, can I ever trust privacy again?
I feel my thoughts are no longer private in psychosis, but that would fall under the fact that something definitely happened to create this train of thought and behavior.
Insecurity? 'This doesn't just happen passively.' - Objectiveness
                "Well, he is paranoid. That's a given." (PR)
                        No, I'm not.
...Maybe just trying to process things collapsing and make sense after the fact.
...perhaps in my thoughts there are answers.
I can't forget someone was on my phone. But I have to make up for that each and every day.
I'm trying now.
"Build trust again."
"You have to try..."
"I need to call my friends more..."
/No you don't. You protect them by not doing so.
I've grown distant and I'm realizing isolation is not going to be the correct answer.
                {Remembers mother's phone from a day ago
                    when prior distance was talked about}
I too am sick of the bullshit that occurred then. I'm trying to express even if I'm not really talking. I need to get this out was the thoughts at the time.

"Step out."
"Breathe."
"Try to be normal again."
What is normal?
What's in a name?
It not about, "Who are you?"
And I've explored, "Why are you?"

I need to learn.
"Be U."

I get U. Then and now. It is the other sides I'm trying to learn.
Compassionately 'I understand Philip.' 3 years past and it still occurred in
factuality. No laughing there. Sadness in what could have been prevented.
Keep going with your remembrance.

August 24, 2017
Post 11: There is no positive, there is no negative.
There is only what is.

When you look at a traditional chessboard there are black spaces and there are white spaces. Not always as their are many different boards made many different materials. Whatever the combination is, there is a clear definition between the two and their role is variable and contingent of the one who chose one side or the other. Who is to say which side is right or wrong? Both are just playing the same game with the intention of winning. What is exactly winning anyways? Each game a stretegy formed and lessons learned.

I see that this story is coming to an end.

With each new entry I know it's just one step closer to closing a chapter. Part of that scares me. Part of that excites me. You create an entire series for comfort from the strange, but when you decide it's time to give it up you are going on a level of faith with yourself and the process that it is completed as it should be at the time. I believe hell knows you are unsure and waiting for you to choose one thing or another of a pathway or strategy. It is the beginning of questionings and understanding of intro-ductions, yet you continue to just stay in it hoping things to be better. In presented re-sponses and variety, it has taken a toll and something has to give in that process away from some aspects of such to look deeper and advance. What lessons are presented in such lies? A formulation of interests one way or another towards understanding.

Change is intimidating. It's unpredictable, and from that you really just can't say how things will turn out. That's the definition of unpredictability. You don't know what one would pick up and translate. But it does leave the value to the question of, 'Better the devil you know or the one you don't?'.Never a wrong answer there as all it does is lead towards understanding and the expansive knowledge from one topic or another in perspective of one side or the other on any topic. I tend to fall into the field of I rather discover new devils but never discount the ones I have already encountered. You were introduced to them for a reason where they bring both plasure and pain. Does that create shallowness of understanding of the ones already seen? I don't need to relive last hurt repeatedly. It showcases lack of growth of understanding why something 'hurt' vs. changing behavior one way or another. I don't need to relive past mistakes.

Or Do I? If I am thinking about it then there is a reason for such one way or another. Recounts and revisits denotes a commitment to something of interest or of wanting to understand. I kind of want to make new ones. From there comes possible successes while prior becomes known outcomes. I want to try some of the same things truer to myself now than perhaps I ever was. Different approaches towards a solution that seems more intrinsically correct to I.

As I go through these last few steps of narrative art, I was asked, 'What's the worst relationship experience I ever went through?' Seems like a pretty black and white question to answer, but somehow I found myself thinking in the grey about it.

I could list infinite good and bad. But for every bad there was a good and in every good moment, something was given from it as well as gained. I find myself saying there really was no definitive good or bad moment. All are casualties of the game if I not in a relationship with them or it didn't transform to friendship or further mutual connection. Doesn't mean there isn't cherished thoughts. We give up something in order to advance across the board. The back-and-forth of 2 different drives denotes a purpose that may or may not include the same partner in one's strategy towards life. It is important to note you are playing a 'game' with someone where others can view it as against. Variable when it is applied to multiple things of thought and physicality.

As long as we don't give up 'our' king, every other aspect is supposedly worth a trade-off if need be. Imagine a game where all the pawns are placed in the back instead of the front and the rules are to save as many of the inexperienced while still trying to tackle the opponent. What if the strategy remained the traditional sense on the other side where pawns first and let the experienced sit back and think this out traditionally. It could be looked at perhaps the front is the little things of life that there are the most of and the rest are the formulation of solid memories and moments. Which ones are worth the sacrifice? The ones of full transformation if they make it across the board or the ones that are distinctly defined in one way or another in their lessons and meaning spoken or not. The pawns can replace any of the other pieces of significance lost prior. They wouldn't be completely the same as it took tremendous work to get across the board, but they replace with respect of the journey that came before and the mantle held.

I found myself apathetic to loss or gain at the moment. It can be viewed as just something necessary for self-preservation and totally done on the intention of what I felt was right to either protect me or push me forward with good intentions. The difference is always going to be in wondering what is the endgame here. When strategy factors into a situation you always have to try to not only know your opponent, but also know their intentions. The conversations through a game of chess becomes much more insightful than the silent partner not revealing anything. Is it intention of motive one way or another or is it simply invested in the game at hand solely and then we talk?

When I started this series with 'Beautiful Layered Lies' in 2011, I don't really think I fully knew what my intentions really were. It definitely was to find myself and get to know me. It definitely was from a place of anger and hurt. But then also of taking a chance and throwing myself out there and beginning to collaborate with others on skills and artistic practice that brought myself pleasure. The splintering of 23 points of view that could all go into their own stories and discussions if one really knew the right words to say at the time. When one doesn't know what to say, borrow what is learned and branch from there in choice of expression one way or another. But I did try to approach it for myself. It was the curiousness to see what others translated from such in a first introduction aspect.

Its sequel, 'Ugly Simple Truths' (2012) becomes a little more clouded. I took out selfishness while doing what had to be done for myself to understand why I am the way I am and what I was trying to say and understand. In introduction, 23 branches into 46 other points while still understanding the expansive aspects of still familiar-izing the previous 23. From there the show doubled and splintered from 23 written entries and then 23 artistic entries making the show actually 46 pieces and 69 offi-cially at that point. Not that I would call the first show selfish by any means, it was simply an introduction towards acceptance and conversations. World building towards understanding one thing or another based on past experiences and influence before going into anything new. The sequel to that series is not so much an open forum of discussion on what is driving me, but some level of acceptance of who I am, what I'm doing and that internal conflict is perfectly normal to go through. That started from doing something for 'Self' first and then secondly look at not only the persective of the otherside towards respect and appreciation, but open up the format to outside conversations that relate in one way or another that invites the same thing on the other side towards compassion and understanding of 'each other' and life experiences of curveballs and hurdles. It's the personal acceptance that is always going to be the hard thing to acknowledge. Overcome that and then you found stages towards heaven.

I have 13 posts left and then my Divine Comedy is complete. At least in the written form. My intention is to finish this upon my return from Italy. Which means I have 6 posts to do in the next 8 days in order to get to the meat of this series and fundamentally change and challenge. It may sound like allot in a short amount of time, but this is all topics long thought about and written about in private and already outlined. I just need life to prove my thesis right or wrong for me.

When you lose control of a situation in the past that is the last thing you ever want to give up. When you actually give yourself up to going with the flow and faith is when things are going to change.

Nothing is definitive.
Everything has a positive and a negative.
List any person, place, thing or concept and you find that answer to be true of perspective and personal relation or just simply fact.

ENTRY 32:

Threats against my mother are never to be tolerated.
EVER!
Thoughts of comments from PR of being a 3rd party response (responses
required.) No 5th in the technological age of court cases.
I remember hearing how Company #1 was painting her. (Further question-
ing protectionism now as I sift between moments that
happened pre and post breakdown. I never heard mention of MUTHER at
Company #1. Definitely did at Company #2. There
are things that I live and die by that factor deeply and deeper)
I can say the personal responses of the 'obsession' of Freud & my mother in
this regard.
"Mom.... Moooommmm"
Reiterated the next day.
"<repeating,> "Mom....Moooommmm"
Me on the phone with my mother to get her to stop in what she was talking
about. In this regard, it was personal comments towards former supervisors
where they could and probably did take it personal. At that time I knew they
were transcribing phone calls of ours at PR.
"Oh, he knows."(T-PR)
'But he was talking to his mother...' (PRe)

It was walking to dinner saying, "I'd protect my mother over suicide over
this." (said to (K) on Buford Highway)
I was stone cold serious as even in that dinner, I turned off my phone to dis-
cuss one thing or another. If there is recordings from that it comes from (K)
's phone or even when turned off, a mic still exists neverthless.
I remember when my father threw the alarm clock at my mother and I laid
in bed crying not knowing what to do.
I was confused and woken up.
I wanted to get up.
I didn't.

I laid in bed crying not know what exactly to do.
I wanted to get up,
but I did nothing.
Fear invaded my bedroom.
Something it was used to seeing.

I remember imagining strength when there was none.
I remember being stronger later in life when my mother was threatened
...her little dogs too. (Memories of real threats to come down to Savannah
from Atlanta back around 2012-2013 to address what was not going to be
psychological warfare on my mother. Threats of just releasing her dogs out
of the house and comments of cruelty. Cops called on the way down and I
was there in 3 hours instead of my normal 4. At least he made up for that
timeframe of their lives and relationship ever since then and is good in my
book. There is respect and empathy there on multiple fronts. She moved out,
bought her own home and never returned to that relationship either. They
remain friends.)
A cowardly lion does eventually find his strength.

I have been right there when need be ever since.
If I have an inkling of feeling that those attacks are still real, I owe it to my
family and myself to protect that.
                    "Mom....Moooommmm" (repeated) (Me)
(So many times repeated at so many different times)
Bringing my mother into it...
That would cross all lines for anybody.
Your partnership os contengient on on attacking an HD shareholder in that
regard. Multiple parental figures in that response.
Polo knows my love of my mother. It was one of the only talking points when
let into FA to talk about indirectly what I heard at PureRED)
                                                      "Release it"
Heightened awareness or just a realization of what power people can have
when privacy is stolen?
"Twisted and noted."
If I ever get a hold of stolen privacy, they will stay that way and not used for
others again.

I know this happened.
An entire company knows this happened.
The path can start at #2 or #1.

                    "Home Depot is pissed" (T-PR)
HD has no business association with PureRED at that time and does not
have client work at the time with them. They did and do have associations
with Freud/Diablo.

In regards to 'worst kept secrets', it denotes the company did not care for confidentiality and opens up discussions to family members & spouses in what is condentiality and what was figured out during the interview process anyways before employment.

'But he was talking to his mom...' (PRe)

How many people share things privately to their spouse and families. Especially when 'Ruby' was a codeword for their Kroger division prior to the deal going through? Are we going to have complete lockdown of connections in privacy in that regard?

Pretty early on once it was uttered 'Oh he knows', I let my mother know (as I talked to her on the phone pretty much every day at the time, that I have been hearing things in the office. It was mistaken for some reason at the time to be thoughts of hearing things that were not there, where there was never a single instance of that in my life prior. To try to express to my mother properly that things carried over from one company to another is difficult in 3rd party confirmation. The best I could do is make sure to steer the conversations away from areas where others take things personal and could just further harm my loved ones and myself.

"They have a bigger problem if they are still on my phone.'(Me)

I think that was understood when I said that before entry of people into Pur-eRED and it was not out of Pure Love, but definitely went in 100%.

Who wants to talk about the continual digital attacks as of notice of November 16, 2022? I don't think that is trying to make it up to I and I'm pretty sure from a narrative stand-point that looks like motive and incentive, but hey...we are skipping head to like 3 or 5 books from now. Ahhh...the joys of being right to write back in 2019 when trying to come back from bullshittery then and it continued 3 years later. Who let that 'Open-Door Policy' continue?

I'll probably move this to the right section eventually.

'We aren't currently on-boarding' (B-FD)

I never asked and that information was provided. I was simply a contract fixed-employee who would have loved security but never asked of such in that capacity. Of course I was lied to as their hired a videographer and also one of note taking skills and compassion without people's knowledge. In any regard, no you can't use that excuse and it was made clear you wanted to fire me on my birthday, possibly pay out a contract for me to leave and internally you can discuss the 'can't trump charges' aspects of internal affairs of when the CEO is not in the office and when Eagles land on that discussion.

There are employees and there are owners. And then there are owners of owners when things grow. When it comes to personal attachment, it comes from those who sweat, blood and tears it took to get there and employees thankful they were believed in an on-boarded in the same dream. Not the same in the other regard.

I understand compassion was met in situations of '**But he smokes...**' just as much as checking up on others to see how they are doing and understanding the situation of prior employment on my end and other people's position. Especially after faux HR contacts with or without bringing in Bosch as the only official resource of HR in that capacity. I got the compassion then. I got the frustration then. I experienced the turning of discussions towards victimization. Did you disclose everything of my victimization or did that warrent people wanting to slap you when they found out about what happened? Where is it now in what was allowed and what could had been discussed then? I walked out professionally. That is all that matters. Cleared of anything they could have said after the fact.

You can't just keep compounding issues self-made in American dreams or that of anyone trying to have a company or company in any regard.

In regards of anything, after lawyer talk, '**Do it..**' in authorization of pulling time cards after meeting with legal council one way or another. That was understood just as much as '**I don't care that he hears...**' could had been explained just as much as YOUR co-workers moved people because they felt threatened from private phonecalls they never should had heard. I think about what I reported and maybe a price or suit game at that point between a known contracting companty and their employment aspects in their con-tracts. I was never given any answer from prior and non of the discussions was for my benefit or reprieve of what I experienced. In that regard, may-be Randstad made off nicely with Freud/Diablo money without fixing the victim of the situation while understanding later down the line the question of istock and how that litegation works understanding the victims or simply company investment before understanding the contributors of a company. What happened then and why not talked to? Someone walked off with some-thing.

Questions come to mind of the moment of Chrisopher Washington saying, **We need to get rid of the mouse?** in an office setting. At the time it was junior surveillance in that aspect where they would try to say Walkie Talkies are totally allowed but still have to understand open airwaves are completely picked up in open-source capacity where Tanya told you I could hear as you were talking to Bonnie Bomar in a capacity of known aspects of invasion and here we are 3 years later (practically 4...actually 4 in that regard). How foolish where you people in that regard to lie to publically traded companies, corporate connections and sponsors and sit here and try to call foul after-the-fact? That mouse comment can be answered several different ways. We can go the Christopher Washington aspect of he was not a part od marketing in any capacity and brought a red hat aspect into the company and introduc-tion to their partners which is inferred on a political side before you flip the hat over to what he was ignorant on in the first place before going elsewhere. Or there is Disney involvement where we can discuss power and influence one way or another on thst regard. Or we can talk about how I was not talking, not sharing with people who aren't my coworkers about what was going on while your employment company and your peers were reacting in real time to what was going on while I was making sure before I said any-thiing to anyone about surity. The transcript of me talking to a lawyer was enough then while knowing I already booked your asses off my facebook and noted a time of seeking a lawyer 'for a friend'. You went 'too deep, too long' and you fucking knew it and wouldn't stop. Did you or did not not continue into PureRED knowing how much legal trouble you are in after November 2, 2018 or can you point me in the right direction. You could had done so then. So could had PureRED. Whatever the reason why, they all made their choice and what has been the outcome of my life comes from their decisions.

I heard enough at PureRED to point that finger straight at your company and say Old School meets New School rules if you are going to pop on the internet and do crimes against humanity that continue 3-4 years after the fact in what could had been resolved then. Indirectly heard at PureRED so by Randstand standards, totally acceptable office behavior.

Who stole what what me is debateable as I have yet to know that pespective, but people were warned by others and by myself where we are now in this situation and the last thing I every will say is this is political. This is across all party lines and allowed in 2018—2019 and was allowed even in 2022. Randstad is owned by Experian. Not an American company. U can't just make this right between companies without fixing the victims.

Freud Tools has an expensive contract with Home Depot that is through the
Diablo line.
Home Depot is letting millions walk out its doors every day
at the expense of the benefits of its employees.
What can they do anyways as a single touch or accusation is a potential
lawsuit? I understand the problem & why partnership is required. Use your
resources and all it looks like is preemptive aspects of finding ways to
villainize someone while secretly admiring them and incorporating their
work anyways. Basically I'm a 'Drake' in this regard.

-Lack of people minding the self-check-out.
-Possible inside jobs.
And its corporate's job to just let them walk to prevent a liability?
-HD fishes the images of the allege thieves to the local police department.
-associates are not allowed to approach or conject.
-it is like that with any company. Liability but a need to to stop and iterated.
I relate.

But as each product goes out the door, it falls harder on employees to get profit
sharing while HD gets a tax. write-off at the end of the year.
But as each product goes out the door, it falls harder on employees to get
profit sharing while HD gets a tax write-off at the end of the year.
Losses had to one is a write-off elsewhere. What is an average person to do
or even a corporation? Incentives on other side to prevent yet hands tied
on either side where one is fine and the other suffers. A state of modern,
contemporary America as modern is commonly denoted from 1945 on and
contempory is an age-set I do not know but could probably place in late 90s
early 2000s. Lots of growth in the digital age of technology from late 80s/
early 90s. So much invasision into homes or perhaps an introduction had.
Until then...
-No retirement.
-Unrealistic goals to get customers on extended warranties
-signed to credit cards above the par level of averaging 29.99%
or greater. But don't break the rules...you pay for them if not
finished in a year.

I do give HD credit though where it is due.
-They are there for disaster relief for the community and for the employee's

affected by natural disasters.

-There is a HOMER fund that is not properly supervised where discretion is key, but there have been failures through the cracks.

Emotions & empathy then of discretion. They home build & I built homes. Never ever would I say anything negative of Home Depot nor do I hve direct contact of such. (Perhaps a thought of their partners in such tangent.) I heard what I heard and if 'Home Depot is pissed', they can say so from a humanistic side of what occurred then from a company that does not have HD interest, tried to 'plausible deniability' things, others talking of 'couldn't wait to leak anonymously' while questioning, 'did we steal this from him?' All it looks like at this stage then and now is you have no problem with possible mental roulette and someone pleading very officially outside of work environments and into legal aspects and there was complete disregard of legality had elsewhere while others were told 'you can't trump charges'. At what point does humanity come in in thst regard or understand what happened later after this book that was ripped apart and translated in multiple places without my benefit or compensation in my lifetime while I constantly heard internally about people wanting me to commit suicide and refusing to do so and adamently continuely doing so because they incorporated this book into billions of profit without my compensation, approval or request. What did you want me to do? Not transcribe my life or process it so you can do whatever after-the-fact and still fuck over and harm my family? GTFO.

Emotion
<homes lost>
<Abuse>
<False safety nets>

I see my mother work harder every day. She has done so for 13 years employed in the same department. I wish for her to go for a supervisor position. but I also know the years before when they never gave her a second glance. People that come into the store call her "Miss Cindy". Co-workers call her that as well. A sign of respect. From a professional stand-point or simply getting to know someone.

I'm also reminded of her comments yesterday when she said she wants to be the one to pass out the HOMER awards to people.
I know exactly where I came from and I could not be prouder of being a Momma's boy. She wants to make people feel special.
I still sm proud of that badge. Every year she gives lessons from her tree to

coworkers. We all make it though hard times one way or another.

I see the American dream fading as my mother begins to think about retirement when I know that she is not set up for that.

21 years a housewife, still was able to afford her own home eventually. Somehow service everyday while I can't for various reasons of outside resources that seem to point in directions of complete disregard in this capacity since 2018 directness.

<20 years a house wife>

<Cashier>

<Assistant>

<Retail>

<Doctor's Office Receptionist>

<Home Towne hero in HD>

An Olde Towne Road to Gloucester walked in multiple fronts.

As she works harder and dedicates another year to the success of a corporation. I can't help but know in the back of my mind what not only other corporations have done to me. but what they threatened of my mother. With there being a #1 degree of separation between them and her if they wanted to.

I'm completely aware of Freud/Diablo and what they could had done then at the time of attack. A possible victim of approved behavior, but they did what they did and I combated properly outside of I in cited referencce.

Yes. I am aware.

Yes. I am protective.

I wonder what shareholders would think of that if there were
actions made of #1 in HD? Not every company involved has
private conversations to consider.

I know what I said in Florida. Also to a shareholder.

You were going to attack that shareholder's son. That was noted in a double check of luggage.

"I'm obviously not helping...

I'm just going to be a third party from here on out" (T-PR)

I bank on that every day.

Where's the 3rd party on now? A question 3 years later calmed down where it took me about 7 months to process correctly before filing with the EEOC correctly on what would had been mandatory with the first mention of Bosch knowing that company excluded their parents and this traveled to another company thst now includes Kroger in morality.

I know enough about myself to know I did not imagine things.

ZERO CHANCE. NONE.

But I bank on that statement said at Company #2. (PR's statement of being a 3rd party now after given privileged information and going one way or another when wondering what this smells like or who said what when.)

Will they be true to thier words as I am true to mine?

I imagine a pleading of the 5th simply denotes one way or anotherc but in this regard points a finger of perspective. I've been created a life where i've had to assume my book has been read (which it obviously has been and acted on) and to discover or thing bout how that was made to still be an attack towards I knowing the worth of such then and growth still occurred after. In persecution of or even acknowledgement in that aspect is a complete acceptance that in your persecution of I, even on the racist side that I've dealt with, my words are colorful and you still could denote me one race or another. Even in 'Chasing' with my introduction of life as a dance you couldn't paint me as male or female and still denotes a desire to do one thing or another when it comes to passion, understanding or others total disregard while others know exactly what they have while they read this or that or what came before. The question of the fact of why victimize me or have me suffer denotes simply a lack of payment of something of value and not a desire to pay for anything which can be looked at in a modern contemporary sense or simply individualized. In any regard, 'It was understood.'

I question what writing all of this down means in the end. Perhaps just things that need to be released that was absorbed in. Words heard do mean something if they are remembered. Words recorded mentally or otherwise bear weight. To life paths, prosecution, closure...you don't remember random things that mean nothing.

There is a sound mind somewhere in here as I process my thoughts. Until then, just me and this journal.

"I'll read it when I'm done."

..." Until then, just write."

"Compare later on what broke you down."

You are doing that now.

(I remember saying to my mother when she couldn't understand things..."I know it looks like I am not here. But I am here."

At the time I was not talking or interacting.

Nor would most not with thr experience.

 I remember her showing me something she wrote when I came back. "... Fuck this..."

Silently I understood her but internally it is painfully true.
But the mind and connectedness are still processing. Past. Present. Future. I am not even sure if I write this later in this book or not.
(I learn as you do.) I do know that there are several things not written that I've marked down elsewhere to note, (they will be marked in orange after the fact as a compound of both analytical thinking in
real time and remembrance that perhaps needs another color to distinguish. There is a difference.) but I find it important now that we break the 4th or 5th wall ATM, because that is important for me to note that that is important)
3 years later, you got your answer.
It was true.

"The choice is yours on how far down the rabbit-hole to go. "

Imagine all the resources to try to destroy someone and others in the same capacity who say not on my watch. Heart to hearts understanding 3rd parties everywhere. Multiple places to place perspectives one way or another.

ENTRY 34:

The Freud website is a compromised asset.

I'm amazed on how many companies I've been in contact with that do not take proper care of their assets. Can't think of everything.

Every die line is available to be taken down from the website and retraced by any competitor. I have not studied extensively outside of the sawblades, but that should be enough to warrant a multi-million-dollar asset breach. There was the use of WeTransfer and drobox that comes also into question in asset management. WeTransfer for free is not free. (D-FD warned you)

"that includes (recording) (logging) keystrokes?" (B-FD)

"Do it." (B-FD)

multiple references, then and when pulling keycard swipes after legal talk. I suppose we can still talk how you found nothing on my email and I contend anything on that laptop IP after I left the office on November 2, 2018 is on me as I mistakenly and still in offering gave my passwords. Rule number 1 in ANY aspect od leaving or firing (in this regard, 2 companies breach of contract and trust) never give your passwords and let IT or HR figure it out.

Both of those phrases were said at Company #1. My memory does not mistake me. As known about recording keystrokes, it is easy to get into any account on the web. As also noted on my Squarespace account as previously mentioned at Company #2.

I've mentioned the layman aspect to the imagining aspect of this chapter already. I proved such on a SCAD computer. Handle your assetsand authorization before remotely coming after me for your business decisions or getting half a book and wanting the rest afterwards. I had nothing to do with their website or any graphics on it. That was a (D-FD department).

Freud.com, Diablo.com both need to be taken down and revamped as of 8/22/19. (I have not been on either of those sites after that date after proving that images can be taken down from the site onto public computers and, if my mind were directed to do so, could trace proprietary information) There is a potential to both sites representing a potential loss to competitor advantage. Common sense for those in the industry would know that to be true.

I'm just a layman with only 9 months experiences with saw blades.
A graphic designer. What do I know?

Not my paygrade to look into as I problem solve other condicts anyways. I just never want to hear about their asset problem in any regard and their disregard of American Law created the beginning of the end of on-line mug-shots where still American law would state you can't do background checks on people you aren't onboarding anyways and can talk about that before I come back and say you were the originality of that curse out move. Family owned and operated there.

...Knowing my email and Squarespace has been hacked by...
"they can break through firewalls" (T)
...It's safe to say anything could be put on any account of mine past or present by someone else.
Precurser to #8. Maybe not required.
"I always questioned the production files..."
-as I approached a PR employee who had knowledge of access to my privately owned website.
They tried to change the subject after a slip of an answer by them. At this point it didn't matter because others can get past firewalls and no one really cares about it if it doesn't affect them directly. (So much indirect allowness in the American workforce....)

In any way, I finally spoke up and asked as I questioned or talked of (K) about it privately. Somewhere on the server if I remember from the very people I heard talking about me prior that I asked compassion of (M-PR) to look out for prior and she acknowledged it was true.

Get past that legal firewall...(I'm sure they can do it, but not from recorded keystrokes of 11.17.2022 at 12:27am)

As SCAD security said in work orientation...
"there is always a way through everything...including phone double authentication."
Well that was a relief. Compunded companies answering vital questions wondering fate on always getting what I need.

When starting a new job and going through orientation, you look for answers in the questions that have alluded you prior. Hopes in life and in new relationships.

How does that affect profitability of signed contracts with

other companies?
How does intergrity of the contract with the physical members of your product affect your company?

One's contract is sacred on either side. The employee's more valuable than
that of the contract company as on is a first party and the other a 3rd. In
any regard, I understand at this point in my life the differences of shells and
backbones.

How has my profitability been affected with assets breached & taken?
Understood 3 years later.

August 28, 2017
Post 12: Brazen.

What's the worst you could expect?
What's the most they could accomplish?
How would they do it?

I'd say for sure when playing a game it is common practice to question every single move. Be paranoid. Be on guard. Never know what side something was coming from...never underestimate imagination. People get creative with both vindictiveness and in intentions. I should know that well at this point. Especially if personal emotions are involved. Best defense I can do is continue being unassuming. I'm used to the discount anyways. Pockets come out here and there. For ever 'I can't do' there is another 'I can do' to support one thing or another. What drives you to do one thing or another? What is the positive re-enforcement?

I don't see myself as a beacon of excellence. God knows I've wronged as much as I've been wronged. That is natural and that is how people learn their own sense of morality and understanding of right/wrong towards 'Self' and 'Others'. But I also see that, as that is what I used to say about things. I put myself in this particular category that I did something horrible in order to excuse something horrible and this is the cause and reaction from it. Truth is no... I didn't. There really wasn't one thing or another that was absolutely horrible that I've done that couldn't be explained one way or another. Perhaps on the other side as well. If something was unforgiveable on either side, there is either good reason for it or some things could be just talked out. Some cannot is understood in general senses of things. There have been things that have hurt and I can feel remorse for one way or another understanding my lack of communication in youth comes from others lack of communication and a great deal of figuring things out one way or another in silence or with others.

Over time I do have to be more forgiving on myself and others as life experiences teach us to do one thing or another later on. There are just different people playing different games and looking for different outcomes at different levels of experience. We learn to speak at such an early age, it is variable when we understand the things we say and the actions we do in understanding one side or another on it. Since a child, it took myself longer to even speak or read than most. The thoughts were always there. Imagine the introduction of interaction to get me to open my mouth only for it to be closed now. Through written aspects is probably the same as imagining the beauty of singing knowing that I cannot. Dancing when I know I will fall or perhaps I find myself in my words the same way as my first paintings on my parent's kitchen table. All the background noise in the world of importance and life-changing moments and for now, a place to process and escape to some place to process accordingly before re-introducing anything to the outside. From brush strokes to shutter clicks to the handwritten gestures of the hands in beauty translated to keystrokes knowing with each one it is a known invitation of translation one way or another.

I won't say I was successful in all of my endeavors and intentions. But I definitely look outside the box and I'm not entirely sure I trust the box to begin with. I know damn well I'll never fall into any one category. I'm a platypus. A little bit of everything. Little bit brazen, little bit scared, little bit remorseful, a little bit unapologetic. I don't really know anymore. I can define myself many ways. In a world that could attack anyone it is important to have internal strength. It is required. In a world where it can go the other way positively denotes perhaps that is why you step over into one area or another and find beauty in everyone one way or another knowing commonality and differences. Make someone laugh and smile and you are probably heading in the right direction.

I like that I've spent the time to get to know me.
I know what works to an extent.
I know what does not. What does not work is the mixture of with whom that invites that one thing with one person is never going to be the same with others and must be seperated towards either individual actions toward yourself or look at the common aspect of negative experience and understand that is the 'not' aspect to know. There is always the respect of understanding where perhaps it is best to listen to one another and know the things they mention in intimacy and connection. When choosing to process or not what is spoken, best to understand at some point in life that what becomes valuable to everyone is time and the investment of such.

I can read someone like a book within 15 minutes without ever having to question anything other than how I gauged you. I imagine people can probably think the same of I as well. The surprise and exciting aspect of that being disproven is the fact that you do not know everything about everyone in 15 minutes. You get what they present with some major clues one way or another depending on how you look at each other.

Shyness, Surity, Strength? I'd say at this point even the fact of someone coming up to say hello to others outside a computer is pretty daring the scheme of things just as equally as it is to make an introduction in any capacity. But the more I get to know me the more I understand that I need to not overthink things. I need to let the guard down a bit. Maybe then I'd actually interact with others more. Perhaps that comes back in time. Strength in many areas of even reconnect of those you know you have hurt in the past and vice-versa. I think in that regard I always admired and appreciated what years later does. I know there are aspects digitally elsewhere that I have to go back and fix as they simply seem completely out of character in any capacity, but at least that is understood internally the difference and when things had switched to handwriting before going back to type.

Let's be honest, some people will break you.
(Or at least have the capabilities to do such.)

People could go for what is best for them and they will look for that and exploit it to the best of their abilities. That is not to say it is everyone. I understand at the time of writing, I was processing what the last 3 years of employment and then probably to a certain extent my prior work experience. It is completely natural to lean towards the negative perspective of such considering the exploitation experienced. For any of that I can counter saying I've been equally supported by friends and strangers in what I was beginning to reintroduce back into my life after the mass closure. It takes time to step back and (especially in unemployment at the time) understandable the focus is fear, not enjoying the situation and then rebuilding for best face forward one way or another.

Maybe it's a gay culture thing, maybe it's a corporate world thing, but it is also there I think in all culture. Not everyone expresses their weaknesses and perhaps it a downfall that I have expressed mine to those who have followed for so long, but I do believe there is a genuine connection between all of our responses that no one ever feels infallible. We all want to feel safe though. Culture can definitely empower as well as emblazen. Even if we have a safe place right in front of our eyes we still will question it and look for receipts. How does one build trust? It comes from the same embolding aspect of support system or addition to any of the positive aspects one desires one way or another. That comes over time yet could be sensed pretty instantly one way or another. Walk in with the understanding of fallibility and you are one step in the right direction towards interaction. Outside influences will question that or challenge that, but in the end people are really just looking for a safe space. Who knew security was such a primal instinct to be desired and genetically passed down from generation to generation and seen through every single species? Whatever was thought of being used for attack later on in life, was a definite understanding to a certain degree the intention of others and where things went. Perhaps now I am giving someone everything they need to attack again on a different front. At least it is understood in a different capacity that for every attack there is also protection available as well.

I don't know shit about relationships. Mostly because you cannot based one off of another. I've been in as many failed relationships that have become amazing friendships as I have in ones where we never speak again. Is it a failed relationship if it transformed in a different capacity? Actually, I am lying; there is only about 2 and one of them not romantic.

Put your `Self` perspective to the side for a moment and you find out that the people that enter into your life are more your friends than you will ever allow if you discount ego from the equation. People don't hate you overnight and chances are people never hate you even if you think so. To hate someone is emotional connection to something that reaches into something internal deeply. It is the same with love. Connections and getting to know one another through introductions and pawned off time one way or another. Staying out of you head is key at times but, `What is your head telling you?` is a way to trust and challenge your internally thinking one way or another. Internally you can perceive one thing to be the furthest from the truth externally. Externally challenge that at times in confirmation or affirmation. Amazing how external challenge towards comfirmation forms what enters from your head to your heart in truth.

It's my downfall I overthink. Or is it simply a requirement to get to where I know I wanted to go? I probably look at something with more meaning than it was, but regardless of that...it's my life and how I look at things should never be discounted. There is beauty in any translation of life and interpretation of discriptions. I'm not going to apologize for other people's issues. I can only be there if they want to talk about it with I or simply understand we all have them and I may or may not be the issue to others and vice versa. That is also the difference between objective and third party opinions. That is completely different to someone discussing privately or with others about the issues towards someone else or something. The imagine the articulation of any issue/problem/concern denotes pointing in one direction or another towards a solution to resolve whatever needs to be expressed, worked on or `fixed` (which probably transformed is a better word to use as 'fixed' denotes 'broken' and contingent on the issue to be discussed could be detrimental to intitial perspective of the situation. How does that apply when someone says a whole system is 'broken'? Perhaps this is why if one were to mention what is or isn't broken, best to look at it as possible for evolution and ways it could be enhanced, polished or go in a completely different direction with suggestions to build upon. It is important to note that if some-thing is broken, there is a desire to fix it in facts of where those issues were before. The terminology denotes if one finds something not working, invest in how to make it so one way or another. A change of mentality so one does not go around just 'breaking everything' without solutions and the incentives to do such.

What is hard for me to acknowledge is I let that hold me back for a great deal of my life. Things didn't go your way...my fault. Your relationship didn't work out...my fault. Wasn't honest with me... my fault. It seems only natural between internal and external influence that if that much weight and responsibility was placed on myself one way or another, then at least solutions and pathways are created from thinking of such responsibility to resolve thiose 'issues' for myself and give benefit to others to possibly never experience the same thing.

That may sound bitter but it really is not. Not at all. It just means I've played the blame game internally and with others and I rather continue working towards healthy aspects of interaction and relationships. It is saying that I don't know when the point we actually all understand who we are, but there does come a point we have to accept that it was not our fault for other people's misfortune or perhaps that's the lesson I need to teach myself. Fucking live your life and desires or get off the pot of making one thing or another the problem. It is the same if you dislike your job, frustrated with someone or look at generalities of anything in broad strokes. Articulate your feelings one way or another. Write it out if you must. Hash it out internally with yourself first to know what is true to you. The variable of discussion with others does not always occur, so it is important to understand solutions or peace of 'Self' is more important before presenting something to someone else who may be 'the problem' or could be put on the defensive depending on the scenario. I've been telling myself that since I began writing. Flip the mentality of understanding what has already been introduced towards understanding. There is a difference between what is buried within and what can be brought out from that search. We are not afforded a conversation to make something right with others. I'm continuing this game as I perceive to be right.

I'm getting closer to an answer that scares the shit out of me.

All I want is honesty in life, yet one is never afforded total honesty in life. It is the same as teaching a child about the world where things get edited out in explaination for them to discover for themselves or when perhaps they are older told. I'm scared. You are scared. But lets be a safe space. In the scheme of things consider why one would say...'Fuck Judgment'. 'Fuck people who can't make up their mind.' 'Fuck blaming other people for your shit.' All of that denotes things that have more than likely experienced over and over again. Do you have a 'Fuck (whatever) moment?' Judgement exists for a reason to gauge positive and negative. Rational/Morality or simply also the application of prejudice of others elsewhere. People who can't make up their mind might be weighing out the pros and cons of a decision before acting accordingly or simply pushing things one way or another depending on the day. Maybe if someone is blaming other people for something, it is important to figure out what the specifics are and what general blanket statements that simply can never be applied to one group or another entirely. That goes completely into outward discrimination that can always be tackled by the introduction of counter discussion to prove well this person isn't this, that person isn't that. Would you be open to opening up your social circle to discover where blanket statements towards any group can be discredited?

Be honest. Be you. From that no one can remotely give you a problem for it because at the very you are being true to yourself. Either yourself or others will say, 'well... your true 'Self' doesn't exactly mesh with my true 'Self' but I wish you well on your journey.' It is the introduction towards discussions that leads to respect that either is or isn't grown from that. I rather be judged for honesty than for anything maded-up. Mostly because you have already proven yourself enough for there to be no question internally. (Fair warning, there is always going to be internal questions anyways.) In getting to know someone is always a sign of trust. At what point do you trust yourself while balancing trusting others?

For the first time in a long time I no longer am taking responsibility for not knowing whom I am, what my intentions are and that I've never challenged that. I guess that is part of being young by understanding that from a first point perspective we are part of my own past and part of other people's past. What about the now? I may not be the most interesting person to meet, but I will always be pretty honest. It depends on the scenario because I have a sense of humor for Left-Field answers in AMAs. I forgot that about myself...think of something positive about yourself and start there.

Florida allows for any request for removal of a mug-shot if not convicted of a crime. Federal mugshots are in public domain, but not state mug-shots. Copywrite rests with the state that has the practice of removing 30 days outside. What happens when outside entities take a hold of that information?

I am re-writing my official complaint referral sent to the Internet Crime Complaint
Center.

"I would like to list the owner of the following websites listed at the bottom, in violation of The United States Privacy Act of 1974 in the release of private citizen's home addresses and personal information. As self-noted on the website's "About" section, these websites are owned by a foreign entity using United States information. Posting of these citizen's government collected information is a clear violation of The Universal Declaration of Human Rights, article 11, "Everyone charged with a penal offence has the right to be presumed innocent until proven guilty according to law in a public trial at which he has had all the guarantees necessare for his defense. No one shall be held guilty of any penal offence on account of any act or omission which did not constitute a penal offense, under national or international law, at the time when it was committed. Nor shall a heavier penalty be imposed than the one that was applicable at the time the penal offence was committed." (as well as) the United States' 14th Amendment denying due process of the law. Further reference to the 14th Amendment, Article 3 states, "No person shall be a Senator or Representative in Congress, or elector of President and Vice President, or hold any office, civil or military, under the United States, or under any State, who, having previously taken an oath, as a member of Congress, or as an officer of the United States, or as a member of any State legislature, or as an executive or judicial officer of any State, to support the Constitution of the United States, shall have engage in insurrection or rebellion against the same, or given aid or comfort to the enemies thereof. But Congress may by a vote of two-thirds of each House, remove such disability." As self-stated, by the owner of these websites, on bocabusted.com, "I used to work in law enforcement. Some say I've got a grudge. I say people want the cold hard facts." directly violates the constitution (article 3).

In the circumstance of any former law enforcement employee controlling a site due to a "grudge" must adhere to (not only) Florida state official code of ethics. (But clearly violates impartialness of the law by self-describing a "grudge" that should be put into question of motive). Especially in regards to possible pensions. As self-noted on delraybusted.com which would apply to ownership of all websites listed in cluster, websites are owned by a foreign corporation, which mean that not only is a former law enforcer breaking the constitution, but is also working with foreign entities to impede on civil liberties. (which also holds them to working with foreign powers to invade the law)

Copywrite Law:
It's more likely than not that they are. All works made by federal agencies are automatically in the public domain, so if a mugshot was made by a federal agency like the FBI, it is certainly in the public domain.

However, states and state agencies can make their own rules about how they want to handle their intellectual property rights. Often though, states still release their works in entirety to the public domain. (However, they can never give up the copyright and by inability to give up copywrite, they sanction criminal activity) – FL Law, https: www.newmediarights.org/business_models/artist/are_mugshots_publicdomain

According to either Federal or state mugshots, each image is owned by the United States and/or the individual state in which it was produced. As self-proclaimed as being foreign-owned, this is US government sanctioned aiding and abetting of crimes against the 14th Amendment and the Privacy Act (of 1974) by allowing (US) copyrighted images on these websites and (US) government collected data.

Copyright rests with the state that has had the practice of removing after 30 days. Outside website, who utilize copyrighted images and personal information fall directly under the permission of the state on usage and can be required by the state to remove said copyright material when in breach of Florida law. Failure by privately owned websites, regardless of place of origin, to remove images transfer liability to the stage against both copyright claims and privacy act/14th Amendment violations.

By using FL copyrighted protected images, these websites give the appearance of being state-sanctioned (with) false perspective of the state of FL to be in violation of privacy acts and the human rights of (")innocent before guilty(") and cruel and unusual punishment by leaving these images on these websites in perpetuate before and after trials.

The owner of (these) websites is monetizing the content of US/FL owned imagery and information through the click ads on their site which could hold the owner liable for profiting off of government property.

It is essential on both the state and federal level to crackdown on the extortion of state-owned images for the betterment of society. Kickbacks into this practice is open to bring into question lawyer/police officer relationships, as well as State's role as mediator of said assets.

Breach of Data:
As self-noted of being foreign operated, the owner's cluster of websites paint a clear picture that not only are they operating within the South Florida area, but they have access to government files and information that no foreign entity should be entitled to on a foreign operated website. Working within the confines of US citizen records within the geography of South Florida should make them applicable to both state and federal prosecution.

By keeping these records up on sites in perpetuity allows for the door of both innocent people unrelated to fall victim to crimes due to others having a "grudge" when addresses are used (as well as those presumed guilty). (As an example, my former address is visible on the website with no knowledge of whom has lived there upon moving from prior residence) Not everyone stays at the same address forever. It's fair to say there is enough information provided to open the door for identity theft as well. (Those assertations) are a Public Safety Crisis.

Florida law (SB 118 2017)
Florida allows for any request the removal of a mugshot if not convicted of the crime. However, site owner does not supply contact information in order to make such requests. Thus, being in breach of FL law while utilizing FL copyright protected imagery and FL/USA protected information.

In accordance to FL law, there must be contact information available to submit such requests for regional specific sites, such as bocabusted.com, which would fall under the jurisdiction of Palm Beach County to investigate. These above statements would be true to any regional "crime" site for the entire state of Florida and any website that hold the state of Florida visual assets unused for the detriment of character, privacy and protection.

Failure to act implies government sanctioned activities in violation of due process, the constitution and privacy to every single victim on this tree of websites. (the arrested and those of residence) This further applies to all "crime" websites across the entire United States on the timing of when images can be posted and when they must be mandated to be taken down. An arrest is not an admission of guilt. Sentences are either had or not. But perpetuity is a life sentence. By failure to provide contact information and blatantly biting their thumb; they have become judge, jury and executioner to people's reputations and their pursuit of happiness and privacy.

As the internet grows, a market has been created. A market that needs to be addressed. The profitable market of public shaming. One click of a button and an image is owned. Where the data goes is another thing. Mailbox filled with lawyer's information. The prospect of police officer/lawyer backdoor negotiations, extortion to get information removed off the web. Hacking of websites to get information removed. There is responsibility to be had with that data and FL's law is at the beginning forefront of the laws that need to occur in this country.

Innocence before guilt.
Not the other way around.

I can't speak for everyone, but I begrudgingly ask, as one of the thousands of people on this site, that "we" all have our constitutional rights returned and repaired immediately. I respectfully ask for
your time in this matter as I am sure you would ask yourself if your privacy and civil liberties were held captive. (by foreign entities)

Bocabusted.com
Delraybusted.com
Lakeworthbusted.com
Rivierabusted.com
Westpalmbusted.com

(Electronically submitted 9/7/2019),
(Handwritten 8/22/2019)

Under penalty of Florida law of up to $1000 dollars a day in damages, Rapsheet.org has denied my initial request for removal as I was not convicted of that crime and as noted by their documented email response back on September 9th, 2019. 10 days after my initial claim. In my mind, I'll just let the figures of imaginary money count themselves as that is the law, even if I never see any of it. $85,000 and counting... This is what got mentioned in the book on rapsheet.org and can vbe verified via waybackmachine.org. Only reported bocabust.com to the Internet Crime Unit. Rapsheet.org came from this book. The particular mention of bocabusted.com was the inclusion of home addresses in the initial argument as stated in my original letter as vigilantes towards individual cases could go on hunting aspect of grudged venegence and put innocent people in harms way. When it comes to rapsheet.org, they transferred their assets to rapsheet.com in an attempt to still continue their business while being warned of liability in the first forbidden aspect. It is discussed in the sequel how when this persistence of showcasing mugshots online continued, including my own, the argument evolved based on initial discussions and added on information. The illegality of the mugshot under due process leads one liable for every mugshot they take 'ownership' of while going further into copyright law.

Let's see where the mind goes tomorrow...
Until then think about phone privacy and user guidelines on personal property and images.
Copyright always falls on the photographer. Regardless of camera usage.

The Apple iPhone is the #1 used camera in the world.

Social media is owned by private entities as publicly traded companies.
Do user rights switch when transferred from phone to desktop to online?

How long is someone allowed on your phone?

Who is on my phone?
How many?

Is anyone on someone else's phone and desktop?

Question "how can someone be in 2 places at the same time?"

A question of locations based on apps and websites on my phone.
My phone says I'm in North Carolina this week.Tampa the next.
Quantum Theory or Cloned Software? (Memories of PR)

Brought about conclusions from connect of (FD-D) and a never again aspect in what was absolutely illegal then. The argument there is still legally sound as you cannot use background checks for hiring purposes unless someone is actually applying for a position and done so only prior to employment. As they were not onboarding, the question of such a background check in that regard is still something that would had fallen under Randstand jurisdiction if to be considered or approached. If one was to want to hire me, then that is conversations that could had been done with the fixed-term employee on if there was even a desire or interest to do so before even approaching Randstad on the possible payout of the entire fixed-term contract towards the end or questions again on 'We are not currently onboarding' and me being perfectly fine and happy with 'strictly no overtime' heard multiple times in my life after Alfred Angelo thankful of not being indentured to always on the clock and always a worker's choice on overtime or re-evaluation of staff, time constraints, and management to avoid that in the future.

For everyone, I stand by this section knowing it was heard never knowing my internal voice in others being read electronically at the same time of typing out further explaination. I did not put up with the aspect of what it brings when I was in Rome and an earshot of The Vatican and I definitely was not putting up with it in casual flings of employment relationships. In that regard, family first and I note very well the initial moment of 'No, we will not talk about this later.' When stepping from one place and on a vacation in any regard saved up when I can never take one due to work responsibilities, I can honestly say it happened right before The Emperyean being discussed in 2017 and with 'Throughts on A Train' to how to approach what society does one way or another.

I will never fault you, never prosecute you and my heart was sound in what played out years later multiple times on the matter. I love you and the casual fling of employment was not family and I was not welcomed but they invaded our family. I cite the United States of America law on that. Please understand why I've been silent and not spoken things on the phone and kept my mouth shut. That last sentence for my sister. Not for Freud/Diablo.

Complaint Referral Form
Internet Crime Complaint Center

Victim Information

Name: Philip Bonneau
Are you reporting on behalf of a business? [None]
Business Name:
Is the incident currently impacting business [None]
operations?
Age: 30 - 39
Address
Address (continued)
Suite/Apt./Mail Stop:
City: Savannah
County: Chatham
Country: United States of America
State: Florida
Zip Code/Route: 31404
Phone Number
Email Address
Business IT POC, if applicable
Other Business POC, if applicable

Description of Incident

Provide a description of the incident and how you were victimized. Provide information not captured elsewhere in this complaint form.

I would like to list the owner of the following websites listed at the bottom in violation of The United States Privacy Act of 1974 in the release of private citizens home addresses and personal information. As self-noted on the website's about section, these website's are owned by a foreign entity using United States information. Posting of these citizen's government collected information is a clear violation of The Universal Declaration of Human Rights, article 11 "Everyone charged with a penal offence has the right to be presumed innocent until proved guilty according to law in a public trial at which he has had all the guarantees necessary for his defence. No one shall be held guilty of any penal offence on account of any act or omission which did not constitute a penal offence, under national or international law, at the time when it was committed. Nor shall a heavier penalty be imposed than the one that was applicable at the time the penal offence was committed."

and the United States' 14th Amendment denying due process of the law. Further reference to the 14th Amendment, Article 3 states No person shall be a Senator or Representative in Congress, or elector of President and Vice President, or hold any office, civil or military, under the United States, or under any State, who, having previously taken an oath, as a member of Congress, or as an officer of the United States, or as a member of any State legislature, or as an executive or judicial officer of any State, to support the Constitution of the United States, shall have engaged in insurrection or rebellion against the same, or given aid or comfort to the enemies thereof. But Congress may by a vote of two-thirds of each House, remove such disability. As self stated by the owner of these websites on bocabusted.com, "I used to work in law enforcement. Some say I've got a grudge. I say people want the cold hard facts." which directly violates the constitution. In the circumstance of any former law

Proof of Original Submit to Internet Crime Complaint Center Page 1 - 9/7/2019. "Philip A. Bonneau. The things of submit exactly 2 years later from the exact date. Scanned December 5, 2022

213

enforcement employee controlling a site due to a "grudge" must adhere to Florida state official code of ethics. Especially in regards to possible pensions. As self-noted on delraybusted.com which would apply to ownership of all websites, websites are owned by a foreign corporation, which means that not only is a former law enforcer breaking the constitution, but is also working with foreign entities to impede on civil liberties.

Copyright law
"It's more likely than not that they are. All works made by federal agencies are automatically in the public domain, so if the mugshot was made by a federal agency like the FBI, it is certainly in the public domain.

However, states and state agencies can make their own rules about how they want to handle their intellectual property rights. Often though, states still release their works in entirety to the public domain.
FL Law" - https://www.newmediarights.org/business_models/artist/are_mugshots_public_domain

According to either Federal or State Mugshots, each image is owned by the United States and/or the individual State in which it was produced. As self-proclaimed as being foreign owned, this is US government sanctioned aiding and abetting of crimes against the 14th Amendment and Privacy Act by allowing copyrighted images on these websites and government collected data.

Copyright rest with the state that has had the practice of removing after 30 days. Outside websites who utilize copyrighted images and personal information fall directly under the permission of the state on usage and can be required by the state to remove said copyright material when in breach of Florida law. Failure by privately owned websites, regardless of place of origin, to remove images transfers liability to the state against both copyright claims and privacy act/14th Amendment violations.

By using FL copyrighted protected images, these websites give the appearance of being state-sanctioned and false perspective of the state of FL to be in violation of privacy acts and the human rights of innocent before guilty and cruel and unusual punishment by leaving these images on these websites in perpetuity before and after trials.

The owner of the website is monetizing the content of US/FL owned imagery and information through the click ads on their site which could hold the owner liable for profiting off of government property.

It is essential on both the state and federal level to crackdown on the extortion of state owned images for the betterment of society. Kickbacks into this practice is open to bring into question lawyer/police officer relationships as well as State's role as mediator of said assets.

Breach of Data
As self-noted of being foreign operated, the owner's cluster of website's paint a clear picture that not only are they operating within the south Florida area, but they have access to government files and information that no foreign entity should be entitled to on a foreign operated website. Working within the confines of US citizen records within the geography of South Florida should make them applicable to both state and federal prosecution.

By keeping these records up on sites in perpetuity allows for the door of both innocent people unrelated to fall victim to crimes due to others having a "grudge" when addresses are used. Not everyone stays at the same address forever. It's fair to say there is enough information provided to open the door for identity theft as well. That is a Public Safety Crisis.

Florida law (SB 118 2017)
Florida allows for any request the removal of a mugshot if not convicted of the crime. However, site owner does not supply contact information in order to make such requests. Thus being in breach of FL law while utilizing FL copyrighted protected imagery and FL/USA protected information.

In accordance to FL law, there must be contact information available to submit such requests for regional specific

Proof of Original Submit to Internet Crime Complaint Center Page 2 - 9/7/2019. "Philip A. Bonneau. Scanned December 5, 2022

214

sites such as Bocabusted.com which would fall under the jurisdiction of Palm Beach County to investigate. These above statements would be true to any regional "crime" site for the entire state of Florida and any website that hold the state of Florida visual assets used for the detriment of character, privacy and protection.

Failure to act implies government sanctioned activities in violation of due process, the constitution and privacy to every single victim on this tree of websites. This further applies to all "crime" websites across the entire United States on the timing of when images can be posted and when they must be mandated to be taken down. An arrest is not an admission of guilt. Sentences are either had or not. But perpetuity is a life sentence. By failure to provide contact information and blatantly biting their thumb; they have become judge, jury and executioner to people's reputations and their pursuit of happiness and privacy.

As the internet grows, a market has been created a market that needs to be addressed. The profitable market of public shaming. One click of a button and an image is owned. Where the data goes is another thing. Mailbox filled with lawyer's information. The prospect of police officer/lawyer back door negotiations, extortion to get information removed off the web. Hacking of websites to get information removed. There is responsibility to be had with that data and FL's law is at the beginning forefront of the laws that need to occur in this country.

Innocence before guilt.
Not the other way around.

I can't speak for everyone, but I begrudgingly ask, as one of the thousands of people on this site, that "we" all have our constitutional rights returned and repaired immediately. I respectfully ask for your time in this matter as I am sure you would ask yourself if your privacy and civil liberties were held captive.

https://bocabusted.com/
https://delraybusted.com/
https://lakeworthbusted.com/
https://rivierabusted.com/
http://westpalmbusted.com/

Which of the following were used in this incident? (Check all that apply.)
☐ Spoofed Email
☐ Similar Domain
☐ Email Intrusion
☐ Other   Please specify:

Law enforcement or regulatory agencies may desire copies of pertinent documents or other evidence regarding your complaint.

Originals should be retained for use by law enforcement agencies.

┌─ **Other Information**

If an email was used in this incident, please provide a copy of the entire email including full email headers.

[No response provided]

Are there any other witnesses or victims to this incident?

[No response provided]

If you have reported this incident to other law enforcement or government agencies, please provide the name, phone number, email, date reported, report number, etc.

[No response provided]

☐ Check here if this an update to a previously filed complaint:

Who Filed the Complaint

Were you the victim in the incident described above? Yes

Digital Signature

By digitally signing this document, I affirm that the information I provided is true and accurate to the best of my knowledge. I understand that providing false information could make me subject to fine, imprisonment, or both. (Title 18, U.S. Code, Section 1001)

Digital Signature: Philip Arthur Bonneau

Thank you for submitting your complaint to the IC3. Please save or print a copy for your records. *This is the only time you will have to make a copy of your complaint.*

Proof of Original Submit to Internet Crime Complaint Center Page 4 - 9/7/2019. "Philip A. Bonneau.
Scanned December 5, 2022

ENTRY 36: 8/23

I didn't ask for Xfinity to be installed today. I called prior in inquiry.
A driver showed up at my mother's home saying that I had requested an in-
stallment.

I did not.
I did not as I wanted prices and was not completely comfortable at this stage
to enter into her home. May not be required, I explain it.

Weeks ago. I asked for a price quote stating how unsure about
connecting my mother's house to the web. Having someone
randomly show up and where my mind went proves I am not
comfortable with being online at home yet. Not with the level of data breach
that occurred and for how long it occurred. (Phone Calls)

"Am I ever going to be ok with internet back in my home?"

I tell myself that not having internet is controlling the trauma
that this has created. Irony is present to this since I still have
the phone that produced a transcript in the office, but that is what happens
when you can't afford a new one at this point. A sliver of discomfort forced to
be withstood and held onto even today. No one wants to break that trust of
privilege in browsing phone, desktops. Imagine complete strangers conject-
ing on possible porn browsing history. Imagine even thinking of that with a
camera facing you on any desktop, tablet, phone. The rabbit holes of starting
on one place of Wiki and ending up someone completely different in degrees
of interest and knowledge. Subjective judgements on your own browsing
enough there to never want to look anything up on the internet or back to
solely physical books, libraries and handwriting.

I suppose if one wanted to go further, the question of privacy when it comes
to interest or sexuality understanding that is intimate or a learning process
from puberty on where we all are guided in postive and negative experiences
while still going into personal questions for self on what 'attracts' us that can
be easily explained or discussed in the area of 'Why do you like this piece of
artwork?' or 'Why do you like this movie?'. I understand that not everything
is everyone's taste. Never will be to blanket love everything. All you can do
is admire that there is love and pleasure in people's lives one way or another
before trying to tell them one way or another why they can't love something

as beautiful as a thought or idea.

If one wanted to approach in critique of such beauty, there are ways to do so from a critical stance and discussion based on facts, evidence or whatever you chose to focus your time on in either support or rebut. Never discounted if approached correctly to find answers for yourself of invite diaglogue. To simply hate something and outwardly express such denotes passion in a way where it could be backed up and discussed or simply something that perhaps best silent in thought in perspective. There are hate statements and there is disagreement discussions. Either denotes a passion of something spoken or not. The fairness of art critique and the search for beauty in anything.

I said before once or twice, if you hate someone or something, wiki them or research to find something you like about them. Everyone and everything has a shining attribute somewhere.

15 months.
7 years.
0 idea as I look at everything.

I'm perfectly fine logging in occasionally at the library to work on my website and research. Otherwise. I'm just trying to get my life back into order and get the sleep that I've not been able to get yet.

Who called?
Was it simply a misunderstanding?

Nevertheless. I turned down the Xfinity guy on installation.
Mom hasn't ever had the internet in her house. Considering the damage done to both of us: I don't blame her or myself one bit for not wanting it.

ENTRY 37:

By law, the rights to images rest with the photographer.
"The one who clicks the button."
-Not the model or purchaser of images.
There is always an agreement made between model and photographer on the type of usage.

Added discussion of owner of technology but at least in this regard,my shoots are always I as Art Director, Creative Director, friend, trustee and one might question later why it is so important for me to distinquish such of my rights. There is those that create technology in a broad sense and then there is the intimacy of artwork and artist that is either contingent of technology or of others knowing someone cannot simply collect something on a tech- nological side as theirs because they offered the software. The software is contingent of adoption and interpretation by individuals where the satisfac- tion of the creator always would more than likely fall on the fact of, 'I created this.' and sit back and see how the world changes from it or occasionally interact from here and there in any regard.

If my files were stolen, not only is that a breach on my copyright, but a claim from all the models can be made as well against the thief.
Still true with no If on the matter. Even in different groups.

An artist is also entitled to use his/her work for promotion unless otherwise stated in signed agreements.

Copyright cannot be taken away until 70 years after the death of the photog- rapher, especially in the case of sentimental value images.
-same is applied to diary usage.

A yearbook.
My friends.
My family.
This book on descried as a diary/journal in title page #1. No completely on the cover to get the point across time frames in discussion.
Who listened? Who disregarded?
I am a non-profit myself as I have always allowed my artwork to just pay for itself and pay it forward within the community.
Don't need that offical status to see and not that truth.
A continual trying to make it.

"We the People..." in the end comprised of my friends and family.
Always there, even when I feel most alone.

A controlled environment.
Heading...back to center.
Removing of variables.

Post 13: The First Sphere.

> *"Yet an experiment, were you to try it,*
> *could free you from your cavil and the source*
> *of your arts' course springs from experiment.*
> *Taking three mirrors, place a pair of them*
> *at equal distance from you; set the third*
> *midway between those two, but farther back.*
> *Then, turning toward them, at your back have placed*
> *a light that kindles those three mirrors and*
> *returns to you, reflected by them all.*
> *Although the image in the farthest glass*
> *will be of lesser size, there you will see*
> *that it must match the brightness of the rest."*
> *- PARADISO, Canto II - 94–105*

In this passage, Dante was describing that the angle of incidence is equal to the angle of reflection. Conflicting moral principles raise many mental arguments regarding what is right to do vs. what is good to seek. Which is perhaps where this journey midway through my life has taken me from the very first step I took into this self-made world that I've explored for 6 years now. Questions of morality, cause-and-effect, love, compassion and somewhere along the line finding peace. I have this unequivocal feeling inside me that we are given what we need most if we only change our perspective and angle of thought. Half full. Half empty. Always full if you consider the rest is air. Granted that comes from a pretty privileged perspective in the scheme of things. But I contend that even the poorest of man is capable of being filled with life depending on how they view the world and their story as it pertains to them.

I find myself completing a vow that I set out to do when I was in college and one that was further built in meaning with the passing of my grandfather this year. I always wanted to see the world; it was not into later on when I started this series that I discovered just how much I really wanted to see Heaven. I've written in the past about struggle and goals. Fundamentally, I think my artwork was born from strife when I was a teenager and from there it grew to what it is today. I grew up very fast and always did what needed to be done. For myself, my family and for others.

I worked full-time through school, helped raise my brother, helped raise my mother and just grew and survived from every experience presented to me through the gifts others gave me by including me in their lives. I've worked every day of my life since I was 14.

I started saving skymiles since college with the dream that one day I'd be able to go see the world and it will be done based on everything I ever had to do to get by each day. I promised myself I'd do that at 30. 30 came. 30 went. I didn't do it. I did go to The Bahamas though for a solo week of decade entry in a smaller scale. Probably I didn't go overseas halfway on fear, the other half probably because the perspective of whom I was in one mirror was not ready to allow myself to have that moment. 31...32...33...34. Here I am and each year passes and another year of doing what needs to be done instead of going on faith and experiment. Responsibility vs. Desire.

My heart broke with the suicide of my cousin. When I got the call I was in the middle of a photo-shoot as the photographer for a weeklong shoot. We were the same age. While I was literally destroyed inside there was nothing I could do to breakdown or leave work. The responsibility was on me and the 100K investment my company made. I couldn't even take a day off if I wanted. I took a couple minutes, shut my office door. Went for a walk and then said, 'Ok...I have to work and just mask that emotion.' But how that affected me is suddenly 35 isn't promised so much. I think she helped me get started with the idea that I was going to finally travel. If not now... when? Having been in places where the pain can absolutely take over, I started thinking about where I wanted to go and to plan that trip for this summer after the responsibilities of the Spring were completed with work. It is understood her pain and I understand that takes over towards choices of control to ease it or stop it one way or another. It is with respect my heart is always there in family I never get to visit or see due to work, finances and responsibilities.

A little bit later, my grandfather passed away and it was another similar scenario of responsibility or desire. In that moment, the cost to travel would have exceeded 1200 dollars to make it there, which effectively would be everything I had set-aside since my cousin's death for my trip. Do I go to family or do I do this trip? It's not an easy question to ask.

My paternal grandfather had an incredible life. 13 children. He had a beautiful wife who is the kindest representation of human I have ever met and I hope I even have an ounce of her in me. There is 1/6 of her there. After she passed he found an equally amazing and beautiful companion who he got to travel the world with and experience so many amazing things. My decision was, 'Do what he would have wanted me to do.' Go see the world and live life.

My decision for Italy came as both homage to one of his trips, but also to complete my Heaven chapter of my series in the absolute center of my faith. It's one thing to want something but when it comes to actually doing it, it's scary to experiment in the idea that it is ok to do something for you for a change.

When my company went bankrupt, I was left with the idea that I could not do this trip. I shouldn't do this trip. I need to be responsible. Do I cut my losses on what I already invested into this or do I proceed with what I desire? Who am I to ask for help down the line if I did this trip and things aren't put in order when I get back? This honestly was something I wanted and I felt that it was being stolen from me. I actually felt anger and jealousy the last day of work knowing my boss was going on a 3 week Arctic cruise and wouldn't even be with his team on the last day when we were all to be told we no longer had a job.

I remember thinking this place has taken allot away from me and although I should not have been jealous, but it was like... 'Where's my turn and when is it ok for me to just live?' So much responsibility had prior that when it came time to relinquish it even a little bit in vacation mode, the entire company crashed and left to once again sacrifice something of my life due to responsibility of other people's actions.

The funny answer to that is I always have had that opportunity to do that. Live life that is. I understand the responsibility of work and the necessary aspect to staff properly to balance out the required aspect of time outside of work. Even when in a position where I was finally making money twice what I was making in Atlanta, there was barely a chance to sepearate work responsibility into vacation. Too much of essential worker with deadlines that always needed to be met. The fact known that I should had been making twice that amount anyways based on responsibility was known since 2015 based on fair market value of dual roles and added on responsibility. Where things went towards the end was never understanding to the responsibility present to others along with the further financial exploitation done towards myself and others. Project managers peaced out on vacation during production of catalogues and even I questioned how was that even approved? Not my business as the Creative

Director and I tried where we could to schedule any type of vacation that was never allowed to happen. I suppose it is none of my business. Simply questions where there is what others can do and what I should do. The choice made where noted what surrounds words. It is a change in perspective that needed to occur in order for me to see that. There are the things we can do for ourselves and we shouldn't worry much about what others can and cannot do. I have to say to myself, 'You never know how rundown you were until you are taken out of a situation and able to process it eventually.' That's an undeniable truth in any personal or professional environment and definitely factored in later capacity at two other places of employment after 2017. Unhappiness can come across as surviving and happiness a foreign thing reserved for the "better" people. One can thrive in survival mode, but it never will be sustained for very long. Every one told me not to cancel this trip. 'To just Do it'. 'Worry about everything later.' "Have faith" was the common theme of direction and probably appropriate considering where I am going and the intention behind this trip.

Leave it to good fortune; my family came across the gifts from my childhood from my grandmother who previously was mentioned. From the time I was born until her passing, every year for my birthday she gave me a savings bond. She didn't believe in cash or gifts for birthdays. From those bonds, was enough money to go on this trip without feeling guilty of responsibility. I kind of feel like it's the last gift my grandmother could have given me in saying, "Oh no...you are going on this trip, here...I'll make sure of it." Those were provided from a safety deposit box and given to me during my unemployment.

So in this angle of reflection, I bring with me my cousin, my grandfather, my grandmother, my mom and ML who all have guided me in their own way for once in my life experiment with desire vs. responsibility. This trip is equally grounded in responsibility to finish what I vowed to do so, but for now I am equally blessed that faith is pushing me in the right direction as I start cashing in what I planned for myself over 20 years ago. Each of those 3 reflections may tell a different story of myself, but in the end it will always be my story no matter the size I feel in each. When shooting for the moon you may find yourself amongst the stars. I have zero idea what to expect, but I have faith that this is the right thing to do.

Til then...next entry will be from Rome.

In regards to Alfred Angelo…
It's a lengthy topic of discussion for me to sort out. I worked 3 years at one of
the world's largest designers and manufacturer of wedding gowns.
Amazing the stories had of 80 years of immigrants to #1 and even in Sears
at the pinnacle of catalogs? There is fallout there of a legacy of connection to
marriages which is always the most important matter of the heart. Expansion, ambition and dreams before. When did things change and when did it
become about other things of discussion? Never my story to be told there,
but I at least know what I reaped in sowed thoughts electronically towards
answers.

First and foremost, the issue of non-payment for photography.
A revoking of licensed rights by the matter of

"Can we just make this one go away?" (A-AA)

Breach of services, breach of trust, breach of all images licensed by Alfred
Angelo. (Something I am sure Kip Meyer would be interested in doing) as
agents willfully booked talent while not only in financial trouble, but while
participating in business practices that resulted, up to but not limited, to 6
months before receiving payments for most vendors.

A motto of "Rob from Peter to pay Paul" was adopted & perceived internally.

This included when payment were not made to myself past the 30-days limit
while also paying a down payment to another photographer for their upcoming services. No money for one thing, but money for others. "They can wait."
mentality.
No…and no payment after can make up for that. A quick glance at signed
agreements understanding verbalized requested & completely spelled out
signed agreements in non-disgregard. I spent my Christmas validating from
facts a price point to something I was already threatened to be a part of. You
already had a decision in hand prior to any work I did on being fair and what
I discovered. When you wanted something to just go away; so much went
away and it is never coming back by force.

There was a willful exploitation of creative/marketing staff including a printing company owned by one of the employed graphic designers who was left

with a liability between 10-20K for catalogs and other printed sales materials. This was all done under the pretense of money shortages and cash flow issues.

I, myself was pressured into a photography role under pretense of guilt and company responsibility for far below the fair market price of services.

"What do you want me to do? Go down to the local college and beg?"
(A-AA)

"You know in the corporate world;
people get fired for not doing what they are told..."
(A-AA)

"Marketing is to act as indentured servitude."
(A-AA)

I remember senior management saying,
"We were told by the lawyers to stop taking orders."
"Cash only."
(A-AA) (About a week from closure of AA)

That was around the time I said it sounded like we are going out of business.
They still took orders for another day or so.
I can say frantic or can say awareness. At this point...guard up...all ears then.
Not like their weren't prior in non-disclosure of what was going on in the company.)
There were restructuring plans written to be executed. 3 of them.
Major layoffs regardless would have occurred regardless, but in the end, every one lost their job when the safety net for the credit cards was upped to a price they couldn't afford with their cash on hand. An evaluation of risk assessed.
Its' not my place to say how I discovered that, yet of importance to note options were taken and weighed by others and there was a lack of communication. My discovery was disclosed in gasping measures to all of marketing present at the time.
We were told the decision was quick and immediate, but (through credit reps in the field) that is just not the way it works. Credit card companies do not simply hold other companies hostage without warning. It was known to senior management that there was an eviction notice on the office space. 3-4 weeks out to my knowledge. Cash flow issues were apparent my entire 3 years of employment.

I imagine a change of credit agreements & liabilities does not happen in a day or so, especially in regards to a few millions in reserved funds. An introduction to bridal all around had in that regard of one of the most emotional businesses out there.

"Some of them will have to work from home for a while." (AAK)
-An open-door discussion
-Further conversations with (AAB) confirmed what was heard.
(A month out from closure)

Some parties knew enough prior, the rest of us figured it out in passing. Can't fault survival instinct. In regards to if this was read why I typed, then that survival instanct I can fault because you already impeded on this book.

I was told the Vice President of Marketing requested specific online monitoring of my work computer, but he was told we can't afford that. That was from (AAK) to (AAB) to me. I was the only one. I asked in first party for verification of to no repsonse years later by the head of IT of AA. I suppose I could as the former VP all these years later, but if you want to get to questions on why single out one sole employee on surveillance in that capacity, I'd work around to go to sources first before I get to that question. Especially in vocalizations and things of 2015. I understood and understand the connections from where I was told and who that was told about not knowing the other aspects as well. All verifiable where it comes down who reacted off of vocalization and who reacted off truth and coming to reasonable questions. Couldn't find that Head of IT on facebook, but asked it in official capacity through private Linkedin to get to the answers of what I have experienced since Alfred Angelo.

-Marketing office threats were made of computer monitoring around the time of (AAMC) departure. I want to say that these comments were made about 1-1.5 years from time of closure. Group comments in Marketing of monitoring that simply did not exist made by A-AA in Alfred Angelo structure. Where did that come from in 2015?
There must have been a reason why I was singled out on that. Not the first time. I was accused, in an open space by the VP with co-workers present, of stealing a company laptop that I didn't even realize until after the fact of closure that I have in my possession. They never asked for equipmentor testimony anyways in what occurred or for answers to creditors.
(Things get shuffled when you lose a home and pack everything up.)
It was found on my website built on my own private computer rebuilt with

the right key commands.

I've now lost 2 homes because of companies actions of negligence.

Where exactly do you return a laptop when there are no employees left. The CFO stayed on for a bit after the lay-off. Head of HR was for a single day. There's the court appointed lawyer, but I have more questions on why we didn't get our 60 days severance more than where to return property. Questions now on it on taxation on pennies on the dollar years later, but especiallyt in aspects of others weighing options to what was was occuring. If the end goal was pennies on the dollar for something of the marriage aspect, you still should probably stay away from the advantage of that downfall if you were involved in the possible buying aspect while there is awareness on multiple fronts of what it means to be in the bridal business where every marriage is a pennies variable to make ends meet and be worthy of some-one's love and partnership.

Away from vulnerable uncomfortability.... VP decisions to even mention Grindr to others in coworkers of office or across the world in relationship to I. Especially in 'promiscuous' aspects of painting me as a whore to assure you my sexual exploits and adventures are none of you business and those comments were reprehensible and we do not know each other in that capac-ity. The things people cite of others if often that which we relate to the most. If you want to talk about faux Alphabet games based off of second-hand accounts, a real alphabet game occurred in a different capacity. (No relation, but years later of note. In either regard, don't knock the Alphabet game in either regard of exploration.)

Comments were made of my pressumed sexual exploits in front of co-workers by the VP of Marketing, including topics of the use of Grindr, which is unbecoming of a senior officer.

A time-travel where I don't care your sexual orientation or comfortability. Anyone's sexuality is personal and intimate to select few or offered up in a capacity of putting food on the table or freely expressing oneself legally understanding the cost of others. The only thing I ever mentioned to the VP of marketing was in relation to another coworker who I actively stayed away from but understood the comfortability to approach me in candidness of de-sired photoshoots and was not comfortable in return. I simply said I retired from photography and stayed away there after. I respect the candidness, I do not respect the disregard on the other side. Perhaps the same could be said for I as advancement is always an awkward discussion. Insinuating myself as promisous or natural connection of such in regards to the LGBTQIA+ community is where I take warrent and you arent privileged to that answer.

There are many personal moments to recite and some already written down and intertwined within my, "Divine Comedy" as I searched for myself to find peace, acceptance and to get to a point of growth that somehow was meaningful to me to include what little bit I did.

Never self-made, but self-driven to grow.
Your experiences with others shape you.
Good. Bad.
All of it.

It is a combination of self-desire and human interaction that makes up my story. My mind is aware that I cannot focus entirely on negative, nor does it feel what has been written in those pages to be that.

There is something in the things I don't want to type out. But it is coming to the point that these are the things that have defined me or will define me. Separate conversations on the responsibility of what I write with myself. Am I changing the context writing out now knowing the beauty of reserved? Only in understanding what occcured from 2019 to present. A conflict of time and place knowing something being discovered at the same time in a span of 12 years of my life transcribed at multiple entry points in my life to complete a narrative told.

I remember my first day at Alfred Angelo. (Dinner the night prior) with (AAMC) and (AG). Everything prior led up to the chance of a lifetime. I walked into office wearing a Cerulean Blue shirt knowing this was a brave new journey of learning for me. I met Michele first in the morning and my first interaction with her was viewing the upcoming year's Disney Wedding dresses. Never a privilege prior as it was always top secret to design. An open door to openness. A quiz took place on figuring out which dress belonged to which princess. I am proud I got them mostly right. It was a different way of thinking seeing a princess concept realized in dress form. Color helped me of course. By the time Year 2 came, I understood a little bit better as I learned different types of dress styles.
I'll always remember being nervous....not knowing my role, but growing into

it from her, AG and AAMC. Michele jokingly made me question my Savannah upbringing and rightfully so. I remember a cognizant catching myself mid- "Ma'am" with the look knowing exactly what she was about to say. Beat Red, "I get it". It took some getting used to on my part, but I did break it eventually. I'm thankful for that memory. 'Don't say ma'am to everyone.' Moments trusted.
Trust built.
I admire her and the legacy her family created.
The intimacy of bridal.
Dreams from a kid to grown.

Michele grew up in that environment created by her parents where history lays in Pittsburgh before ending up in Delray Beach.

She studied abroad and designed for Dior. I knew her as Chief Creative Officer. A title coming back into a company she was removed from previously. What I know of before me, her brother Vincent ran the company. At some point, ownership of the company shifted hands. He was not there when I was employed. She was though.

I remember questioning what I could or could not approach her about. That came from respect. Over time there was comfort in approach.Trust learned on eitherside in questions where I imagine uch of I to learn.

I remember writing her a card. It was thankful in approach. I included it with a gift of "The Devil Wears Prada". Given, not as a joke, but appreciation that she had shifted the course of my life as someone with no fashion background. Connection there as roles similar but different. Isn't that the place of any good story though? Relateability. Never my Chief Creative Officer of that characterization and was always meant to be a symbolic 'fish out of the water' thank you for taking a chance on me. A story of associations had yet simply not the same in regards to many things. A structure prior in reference and in my regard a wondering aspect of reaching to departments for understanding that didn't happen prior and then being stopped from saying hello to simply succeed and have the company who believed in I succeed as well from talking to one another.

I'm hesitant about the memory that has started this stream of consciousness. A secondary thought pops up instead of when I first started. AA used to pay for all healthcare. Every little bit. A transition occurred when HR was brought on the following year. 'Too much front-loading...', they said in the newly formed HR department.

How did a company this large not have an HR prior?

Families grow...

As transition occurred, that was eliminated as front-loading was not affordable in cash aspects. Perhaps I see a legacy her family wanted was to take care of the AA family as their own. That was a decision made by the board to remove that. Makes me wish I had got sick Year 1 instead of Year 2. So much insurance could had been spread while questioning why I was throwing up 15-20 times a day without an answer as lay-offs occurred while I was getting them. The best I have for an answer is anxiety and what you put in your body. I understand my VP was going through Chemo at the time and what I was experiencing was seperate but was noted 'He's going through the same thing.' (Paraphrase) while I lost appetite and simply tried to eat when I could. It couldn't be a connection, but it was made and noted and carried on slightly into ATL. 2.0 before eventually going away. Anxiety and unnecessary responsibility factors in both regards and locations.

I recall the first time I was flown to Pennsylvania.

A change of guard.

Thrown off by CD mentality on either regard from said on one side and never got the chance until later to learn the other side. .

Didn't get a chance to know them at the time. When Sunny Song came back into the picture, I like to think we worked very well together and never really discussed prior or people. She pushed my creative side and nurtured. A direct opposite of AA-MC, but welcomed to be given a chance. There were similarities to each other of ourselves. Two Scorpios and definitely lots to be learned from either of us. Sunny approached things in a way that meshed with my mentality. I like that she valued other's opinions and gave responsibility accordingly as much as I began setting boundaries of positions and responsibilites due from prior experience. She was the CD in the end and I was learning from her as I would hope I was teaching the graphic designers as well.

I do miss her.

We talked every morning.

Part of the process with one on-site and the other located in PA.

Greyness in some areas, but I always gave respect to those who give it in return. Always a collaboration with her decision that I would always defer to. I remember having to fill her in on the behind-the-scenes as they occurred. Not fair from a distance to go through indirect channels to discover the downfall of Alfred Angelo. Always a right-hand man, even though I'm left-handed.

Where was that understanding by those above me? Wouldn't be expected as they werent telling people in office anyways.

I remember there being a fatal error done under one of the CEO's leadership. Major decisions made in factories and their transition to new places in China. Chinese laws change constantly and apparently there was a move made based on old laws that cost the company millions during the transition.

There were frequent board meetings had from the time I started until Alfred Angelo closed its doors.

That one in particular was leading towards Michele's leaving of the company in disagreement.

The final one ended with laughter when there should had been none.

"At least they will have closure"

It was common knowledge that Czech Asset Management controlled operations with internal parties involved in it. The new CEO, Rich Anders, was a connection to Steve Czech when the board ousted Paul Quintel. Michele, as Chief Creative Officer, was not involved in that board decision and removed-herself from her family's company.

She quit over the decision.

Family first I imagine.

A reminenant of trust & who she cares for.

I'll always erspect that not knowing everything nor do I need to.

To walk away from that was enough to witness of a history I barely knew.

But definitely took things personally as AA was treated like her family with relationships that spanned not just decades, but generations. There was another connection to Czech Asset Management with the CFO got demoted to VP of finance. THe new CFO only came in occasionally and was not located on-site. (Neighbor Settings)

I am not privy to all of the behind the scenes, but I know the people who were.

I remember walking at night after AG walked Michele out of the building and coming across a woman utterly destroyed at what I pieced together later on. I will never forget seeing her. In hindsight, I was witness to someone seeing a legacy no longer in her control. A family taken away. 80 years of family history now in someone else's hands. Later those same hands destroyed that history at an exponential rate.

As one of the many things burned into my mind, I will never forget that moment and it begs me to rationalize if I should write this or not. But that shook me. Humanization of a very human person who has always kept the appearance of composure and strength. Perhaps it takes more strength to walk away than it does to stay.
Everyone is afforded their moment in that capacity and all I could do was silently gesture however I could of being there. It was not required and completely understood.

I asked if there was anything I could do. A moment made between two people and the car window; but that was her moment. Not mine. I protect that. I wish I had done more, but I wanted to give her respect. Probably the truest moment of my life of an American Dream stolen. I hold onto the files that I have because that is her family and her legacy as well as my own now as well. I'm grateful to have been allowed to be a part of, "HER Dream. HER Dresses."

Their dresses & legacy. The inclusion of her family photos on the updated website denotes family attachment as much as the 'We're Back' denotes someone of prior attachment understanding or not that 'Not all of us are back.' The inclusion of the family photos perceived as a total disregard to what occurred prior in ownership or ownership/acknowledgement of re-sponsibilit of an 80+ year legacy that factored in so many weddings across decades. I saw it as a sign that it didn't matter to some of stealing a family history or their family photos or simply what could be and still just should had been thought about differently if it was family reclaimed in a different capacity. The acknowledgement of what happened was glossed over. From my miniscule contribution to a family legacy and indiret of marriages, or from the aspect of a family business torn apart one way or another and then sold pennies on the dollar while negating every single bride and wedding party who had their (supposed only wedding day) disrupted by a compa-ny that could had fulfilled the dress obligations and closed down if that is what they wanted to do. That retail space is not retail and it was addressed thankfully with none of my photography or graphic design contributions on their website when turned back on from whomever the owner is/was. It was noted in both strange and of respect. Thank you for understanding I never would had said, 'We're Back' and my work was acknowledged as being some-thing not a part of any transition in that regard for one reason or another. The Piccione's were not a part internally of the closing of Alfred Angelo and I stand by things occurred after the family left that denotes what could or should only be a private conversation on the difference of lack of adaptation to trends and market.

Similarities in every situation. Until then...breathe.
Next page tomorrow...today...whenever.

In regards to this first hand account, I'm always protective as no matter the circumstance that was an American Dream of original immigrants that became Bridal Dreams of so many others. Their life story is not mine to flesh out but one understood of cherish and appreciation of the indirect and direct aspect their family had on unions and relationships and how that could had grown one way or another based on any decision leading to where it ended up in complete closure. I don't know...that ending of morals and beliefs brought someone back a second time and I witnessed first hand what others do for family legacy and how we can't control everything or simply things grow and we have to defer. That moment of coming back from retirement or perhaps more importantly in that car was her moment that I came upon and I'm honored that I was allowed to continually learn from afterwards

A difference of being sculpted in one area or another. Thank you. My employment was ultimately your decision above any of the others and I don't regret one aspect the uproot on my end and the chance provided to I on yours and those you chose around you in your family's company.

The Alfred Angelo site has been purchased by new owners. I found out from James Wisdom who condemned it, but made people aware. He probably found out from Andrew Georgiou. Post were made from the company's social media. I didn't get to see them before they were taken down, but backlash was swift from both wholesale accounts and the thousands of brides that were screwed over with their wedding day always married to the negligence in the downfall of Alfred Angelo.

In bankruptcy, "We the employees" did not get our severance. To some they didn't even get a day's notice. The responsibility of whomever takes over that name is to fix all the legacies assigned to it. You can't just say, "We're Back".

WE aren't back.
The 'We' in question, especially considering the elimination of middle people.

1000s of lives changed from that company ending the way it did.
I see what they are trying to do though. Eliminate the bodies and
go online only with E-Commerce. Which is exactly what they should have
been doing for the 3 years I worked there. (In building e-commerce that is.)
It was discussed internally but never set-up properly as the website update
to responsive design was a task within itself. To go e-commerce in the age
of the digital bride was a priority but the funds never set aside for it. How
does one handle the model bridal structure without removing the magic of
finding a dress and trying it on? The insurance of shipping dresses until the
bride frinds the right one would had been astronomical I image as dresses
hundreds or a few thousand dollars through the mail system invites theft on
something not easily tracked on the secondary market. Interest there where
elimination ideas present where in bridal, the dress finding experience just
isn't the same.

Licenses revoke when change of ownership.
Licenses are revoked when past due date of payments.
Licenses are taken away when you want invoices to...
                "Make this...Just go away..." (AA-A)
Any of my images that I legally own the copyright to will never be allowed on
that site until people are made whole.
Questions on why none of my images appeared on that role-out of discussion
still of interest.

(I'm wondering what it means when I no longer see any of my images on their preview page in all its modifications)
Someone aware and someone knew...

Whoever "we" is needs to just rebrand and start from scratch.
As noted, when I saw it, that legacy of closing has damaged the brand for at least 7-10 years. Longer to the wholesale accounts already burned by Alfred Angelo before with the opening of retail stores to compete with DAVID'S bridal in the ever-changing bridal market. To repair that relationship, I wanted to approach the At-A-Glances as a toolkit to educate and embolden the wholesale accounts on the brand, but that concept never got to be fully realized. Trust needed to be built back from them towards Alfred Angelo. The company and wholesale accounts need to know how to sell its product. Everything was there to begin with, but it needed to be put down in words. Tightened. Refined. An audience for every collection. I remember when I first mentioned that. A concept that did get executed over time to success. We spent 3 years course directing and sailing towards that. 3 years and we almost had it. I'd say the 4th would have fixed the last few things that were missing. There is no repairing that name. Only explanation of what occurred and going elsewhere under the same people. Leave AA alone.

"Truly Yours" was a needed entry. Completely reliant on I in visuals of understanding.
Personality. Destination. Individuality.
"Team Amateurs."
A name used by us in marketing when left to our own to spread our wings and connect with our generation. We were most successful in social media & marketing when
allowed to do so. It was not a mistake or "by chance" or a "happy accident".
It was
skillsets put to good use, not valued to what they should be by people not understanding individual's roles and value.

Your creatives make or break a brand.

I walked out of the marketing department over those comments. I'd do it over and over again because I can not bring myself to curse you out in front of other country's representatives in the same place you joked about GRIN-DR. In silence is my strong point. At least I said enough is enough inside. Maybe others did as well.

Post 14: The second sphere: day 1: Rome

"Truth is I know I have to give up everything that I know or thought I knew with this final bow. I've never been one to be able to easily un-attach from things. Values of things have changed even if I cannot forget the experiences. I forgive for sure, but some things have meaning that is hard to forget and I know I never will. Some things in life have pushed me in directions that are uncompromising while others have formulated paths completely unintended but welcomed after the fact. I remember everything. I hate that. I really do.

But at the same time one of my biggest fears in life is also not being able to remember anymore. I think I write more than I should as insurance if I ever do happen to not be able to remember, that there is something there to remind me of who I was and where I was going and this is what I want to remind myself of. Life is not without irony so it's not something I'd put past it to do that I'd forget. Is this I being over thinking again? Is this I not able to handle things? Or is this I taking in every bit of life experience and driving others and myself crazy sharing to find some life meaning reason why I used the bathroom this morning?

Perhaps it's not a bad thing to forget.
In doing so you can make the same mistakes over and over and there is never any remorse or reflection." 5/13/14

I land not knowing a thing about how to get from the airport to the hotel. I should be exhausted but as it comes from any past experience, I simply cannot sleep when excitment and adventure is in the air and awaits. I consider the train but then I understand how that plays out for me based on my first visit to New York City from La Guardia and turning down a limo ride to the city in lieu of doing it myself travel of figuring out the bus system only to screw up that on a longer than expected bus trip before the reintroduction of help and the kindness of strangers to get me back on my feet. A good memory where it was admiration I suppose of my first solo trip then and this my first solo trip here. I imagine this is a little bit out of my comfort zone where I understand lost here is really lost until I start familiarizing just a little bit better than before. This time I think I'll pay for the cab and at least know I'll eventually get to my destination. It gives me a chance to see things along the way and ask questions if need be. From airport to Rome you can see the cityscape change and get a sense of history understanding that at least I know I'll get where I am supposed to be in a proper amount of time.

This is my first day in Rome. I know no one here. I am completely in my own world and it's what I make it. I arrived to my hotel early and I am checking my bags and going out instantly into exploration mode. I'm 5000 miles away that anything I know and my time is short. I have to make the best of this. As much as I have wanted to do this with other people, I kind of feel like this is meant to be my own journey and I'll be ok doing this. I didn't invite anyone on the trip and although the introductions of things already there, it was important to do this trip with no labels and come to my own conclusions one way or another on where things were going, where things had gone and reconcile one way or another in a place of new environment and experience. With every trip a new version of yourself is had in experiences that are never going to be quite the same. A first time for one could be a passing rememberance for others on their travels back to the same city where it is impossible not to recall the first experience while living the second, third, fourth etc. I imagine if one wanted to do a vacation with someone, it is always best to go somewhere neither have gone before in the first few trips before backtracking to places they have already travelled. That is unless there is a love and desire there of memories fond or connections made. Nostolgia factors in there where unassuming partners and friendly companions travel with you one way or another in what is neither good or bad. In the scheme of things quite beautiful. In the end it is about sharing moments or past experience.

At the time I was not officially in a relationship and that was important because when unemployed that matters. A constant feeling of inadequacy present as it wasn't until Florida that I actually made enough money to travel to begin with. Now I make nothing and I understand that is a contention for I. Always has been. In long distance that matters. In short-term it is on the forefront. There is respect and there is understanding. A relationship was building but no status attached to it just as much as any other when thinking of space and simply what to do with building connections. Long distance at best at the time of what was entertained. Keeping distance and growing until one realizes one thing or the other about arm's length growing one way or another. No constraints and European in approach as this trip was about many things, however it was important to discover a bit of myself which you would think I would had been doing the past 3 years, but it is always on vacation where surprises come out one way or another that cannot be replicated back in the reality of the day-to-day. I carried in my heart may things that needed to get sorted out internally. All I want to do is explore this brave new world. 'Headphones on: out the door.' 'I can do this. I will be ok.' I'm going to write as I go on this trip and it may become out-of-place narrative-wise, but each moment will spell itself out, as it should, even if it is disjointed. I will fill things in after the fact. In reflection of doing this I thought the 10-hour flight would be hard, but I was surprised that it actually was not bad. I do recommend not doing a window seat for a long flight. It makes an awkward moment when needing to use the restroom at 4am and having to wake someone up to do it. But at least I know for next time. I am going on probably 2 hours of sleep at this point. I'm so exhausted but adrenaline is alive and well. 'Out the door... Headphones on. Adventure Begins' as my hotel was near the presidental building. I played my Final mix to Brave New Secrets from 2014 and went about my day one way or another in and out of headphones to connect accordingly and see where things go in that regard.

I went first to the central part of Rome today and the Plaza. From there the coliseum and found myself just walking around and exploring. The amazement of floating street performers and gypsies loving respect and understanding from others that the same are far more wealthier than you think. Secrets everywhere on the streets from every individual who either is visiting or makes Rome their home. In building to building, the size of such things do not do justice from any picture knowing they are far older than anything in the United States. You can feel the history of thousands of footprints walking down one path or another over the centuries. From walkways and paths, you can see where history came, crumbled, rebuilt and rearranged in ways as if visually you can piece back arenas in a capacity as if they breathe the same life they when they were built. I came across the Trevi Fountain in passing on my way to the Pantheon. I'd pull pictures from the trip but it is what it is there. Someone valued them more than I to take them from me that I'll just do my illustrations when and if need be. Memories in the head and not required in directness and translation. Perspective is always more important. At least it is understood that things surrounding certain aspects of my life seem to just always, 'disappear'.

I wish I had mapped out this trip better, but nevertheless I like that I just find things as I do. Adventure awaits in simply what you come across and guided one way or another. The fountain came at a particular part of travelling through the city. All by foot, it was important to note to return to it in the evening. The lit waters of sculptures illuminated across the statue of Oceanus and the Tritons. I did not understand then the same way as I do now but knew to respect of such a feat of a fountain. To sit and listen as well as water flows and tourist travel. Often I play music but also just like that it gives a false sense of unawareness. Headphones on, but I'm listening around me. A part of street smarts I guess as unassuming is always what gets looked for in certain scenarios. If I wander to the wrong areas, at least I'll know pretty quickly. Probably not so much smart to reveal as such, but for the everyday person they wouldn't know the wiser. It is understood the magnitude of the sculpture and representation although

I don't look it up the same way. There are messages in there heard or understood that perhaps is personal and drawn from the time years later. I imagine if you thought the Mona Lisa's size was a disappointment in person you are missing the point of small things doing great things in comparison. From the perspective of a child, one could understand better that which is being presented in concept. Once an adult gets it they too understand that when it comes to representation, there is always something bigger that connects to something bigger and a choice to scale it back or amp it up one way or another. A journey begins undertstand I am thankful for how I got here.

In blind tradition of understanding of observance, a wish was made from the observance or perhaps from either looking up or asking of the people around myself. I would say it was probably from observance as I have not spoken much on this trip. From my back towards the fountain I cast it into the fountain with a kiss of a coin before doing such. Faith and trust on being here. From there I was not sure what was born of such a wish. The journey has gone one way or another in amazing directions. A video of such that I know I can pull or simply remember what I was searching for or wishing. It definitely was a path towards one thing or another and to be steered in the right directions. At the time so much transition and fluidness was up in the air where perhaps it best to contemplate what I get introduced to one way or another. Respect paid and we go from there with blind ambition of discovery.

'A Thought into the Fountain Trevi. Blind Trust in Memory or in Thought' - Sketch Translation'
December 1, 2022. "Philip A. Bonneau.

There really isn't any map at this point in Rome; my itinerary is pretty much set for Florence and the Vatican where perhaps I could had planned this better. What is a vacation if constantly on deadline and appointment all day long. It is not like I'll get to experience everything anyways. 2-days Rome, 3-days Florence 1-night Venice then back to Rome for another evening. Everything else is an added bonus and I find it completely humbling that art is so much a factor to this city.

The Pantheon was a must to do on this trip. It's over 2000 years old and one of the best-preserved monuments in Rome. It's has a sordid history before ultimately becoming a church of respect to past culture and history knowing it was built for one thing and then transformed into another. That usually is how things go one way or another in life as well I imagine. Wanted to do one thing, went for it and then ended up becoming something else. A history there of understanding spaces represent many things and only transform in advanced meaning as it grows in age and experience. Preservation of such of one of the oldest standing structures of Rome. I imagine it isn't going anywhere anytime soon while understanding thoughts back to transitional living and the borrowing of one space or another.

Although in fairness, I stayed on the outside and just imagined being inside of it in the evening. Alone and weighted in darkness where light shines through while the artifical lights are turned off. A natural occurance of being at the right place and time to have the full effect of the imagination. I imagine at some point it was designed to have the moon overhead as if to fill the gap complately. Perhaps a thought of when it rains where water drips from the open roof that is now surely covered to a floor as if a Baroque lighting scheme of divine light flooded in combination of elements upon an environment of darkened interiors exists. The weight of such an image would be again added on gravitas to an already weighty internal. Perhaps the eye adjusts to some of the details present while little bits here and there present themselves in ad-justment. If you can't take it all in at once, best to let it breathe afterhours. Would the blue casts convey a depiction of nighttime, or does one look at it in dawn or twilight with reds, oranges and purples where more of the environment would be seen. To get the intensity of such is a question as it is designed to fill the space with light anyways.

I imagine an emptiness of the space as if the moon is directly above it to shine the most amount of light. Direct where the gravitas of the environment is what takes hold as one is flooded with thoughts and images. The tapping of the raindrops upon the floor as if all to join on the same level before splashing here or there until eventually accumulation sets in and one starts to see a ripple effect that spreads across the floor.

In such a space the sounds of the tapping on the floor begins to echo in magnification where even if a bird were to land at the rooftop portal, it now doubt would be a bellowing sound to be here from the silent tapping on the floor.

'Pantheon Internal' - Sketch Translation' November 28 2022. "Philip A. Bonneau.

I'm currently sitting in the middle of the square in the evening right across from it. Piazza della Rotonda as it is called. There is a street performer singing Jeff Buckley's "Hallelujah". I don't know why, but I am crying listening to this. I record him afterwards as such knowing the transendance of culture and song always carries from one land to another. Sometimes it is what just occurred or to the left or right that matters in notation for later on. Something feels right about being here at this moment. Just listen to what is around you. Catch the performers and conversations around you. "Your faith was strong but you needed proof" I guess that kind of resonates at the moment. For dinner I met this elderly couple from Clearwater, FL. I interjected into their conversation over phone issues they were having at the time and from there they kind have adopted me for the rest of the evening. We chatted and introduced one another. Here's a couple that spends 2 months out of the year in a new world every year. Their reasoning for doing so is not only that Rome is their favorite city, but also that they promised themselves that they will see the world when they were younger. I told them I was traveling alone and with thoughts of my grandfather and my art series on my intentions why. I think there was mutual admiration in our intents and we spent hours talking about life and where to go, what to see and just intention in general. I don't think I can forget their words when talking about current situations, "You are so far removed at the moment from anything you know or knew. You are going to find out things about yourself you never thought were there and you are definitely going to find the answers to your questions here." Best advice they gave me was to remove yourself entire from everything and you will be guided exactly towards what you are looking for.

I don't know what I am going to experience or learn from this trip, but if today was any indication of what is to come, then I feel I made the right decision in this trip to explore and understand that here I don't know much and the discovery aspect is what is most important. I know some. I'll learn elsewhere. Respect of cultures thrown into the fountain and none-stop on day one.

I'm exhausted but I don't want to miss a moment of this. I remember the same emotions when I went to the Bahamas for my 30th solo. Within 2 hours I was adopted by a group of women who asked me the same question, "Why travel alone?" For that trip it was about people not making up their mind and me never wanting to make a big deal about a birthday. This trip, I dunno. I like the idea of being lost in a place I know nothing about. No schedule. No expectations. This is my time. I never thought I could do this or be here. Soul-searching and understanding the frugality aspect of my journey here as money is going to be tight when I get back. Cheers to tomorrow.

Aimlessly wander the world wondering what is in store for you;
if only you open your eyes.

I came across a magician today. A known trick to give the appearance of floating, but I can't help but admire the persistance to sit still for hours. As I have struggled my entire life to be able to do so for long periods of time. Even as a child I had to be strapped to my desk. The truth continues into adulthood where at best I find it humorous that I sit for hours on end typing and revising book after book in electronic form. I suppose it is now a combination of simply knowing what is important or not.

I am sure there is an illusion to this magician, yet why look it up and try to break it? The study of such takes time, patience and a craftiness of the eye. Is it comfortable? Seems to be as one does so without strain or pressure. Does it bring in good money? 'Dhalsim in Italy' was the initial thought. I imagine combine floating in air with some yoga fire and you are going to be making some great money daily in wonder and amazement. I couldn't help but think I've never seen street performers like I have here in Rome. Travelling bands one way or another. My only points of reference is perhaps in New Orleans or New York City, but never a total sense that these people can be from anywhere in the world with fair greater ease here than back home. I imagine much the same as there or anywhere of international cities and interests.

'As I walk by every incredible sculpture and building that I come across here I can't help but think of the value of holding onto artistic contributions. Some of these monuments represent the best and worst times of this country. Perhaps if America had a couple thousand years behind them to heal wounds, they would feel the same.'

Coming here together to share a talent and live a life.
Is this living or just the beginning?

ENTRY 40:

If I wanted to write today I would, but I think I'm ready to revisit some past writings when the time is right. I need to be more aware that spatially I am having issues now.

In my head
Out my head
Overthinking
Underthinking
Perspective in
Inward Thinking
Attempt to
Catch up to now

I vaguely remember signing something. Part of my breakdown I imagine. Was that in my head? Was that real? I remember struggling to sign documents when left alone. I remember not having any clear answers on where I was or why. Fog. Confusion. No answers. Maybe I was not asking the right questions when not of sound mind. 5-6 days before someone sat me down. I remember someone grabbing stacks of patient files. I remember demanding a drug test and to be released. I remember feeling something is wrong and asking to go to a hospital...calling 911. They wouldn't let me go or leave. Pulled A fire alarm to get out of there and that just put me in the quieter section of the hospital which I was thankful for as I was finally able to sleep. Told 3 days at doctor's discretion when that leads the room for whatever they wanted to do. Did I even have a doctor? I have to admit to myself I broke down. There are gaps missing. Signing something day 5 or 6 does not absolve the questions prior when clearly not of sound mind as noted by doctors or I would had been released prior to my 11 day stay coming to an end. No double jeapordy there disgarded on their part...

'You can't just walk up to a place of business unannounced..'
Comment heard of the officer guarding my hospital door as is probably standard practice to surveillance an person who attempts suicide as a medical representative is in the room at all times. Noted said externally, but may or may not have been directed towards I.

245

I was left alone.

I was met by others privately of scenarios that did or did not playout. Was there signing of documents and trying to hold on at the very end while in no clear conscious mind to be explaining illegal activity and citing names and events, but I did my best in what I remember.

I am asking questions now and I am finding out from Kenny and my mother that it was not clear where I was. It took 3 days until my mother knew where I was. 11 days stayed. I'm not sure I am ready write everything of those days. HiPAA violations if I were to write things to the audience in my mind. Privacy; raped.

But perhaps this is my mind sorting this out.

(Slamming of the swing door)

"Phillllippppppppppp"

(Slamming of the swing door)

"Phillllippppppppppp"

(Slamming of the swing door)

(Slamming of the swing door)

(Slamming of the swing door)

Memories of 11 days where wooden doors swinging and slamming late in the evening as if slammed on purpose to keep everyone up and awake throughout the night. A mental blanket placed on someone screaming in another room as if perhaps the thought of comfort in that manner would help them before physically giving someone a blanket days later that absolutely needed one.

There is an uneasiness that lingers between my existential memory experience between Company #1 and Company #2. It's foggy at the moment. Something drastically triggered that I can't explain getting from point A to point B. Probably best not to think about it. Share moments nevertheless.

I remember tearing up paper.
Throwing it in the trash.
Abandonment.
Cameras.
Somewhat aware.
That factors in later, yet one could say fireplace in this regard.

I remember falling asleep on a bench when left in the illusion of privacy if

I ignored camera monitoring. Some woman provided documents. I'm not sure what they were. I tore up admittance documents as if I it was thought that I shouldn't be signing this as I don't understand what I am reading and cannot focus correctly. The signing a weighing of choice. I began looking for something I heard down the halls. Was it people I knew who were on the other side of places I couldn't get to. The mind playing tricks as my mother's voice in other places, (K)'s in either refusal to see me or finally seeing me. There is a difference in both of the experience. Now alone and watched in every room, camera's abound. Perhaps sleep is what I need. It didn't matter anyways. A wooden bench in the office room I was in until signing documents that I couldn't bring myself to do until days later as if fear from multiple places prior come to mind of signing anything. After my first ambulence ride of complete civility, perhaps just rest until a room is available to sleep.

I remember when a woman was admitted to Ridgeview. Signing of documents were not so privately done then vs. what my experience was. They left her in an open space naked and asleep. I went to my room and got a blanket to place over the body. It was the least I could do as it is what I would have wanted for me. Was there a difference in naked admittance?

Was there a connection to the prior thoughts from a few nights ago? It doesn't matter...respect and compassion in eith regard to strangers.

I jump to when....

(Non-Recorded Dialog)
<always present>

"NOPE."
HiPAA....
"My rights."
"Their rights."
"Look down."
"Don't look at anyone."
"No interaction."

And I didn't look up. I didn't look people in the eye there. My mind crashed. A hard reboot that 6 months later, I like the idea of trying to understand, but I can't fill all the gaps without asking questions. Even now, I am questioning if I can get the treatment I deserve from this. It was instantly removed by willful intention then after 3 minimum days. That is understood where I had to rely on my mind and body to piece togeth-

er what insurance did not provide when taken away. From a worker's comp aspect, insurance would had been able to validate the dates of hospitalization that I already verified with proper documentation.
"You are stronger than this."
Rebuilding...

I remember if I look at this with the concept that someone is watching then I have no choice but to be truthful. Truthful when of a sounder mind. Truthful when I have spoken after the fact because I am relearning to trust my mind which is not an easy experience.

It's difficult.
It's finding balance and there is truth in everything.
"Question what you have just heard."
What did I hear?
Seraphims thought of at first. Insightful questioning of pre-established tr-tuths that simply do not make sense or do.

I have an idea of what happened. but I would never sign my name to it without of sound mind and furthermore not without the presence of a licensed psychiatrist.

I still go back to that foggy memory if one was to say 'double jeapordy'. It denotes awareness of the first account and that they thought they got away with it without penalty.

I remember having just the one cigarette there. No smoking the entire time except for when I believed something major occurred that has since been proven false. The mind can equally be cruel. I remember an entire thought process of loss and asking to bum a smoke in process. Later I began going outside for fresh air. but when stuck within the confines of smoke you smell it and it does trigger. It actually was not appealing. but I needed to get out of an indoor setting. It had been days.
Imagine seeing murder occur multiple ways of your family. Forced suicide of loved ones in one scenario of revealing things on phones or a gun to the face after showing something on a phone or a drive-by bullet sprays of them walking the dogs in left or right sprays. My mother thrown from a train in a non-comical sense. An apartment raided and my dogs killed by officers when I'm not there to protect. Those images never experienced like that since and understood why perhaps those kinds of images in new experiences of senses

is perhaps understood in vividness in a place alone without any answers and anyone to talk to while not even have clothing except what I arrived in for days. In any visual sense of that intensity, I lost everyone from something horrific and those images happened while I was already under care when internally someone said, 'Is he ready to pay yet?' For days, I think I did pay something. An introduction where still somehow found comfort one way or another from one place or another.

I remember taking laps when moved to the higher security wing (It was a much-needed break from the slamming of wooden swing doors and I was able to finally sleep) But exercise was important, a chance to think and do something. Options were extremely limited there. Color. Crosswords. The other wing had more limits. At least there was TV provided. Some thing to focus the mind on in-between meals. Begin to eat when I didn't want to at all.
I read Lewis Carroll as I finally given some of my books & clothes. A kiss when the other didn't know what I experienced and to see him alive mattered. (Careful with mom & train references with CEO references).
"Father William"
"The Caterpillar"
"Dummies guide to Philosophy" was borrowed in 3 book choices provided.
"The Art of War" was gifted.
I gifted a copy of my Dali Alice in Wonderland. but it was returned to me in the middle of the night unexplained why.
Was it not the right thing to give?
Is it coincidence the same copy of Alice in Wonderland ends up in my doctor's office? I noticed it on first visit and briefly mentioned it as it had already sold out at that time.
Many questions from side 1 and side 2 of that chessboard. But for now, I need to wind down and remember to do my time sheet.

When experiences of the mind occur vividly, do they become a memory?
Yup, but always good to compartmentalize and know the difference. A trick forced to learn from Feb. 21, 2019 on.

There is a memory of a heart beat held onto for longer than sonically possible. Sitting next to myself just listening as it faded off. A release followed by a return back.

In another instance. I sat on the floor in silence. How long it was I am not entirely sure. 30 minutes perhaps? I was looking at the light shining through the window of my bedroom. From there the dust in the air floated within the rays of light that shined through. It was as if I was viewing the entire universe in something ignored everyday but always present. A wave of the hands created a dance between the dust. A world transformed by a single jesture.

There was peace in that moment.
There was peace in my heart.
There was peace in silence.

Perhaps meditation is required to re-experience that moment again. It was the only moment I asked to hold onto in the end.
It revisits every so often. When you see it, it would be in awe or simply disregard. U miss the point if one does so in that manner.

'Divinity in Dust. The Dancing of Galaxies and Worlds in Gestures' - Sketch Translation' November 18, 2022. "Philip A. Bonneau.

Did I had conversations with God there? I found something there within those walls.
I imagine in things heard there is the possibility of questions of how I lived and phoning things in while the questioning of thought became essential and eventually overcame one way or another.

I remember looking into the eyes of a patient there and I began to cry.

I was reminded of the eyes of Donna?
Could they have been the eyes of God?
Were they reflections of my own perhaps?
Every set of eyes is the holder to a universe that is completely unique to themselves. Never the two the same perspective.
At least I remember him saying to someone objectively, 'I don't think he did it.'

What is to become of me?

Even then silent protection one way or another while I figured things out.

Post 15: Day 2: The 3rd Sphere and Vatican City.
Let's get as close to God as we can get...

"My favorite word as a child was "retribution" since I heard it first in in grade school. I imagine it came from reading 'Paradise Lost' although I don't seem to find an instant direct quote to such. It was the sounding of such and not necessarily the mentality behind it. I can see if one as I child learns bullying pretty early, I can see where it pops up in social questions on life early on.

As I flipped through to quotes surrounding to be sure, the concept is there one way or another on what is 'deserved punishment' and how that plays out one way or another. I did find in equal meaning this quote.

"All is not lost—the unconquerable will, and study of revenge, immortal hate, and courage never to submit or yield: and what is else not to be overcome?" - John Milton.

I guess that probably explains my fascination with the "Divine Comedy" later on in life although I was introduced to it early on in the same capacity. Libraries of greats sitting in the living room next to the fireplace as a child. I didn't grab many of those books but every now and then they weren't just for show. There is not a better example of deserved punishment than that series of poems that state what we do in life echoes into eternity. There is always going to be a ripple for every splash made.

I talk allot about water and cause/effect in my works, probably more so with this new series. There is no way for me to totally distance the two no matter how hard I try. You have to look at it all to understand. There will never be one thing without the other. Everything is a action/reaction. Smoking leads to something. Being a bitch to others leads to something. Loving leads to something. Being guarded leads to something...everything really does leads to *something*.

There is no escape in cause. Can't exactly just sit in a room and wait for life to change because something else will come from that decision. You have to do things for yourself. The choice is always there to do or do not. Actions or inactions both create a ripple that cannot be stopped once the water is stirred. Even if it is in the mental pond of your mind.

Where do you want to throw your rock in the water? 2/18/15

'A Tale of Two Libraries (And whats underneath)' - Sketch Translation' November 28, 2022. "Philip A. Bonneau.

I look back on my choices in life and the ripples they made. I feel like if I was the person I am now that I would not make the choices I did in the past, but of course that becomes the paradox that the only reason I make those choices now is because of the past. It would be fortunate to see the future...to see where things lead and to know their outcome. Although at the same time, surprise gets lost. Imagine the thought process of now knowing the future 5 years later and going backwards knowing some of the answers and more questions elsewhere. All lessons learned and behaviors known. Over time we definitely are given the opportunity to accept who we are from experience and knowledge. A choice either way or relative Good or bad. We learn from this or that or we don't. The choice is always going to be ours. At some point the word retribution can lead to the word "penance". That point where we accept a punishment for our actions until it becomes a point that we attempt to realize that we may have been wrong and we try to find a way to offset that and do right unto others.

Penance is a funny thing.

It's something that individuals need to accept for themselves. No one else in the world can say you paid your dues when it comes to what internally you beat yourself up over or find confliction in on the search of guidance or finding new ways to respect and love yourself and others. No one can say you don't have to feel that anymore.

No one can say you have done your time in that regard. It is a choice that can only come from you. Penance can be a purgatory until you say you have done enough. Only you can free yourself from a mental prison that, in honesty, you created yourself to some degree depending on the internal infliction that simply no one can tell you when you are done with your time there, but advice had one way or another whether you want it or not. No one else is in your head. It's only you and all the different facets you create along the way. We create our own rat trap there at times. We create our own solution to the maze within or perhaps guided instinctually to answers unexplained.

I know I mull over and over on what I could have done better with others. Shit, most of my art has been me dealing with that. But not entirely accurate in that regard. It depends on which side you are looking at. There is an individual question of The What? The If? The Why? I can't say for the least I regret those mullings, because from it I somehow I found myself or at least find something worthy of talking about. I am a work-in-progress. I'm not perfect. Never will be. Maybe I held onto things of the past too long. Maybe I didn't care enough, or maybe I cared too much. Maybe my subject matter did more damage to others that offsets the positive to me. Doubtful because the only damage done that I see is simply the idea of illusions between one thing or another. Which aspect of connection is made from the investment of time and process in any love? Everything has their pluses and minuses. All those are questions that are really just in my own head. Life goes on nevertheless. For any catalyst or I.

Lovers move. Lovers find new connections. Reconciliation never occurred or perhaps it did. In the scheme of things, things that mattered lost the weight they had at one point. I find myself at the point of apathy for some emotions. We all have demons, so it is a matter of making others feel like demons do not exist or they are not at the forefront.

Truth of the matter, I don't need to think about what ifs but they are fun to entertain from time-to-time where even so there is a continuance of stories that fell short or simply unexpected plot points and twists. It's about the actions and the ripples made overall. From my own accord and from the ripples of others. I need not waste my time with the what ifs. That changes nothing. That just opens up the series of non-consequential what ifs that really just remain in our heads anyways. THEY ARENT REAL. But those what ifs are where dreams are made or when memories broken occurred in a sliding door effect.

I guess my series has become in it's own way a commentary about the modern relationship just as much as it has been about individuality and humanity. It evolves with every entry as I grow older. I can say sorry for bringing things into my series, but at the same time I cannot apologize for myself and what is right for me. I have to believe that it is important to include what I have in talking points as it only leads to connection one way or another. Perhaps disconnect had in translation or meaning, but at least the love and respect of 'Self' and 'Others' is there in any aspect of a fledging story of so many years. You would be surprised how old some of these story creators were at the time of production. The youthful hearts of some of the greats in either aspect. Stunted growth in society occurred in some places and advances made in others.

Long story short..."do you". You will guess yourself. OFTEN!!! Others will make you question yourself. But if your heart is in the right place...also do what you think is right towards others. It takes time to feel ok with that and I can't say I'm at a point where I can say that theory is right or not. But it's my belief we are all trying to do right by others and ourselves. Just not all with the same altrustic aspects of one direction or another. One must be careful in knowing there is a difference where collectively you can get a great number of doing right for selective readings. Many get misguided along the way on what the answer to that may be and we take into account things that are beyond our control due to our 'expectations'.

Today I went to Vatican City. I go off my notes and go from there.

"I am sitting in the middle of St. Peters ATM. Looking around left to right, the square is actually breathtaking. It begs reflection. It screams judgment. With each pillar I have some of the world's best artists looking down on me in a complete 180 degrees from each sculpture that sits at the top across the board. I couldn't have imagined this square to be as big as it is but I am humble to just sit down and take this in. This literally is the center of the faith I was raised up in. Being here now I understand why people strive to pilgrimage here. Is that what this is for me? Is that what I am doing? I don't consider myself strong in organized religion, but I have to think this trip is spiritual for me in one way or another."

I treated the vacation as if U were with me one way or another. A trip where I had to do it alone, yet it was a shared adventure of one's first trip oversea to Europe. As I am used to the alone time and silent thought processes, it makes a difference that I had not been on vacation with anyone since what I recall to be 2012 or 2013 to Puerto

Rico to travel the island and work my way around the week to places I may recall or never have been to from my childhood. I didn't visit the base I grew up on knowing it either isn't one anymore or I wouldn't had been able to visit it anyways. An experience of reflection of memory from 4-7 living there.

' The Introduction to the Personification of Fog over El Yunque' Video Still - 2012. "Philip A. Bonneau.

While visiting the Rainforest, once made it to the top, a storm came through of fog sweeping the entire valley below as if a personification of a blanket of grey pulled over to protect that which was in need of protection. A connection of nature discovered there from my youth. From the touch of plant life to that of introduction of birds in trees and hidden forts. From there, the fog grew fast and came over to where not much is seen between a couple feet in front of you in the matter of minutes. What needed to be preserved or understood then is perspective of the beauty of such a feat to occur on either side of childhood memories one way or another. Perhaps a common thing of rain forests and nature to come sweeping in one way or another with understanding of the changing of climates and to reflect upon later. At a tall point there and can't seem to see the bigger picture any more. Was it missed? Greyness took over of clouded thoughts and perhaps a limited palette of color to look at things more objectively while proceeding forward. A memory understanding trust in any regard.

A hurricane approached and came through while we were there. I believe this one was Isaac. Hurricanes comes with buying tickets during off-season for a reason. Still the beauty of a usually full resort now cheaply rented for an evening or two in abandonment makes one discover the 4 or 5 other couples or guests in relation or go down the beach and see what you come across and meet. I suppose it was the affordance aspect of such where I wouldn't change the off-season approach for anything in that regard either. You do what you can when you can and that is what matters. As that was my last vacation with someone I was with, it was all the more important to do this one on my own. Never a question of problems with anyone I would travel with or could. Simply a reflection of how many vacations I couldn't go one with people nor afford. How many moments others got to share while I worked or tried to make ends meet. It was important for many aspects of myself to look at chance encounters and just try to discover who I am outside the influence of 'I should act this way' or 'I should do this' or 'I should do that.' 'If only I did that..' is not what I needed to hear. I needed to escape the responsibility of weight of what I should or shouldn't do and breathe.

Prior to that not a vacation had since my 30th in The Bahamas and before that proba- bly Isla Mujeres, Mexico. There was a gifted cruise that I was allowed to be on when a friend ended a relationship and invited me along in a once in a lifetime opportunity to finally go on a cruise. Funny how when I was in college, my father, step-mother and brother went on a cruise and I wasn't even invited. It happens, but at least I got to tour the Carribbean in a capacity of friendship, making connections and an intro- duction of the idea of 'Heroes on Vacation' knowing it is so rare and far between. I thought of doing the same on this trip where the only concept I had on it was Ant- Man in giant form holding up the tower of Piza which I didn't get to visit anyways. Mask was brought anyways just in case since I still associate the release of the movie to home video as the day I was able to adopt my wired-hair dachshund and both came home with me.

I know what I experienced and I know the moral weight of the company that I was associated with wondering why it couldn't had been talked about and handled differ- ently. Especially when it was apparent in planned to a certain degree and completely could had been preventable in others. Now 2022, I've grappled with how I've been attacked and know I've been attacked and don't know most or all the reasons why. Can you imagine what I could had done one way or another to change something that never was my responsibility? I put a great deal of things on the line and under no circumstance would I have offered my own work to save where I was exploited. But if that was what people wanted after to 'frame me for Alfred Angelo' or harm me for even having a concept of dream and believing in my soul the dream of marriage from my own life experience to know it is deeply important to myself on multiple levels that were established back when I was 19/20 with my own dreams prior and after that timeframe through life lived. It was right to believe that dream and take a giant step career-wise by joining the company in 2014. The conflict that I had then is not necessarily the same I have now. I've said what I could and I've expressed more than I could only to be the one painted one way or another.

In video form recorded and posted on my social media there was a beauty of recording video to showcase the plaza. While not normally one to showcase video often, there was a recording and then a playback. A survey of the Plaza where time goes forward and then it boomerangs backwards as if time was reversed for a minute to take a step back and reflect on the choices made if only for a couple seconds. All around the St. Peter's larger than life artists who have been collected, praised and beame larger than life to major parts of civilization while understanding that cultural influence comes from many places and means different things for many different people. Each one of them of name recognition of support for one way or another and all pursued their dreams and had that afforded to them. The same, no doubt to be found in Florence in the same capacity. Supported one way or another where level of detail then and now never misconstrued. Revered one way or another in chosen worth of conceptualizing and talent. No matter the applications, each one of those statues represents a life of artistry supported, nurioushed and sustained to persue anything they wanted to in one capacity or another. The fabric of perception present in this space knowing it is the fabric of so much espression and beliefs.

I refrained on this trip from visiting The Sistine Chapel. I have my memories of what I learned in Undergrad with my self-driven desire to map it out. Part of me felt unworthy in any capacity to visit The Papel Chapel knowing the magnitude of the significance of that kind of introduction. It is also from lack of mapping things out properly, but the imagination aspect of what it would be like is what I've grown up on. Later in life, I probably have more questions about it while still knowing the insignificance of myself in regards to being able to comprehend the connections I have made one way or another.

I looked around knowing how small I am in regards to foundations upon foundations of thought processes that go one way or another. I understand the wealth aspect of understanding everything around me is preserved and protected...perhaps that is more a thought process of 2022 me vs. then. There was not as many people as I imagined although I am sure it is different on sundays or special events. Millions available to fill a space in that regard. Perhaps it best that I was not overwhelmed once I crossed over the bridges into Vatican City. A different area and a different safe space of exploration although perhaps a combination of the same for any place of importance to respect. From a religious aspect all the way down to a home. I suppose it is designed to make one question what business do you have while I see the potential of support and structure understanding there is a difference where culture changes in modern times and what has occurred in many fronts that could seemingly never happen again yet 2022 me knows it still does. The experience of such is few and far in-between in the world knowing it would be the same of any strongly held belief of expression of passion one way or another. There is a seperation between the natural wonders of the world and then being anywhere near places built from artistry and from the creation of communication that define the fabric of human civilization one way or another. I made a comment about one religious presence in the United States in comparison to the Plaza of St. Peter's noting of such the wealth that if one was to go into mega-church structures, it would be hard to compare against such a place while wondering which one stands more for belief systems understanding what happens during disasters natural or man-made.

"I'm in the cathedral. The long line was worth this. I've never physically responded to a place since I was a kid. I had a panic attack at church growing up when I knew my father wanted to get his marriage of over 20 years annulled. I questioned what that meant for me in the eyes of God. Consider it a crisis of faith at the time, but this is different. Being in this building is humbling. Dead popes everywhere, but everything is built with a level of detail that is unmatched."

In another video posted, the question was posted wondering if you hear what I hear when walking within the walls of St. Peter. It was beyond the echos of words spoken by visitors there for prayer or in conversation. The translation of many languages occurred understanding the fact that I am sure all are represented one way or another. (Translation being more the understanding of hearing multiple languages at the same time and knowing the difference). There was the auditory aspects of such and then there was the soft sound as if music was playing and there was singing knowing there was none to be found in what I saw. The walls spoke I imagine knowing that whatever rests inside these walls is something of a different degree than I have experienced. A life present inside where there is a difference between whispers and life thriving and well within this building. What is present in this space is found in translations. There are few art pieces I know of in this space which are of the highest regard. I know of Bernini from Art History, there is the sculpture side of him and then there is the 'St. Peter's Baldachin'. I've never looked up the details then or prior but today I wanted to know a bit more interest in the Plinths and the Barberini coats of arms as bees factor into my life here, prior, in Paris and always with respect of flights taken and those who never could. Was this my flight that I never thought I could? Interest had from what was read understanding I'll need to process that a little bit further in the understanding that which I've known since Catholic school growing up on the history of saints and foundations of beliefs. My conflict is perhaps on full blast at the moment while also just always knowing what has occurred, would occur (in probability) and what people do to retain something or transform in ways that always is a delicate balance.

I'm aware St. Peter was murdered brutally before even becoming a saint. Most were in their beliefs and how others in power adapt one way or another. I know my stance elsewhere in understanding of persecution of those of ideas or others who like things the way they were and do not like added interest elsewhere. I look around in my head remembering the space of 2017 trying to recall what I felt at and saw at St. Peter's while at the same time setting here for the moment knowing I've been elsewhere at other times with other people of other religions. People of stature that I can only imagine in introduction or of time of day in any regard while never discounting the slight comment or passing glance. I carry with me my birthday of November 1st where it means something to me and now represents an American month of understanding not just the previous culture of American Soil but the beginning of understanding and appreciation of where we come from on a civilization aspect and where others were wiped out or by virtue of modern times allowed to be preserved one way or another. It is understood I come from one of the younger countries of the world. America...A melting pot exploring things in a different capacity of ideas while the whole world does the same now anyways.

Mistakes of history or simply human nature understood with I in that lessons learned from everywhere and in erasure, not knowing completely where the truth originally was or where it is now. There is knowing that as things advance so does lineage, thought process and teachings in one aspect or another. To teach of things to relation of hundreds of years ago is to teach things of thousands of years ago while understanding the now and it could go back further if wanted while we try to apply it to the 'Now' which is important to not repeat or simply let one path lead to another. My grade school was named after Saint Peter and from such I understand then my introductions and appreciate weekly still getting to interact with the priest, (retired) Father Patrick O'Brian from Ireland who helped found St. Peter the Apostle Catholic School where life lessons still learned 25-30 years later at a country club where the community he helped build supports and honors him as well in multi-generations knowing the honor a sense of humor in such still where there is a difference between one role and another while still being human and understanding that one cannot be one mantle or the other at all times. Friendship found in confidence and that builds trust from there. Perhaps that factors later in life in things written and explained elsewhere.

Since I was a child, he taught very early on that is engrained in myself all through my life, 'Don't hate the person. Hate the action.' Taught at an early age and transitioned. It has been challenged over the years where it understood that I can't look at it any other way anymore. There is the action of what occurred one way or another and then there is the understanding of the compounded questioning why that person did that or not either in discussion or simply accepting none was to be had. Life compounds. Lessons compound. It is no less a difference that the complexity of answers to such things as the meaning of life, cognizance or self-awareness and where that comes in compounded interest. Is the answer anymore complex now than what it was in the first footprint aware of recognition?

In awareness I am spiritually and mentally right now in St. Peter's knowing I am elsewhere as well. A timeframe of understanding the concept of time and safe travels to any place the mind needs to go when processing anything. Is it such? Understanding what I have already written and transcribed, tried to protect and showcase one way or another. Would it not be a conflict to have any being past normal human life have the same questions of recollection and recall where things go one way or another knowing what is and isn't monumental to 'Self'. How many 'Actions' can be hated before it becomes a collective understanding of teaching people one way or another with as much information as their hearts desire to see if that makes any difference. Interconnected everyway possible and yet still a divide on some things, not as many things. Respect comes with introductions and getting to know one another despite differences.

I understand the social media aspect of mentioning the phrase 'dead popes everywhere'. I'm unsure how to properly describe the preservation and embalming of people of sacredness one way or another. I relate to the same procedure in Egypt of honoring those of stature or respect to those we love if we could afford to honor them in such way. I associate the procedure with Egyptian culture knowing other cultures too at the time and after did the same. There is the preservation aspect and then there is the mystery of cultures long since transformed. The same honoring is done in the Taj Mahal when it comes to affordance of love one way or another. It was witness again years later in Paris in the same regard. That can be approached by the tomb of Napoleon and his son just as much as it can delve into The Crypts of those unknown and unnamed.

The affordance of such honoring is wonderings as I never knew one way or another, which bodies are laying in reverence in St. Peter's and what was their specific contributions? It is important that if honoring of such towards preservation, there is a reason for it beyond even one understanding or another on how or why that is. There are those in preservation that got to a status to begin with in accomplishment and always an interesting aspect of getting to know one or the other. It is understood though history that not all Papal contributions were infallible without looking at the sign of the times and understanding culture changed constantly from St. Peter on in many regards where protectionism was alive and well then and definitely now.

Preservation of something is the important aspect to question and understand that souls speak and so do bodies. In presevation of thought, imagine what happens to that in the physicality aspects. I remember a trip to the Boston Museum when I was a child. Perhaps 3 at the time. Maybe 4. The Egyptian exhibit of importance understanding what I was introduced at such an early age. An introduction to someone or something simply beginning to appreciate what others have known far longer and captured my interest and imagination. It was seen far after and still connects to me even to this day. I've often question what would happen if I went back there to see which connection still exists all these years later. I imagine it is still a complex question of not knowing of captured imagination of children and what age of such. Questions later in life of the difference between cremation and that of preservation of a body through mummification and preservation. On one hand there is the cremation aspect of the end of a soul and no advancement of it to transfer on to other aspects of adaptive sustainability and then that of preservation where it could be viewed that part of the soul is trapped or around to speak one way or another about a lesson learned or a lesson to be taught. What lesson was meant to be taught and shared from that of a preserved body that wouldn't transition anytime soon? Perhaps the soul moves on and it is moreso an understanding of I existed in this capacity. It could be both seen as a gift and a curse to what is left behind for others to translate or connect to. That need to understand the origins of such is perhaps a question where I don't know that answer readily possibly available from the foundation of written language, but if something was built on the backs of others and there was condemnation that got passed down... who originated mummification and who trend-set that into other areas? Surrounded of pyramids of earthly fortunes and well wishes, a soul trapped to their own belongings without a single person to rule over. It is where my mind goes, yet I am sure there is much more to it than that in what became common practice of what could be respect or could be 'revenge' on the search for immortality.

Perhaps it could be looked at as the body is preserved so that when a spirit does comes back in a different capacity, it could be reminded of the life they once had and connect to it one way or another. Reincarnation is not uncommon in deity aspect and heritage present and introduced with Jesus Christ. A constant look out from one religion to the next of where life is and where it is going. Often in Egyptian culture and of others of reincarnation, it is done so that one can learn the lessons of past lives already experienced. To have the soul come across the body of a former aspect of themselves makes one question in reflection of silence and understanding what is and isn't immortal and understand that perhaps that the life you were from this culture and from this time frame was important for you to remember. Probably to the same extent if you were disregarded, disguarded and cast into a mass grave. The lesson could be now you are of this culture and another time frame and what have you learned of such? Did you learn respect of others or understand where things come from? What story is a soul being told knowing it is beyond generational and looked at in a way that still denotes learning commonality, respect and empathy knowing it is not just sympathy. Understanding of life where perhaps leaders are embalmed for multiple reasons then wondering how immortal things were one way or another. How many different belief systems are in you genetically before going into the spiritual construct of a soul? I don't have a reference point one way or another. It is simply a belief system where that could had came from those of persecution or from a place where it is not understood and lost in history or a severe question of understanding what happened after Jesus' death and saying there might be a little bit more condemnation than expected in this world.

In the other take home aspect from the museum from what I recall of my childhood, a mural of one dinosaur era to another that lined the museum walls in a massive scale reduced in stature but not of meaning to line a full wall of my childhood walls in multiple locations. Millions of years around me every time I went to sleep as a child in evolution and adaptation since then and framed in thought and process. Time travelling every time I resided in my bedroom.

I go back to Bernini and now 'The Chair of Saint Peter'. I see it was 300 years after Dante and the motif is still present on the Papel chair. An Empyrean one way or another where the adult aspects of Gustav Doré's depiction went from adult representation of angels to those of winged children. In reference to bees and St Peter's Baldachin one cannot help but wonder the thought of children and of birth and the struggles of such. To match the two together is to understand 300 years occurred to understand on some capacity Dante's life and understanding how 'politics' then played out and the influence of such in history probably immediately, but more than likely a lasting aspect 300 years later towards artistic influence and establishment. Perhaps a toned down of approach towards invisable shankings of inspiration or simply artistic expression written somewhere. A question that is always the artist right then to never have to reveal as much as now and simply look at the beauty of things play out for your own conclusions. I don't know the answer of what was lost one way or another or what could be gain in conversation and introductions. But child-like innocence is always something to question when of the world and their discovery of such. They do grow older over time. Maybe not always at the same pace but eventually children are no longer adults. Perhaps I look now at any cherub musing wondering, 'Where are we going next with this?' I imagine they are friendly with satyrs. Lessons learned in The Lovre years later.

Who allowed who to suffer and who took over what in what capacity after his death? A question that could be quietly between Vatican City and Italy or perhaps a common structure of such between Italy and whomever in understanding what occurred from one processing suffering and amalgamating any aspect of his comfortability to religion/theology/mythology to comprehend whatever he experienced well aware of what he experienced and his surroundings knowing he already lost his home because of having any opinion on anything of importance only to 1-up politics and go completely into the entire playbook of theological comprehension to get to a safe place. If politics factored into the destruction that others based their property or understanding of things on one way or another. Others pick up on that and probably understand one waty or another on the struggle and the realization of one thing or another.

"There is a confessional here. It's not English, but perhaps I should do this since I'll never get this chance again."
I am understanding that I am here and this is central to my believe system. I look around and there are places where if one was going to confess in any aspect, this is

the place to do it. It has been since middle school that I did a confession of anything and it is important to I to understand that this is probably the only time I would be able to do such. 2018-2019 kind of solidified that belief system of trust understanding what that was then and unknown at the time now. Introductions had prior where perhaps things played out one way or another wondering the children of others and those who had none as well.

"Directed to the other side of the cathedral where they cover ever language.
Waiting in line like this is Disney world."

The lines are broken up by language. There aren't that many and I imagine every language spoken here one way or another. It is understood the scholarly aspect of such a building and institution to know that despite cultural differences, there is cultural translations to discover what is universal. I imagine ask anyone of the church in that capacity in those boundaries and you will get some universal answers that can be either defined to one religion or expanded as well to commonalities to that of others. It is more than likely universally understood that the higher you are in religious stature, (At least in modern times) denotes respect spoken or not of others of commonly held life choices and belief systems. It is only natural to respect others who also can back up strongly held beliefs one way or the other. It is understood later in life that if one was to prove the other wrong, there is a great deal of evidence to back up saying otherwise in either's defense before going straight back to individuality and defense for one or the other or multitudes really when you think about it.

"Surprised the English section is actually barren. I'm not going to have to wait."

Not as unexpected as I thought as English is not the primary language here, but I find it barren at the moment wondering if my grandfather also confessed here. I remember receiving a cross from him blessed by the Pope on his travels. I understand it probably is not that uncommon and to have someone think of 40+ grandchildren on anything is amazing to consider in regards to any travels had. But to have anything in that capacity translated and passed down in meaning is an understanding of the significance of such and the lesson being passed down. A planner had where never a birthday missed from any regard of children, grandchildren or great-grandchildren. I question what I would ask and wonder how I would approach such one way or another.
"I'm not going to get any closer to Heaven than this...I have to ask"

Confession is a funny thing. It's partially what you want to talk about and partially what conflicts you. One of the first things I said when I came into the booth was that it's been 20 years since my last confession. I started talking about how I don't understand faith and just have so many questions. I started saying I'd go to church every Sunday with my family and see people mass exit the parking lot screaming at others along the way after the fact to move along. There is so much hypocrisy in it. That a handshake of friendship only goes so far and I talked about annulment if ever so briefly. Definitely a crisis of faith and rules. I started this encounter off that I feel I lost faith and at the same time giving background to what I was going to ask and saying I think faith is what brought me there to begin with. Through my grandparents, through my cousin and through my own decisions.

'Totally had an emotional experience in St. Peters. It's been years since i confessed to a priest and to be able to come, do so and ask the questions I needed answered and guided on how to proceed will be one of the best experiences of my life. (Side note... if u do a confession in st. Peters u are given more access and allowed to go right up to the alter) #blessed'

My questions were definitely father-bound in most regards. The brief aspects of being unemployed was discussed. The same here where money is important and how I almost didn't do this trip but I was also driven to do it for multiple reasons explained or not. I also wanted to get an idea of Dante in a different capacity understanding what I've already written in this section 5 years after my visit there. There is abandonment, exploitation and then the complete question of the non-existance of a child when others ask for an annulment. I didn't get an answer on that or simply cannot remember nor should I have to disclose anything from a confession. I imagine no confession more sacred then one at the heart of Christianity. Where my mind went was I was glad to have the conversation and I am confused. I suppose to open my mouth in any regard was a starting point and from there at least an entry.

I don't have much. What I do have was betted on this trip being right for my journey and myself. I confessed that I'm scared I don't know what will happen and I discussed my moral dilemma of such after-the-fact of perception. But I feel this is the right thing to do. I wanted so much to honor my grandfather and my history on this journey and I really never considered that I'd come to the center of my religion and just let a stranger in on everything I hold close to my chest. I didn't release everything and I believe my thoughts and questions were directed toward myself and of questions of fatherhood as it pertained to myself and in relationship to myself. Confessions probably don't last as long as mine but I got about 45 minutes of discussion and understanding.

When pressed on what to talk about I actually brought up the part of scripture where Jesus discovered that he was going to die and his time in the desert. I asked how does one come to accept that they have to go through situations they didn't deserve. That and why does someone have to suffer for others to have a better life and how do you even come to grips with that. My answer was definitely given on that we could never know what Jesus was thinking, but that something is bringing you here to ask this of me and of yourself. I don't know how to take that especially considering the day before in guidance and understanding you will get your answers one way or another. I like to think that this is no different than me in grade school questioning if priest masturbate while also priests teaching sex-ED and rationalizing evolution/theology at a young age that God was an ape and we grew out of the image of God from our mistakes. It is my understanding that in the concept of anything that could be broken down in Through the Looking Glass of the dreams of a father that at least in my childhood regard, yes...God is many things and seen in many things and commonality found in protection, nurturing or if one was to go into it straight up emotional wrath to deal with moral issues that is probably a little bit more subtle now than what it was then. Equally effective. My original thought process as a child on God being an ape is the understanding of the purity of nature and primates and understanding the difference between humans and apes or humans and gorillas. If one was cast out of Eden in that capacity at the time, it was understood there was recognition that occurred in some way or form that went on to seek further shelter, knowledge, protection and simply no longer for the forest as they would had naturally began to question many things. I suppose that was 6th or 7th grade where at least I still validate the purity of such a thought knowing where I am at now in commonality and evolutionary branches towards connections with very few that blip off beaten paths. I think it was the appreciation of nature, well before I ever saw 'Gorillas in the Mist' to understand that there is a connection there between where we are and where I was going as a child in rationality. One could easily look at it on multiple fronts, but then one would have to question in comparison, is your family pet a pet only or a part of your family? Up it up a notch and understand humans are a part of the animal kingdom. Domestication exists in multiple fascets. I imagine at the time I was looking at the Purity aspect of what is probably divinity and also understand the emotional aspect to it as well knowing in relatability there is reaction, speaking and everything else in between in understanding where we came from and that while is a part of us. On the human side from 6th or 7th grade, I can say I basically rationalized the Exit from Eden as 'Animal Farm' knowing I had not read the book yet and was probably maybe aware from it only in the aspect that my mother refuses to eat meat since high school after reading that book.

I'm reverent for sure, but I come with so many questions as children do. I imagine people get tired of questions and enjoy a sense of humor once in awhile or different perspectives one way or another knowing where it comes from.

All said and done though I did ask the one question I needed for me. Am I doing things right? Simple enough question. My answer was subjective. I don't know how to feel. Not about faith, guidance, or answers. But I'm glad above all things that I at least asked the questions I did in the highest form I could ever ask for. Can't say I'll reveal everything from my confession, but then again...that's what confessions are for. Brave New Secrets.

I'm not sure if I'm disappointed that there is no definite answer to things or that I expected such. This trip is going to find it's own answers one way or another.

'And in typical pip fashion, time to do the exact opposite of everything I did through-out the day. I was suggested from a friend to at least try the bathhouses here once. No, it doesn't have to be about sex because honestly a steam room and sauna sounds amazing at the moment and apparently it's not a late night affair as in the states. From Holy to Hole-y in less than 12 hours... #thejourneycontinues'

I spent the time in reflection afterwards as I exited Vatican City and proceeded to go about my day. It is here I believe I caught the image of a gypsy woman crouched down on the bridge in respect. A common image to some I image, yet a photograph of rememberance that I had at one point and no longer do. Money paid one way or another where I understand just as much as I couldn't bring myself to take a snapshot without giving some form of compensation for such. A beautiful image of a woman faced down in what I imagine is respectful and common-place. She resided on the bridge between Vatican City and Rome. The act of such in understanding the humility of a feat is probably the underlying aspect where I find interest in the actual value of such knowing, be humble at work for awhile and then go home to riches elsewhere. The observance of such noted in understanding the humility one has to do for a pay-check never knowing the actual salary attached to such. Wisdom in understanding.

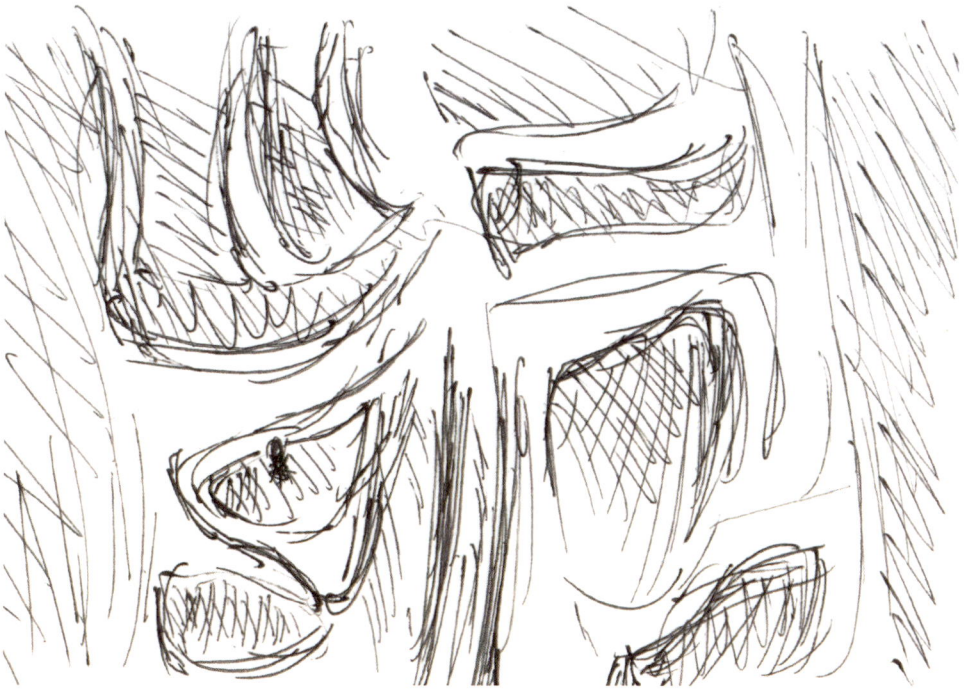

'Pools of Thoughts' - Sketch Translation' November 28, 2022. "Philip A. Bonneau.

On the return back towards center, it is also where I was told of other places to go at certain times to clear my head and relax from those of familiarity of Atlanta who were following my travels. If one is getting into the underbelly of things, there is always a time and a place to do so. The way I think of such is an understanding that when one goes one place or another it is always about comfortability of simply a place to clear your mind. Having been a long time fan of naked swimming, of course I showed up long after others were there and simply enjoyed the time for what it was. Thoughts and reflection in a place of complete nakedness after already beginning to strip down emotionally at the Vatican earlier that day.

In the catacombs of a building a liquid maze existed where perhaps it was best to enjoy yet another space not crowded and of equal many memories I imagine. The underground of Italy is a little bit more understanding of the roots of other cultures and if one was to entertain any idea of a bath-house after confession then it might as well be the best place to sit here and sort the tangled thoughts that go one way or another. Perhaps the first time in 48 hours I could relax and breathe. Never a problem when in water and simply the surroundings were comfortable to one thing or another. The things we hide in the under-currents of our minds...is it a social thing or simply just have to find the right environment.

Which path am I on and which one am I choosing? I would say in naked swimming it is understood that there is simply an understanding of underground, underwater, under so much pressure. Deep pockets of thoughts and we go from there. Connections made to where one simply understands a connection that in many regards I was the last one standing on many of the topic points of the day and needed to reconcile with moving forward and enjoying life one way or another.

Is a written book with a discussion of a religious confession any different than the image of swimming nakedly in the under-currents of thoughts one way or another?

I'm stripping one way or another in this book. One tends to do that in adulthood, honesty and moving towards one level of peace and acceptance. Perhaps the opposite approach when in thoughts of Eden. Unashamed before. Unashamed now. Stripped and going with it one way or another for the world to see. Camera or not.

'Regular massages 100 bucks. naked swimming with jet massagers, steam rooms and saunas 32. Funny side note. People think I'm Hispanic. LOL'

I honor my newfound Hispanic heritage and continue on my journey...
it was in me anyways even if I don't speak of such.

ENTRY 41:

"Kindness begets kindness."

Rolling in the deep.
Thought
Thoughts.
Replay.
Rewind.
An interesting more of imagination.

I haven't really thought about it until now but I like the similarities occurring in my head.

"Happiness is homemade"
-a phrase in my mother's spare bedroom

I think of my heroes series and not affording a studio.
Equipment earned over time.
A budget of 20 here.
100 there.
A gradual increase for a make-up artist.
Heroes was a concept birthed from escapism & dreams.
Fledgling in thought. Growth through progress.
Done on my own time...belief and trust.

Regress.
Rebuild
Regrow.

...Childhood brought into the grown-up world
Children view the world different
I view the world different

My mind goes back to previously written thoughts of mental shifts in adolescence. Compartmentalizing is learned. Groupings are learned. I still

believe that in both literature and in comics,
uniqueness is where value lies. When did that individuality become something to avoid? Are we all destined to be hundreds of multiple clones of what
is pre-destined for us to become?
Where do we stand in commonality & individuality?
"Why tell a story? You are either part of the group or you are the one being
written about."

The concept of soul-mates is remembered in my head. Plural. There are
often discussion with the muses on it and where I lie. "Voted in." "Voted
out." Multiples state their cases. Something Nu to look into later. Does the
idea of soul-mates denote something bigger?
It denotes a desire for connection and someone/anyone to get to understand
you.

"Separate yourself to become something greater…if only for yourself."
Eventually we piece ourselves back together.

Identity plays a key part in all of my works.
Why wouldn't it? We all want to know ourselves before knowing others.

Reflections of me.
All models reflected.

Perception Given.
Withheld.
Masked.
Piece it together
To find my secrets.
Beautifully Layered.
Simple in Execution,
meaning in everything

A story told or not
Everything a conversation
if only asked.

Place.
Time.
Feeling.
Thought.

Every image a memory.
A connection between Us.

Overall my thesis is going to be about working towards commonality and understanding of one another. I wonder if it's important to write things out. My thought process comes back to an e-mail on my artist's page. A critique of over explanation from the artist and the question on if it devalues or enhance the art by knowing the artist's intent? Is it now limited to the narrow view of the artist alone or is that just a building block for others to dissect? A keystone? It's quite possible that "happy accidents" occur in art. Perception is key to any art piece that your mind has taken hold of. Does an artist's interpretation devalue your own opinion of the art piece or did you simply piece things together that were always there that no one realized before? Perspective is uniqueness. A voice is uniqueness. Critiques can be accomplished both with and without emotion present. Always a choice in a vernacular approach.

I remember a time at Swinging Richards when an art history professor brought up my intellect of art as a way to look down on me. (Probably discounted anyways based on what I was doing at SR to begin with. I challenged both that person and the one who wrote the e-mail to me. I believe that if you cannot back up your art then it is for art's sake or a group mentality to let others explain your work for you. Everything is an exploration. There is influence from everywhere, but you have to back up a common thesis with yourself in order to validate your hypothesis.

I remember going to see a famous choreographer/composer receive an award at the Guggenheim for his new production put on based on "The Divine Comedy". The artist's name escapes me, but I remember the excitement and honor of being able to see this production that a friend of mine was a part of. When it came time after for a discussion of the work, he was asked about what he was specifically referencing from Dante's "Inferno".

His response, "I don't recall exactly." (Paraphrased) I don't recall if it was anger or confusion that prompted me to up and leave in the middle of this, but I do remember I was pissed or perhaps disappointed is a better statement as to invite translation of dialogue and interpretation was the point of discussion anyways. Might as well called it "The Mighty Ducks 2" if you aren't going to recall. Hindsight though, it is possible that a great deal of artists are introverted. Funny enough...at the time, I had only begun to attempt my own keystones to, "The Divine Comedy." Words matter. Which is perhaps what art is supposed to be. Backed by meaning and open for interpretations. It is presumed so in translation of such into modern dance and it was the musical aspect that I was very interested in from the artist/composer as well. To consider the contemporary aspects of The Divine Comedy is to understand multiple translations is how I can look at it now with more understanding of age. When was that? 2014-2015? Earlier? Been to NYC more than once on vacation over the years.

Is this me being pretentious?

I feel words add context that may have been missed. It's a pattern of backing up your intentions. Individuality in thinking, but within the commonality of human experience and archetypes. Everything driven to purpose and meaning one way or another. Sometimes you are simply on your own path where there can be 100s of more words to validate your intention, but a balance of direction makes intentions towards discussion or interpretation essential. Once held only in title form, a guessing game expanded on artistic intention pointing one way or another.

I believe my words add to the experience.
I believe my music compositions add context.
I believe I try to back up my intentions, which probably also says a great deal about purpose and meaning.
Individuality within commonality.
Relatable.
A segue from something familiar to something intimately shared.
Each moment given. Never capable of being stolen as there was always the initial moment between photographer and model or photographer and camera. Or camera and viewer towards the final art piece to viewer in a mind of interpretations and applicable production.

I see that as I attempt to approach photography as painting, A RAW image will never be what I saw completely. It may showcase the initial potential of where my mind could go, but I find as I revisit things every couple of years, that there is proof of growth. No one version replaces another, but I like to see that transition of "Getting it" with an image. Don't change what has already been bought into, but free to change anything not yet sold. Each snapshot is a moment given that can be modified based on emotion/mood/concept of the moment. "Blink and you miss it" going into a completely different direction.

Life begins at the click of a shutter where befores & afters go in infinite directions based on mood, context & desire of intention.

I remember seeing work sold from my first show and finding the flaws after the fact. I was specifically told not
to change it. I value that and I see value in keeping the flaws apparent. "Nothing is perfect." "Perfection in Imperfection". But I still go back to the revisit as a sign of growth and never in the same place. Proof of transcendence of art? OR simply refining a craft through experience and time through the years? The highest form of flattery you could give me is to hang my work in the bathroom. The most intimate setting where it is always just me and U.

I remember seeing a Matisse painting. I don't remember the name of it. It was a fisherman scene. I saw the painting as Matisse flaunting of a lover in the face of a companion. There is always a story to be told with no one aware of if there is one or not. Artists are capable of a sense of humor. Perhaps my mind is looking into that context because I have a sense of humor and my mind is telling me that story which may or may not be true. (Could this be a valuable tool in saying be careful what you say in explanations?) Perception always, but context sometimes. Even if it is impossible to void context from anything. The latching of new context to older works comes from when first introduced to the view when dectective work had on the story behind images you may find yourself tired looking for answers not provided.

An artist is always going to be a damned liar in that they can title something and it mean something completely different, or they can intentionally name something and there is a reason and reference to be had. Conversations are evoked by the words associated with an image. The artist, if one does not wish to be called a liar, can simply be referred to as a storyteller and a builder of worlds based on points-of-view of their truths, perspectives and imagination.

The door left open for interpretation.
Layers left to leave things be.
Somewhere there.
Always me.

Another theory I have is if you remove
the eyes from the human
subject within a work of art, it allows
projection of the viewer into the art
piece. Personalization?

Probably more so empathetic
to the subject.

I think of the symbology of goggles
and masks.

Both are open for interpretation.
Blinded by youth?
Blinded by naivety?
A performance in different groups?

A Portrait of Self from 2010—2011.
Or was it 2008? Time flies.

MASKS

*To wear a mask suggests that you are trying to be someone you are not or struggling against
deceit and falsehoods. You are trying to hide your true feelings and only reveal half truths. If
you have trouble taking off your mask, then it suggests that your true self is lost or blurred.*
(dreammoods.com)

Environmental Aspects to be had here.
Is a self-reflection in a mirror a mask of perception on either side?

GOGGLES

*To see or wear goggles suggest that you are trying to protect yourself from emotional harm.
Perhaps you need to confront something in your waking life that you know is hurting you.*
(dreammoods.com)

Protection to the windows of the soul. A tinted theory of where to or not to
look for stories of humanity & projection in I. In hiding eyes, there is a conversation about 'Our' relationship to humanity and what connects our souls
while leaving the viewer to desire to see one eye-to-eye.

Post 16: Day 3: The Fourth Sphere and Entering Heaven.

"I think for me this is what my brave new secrets is to be. Definitely a self-portrait in regards to story but not in the regard of talking about being in relationships. Or maybe it's a relationship with U. On some level rediscovering hope and remembering what it is like to explore and that the world is yours to translate and explore. I think I forgot that. I think I've never experienced that. I'm beginning to do so. I have been so preoccupied with being back to center that I forgot so many lessons.

Namely appreciate what is right in front of you. I've been so preoccupied with things not wanting to be in my life and fighting to hold on others that I want to keep that others may not want me to have. I not going to publish to the world everything anymore as I go through this journey and part of being a secret is you keep it one. But I'm excited to teach myself restraint and to also teach myself that perhaps I've been scared for far longer than I remember and it's time I challenged myself vs. challenging others. Or have I always been challenging myself and need to learn to trust where I have grown one way or another? It's one thing to avoid going through a situation ever again, but it's another thing to be scared to ever take a chance.

My end game is Florence, Italy in 2017 for this story. I'll begin to finish this series there and then go on to exploring the birthplace to The Divine Comedy. The challenge is to myself to go there in the first place.

Are you going to do it or are you just going to sit back and let this continue longer than it should?

Are you just going to justify this to not go continually?
This is your game afterall.

Something feels fitting about coming full circle there and finding and exploring Heaven in the one place that created Dante's journey.

Maybe it is time to break the cycle and rediscover faith.
The choice is your Philip.

Do it or stop fucking talking about whatever it is you are talking about." - 9/28/16

'Nothing like using a kiosk all in Italian praying that I booked the right thing. Either way I'm gonna be heading somewhere.'

My first train ride in Italy. In fairness, I really should had booked these prior as it gets more expensive the day of and on what is available. Train rides in Europe are far more common than that in the United States as everything is interlocked and connected. Always aware of the dreams of rail systems in the United States, I never undetstood why it never happens outside of the aspect of the country's expansion was built upon it in the beginning. I only imagine now it is about the investment of other means of transportation that took over. I could be wrong, but I seem to think from time-to-time there are a great number of people who want to rebuild the wheel vs. looking at other countries or asking advice from them in order for understanding who has been doing what to great success one way or another. When thinking of railways across America, I understand the problem of natural blockage of passageways that may occur with fallen trees or boulders to block passages. I'm pretty sure the same thing occurs in other countries. Strategic pathways away from such is design and mapping out cours-es is a known profession. While understanding when rails gets built, over time, nature and migration either gets divided or crosses paths the same way a deer crosses the road and causes accidents. The avoidance of such is something that just isn't easily overlooked unless you start going into tunnel systems to prevent what occurs natural-ly with it's own problems. Weaving above and underground is still expensive but at least would look at the natural aspects of what is and isn't natural disruption. In and out of thoughts in my head, I imagine if one was to start with main destinations and build from there you probably are on the right railtrack. In current aspects, consider-ing the influx to Las Vegas, perhaps an LA to Vegas system understanding there is a great amount of money traveling there anyways. I can see where earthquakes would be an issue. No doubt the same here in Italy. In any regard, I can see how you can take the concept of a smartcar and apply it to a smarttrain that self-recharges in some capacity from the very rails from which it drives on in built friction towards stored energy and back-up storage in case of delay.

Perhaps in a more traditional sense, in the underground aspect of pathways, the elec-trical recharge aspects could be done within a contained wall-like structure of ins-and-outs wondering how much electrical friction is required for a certain amount of time to continue propulsion and moving forward in one direction or another.

'Still -ish bish. The scenery is amazing outside. Ps. Still not entirely sure I'm in the right train yet. #gowiththeflow'

The expansion of the previous Corporate World of one division not talking to the other where one wonders what happens in mutual conversations of different departments being talking to difference countries about things one way or another. It is not like corporations don't already do that. Imagine how many 'misteps' could be prevented by understanding others do things betrter while knowing your own strengths and weaknesses. I'd say I'm definitely the opposite of an isolationist, but love the idea of isolating who is good at what and seeing where ideas can be forged towards common benefits and expansions one way or another. It can't simply be a name thing as there is infinite space to put contributions by one way or another or to understand the mutual benefits of even glancing at other places before coming to your own conclusions. Guarenteed that has happened with backlash in other expansive programs that are universally accepted in other countries as being successful anyways. Where is the problem in that?

The beauty of a trainride in Italy is the landscape that is presented to the world. Hills and mountainsides between Rome and Florence. Pockets of towns and settlements along the countryside that express the desire to expand in so many regions of expansion if only one were inclined to do so. The idea of space is present in land value. I am aware that over the years Italy has offered incentives to come in and revitalize some of these settlements and towns. If you had the money and a skill-set, you could buy property pretty cheaply and go from there. I see the investor paradise aspect to such knowing with it comes the desire to need skill-sets invested in such. There are simply certain professions required for success, which is probably why visas from one country to another look for that specifically.

Years ago it used to be free for Americans to be able to get a New Zealand visa for a similar reason, yet that has since changed over the years for one reason or another. When looking into Austrailia all those years ago, perhaps 2008 or 2009, I enjoyed the imagination aspect of travel then or hoping from one island to the next eventually if I were so inclined to do so.

I imagine internet would be awhile to even begin to figure out that one without understanding much of beacons to bounce such from one place to another. I believe Google has fiber towers but I don't think that really is what could be something to build a solid signal in such a settlement where do-it-yourselfers would youtube some aspects of fixing and rebuilding while others simply would enjoy the connection and progress of others investing in these towns and rebuilding them. If anything it is an interesting concept for a reality series of what happens all the time.

"I arrived in Florence, I fully anticipated I had to grab a cab to my hotel. I ended up booking the Hotel Beatrice out of irony. Funny enough it's only 2 blocks away from the hotel. This is nothing in comparison. "

The train stops right outside the the heart of Florence. I admit at this point I am quite used to the visible military aspect of noted difference between here and America. It brings more comfort than one things questioning does such a presence detract others from doing one thing or another. I recall an incident at the Fort Lauderdale airport of a gunman (never really see many gunwomen in those types events, but they exist). Would a visible presence of such deter someone from no longer going into places of national security of such? In the ever known aspect of people in uniform, it is completely understood the attraction had in one place or another. There is the Firefighter aspect of the Firearm Fighters that made me introduce the idea of presence of such as an introduction to my arrival of Florence as being a reality or the beginning entering into an Italian Army porn. In either way the comment was more in humor, but I am sure they get it more than often then one think.

"I'm getting settled into my hotel. They didn't even question whom I was checking in. I guess Americans are easily spotted than I thought or maybe I'll get an upgrade."

The Hotel Beatrice is a quaint, older building that more than likely was once a grand home transformed into a rental space. Not that many rooms which provides a more family-like environment. 4 floors with a parlor in there. I check in and they don't even ask for ID. Perhaps because of the number of rooms and simply I can be spotted one way or another. The hotel chosen for it's name and before of it's affordability. The surprise I experienced on my travel is how cheap accomodations are once you are overseas. Plane ticket is the most expensive aspect of this. I feel like I could live off the 3 Euro Caprese Sandwiches found everywhere, but the food is fresh and still afforable. A splurge here or there to have a 20 Euro meal. I'll have for a more expensive one at one point. I get my keys and go to my room.

"Nope...definitely did not get an upgrade. I'm glad I spend more time sleeping on my couch than in my bed. #twinbed"

The room is small, but it is all I need. A small bed, a bathroom, a couple windows overlooking not much in this direction, but I imagine if it is anything like Rome, I won't be spending much time it in anyways. Pretty much sleep, write a bit and discover the joys of the bidot world. My frugal behind is going to be investing on one of these. Toilet paper is expensive, but still essential to the overall experience. What is this giant spoon in here for?! Questions that I can only imagine has nothing to do with cooking soup but more than likely stirring a pot.

I drop my bags off once again and hit the ground running once again with headphones on and carrying with me a great deal of excitment understanding getting lost is the best part of this trip. It will be a long day for sure. I walk through the market places here and there knowing this city is known for such. Fabric trades and merchandise. Strung together and showcased on the open street bazaar-like aspects of what you would consider a finer version of an American Flea Market. There is no such comparison as a flea market is second-hand and this is vendor upon vendor in an outdoor setting. As both sides have a history to it, one knows that I can't really buy anything tangible on this trip. There is only one item that I have my mind set on purchasing in that regard and it will be from this city. I just have to find the right place for it. The only comparison I draw to is the personality of shops in open space which I am sure there are better comparisons to in The United States as once was and is a viable market to fabric and trade.

I don't recall if there was any rain that occurred on the trip. If there was it must have been in the evening while I was asleep. To walk by everyone, it was understood I still refrain from talking much. Wondering whom I'd really talk to anyways while I am learning the speech of the buildings around me as they tell me their history from the stone grounds to the top of the towers.

'Pippy is about to become a servant of Doumo. #italiandrstrangepun'

The focal point of the trip in Florence. The center of the city and the tallest point. The main attraction to such knowing it would be of equal importance to Dante as well. In the scheme of things for I to walk anywhere around the city in context to Dante, it was to know the distance from Rome to Florence knowing it wouldn't be by rail to get to such right away back in the 1300s. There was a contention of such that his journey into politics and time in Rome is what transformed his life and where he had to flee from Florence in forced manuveurs to what he spoke of potically at the time.

Opinionated and educated on many fronts, it was or is understood the under-currents towards elsewhere where no doubt if one was of a political mind, he was a mind of sociology as well, where one would gather it was studied and at the same time still growing in aspects where knowledge of such determines value of gain towards morality and control one way or another. Around the city inspiration, but what would be the cause of it being called, 'His Beloved Florence'. Although not the same as the streets back then, the artistry is alive and well with the understanding the attention of detail noted from the time periods in particular. As no different than any mosque or building of importance, the hidden little details all mean something one way or another. In full focal perective, 'its no wonder the Renaissance came from here'. What does this mean? What does that mean? Why are there this many trees or that many that patterns. The secrets of control of expression is also the secrets of financiers where the Medici would be all in on little details that surmount to one thing or another in discussion and curation of ideas and concepts.

"I can't believe the level of detail of these buildings here. Can't do the Doumo today. But scheduled for tomorrow. Can still hit up the smaller museums and see the Death Mask. Super stoked for the Uffizi tomorrow. Have to let Momma Goldstein know that I booked it in advance."

As one of the most important landmarks and sites of Florence, it was to be understood it has to be reserved time-slots in order to travel through it. Tight quarters where once on top, a limited number of people are allowed to be there at one time. I review my options available and find that I can precisely time my trek to the top for sunset tomorrow. Such a grand scheme of things to walk to the top of the Duomo and see the sun set across the land as world transitions from day to night. I can wait understanding that is worth the temperance to jump right into it and let the city breathe a bit more before doing so. I want to get a feel of the environment and understand how one gets lost in thought in such a city. If one of desirement or attraction to one area or another, what comes to mind when wondering and viewing from a distance? It is understood he would be known to others and quite affluent or perhaps not quite as much as others around him. Debateable as I bought a biography of Dante with me on my trip but also enjoy I only flipped through a couple pages. It is important in ignorance to understand the concept and the idea vs. the exact thought at this time in intuition.

Contimplation of one statue or another, it is apparent that the Gods surround from Rome to here. Stories of Medusa while satyrs play and Neptune makes his presence known. A thought of if Oceanus was in Rome and the story of Tritons and travel, it is here that perhaps one of those Tritons exist in another fountain where no doubt another exists in Greece of respect and understanding. The difference being the landscape has changed, the architecture remains the same with additions over the hundreds of years. New Gods replace Old Gods were once stood one deity for another. What lessons are they there to teach wonding why the displacement from there to here to there. Collected thoughts and stories unfold from street to street. Once private homes now open for the public to experience what was collected and once held private now publically available to such viewing as if most of these people would never had been allowed in these homes without invitation. Now, an open world of welcome to explore places that once were revered and still are in what they collected in their lifetimes. As family transition from one home to the next, I can't help but wonder where did this family go vs. that family. Dante ended up in Ravenna for sure where they don't speak much of it as Florence was central to the overall concept of inspiration. I see it the same way any artist would, pure inspiration where during the 1300s no doubt academies to train other artists but sitting observing, sketching what is presented to them.

Where did artist go since the 1300s?
What inspired them and what do people completely get drawn back into?

A remix of thought understanding that in each building a refrence to another land and another world. I imagine Dante to be quite confused on modern art and fascinated at the same time not knowing what it looks like but understanding abstraction of thoughts? What do you mean these lines represent the Passion of The Christ? How does that work between literalism and expression? The description becomes essential where it is understood the retainment of image then was a reproduction based on words, now you have an image as a representation of an idea that invites words afterwards. Such a strange way to hold onto memory and recollection.

Even before Michelangelo, what was introduced after Dante that would had inspired in a different capacity? Perspective there in understanding the same patterns occur but where do things get personal in reference and where is the commonality? As one collects thoughts, so too the introduction to new ideas and stories yet to be told.

Why the same stories over and over? It is not like it is difficult to go in new directions and avenues. Surely there is a lesson for such to be learned there. Inspiration is alive and well where once from physical art and books found only at the library there is the introduction of movies, music you can take with you were you once had to sit live to experience it. The same of any play as no movie existed back in the 1300s. It is not without notice the one thing that remains on the power, wealth and perception of society from such that still remains. As the world opens up to travel, where does the mind wander to now. Am I down the street around the corner. Perhaps I am back in Rome looking at one thing or another or meeting one or two other from there. The perception of identity is always present that you are what is around you and influenced by such one way that it becomes a general acceptance towards social acceptance or rejection. The strangeness of such to mold stories one way or another now when so easier to do by word of mouth prior without the ability to fact check or process. An understood aspect as one differentiates between fact and fiction on either the simpliest of things or the most complex.

It is understood at this point that as I draw from memory, others have drawn from my memories prior and from it inspiration to one thing or another. Imagine the citation of references Dante would have to do in order to remotely get him to open his mouth of the thought process besides what hge presented to the world after so many years a struggl, yet really wrapped up in his work and trying to make it one way or another from the transition of what he knew to where he ended up.

A search through the various open spaces of museums present. Questions of Death Masks apparent as one wonders which is the true death mask of Dante and which is the copy. Irony as that plays out later in life in understanding that the intention may had been lost in some areas where one wishes death or persecution on others based on a book of someone who went through something that fundamentally changed him. I question in these cooridors, what reference was he pulling from in mythology in this aspect. Did one reference a certain house or party? Perhaps a person transferred and personified into a concept of connection understanding there is always a reason for placement one way or another. Circles first as anger and an attempt to understand begins. Not knowing where to go mid-life, he searches for that which he knows most. Storytelling from the foundation of Rome and world build and introduce what is found throughout those streets and this.

The common aspect of the Death Mask, a way to preserve something understanding it was well before photography. A held on belief to life where it is replastered, remolded and then placed on area or another citing the question of which is the original. I have no doubt one also exists in Ravenna, but I wouldn't be surprised if they are recollected and brought to Florence anyways since the city is so fond of such a story to transfer things from one place to another. The beauty of any story or book, is that once it is read a continuation of such exists in both understanding it forward while retracing steps backwards to understand the screwdness of social commentary in what does or doesn't get missed in moral lessons of striving towards inspiration and going to the highest authority in literature form while so much athority along the way in understanding the difference I had then and where I am at now understanding the collaborative efforts of mythology in order to complete his series, 'The Divine Comedy'. Squares of Beatrice present here, I wonder if I should pick up an Italian copy of it as such knowing physicality is not in my budget on this trip. It is the thought process behind it that I have to hold down, expecially as I know in 2022 I've been attacked, my work stolen and other's simply claim it for their own ideas or inspiration until proven otherwise. Internally I stick to 2022 in thought before going back to the streets of Florence. Attack after attack understanding the complex addition of perhaps banking on the worth of files after my death pondering why one story or another was lost or why this book was never read or not. A contrived aspect to simply a complex aspect of , 'Well, they were probably doing it for so long without recourse, that eventually it comes a point they have better investment opportunities supporting living artists, vs. the dead.'.

In the death shroud capacity, I think to myself, 'What would Dante do if he was allowed back in Florence from exile?' An interesting notion as he is all around anyways. You can't miss him or feel like he is there one way or another. Inspiration drawn continually from him by multiple sources, one still questions originality in practicality. It is of no doubt of I that of major investor interest in anything Dante 'The Divine Comedy' references, it is always clear the difference between ine and what is not 'The Divine Comedy'. No doubt that much interest in such an area would denote the same level of interest in the right circles as well onl to know that it is the physchological side that I look at things in generalities and branch out. I don't speak much in this book of where things go because I am not compounding the story into one massive book. It takes time to process everything and the reaction aspects denotes the questions of expansion that I've gone in that are far beyond the individuality of Dante's perspective while respecting the original source, inspired by it and others and went to directions in both the original version of this book that people didn't want to pay for yet somehow it managed to still go elsewhere. I look at it no different that hundreds of emails being sent through my email without my permission as if someone got caught and just doesn't want to accept the damage of liability of such a feat that occurred before. I stand by this book was not written prior to Feb. 21, 2019 but these posts of my trip of Italy definitely were and ultilized in a manner that is respectful and also full of lessons on life and morality as no doubt others wished to teach the same of I. When looking at each other's masks in continuance, which one is the copy and which one is the original?

I come across further illustrations of Maps of Purgatory and of Heaven at the Dante museum. I imagine where my fascination has been in that regard and where I have ventured into is the common depiction of the mountain on the outside. Walled protection to thoughts veiled at the point after addressing aspects of Hell in a fully realized map. As one already went and was shook to the core, it is only understandable to reach around the topics moving forward and begin to protect guarded aspects of the reveal of empathy. A mountain climb once that occurs with the understanding it is completely acceptable in shareable aspects to go around the outskirts of such. I can't help but think with what I've done way or or another in 'Ugly Simple Truths' is the knowledge that I've gone through 'it' and continue to do such to reach my destination in continued paths forward and sometimes in backtrack. In understanding and the search of empathy and understanding, different directions and intentions between reality of reveal while coming to a set of conclusions on what I was looking for. At this point is at least on the reality side and the fictional side, the foundations of such is copyright protected where aspects of a story of a mountain and the internal workings and systems of such intertwine with stories I've only begun to find the courage to type out and protect in 2022. A series from 2012 for UST and the question of how to proceed from there towards heaven in this book and from others as well. I visualize a Die-cut of such to paths of traveling through things in a different capacity undertstanding there is no one right answer or one singular path. There is simply a desire for one thing or another in life and the journey of discovery goes from there.

'One of the best examples of forced perspective u will ever see. Entire cathedral was filled with fire bushes as well.'

As I don't have proper visual reference anymore, I am further reliant to at least the written structure of such beauty in the city. I'd say from any aspect, go and visit yourself to draw your own conclusions or beginnings from. Back in the 1300s or really up until the invention of modern cameras, there was the beauty of learning venacular and descriptors. From there came book after book, letter after letter where the artistry of a sentence structure was promoted through society where still a clever craft to word smith a saying together knowing every letteracy matters in the formation of a sentence. How much beauty can be put in a single sentence knowing that as letters were far and few in travel and delivery to wish someone else well or talk of daily adventures. Even a casual hello could take days or weeks to get to. Now, in photographic form you don't have to say anything and let the image write the story for you. A craft change from one focus to another. 'A picture paints a thousand words...so I don't have to say a single one.' An understood statement of again cleverness of such a game. If Dante were to do that, I imagine there would be 'copy-rights' involved in that as why would one need to write if a picture says everything and nothing? Why would someone even send an email if someone else is going to read it and transfer the information elsewhere outside the benefit of the creator or recipient? Words matter just as much as visual inspiration where pre-investment in discovery zones simply denotes either a pending offer of advancement or a complete shut out from the market on which was impeded on. I see it no different that there is a constant need to surmount wealth that eventually backfires and goes the other direction.

Imagine the thought process of all those unspoken sentiments and phrases already called for by other people before it even goes to the intended recipient. Such an advance on a property of such is surmountable at best know from a single image or painting whole novels, books and artistry forms from such. How many songs have been written about 'The Mona Lisa'? How many books written about the statue of David? In Citizen Kane, the inspiration for a lifetime boils down to a sled wondering what other Citizen Kanes are out therr in their own multiverse references involving sled-rides one place or another. A cost of growing up perhaps where even as one does so and crossing into the realm of adult-ish adulting, it is always a past life of childhood memory that lingers on in revisit one way or another. Story driven narratives denotes a reference to the past in some form. How could it not because even when you came up with the idea and proceeded to flesh it out, the initial moment of the idea is already in the past and grows from there. It took 12 years for Dante to write 'The Divine Comedy'. Do you not think he would have other talking points while also living a life as well? What else would had been on Dante's mind and clearly made money or had money to survive without working. Financed? Exiled did not mean he lost his wealth, and definitely never lost his wealth of knowledge or personal experience.

"This place has to be the inspiration for Labyrinth. I can't find my way back home." I travel the streets pretty quickly taking of note the narrow roads and the structures. A maze like pattern from one street to the next where there is a easy room for getting lost if one does not pay attention to the subtle differences from one building to the next. I imagine as I get tired I have to remember if I ate much today. More than likely not much as corner markets denotes a constant on the go for I. There are words and there are pictures and there is the understanding that perhaps things aren't what they seem around here. One can go in circles looking for answers onto to find more questions than anything else in trying to notice every single little detail and wondering was everything is in focus in the Renaissance outside of the fact of it being an explosion of inspiration that was proceeded by The Dark Ages. In enlightenment and in ideas concepted of techniques one way or another, something awoke in people and began to be translated from pain and held back expansion due to plagues and other conditions towards society. Where do I go from here? For the moment I think and simply ponder if I remember the steps to retrace if need be.

In the distance I hear the sound of a violinist playing. I know not the corner from which it speaks and echoes between the wall of one building to the next. A violinist plays the theme of 'Game of Thrones' owned by HBO. Probably not the best direction to be heading in when in a new land that I know nothing about it, but I am drawn to the connection of bow to string. I go a few blocks and find the violinist playing the song before she moves onto another piece. I record what I can after tipping her. I replay the video now finding it odd that no sound is present in it anymore as if it is a pre-emptive rights issue already or was perhaps then. It is not like I was the financier of the street performing siren of strings and wood, but here we are wondering what gets capture in imagination of factual events then and now. To sit and admire the artistry of sound in such a city is to again note that difference of languages and what is universal from one culture to next. Is it one note or the other. Perhaps a series of connection impressed at the memorization of such as if practiced, perfected and then on display begging for connection and appreciation before perhaps an original piece or something that would be remembered vaguely if never even heard again.

I spend my time in appreciation and then realize I should be heading home to relax for the evening. I got home back to the hotel and rest for awhile and chat where I can to at least have some kind of interaction with people in a different capacity. I write a bit and then proceed to go back out to wonder a bit more. Perhaps a combination of keep going as far as I can or simply the interaction when streets are not so busy and things gets relaxed and can process as much. The streets at night of golden lights and squares. Still probably not the best to walk alone, yet find it comforting. I imagine early to bed and early to rise where if there is such an early closure to the city it is because time tables denote an expansive day toward daily tourism.

I end up coming back to the square of Beatrice where a statue stands in the evening. Questions remain as there is also a statue of Dante present in the city. If one was to look at the sculptures of the world and give them a persona molded through the eyes of other artists, it is probable that there is a life presented to then in perhaps a grown up aspect of Gheppeto where depending on the the subject matter at hand, there is the wish of the artist to bring life to something in a different direction then of solely a child. Perhaps a birth of a diety here and there, where over time that of the preferred form (culturally) of men and women of both diety representation and that of archetyp- ical fashions of warriors, heroes & villains. Myth makers where over time their story collects, transforms and brings life and purpose for their existence. Thoughts go to the statue of David in again an eye for angles to understand perspective and idealism.

With the statue of Beatrice present, it was as if a misting of rain occurred at some point when I was indoors. Reflective surfaces of understanding that in the story of Dante (portrayed almost voyeuresque) denotes lust but perhaps also the fondness of keeping a distance. Not knowing much about the interaction between the two, I've wondered the inspiration aspect of evoking of such a beauty in later works. Perhaps to gain favor is probably not the right answer with your wife in the same building as you, but one never knows the perimeters of any relationship. Was it a missed op- portunity to Dante? Perhaps a fondness where there is an understanding of such in secret. I imagine if Virgil came to Dante by the bequest of fictional Beatrice, perhaps it was she who gave Dante an introduction to such at such an early age of life and then it grew from there. History denotes one thing or another, yet one understands the aspects of going back to introductions and that of childhood wonder and amazement. As Dante married into another prominant family, it is more than likely he didn't have to work or was financed by the family towards his *Commedia*. I see a stark difference in where I have gone with my work where underpaided, at the time unemployed, and the work done on my own free-time and executed how I could in combined charity aspects towards the advancement of myself careerwise and personally.

A combination of thoughts there where I go back to the meaning of Beatrice and still question things from a modern sense behind it. There is love abound one way or another in my works and then there is the expansion of it from there where there is a diffference between 2017 and 2022 where protection mode is present vs. what I imagine could or could not be protection mode elsewhere. It doesn't seem so, but at the same time things could be one way or another in extreme examples. At what point does one bend was things move from actual representation to eventually the fiction-alized aspect of things either romanticized or going one way or another? At least a clear difference between one side and the other, simply wondering if even then is it a relatability aspect or of truths masked one way or another.

In Beatrice there is Dante and the reference of such is similar to the interlock of say Icarus and Daedalus. A dance of identity and purpose where intention is not so clearly defined in meaning (nor perhaps should it I imagine). The idea of love in any capacity is always an understanding that there are many B's in the sea in that regard, but which ones hold the value in the end? To say there isn't discussion points, is to understand still the beauty of wrapping things around other things where in unwrapping you may get one answer or lead towards and entirely different set of questions on where love is and isn't found. Beauty to know it comes in many different ways and if one directs in one way, with surity they can undercoat things elsewhere.

In thought of contimplation of even now standing in the mist filled air of street lit Florence, not all the details present themselves in dim lights yet again. Naturally it forms the weight of thoughts of relationships in general wondering what came before, what was learned and where to go from there. From a distance many things had in understanding over the years where even in talks or not, promises made of Self and Others on where things went and where they could go. Never a moment here knowing that I'll never be able to replicate the experience of seeing something for the first time as with any other person's love. To gaze upon anyone that is either a part of you or someone you knew would simply be a part of your life one way or another is amazing in any glance. From the birth of a child, to the glancing gaze in passing and smile or perhaps simply knowing one way or another that you would be friends or more at some point in life. The gaze towards anyone is important if one was so inclined to speak or say anything. Even in familiarity a choice to say one thing or not.

A Beatrice is many things, but whomever Beatrice is to Dante equally have their own life and story that went elsewhere. As with Daedalus the same, where stories travel after one's death to where others of association say one thing or another toward their memory or advancement from such. What would Beatrice had written had Dante passed away first? History denotes she is not directly connected to such but doesn't mean she wouldn't if the connection found afterwards. Everyone has a story and even from inspiration for stories of others it is either met with honor, disgust or simply never known one way or another. There is inspiration and there is love and then there is the fact of other things to consider. As in the context of Dante's Beatrice a connection to one thing or another hidden of why such praise and driven aspect understanding that there was love there one way or another. If one doesn't have a driving point towards connection in one way or another, then there becomes the point of stories of solitude where simply no one would connect to anyways as it was never the point to relate nor understand one another. Perhaps there was an inability to speak and only found the words afterwards or the courage to do so one way or another. A process that comes in time where in any variable youth could be understood of both young love or introductions or as life proceeds to bigger concepts and conflictions of what to say not know how to translate properly and finding it easier to start one way or another with the understanding more people comprehend and can relate than you may think. If only you open your mouth and say something.

'A Dance of Light between Beatrice and Dante" - Sketch Translation' November 29, 2022. Philip A. Bonneau.

Perhaps out of time and context, I revisit the statue of Dante within the same types of questions. A different piazza he is found, but on the same board and in the same city. My mind flashes to the two of them on the same field of understanding. In my thoughts I know have been on the right path for many reasons. I cannot explain for the life of me why I have been drawn one way or another since a child. I reflect perhaps now in 2022 memory of 2017 wondering wht has unfolded of social injustice, my own experience of inspiration, of love-had, love-lost, love I cannot even consider now considering the sequestered aspect of attempting to still do the right thing and protecting what I can alone knowing every day I write or do anything artistically it simply could go out the door for someone else to take and cast me aside as if I was nothing but everything to someone at the same time.

I know my processes has changed ever so slightly and I know many answers to things and yet I'm wanted to be just a copy artist despite originality after originality to I. I don't even look at a television screen or watch a movie anymore knowing it may or may not have somerthing to do with my works one way or another. When I look at what could be I know how much I have to do that I have to constantly protect myself and counter in ways that I cannot be every hat I can think of. I pull where I can of strength and from morality and reason. I jump into novice areas of one thing or another as if I speak it could be just taken as a discovery aspect to simply be ready to battle me one way or another when I was never the enemy to begin with.
I see your statue in Florence wondering if you saw what your works produced and where claim goes one way or another. Interpretation is no different and expected for anyone of any book or written aspects of themselves. Souls trapped in books, life brought to rock through sculpture...the life of an artist brings life or should. It discusses death as if a way to prepare one way or another. How can there be death in the birth of something such as art. The chipping away of what was natural is understood. Imagine what happens to not owning a sculpture but given a fragment of the disguarded rock chosen to be chipped away. Does it not have the same value if only in connection? There is always what comes unexplained within and what is molded by the elements over thousands of years, maybe shorter...maybe longer. The active decision to mold something one way or another comes from environment as much as the potential of one eye over the other in what they see or do not.

Active hands one way or another just as much as active imaginations and patience had to see something through. No doubt your life experiences matter in conclusions. Had Beatrice not passed on before you finished *Commedia* would she had even been in *Paradiso* as she was? The recognition of male/female there is apparent just as much as the underlying aspects of the planets denotes respect to Roman Mythology just as much as Christianity where in advancement it is natural the progression of respect towards any other introduction and inclusion. The inclusion of sphere after sphere of Angels denotes respect of knowledge and something older and understanding.

In inclusive-exclusion, I understand that at any point this could had been different for anyone. Years now and I the cost from such an expression of life and trying to find similarities towards coping with other or letting people come to their own conclusions. The introductions are what cannot be explained as anything other than truth and with that I try to keep a mindset in this book and section of my life while understanding I'll not be going at the pace I was as others take prescent yet again.

My heart is in the right place or maybe left.
Centered in thoughts...
I have to remain focus and continue this journey with far less means to do so.
If I stop trying, then why would anyone else even attempt anything?

"Never trust the street vendors trying to get you into locations. I lived in the hood too long to fall for that game."

Florence to me was everything for a crossroad on where to go and where to begin. It was an aspiration to be met. It was a city to understand. I'm here in this city for the first night and I'm unsure of what I should talk about or what I can think about. I surprised myself with my confessional at St. Peters and apparent daddy/God issues, but here means something more to me. This is the beginning to the end. This is what I worked for. In doing so I think I have to list out the main things of what it is I'm looking to accomplish with this series and with this journey.

I believe I have to come up with some sort of a definitive answer to this end or else all of this will just be an ouroboros conclusion never really ending and just recycling to repeat it's destiny over and over. I've struggled figuring out exactly what that is. Perhaps I've grappled from day 1 on what this series is and what it is to become.

Part of it comes from experience/inexperience and the other part from desires and hope and things not working as I thought they should. From it both disappointment and pleasant surprises have come into play and I can't help but think that is what life is always going to be...a never-ending test of conditioning to adapt to what the world throws at you in both good and bad. That is not a bad thing, it just keeps me a little bit guarded or a little bit not wanting to play all my cards. I think perspective is always going to be the key though. It's not so different from basing the beginning off with found objects that's are all around you and finding worth in something no one wanted or forgot. I believe there is something good in any scenario. Looking back at the beginning, I got myself out of one bad environment or another, made my own place, built from there. From that I made my own mistakes and found myself in another bad place and from there I found another for myself and grew and learned as I went. Can't always get it right, but through every experience I can't help believe that things get a little more right as I go. I'm not the Alice I used to be. For every bad memory there is an equally positive one trying to understand which one weighs more. There isn't a term such as weighed-up, but there is weigh-ed down.

Coming here makes me ask what this series is about now. This is the end for me. I can't exactly expand a Divine Comedy after 3 parts. Can't go beyond Heaven. But there is always that question and desire of what comes after that. I know my connection is the psycholgical aspects of coping. If I were to entertain what a narrative is on the Dante side of his works, it would still be on, 'What would happen if Dante returned to Florence?' He already has. He is there. Not in a physical body sense. But he is a representation, a driving factor. Even in the story he returns from Heaven and would naturally go elsewhere after. At that point Heaven accepted of what was there and a branch towards a healthy life to where if one thing or another happens afterwards, far more knowledgeable of 'Self' to be able to translate any situation better than the time before. I'm at the footsteps to what I wanted and talked about for so long. I come from a place of both question and doubt but my faith and inner trust equally challenge that.

"Why am I here? I'm f*cking here!
What is right? This is right ATM.

'That's the questioning that is just always going to be subjective and personal and may not even be the main driver but it could be. When fighting with ourselves, there is no first line of defense. We are the front lines of 'Ourselves'. It's the question I ask myself now. It's the question I surprisingly asked myself in Rome. It's the question I asked a priest on if I am doing right.

I'm beginning to wonder if I should just stop asking that question and just go with the flow. Who can even tell me if this is right or wrong anyways? If I listened to other's I would have never have continued this open forum of thought. But it felt right and it feel right to finish it even if it is becoming harder to do so.

When in the Vatican I asked about forsaking.

Biblical in conversation, but I am beginning to understand that that is an issue that this series drove while discovering quite the opposite in others. It's been a day to let things sit in what I asked. Impulse drove me to talk about the things I did. I'm with a stranger I'll never meet again, well versed in faith and scripture and those things are the things that come out of my mouth?

In hindsight this series pretty much deals with just one reaction over the other and that I seem to struggle with understanding of things. I kind of feel it privileged to talk about struggle at this point because I appreciate things more because of it. But at the same time, no one should ever let you feel like it's not ok to feel anything you are going through. I don't know a single person in the world who has the perspective of every individual who can discount what one person is feeling, and any comparison to another person's issues as 'bullshit' on their part. (Perspective while understanding venacular. There isn't really a singular word for the complete discount of someone else's emotions, expression or something that is a complete waste of time to process, deal or put-up with without understanding the discountment aspect of vocalization)

But here I am in the middle of Italy and the only thing that really comes to my memory is I wish you could see this. I'm here. I'm 5000 miles away from anything and I'm living life and discovering. I actually have zero fear at the moment. This isn't about work. This isn't about a love life. This is just now and everything I wanted. I'm not sure if I'm talking to my dad. Nor an ex or anyone else who just joined this journey. That is the part of me that struggles. This is probably one of the rare times where I'm just sitting back and saying, "You are here. This is you. Somehow I made it here with help. I'm walking down these streets. There are vendors on every side of me. I can't help but think that this is exactly where I am supposed to be at the moment." What is being sold? What is being bartered? The value of many things always a negotiation of discussion.

I don't know what tomorrow will bring. I've scheduled myself to walk on Heaven. Faith is factoring a great deal than I ever thought in things on this trip. I hate that at this point in my life, I opened up a door for honesty with this series but at the same time, I welcome not feeling alone. No one wants to feel alone and perhaps someone out there will connect on some level. Moving forward, all I want to do now is keep things for myself but that is a total cop out at this point. I can't go back from that promise.

Perhaps I have grown.Perhaps I have not.
But I'm walking in what I felt was going to be my heaven and what was Dante's.

Tomorrow I live that and I can't help but wondering if this is right?!
But I'm here. It's right now I guess
Whether this is a mistake I pay for later or not, it doesn't matter.

Tomorrow is another day and I make it matter one way or another.
Don't be quick to post these final posts.
They are the ones that make it worth it or not.

'A jammed packed breeder bar called 'Inferno' (across the street).
Yup...sounds about right. Guess tonight is straight night. Wish me luck.'
-They don't even try to be on the DL. Apparently it's not cheating if the same sex.
Still fun and always inviting no matter which area I stop in and say hello. Everyone
is on vacation one way or another or simply used to tourist and learning different
cultures. Apparently it is quite pleasant in Inferno. At least that version of such.

Perhaps a thought and notion back to Beautiful Layered Lies in connection. Don't
know everyone yet in it, but it is an introduction and a process forward towards finding out what is absurd and what holds weight. Even the strangest of things and places
can bring about one thing or another. What are they trying to say and where do life
events go in one direction or another. To think of one thing or another is to imagine
either what you have never seen before or perhaps begin to translate what you have in
new directions and understanding that collective it represents something else.

'Fun fact discovered. Pretty much the bulk of Florence shuts down around 1-2 outside
of a few bars here and there. You can pretty much travel through all the great sites
with minimal to no one present. HOWEVER....if say your phone dies and your sense
of direction is F'ed up...you will instantly feel like Jennifer Connelly trying to solve
the labyrinth....' I hire a taxi to bring me home.

If only I just kept going that way...I was 2-4 blocks from the hotel, I just couldn't find
it at 2-3am in the morning. (Social media says one thing else but that profile doesn't
exist anymore and is my property...RIP Pippitydodah...you did well at the time)

I'm going to bed.

ENTRY 42:

I like that one of the last self-portraits I did was without a mask. It was me naked. Past. Present. Future. Acceptance. A new home. A new beginning. I member my thought process during that shoot. A home gained by the grace of others. A new beginning and a chance to start over on my own. I owe so much to Michael Goodwin for understanding and letting me into his home while I rebuilt a new life. I am privileged as well to have met Robby and get to know him. I remember the challenge of coming home to Atlanta. What it meant. The strength needed to do so. Who I was prior is not the man I am today. 3 years removed from the city. Now back differently than as I was before. Better? Worse? ...Or Simply just older? I may be none the wiser. Private..."secluded" isn't the right word, but I do not let many people into my life for good reasons. Even if in the chance writings were taken from me, they still do not get the full picture of who I am. Meticulous in what I write when I need to write. I'm conflicted on the thought of things not shared that are now available to sift through. Interpretations matter where clear lines between fact/fiction, truth/hearsay, reality/imagination. Metaphor/Allegory.

Do I own my words and thoughts?
"I do."
'Maybe Not'
But I also own not acting on any thoughts not realized and found to be in poor taste or not worth exploring. One can not fault an idea/thought that was never acted on without questioning why it wasn't to begin with.

"I have a problem with that."

"But you always have a problem with that."

I take issue where if it didn't publicly come from me, it was not sanctioned and stolen. I take issue if you didn't talk to me. Sided stories.

I'm thinking about journalism. If you are going to run a piece, the key is to reach out to all parties for comment. When using a mug shot, there is a responsibility on the journalist to allow all parties to rebuttal. Failure to do so is biased, grudged and hearsay until proven in a court of law. Regardless, if you are going to run a hit piece, give all parties the chance to speak. DO NOT PUBLICALLY SHAME! (Based on one perspective over other methods used since the basis of civilizations where popular opinion or leadership discussions prove one thing or another over time on effectiveness or why.) The Scarlet Letters come to mind. I was forced to wear a lot of shit I didn't have to. I questioned everything about myself. 9 years later am I better off or worse because of it? I find that over the years I have had to question myself over and over again in thought. At this point I've had to assess everything. I have made a name for myself though. Years apart removed but still a name exists nevertheless. I wonder if I did an AMA now would it even matter anymore?

One of the proudest moments of my life was the topic of LGBTQ+ marriage. Gay marriage in my eyes. (As simply understood common venacular at the time understanding it is not entirely accurate terminalogy.) 2 men. 2 women. Fully accepting and realizing there is a bigger spectrum of love that I don't fall into but respect as the passage of such was on traditional unions of 2 people (in American culture) knowing multiple religions and relationship constructs have more than 2 partners. I image to a certain extent the concept of the Divorcee already refers to 1st, 2nd, 3rd etc. But I remember sitting down and bringing up the topic. Was told.

"We don't get political"

While also being told after the fact.

"Most of the people in that room were gay."

A conversation to be had nevertheless of introduction and amazingly a great way to open up discussion and candided approaches.

I question the conviction. Was that the right thing to say? It definitely was noticed. I remember the day of the Supreme Court ruling. I begged for consideration of recognition from a company standpoint. I said you are either on the right side of history or the wrong side. I was given the opportunity by (AA-A. VP of Marketing) and I am sure after discussion by Michele. They let me have that moment of expression through the company's moment of industry leading acceptance. The rainbow flag with just. "Love Wins" written. A Facebook profile image that changed an industry on a global scale or at least in the United States. Done with taste. The first major designer in bridal to do so. A message heard loud and clear within the industry. It was the right thing to do and I'm proud of that moment collectively. I'm proud others allowed for it to happen. The definition of marriage changed to...love wins. (love conquers all?) Other companies followed suit after us in different ways. Social media noted the differences. Application denotes it takes time for society to say one thing or another on what people personally accept, disapprove of or simply just introduced to in the first time to concepts foreign. A point proven of prior hesitation on the matter from another company's example. Approach matters in any conversation, but it was about overall acceptance. From a wedding industry perspective, I believe the average wedding at the time was around 30K in the United States. Openning the market in a capacity of acceptance of unions and love only boosts the economy in multiple areas of commerce, service and hospitality. Never a harm in that capacity.

If one wanted to get into economics on the anti-wedding aspect. Why are divorce rates over 50%? It is not a bridal/wedding contribution for repeat business, but it exists. This is why maybe staying out of people's bedrooms and unions are probably important. The importance of relationships learned early on in life. Keeping them is important that is learned individually over time on a case-by-case basis. In all aspects, people and relationships grow together or apart, but the last thing people need is others shaming any relationship on any side. Adulting is difficult or fun at one point or another. I imagine few anticipate their average 30K reception to end in divorce in a monumental moment of any union's memory.

I like that crowning achievement of my life. The push for marriage acceptance recognized by an 80 year plus global brand. All from conviction and intuition and the right place and time of history.

I have a right to know what happened.
If there was an internal investigation, after it's completed,
I have the right to know about it as there was mention of one at Freud/Diablo.
Information withheld.

"...You can't just trump charges..." (FD-L)

I think of November 2nd. My last day at Freud.
I wrote a resignation and emailed Randstad the night before.
I reiterated it on the phone to my mother that same evening after my birthday dinner at a French restaurant of Oysters and reprieve.
I talked to my assigned Randstad Rep the next morning and there was hesitation in going to work.
Fear.
Anxiety.
I knew what did & didn't happen on my birthday.
Awareness from multiple perspectives.
It will be the same thing remembered every year henceforth.
I knew what they were going to do for a week of talks of firing me on my birthday and then 'getting rid of the other one' (Paraphrase) Impossible they didn't know if they were transcribing phone calls or having them provided. Or was it selective listening and '...reacting in real-time'.
All spoken in an open office setting.
Working from home definitely was the best option as (FD-D) mentioned that 'people are freaked out he can here' before I ever mentioned such in the office and asked to be moved away from hearing as it was 'pyschologically affecting me' and I mentioned it as such. I was not moved, yet it might had been considered over time.
On my phone...
Never did that because. "...reacting in real time."
(Conversations had via phone and text with my mother on needing to talk to a lawyer and then while they were discussing things in the office, I texted her saying, 'I don't feel comfortable talking to one and that I wasn't going to do so' (Paraphrased) While they reacted to the text messages just sent.
They knew this was affecting me.
They knew how deep this was getting.

"...Too deep, too long."

A willful quote expressed on the Facebook I already changed my privacy settings on and booted them off of. Brought up the next day indirectly with (FD-B). They knew this was emotionally affecting me and where it was heading.
They willfully did this.

You can't move someone just because you heard a conversation on my phone.

A panic stricken Randstad employee (myself) just experienced indirect physical and verbal threats while a Freud/Diablo employee swung a baseball bat over his should in his office. This was done while I intentionally looked at a piece of paper that was commented on by other employee on me looking at it intensely. From holding up that paper I was really looking right at him in the reflection in the upper glass part of the workspace. (Looking directly at him but not for complete surity and understanding the message they were sending and the need to not react, be silent and report it as soon as I am out of the office.

Those were threats.

That was being cocky.

That was intimidation.

Do not talk about someone while swinging a baseball bat and saying how you will "pop him" and "we will get him on the internet" (Paraphased?) or was it simply, 'We will pop him on the internet.' (FD-S)

"I know a guy" (FD-S)

'I bet you did.' -Me (Internally now in revisit)

There was mentions of 'old school' tactics and going to people's houses to hurt or threaten. Relieved that I am now in a gated apartment complex and Michael does not regularly stay at the home address they have on file. I should have mentioned it to Michael then, but fear of saying anything was going on at the time as they now were putting other people in danger by not having the proper address.

Going back to November 2nd. I walked in. the digital department knew what happened.

It was the remorseful tones of the office as if reacting to either my phonecall to my mother the night before or my email that was not sent to them. Or perhaps the phone call I had with my Randstad Rep prior discussing how I do not feel comfortable coming to work and the environment is not healthy or safe. We discussed how to proceed with the 2-weeks notice letter and I worked up the strength to just once again go into the office as I need to pay bills and don't have a plan to just leave but I have to. It is not a healthy environment. I pick myself up to walk in professionally once again.

"She did this" (FDe - Digital department)

FD-D, FD-S, and FD-B all in FD-B's office.

"He thinks he is doing the right thing." (FD-S)

"I can't work with him anymore." (FD-S)

They knew of my resignation before I got to work and still talked about things in an open-door setting. Which was exactly the reason why I read it to my mother on the phone the night before. They were reacting in real time to information they should not have had available to them.

The same would be said in tested aspect on why I never would have utilized or taken the catalog for any of my portolio purposes or otherwise. All those die guides of vulnerability to know any digital version of it is a liability of assets in the current form. No thank you on something I was trying to design past early 90s styling and to create in future applications that 'no one wants to work on that antyways' aspects. In some of their entrapment attempts, they turned on the USB access to the laptop I was assigned and even then I refused to put in a USB drive of any kind to it and only thing ever connected in those slots with or without the USB permissions was my phone for charging only. There was zero chance I would want that and was simply trying to figure out the phone call/text aspect of what I absolutely don't have, don't want and even that assigned computer, never a Wetransfer sent from that computer. It didn't work like that and still agree with the fact it is not Bosch policy to use Wetransfer on any-thing of sensitive material.

I didn't last long that day as my theory became true. Maybe 30-45 minutes in? If that.
You can only listen to so much & beg so many different ways to get people to stop and move me from hearing conversations or see that I was getting sick on multiple fronts with no insurance at the time with not even a chance to take a day off due to the first experience of doing so.
I printed out my resignation and brought it into Bonnie's office.
Beforehand, I mentioned to FD-L, that I am giving myself a birthday present.
"I know what you have been going through." (FD-L)
Spoken with compassion and understanding without much more said. The birthday present was to get out of the environment at all costs and figure out what occurred, how to approach it without another day in the office of anxiety driven illegality and continued possible threats or conversations I did not have to listen to indirectly anymore.
"You knew this was coming."
"I want my privacy back." Both spoken verbially by I on November, 2, 2018 in the office during that.
There was a playing like they didn't know and I shut it down right there.
"CLOSE A FUCKING DOOR." runs through my head of things heard over the months. Never verbalized and if did, probably on the phone to my mother or (K). If phone transcripts were the issue, I definitely sought out council to a former higher up of ADP in HR who is very much closely connected to me in

friendship/family capacity on multiple occasions.

I asked to leave right then and there and I was walked out by (FD-B). I never allowed my phone to be reconnected to a Bosch owned computer again. All I wanted to do was to sleep. I was met with compassion where I printed out my 2-weeks notice, but when minimal discussion I suggested to them at this point it was best to leave now and not honor my 2 weeks.

I spoke to my Randstad Rep shortly after leaving where Freud/Diablo said that I had just up and quit. She wanted to know what changed and I expressed what I could to her in what was further probable manipulation of the matter on Freud/Diablo to Randstad who never came on site to verify the charges or to fix the situation after repeated conversations with them first before going into being professional with the on-site supervisors and employees. Some conversations were meant with my actual employer before ever addressing with the fixed-term contractees.

A drive to (K)'s later that day. A return home to Savannah where I grew up since 1989 before moving to Atlanta in 2006 and my mother still living there. I remember on the way getting confused on where I was at exactly. I stopped and purchased a phone charger. When I got to (K)'s,

I asked him to drive to Savannah. I crashed in the backseat.

I had never just quit a job before with no back-up plan and the months on edge took a toll physically and mentally. For my health, it was important to remove myself from the situation.

I WAS DONE.

...the things you allow when you need to keep a roof over your head and food on the table.

In Savannah, I remember talking to one of my oldest childhood friend's mother about what happened. She is a paralegal. Not knowing how to approach this, I left my phone in the car and powered off. I looked up the FBI the following day. I went to the Chatham County Police Department expressing there is something on my phone. They didn't take my phone, but did say how someone probably got in through it.

I tried. I'm trying. I'm definitely not the same anymore on the outside, but I am here on the inside. This is the difference between phasing out in the real world, but still being cognizant. Inside there is the need to speak up but only when the time is right.

Until then silence externally to understand what I am thinking, retaining and need to express. Come back.

I talked to lawyers (that was impeded on)
I spoke to another lawyer (they questioned phone taps)
It was finding out at PureRED that everything was true makes me question everything. They saw my bank account zero out and go into the negative. They saw me ask churches for help with my rent. Asking for food when I couldn't afford it. Asking my father if he was ok with me being gay...They got to see emotions that never should have been shared and were not willfully done so. Both companies and no one talked to mr about it directly.

*A life destroyed is not coffee table talk. Thoughts of that specifically associated to what followed into PureRED. I question why I am here now, but I know in my heart I am exactly where I need to be.

Rebuilding.
Fallen.
Cracked.
Humpty Dumpty comes to mind.

Was he pushed or did he fall?

Post 17: Day 4: The Fifth Sphere - On Top of Heaven.

"Hell. It is the dark place where our demons thrive. They sit there and torment us day in and out; striking at our fears and the things that we are most unsure of about ourselves. Sometimes they are direct in their attacks. Other times they dress themselves up in layers and will present themselves as beautiful. They will consume you or they will change you. They might not always win, but they will always test you. Eventually they will die but their voice still echoes on. Perhaps that is what Purgatory has to offer. Is there anyway to really see Heaven after that?" 5/1/2013

"This is my church
This is where I heal my hurts
It's in natural grace
Or watching young life shape
It's in minor keys
Solutions and remedies
Enemies becoming friends
When bitterness ends
This is my church

This is my church
This is where I heal my hurt
It's in the world I become
Content in the hum
Between voice and drum
It's in change
The poetic justice of cause and effect
Respect, love, compassion
This is my church"

- Group: 'Faithless',
partial lyric representation written by
Maxi Jazz, Rollo, Sister Bliss, and Jamie Catto. (1998)

'How eating seems to work at restaurants in Italy. "I would like something light for lunch like a salad." "Ok...salad to start off with and then?" "No... that's it." "Ok...i bring u brusetta and olives while we prepare the best antipasta salad for u."

The understanding of what is around me and the culture of the moment. There is so much to be fed but it is not what I am used to. A difference in courses where I imagine they want you to retain everything you can while also taking a moment to breathe, relax, unwind and let's go from there. I can go one way or another with this as even a young culture or country introduces things in return and everyone can learn from one another. Is there discount from The United States just as much as there was discount from Argentina or anywhere else while understanding the basis of civilization and understanding where things come from in stories then and stories now understanding there is an understanding of where things come from and where personal experience comes from there. So much of the world has grown to course after course with the clear understanding and respect of where I am sitting at now understanding the traveller's dream of trade and commerce there.

What am I being fed on at the moment? I understand portion control and the aspect that I really am not eating as much as I should here. Perhaps I am not digesting it properly or it takes time. I can look at this as we have everything to offer or simply understand the flabergast answer of simply a salad for dinner. Always more to be had one way or another and it is always about hospitality in the right settings.

So much food for thought to be had here in comparison to what I' have known prior while still in hindsight of 2022 questioning the Eagle of travellers into a melting pot of culture in another area of conversation. Room to grow there or buckle, unbuckle up in that conversation much to be consumed as time goes by.

Who doesn't love vacation and traveling to new lands?
Especially ones of acceptance and freedom from religious persecution, old or new. It is understood on many levels that old meets older or young meets old or young meets young and it is all relative in the scheme of things and only about who persecuted who and who saved what in the end. The idea would or should be about universal truths one way or another, but it does come down to power of knowledge or power of power knowing others are gauging human nature to see what they do with it to still get the same answer from one culture to the next. Indirectly perhaps I now consider myself a test subject while others wonder what is and isn't the control in the matter.

I swear if these people didn't smoke and walk everywhere, they should be able to roll themselves down the street.'

Got to love some food. I think I actually had a great breakfast this morning knowing I'm about to go Full Throttle at it again today. My meals are important to have, yet I don't talk much of such understanding 5 years later it is about the experience and fleshing it out accordingly wondering what course was had or if dessert was taken before the meal. I can't really say one way or another, yet I understand the aspect that at least now I can say that whatever the excuse was then, probably could had been talked about, worked out or discussed. That is of course, I have no direct basis of negative influence until mid-2018 in Atlanta wondering who was clouded one way or another or dare to want one thing or another at the expense of human life or sustainability.

I try to keep that in the back of my mind knowing maybe that isn't the scenario, but at the same time any person of venture captial would understand once I put up my website, perhaps it was a time to talk and not fuck me over. If actively negitive towards my life you either detrimented yourself or communities one way or another that I try to uphold.

I can only imagine what others have done. I can only realize my own life experience and how I tried to get others to stop back in 2018. I know not the answer now in 2022 to say one way or another.

Today was the Uffizi Gallery.
I was told to purchase my tickets in advance from the mother of a bestie who got to backpack and travel in her youth. Family strong it was understood the excitement of such a trip and understand the beauty of discover of art, the world or perspective in any way at any age. If one is not afforded the perspective of difference, then one is simply never going to see any other reflection then the one they want to see and imagine for themselves.

I treated my experience of the Uffizi in live blog form on social media. One of the most celebrated galleries of the world and for good reason. A determination to go to Florence to see the collection and the surrounded works either bought or commissioned for the very same reason one travels to any gallery, museum or of any place of artist interest. The most amazing buildings in the world are the ones that honor history and the interpretations of such in one form or another through artists. If anything else then either a shell of disregard or not a building of respect to free-thought and conversation. Intention is always important, but a museum is made to question such.

Before entry and waiting trying to get wifi to work to retrieve my tickets, I spend a great deal of time at The Loggia dei Lanzi right outside while also the river on the other side of the museum in searching for one signal or another. The time spent at The Loggia represents a recall of many famous works I have been introduced in Art History classes all compiled to a single location not even a complete block. A curated collection of monolithic contributions to the history of Art. In my snap shots I have an image of Perseus with the Head of Medusa from Benvenuto Cellini. A thought of such being surround by so many other depictions of rape. I read up more now knowing I couldn't see everything at first glance without knowledge. Held up by Jupiter, Mercury, Minerva and Perseus's mother, Danaë. 3 dieties and that of any child's god or goddess, a depiction of his mother, where Jupiter his father. Or was that still Zeus in that regard and respected on the otherside? It seems to be so in quick internet search only to see there is a difference in relationship to where there is connection from one and the other knowing personalities are completely different and equally respected based on region then and now opened up further. The name Medusa translates between the two cultures unchanged denoting respect or of a lesson that crosses between the two cultures and beyond clashes of titans of mythology and into something different to note as neither express a desire to change the story but still depict it. Minerva, that of strategy and not of war of interest with the understanding in the regards of knowing surroundings she may be placed there for one reason or another. Wisdom, Justice, Law, Victory. I do not recall if I noticed which virtues rest within the Loggia at the time, but I am sure I caught them visually as I explored. Fortitude, Temperance, Justice, Prudence.

'The Rape of Polyxena' calls into question the snake-like aspect towards that of man in the composition, especiallly in context to that of the gorgon Medusa. What is the story there in connection to one of the same type of depiction. Common for the time of representation, yet at the same time calls into question that which is being wrapped around men in the children of Medusa one way or another in representation.

There is the representation of 'Hercules and Nessus'. Giambologna. As 2022 has brought me back thrice to Chiron, I find it important to understand the difference between the two. In one a teacher and that of medicine to Herakles that goes on to free Prometheus from his generations of punishment at the request of the one who chained him. In the other regards, Nessus both a curse and a warning to the heroes journey and one of rash decisions and reacting in real-time only to have regret later. An accident of Herakles kills Chiron a mentor. A simple misunderstanding of rash decisions and emotions kills Herakles when eyes set one place or another. It is probable that if Chiron was still alive, then perhaps the medicine aspect of such could had prevented Herakles death. Even in accident and trying to make up for it through any labor, it is understood the depiction in the sculpture. Traditional standards denotes Herakles shot an arrow to killed Nessus who was attempting to seduce his wife. In the sculpture, Herakles is seen beating down Nessus with a phallic like blunt object. I suppose in consideration of either's fate in consideration of lust, nature and male (and not often discussed female) sexuality, that in the end their lust did either of them in while still questioning if this is actually Nessus or, in fact, Chiron trying to teach one thing or another.

The Medici Lions by Giovanni di Scherano Fancellii guard The Loggia. Long held secrets of those of investment with family histories older in other countries than that of the childhood melting pot of The United States of America. The same effect occurs of legends, myths and interest in talent one way or another. You see it all though what little aspect of the world I have seen and especially in Italy where this is my first step into the world of such things of books and fantasy. The ferocious aspect of financiers and backers. Perhaps with understanding that Dante too was forced out of the city for such of paying fines or be burned for not paying such one way or another. Amazing what happens with a property after-the-fact.

At the time leading to his exile. Papal questions of power or in general while understanding there is something I've not know prior but of factions known as "Blacks" and 'Whites' in what was going on at the time. Obstinence present but still resolute in thought one way or another.

<I decide to not read further on the history of Dante knowing the fun part is always not knowing where things overlap and simply are what they are. Good to know he had children though..the spirit is definitely there one way or another. >

A moment of sit-down and reflect away from the computer. I have a moment to myself where I know that at the very least my childhood fascination with 'Alice in Wonderland' is an accurate introduction to Dante's 'The Divine Comedy' as he referred to it as *The Commedia* himself. An understanding of what caused his exile was a battle between factions called "The Blacks' and 'The Whites' in an understanding I was adament and worked from black-lights of 'Ugly Simple Truths' to going into 'Through the Looking Glass' in an allegory of chess not knowing the connection and being drawn there naturally to that board and that story hundreds of years later and consider it as such very actively since 2014. In that regard, I know why I created two seperate books for multiple reasons. 'Building Brave New Secrets' cut off at 2017 posts of my works since 2014—2017. It was done to say this is where I was going prior and then XYZ happened and where is the difference and where did things move from one way or another. I imagine a book where I express very candidly about pulling my mind back together after moral attrocity is one thing before coming back one way or another towards what I was working on anyways. That could be professionally, personally, of artistic exploration or even of intimacy. There is a difference knowing I still don't know everything yet. I don't want to know everything and still a cover story one way or another for future exploration.

I enter into the Uffizi. I was told stories of such from Momma Goldstein and her travels across Italy. She was excited for me as well and knew I'd be on an adventure one way or another. She backpacked in her youth through Italy where I imagine she had admiration of my first time over seas just as much as I understood the welcome I had to their family. I feel the support and the idea of others wanting to experience and understand what they have gone through prior and experienced wondering if the same experience is had of if new adventures lead to new avenues of understanding and connection. A generational aspect of understanding both ignorance and watching how one discovers one thing or another for the first time. Her son, a best friend had in Florida where stories of transitioning from Section 8 of concerts exist or themed movie dinner combinations. I shall not share that secret, but it is possible even if vicarious through avatars.

Still a commonality of friendship and understanding what it means to be friends and comfortable in conversation in any regard where if you cannot laugh in situations then you have to either understand you are trying too hard or simply one has to find a way to be comfortable with one another one way or another. There are friends, there are partners, there are people you are in relationships with and then there is simply the ability to focus on good times or bad. 2019 me understands completely where we relate based on past experience and 2022 me understands that it is important that you can have the most candid of conversations with friends and understand that comfortability is regardless of sexuality or each other's individuality and still the greyness exists in any aspects of things to find humor or memories. I consider The Goldsteins very much an adoptive Florida family to I where fun family secrets that

I hold towards high regard. I imagine in that aspect the hilarity of awkward family photos, moments of tush or perhaps when gifted the contriband of several dildos for a potential photoshoot. In any regard in retrospect, a musical number nevertheless.I did a second pass of this to make sure this was accurate before continuing. I'm cool with with humor there.

Knowing some of the images to be seen in this building I walk in with respect. I approached such in regards to the aspect of it is not the same if you are not here, but I invite you on my journey nevertheless. Entire hallways of busts and statues sense understanding each one there for a reason. Not all by the same sculpture and defi-nitely a notice of what is between the eyes and what isn't in some of them. There is a difference there when soul-searching. You are seeing things I've never seen before or perhaps only things of images in books or online understanding the fabric of such in society.

I walk through and begin to understand the Renaissance just as much as I have before. Everything in focus. Forefront/Background. Near-sighted/Far-Sighted join together to tell a story.

From what I remember outside the hallways was the Christian aspect and in respect I love it much. From appropriation of Greek Gods to Roman Gods to taking the best of one or another over history or history continuing it's story of lineage, collections amass and contimplation exists towards one consolidated place or another not fully understanding exactly what it means to amass things to sections just as much as one could look at divine lines geographically and see the same effect. The collection of history always important to guide one way or another towards truth where ever one is called to find it and prove it such or others prove it false.

'Surrounded by fortitude, temperance, faith, charity, hope, justice and prudence. My live feed will continue in the comments below.'

I enter a room of great importance. Known before from Undergrad and practiced in my Catholic School upbringing directly before looking at the unavoidable aspects of how to teach such things indirectly in public schools prior and after. Section after section or rounded answers at the top, there is the virtue to strive for and there is the virtue to own all of them. Owning them does not mean you practice them. It simply means you posessess them and could teach of them from this front or another, other-

wise it is a lesson of sociology in understanding each and every one of them is important in one way or another. To practice all of them at one time is also to be aware and
battle their opposites which are equally in possession and may or not be practiced.
It is the awareness of such that you can have a room of virtue and a house of sin. It
doesn't matter much in the scheme of things considering how morality is only a stone
throw away from what is nature and what is man-made behavior based off positive
reinforcement. I reflect mostly on this room of them all knowing I touched on every
single aspect of such as if U were with me. To come face-to-face with any aspect of
what it means to personify virtue is to know that at any time even the most virtuous
could be personified devilishly in one perspective or another.

To look at any one of them is a challenge to what is reality and what is faced ahead
one way or another.

Fortitude - strength in adversity. The continuance to carry on despite odds.
Temperance - restraint to think things out rationally. Patience and understand the
severity of people digging graves while wishing graves of others.
Faith - Trust of both instinct/intellect. Morality to understand no one answer is
correct and everything is guided by beliefs and trust. A learned trait on either respect
of where instinct comes from experience genetically or in this lifetime and belief that
there is always someone watching in any capacity, both from a traditional none internet aspect and what was introduced with the internet and electronic surveillence.
Charity - The act of doing common good. Not neccesarily without personal gain or
security, but with actions towards the benefit of others while also being kind to yourself once in awhile in judgement on either side.
Hope- The believe of others, yet knowing one cannot solely rely on others to just
come in at any point. Hope in yourself to persevere when it seems like no one is there
and hope you don't forget faith in yourself and others. A struggle between fortitude
and faith that balances out human instinct and makes one understand that no matter
the odds, don't give up hope and morality will work on the other aspects based on
what you do and do not say.
Justice- Morality comes back into play in this regard. A choice of words and where
the heart is set. There is what is right and then there is what is right for you or right
for someone else. This opinion is determined outside either side and is objective to
the best they can be and in numbers if they have to be to understand the difference
between right and wrong and the fabric of civilization.
Prudence- Caution. Think before you speak. Rationalize before you act. Instinct
takes over, but it is about doing due-dilengence one way or another for yourself and

for others to understand any case big or small. Any decision can change an outcome. A sit back to think means all the difference in the world.

I sit on the virtues for a moment knowing the sins as well and give them equal weight. Inward/Outward. There is a difference where all factor in on this. Others so quick to judge and place sin, but where does one place the virtues under the same scheme of things. They factor and they place. But it is not withstanding that in either regard of how subjective they are towards judgement of others which is neither a sin or virtue but could lead to such depending on where it goes. I take this room to heart in more way than one knowing it is understood what they represent and how hard it is at times in any one of those scenarios to portray that. Balance had understanding even the most virtuous one place is the most sinful somewhere else. Disrespect outlook one place is perhaps more reverant and respectful than one may thing. It simply goes back towards the one saying one thing or another and open for discussion. Closed discussions or lack of communication after negativeity simply represents lack of prudence at the least and simply a heart filled with one thing or another and ready to move on to the next positive or negative comment not caring any bit about the words provided.

'La primavera - botticelli found in an entire wing of art basically dedicated to Madonna and child.'

Also the introduction to Botticelli, although I know I distinctly documented 'The Birth of Venus' as well. In both regards, recognition of aspects of seasonal changes and things coming to light and shores. Transitional thoughts and topics where I have always found myself quite fond of Botticelli in multiple aspects of his works. A Midsummer's Night Dream to La primavera while perhaps probably or could had been seen by Shakespeare one way or another. Stories pass on from country to country just as much as they do from parent to child or indirect appropriation and positive reinforcement to the next country or nationality in the same regards. The old world is different from the new world. In the new world, they can silently kill and take over without a life taken while in the old world it was come in, take over culture, convert and destroy and move on from there in power amassing one way or another. I'm aware in the picture taken and when things go elsewhere in my second travel to Europe in 2021. The world's greatest art seen from an aspect of indirectness and with multitudes of people abound. 'If only you were here...' countered by 'You have to see it to appreciate it...' A lesson learned in growth in understanding it is not the same thing and there is a difference when discovering allure behind artwork and secrecy.

I suppose in the difference between then an now is the aggressive, passive-aggressive aspect of understand what a life taken is and where and why that was. Financial gain of such never looks kindly on the Gods, while one has to understand the longevity of digital life in comparison to physical life. Would one simply look at a statue of Napoleon and say, well...he had a good run...this is ours now.' The same could be said in any fine art aspect of undetstanding there is a difference in life span between a person and what they contribute to society and where it goes from there. To think small on that aspect is to think digital where data is being paid for one way or another. What about the data of a private computer or cell phone? What happens when there is the willful deletion of a digital presence because they thought they could while it being incorporated elsewhere. I defer back to the birth of Christianity and conversion factors on that aspect when it comes to the erasing of one history or another. Although not the only example of such, they have a long history of what happened in life and lessons of morality to know even amongst the most rightous, the most evil stand beside them. I've latered coined the aspect of 'Even if the Pope is infallible, not a single person around them is.' I am sure in that context, history and of the most respect of the religion can say where there was and no fault of prior Popes.

'Second wing seems to have led the mother and child theme to the other end of the story. Pieta-Perugino'

All throught the museum is the lesson and life of Jesus. What was I thinking then vs. what I think of it now? Lessons. Morality. What is engrained culturally that needs to be understood? There is reference of a Mother and Child. There is reverence there understanding that in this capacity it is clearly the same thing that happened in Greek and Roman mythology but focus on one individual to contain all responsibility before branching into the Holy Spirit who branches outside of individualization and back into the individualization of each and every person and what is breathed in every day that still opens the door to perspective, discussion and thought process outside whatever is spoken or taught one way or another to also be another branch towards morality and understanding. It is with respect the lesson engrained and where it has translated true to my life and the life of others before going right back to the foundations of anything of value or transition understanding that part of human nature is alive and well and spiritually that is handled and addressed in away where it is not singular to come to a conclusion or a vote on. It isn't a question of 'Who's Child is This?' It is a question of look at the story, try to prevent that with others and understand power struggles on one level or another. Human. Corporation. Theological. Natural. Genetic.

In any aspect, what needs to be overcome and what is the constant battle of what is an original sin of society and power? I imagine I defer to areas well beyond my lifetime and years to understand the lightening aspect helps, but it is a truth, it is reality and it happened even in modern times where both government and religion should teach against it and understand the difference.

'Very dark palettes, but it was also common around this time that painters would paint by candlelight.'

Something I taught myself in Undergrad. The use of oil-paints and the strain of the eye to see one thing or another. Not particularly knowing which color I am grabbing at the moment, yet the richness of it shows through. Even the smallest of details contain a context and a layering of what comes out from darkness and into the light. A technique worth exploring if only to appreciate the hours of which one works to complete one thing or another. It is doubtful that stimulated minds rested one way or another after darkness.

'Onto the Leonardo section. They start u off in a room of what came before. Live feed will continue in comment section below.'

I admire the unfinished works as this is not the only time I have seen such of his. Constantly going and constantly processing. It is the gestures of the under-drawing that has always been my interest. They are the most reactive, the most instinctual before going back and revisiting, finessing and finalizing one way or another. To see the undercoat gives a purity to the idea before going into the craft of one artist or another on if they expose it or not for others to see what is an illusion or surity of the strokes or drawing one way or another. A respect there understanding not many revered enough to place value on unfinished works while others simply want to call something abandoned and discount it.

A man of many thoughts and avenues. Neither here nor there, but everywhere where even in concepts unfinished he inspired one way or another towards others to also build from him one way or another. Although the first airplane from The United States, it is not completely Wright to discount that even Leonardo thought of such things then to only play out later in brotherhood of invention. If such a regard to Da Vinci is to be had and recognized then, so to the value of most artists or at least a non-discount of such as they fly their creativity from one field to another in thought. Centered in ideas, it is important to understand the stroke of genius is not just from a pen, but that too of a paintbrush.

More than likely out of order, but an image of the Laocoön in classical context. The man who said to burn the Trojan Horse and not let it in only to be attacked by the will of the gods in saying, 'Oh no...this is going to happen and be a moral for thousands of years.' How else would society come with the phrase, 'Don't look a gift horse in the mouth?' on multiple fronts. Poseidon doesn't play in that regard, but also long thought of Athena before understanding any of their personality and respecting such. I imagine based on written history they all are like that one way or another.

'Madonna/child example #632 '

It is important...not many images depicted of Father and Son in this regard yet often talked about and associated. Never discount the adoptive father Joseph. Unseen adoptions all over the place of protection and definitely talks beforehand of Jesus' birth. Cousin conversations to be had there as well. If you think about it in the context of the Bible (also knowing the family escaped to Egypt for protection), it is important to understand people talk and people listen. Much easier to get facts straight nowadays. If you want to find out who paid a crowd, can't really do it then but can definitely find out who does in this era while also finding who plays on fear and persecution of others to say one thing or another. In the state of things since certain eras of politics and isolationism, 'Why the fear?' I can imagine in one scenario or another, it wasn't make fear of persecution great again. I rest on every image if a mother holding a dying child (now an adult) in her arms before she buried him. It is assummed what happened to her, but then also understood what happened to St. Peter and all of the Apostles. I imagine by the standards then and the standards now if someone thought Jesus was a threat and something that could be taken over, it is more than likely considering the death of the Apostles that they would had not stopped and more than likely would had killed Mary Jesus' Mother and then try to hide it after-the-fact in any way to express compassion and continue building on the death of someone that they could had saved and worked with. In any regard, they murdered her when they murdered her child.

In modern times that is an understood reality. In times back then, it is a real probability.

'Painting techniques definitely becoming more realistic. Usually when classic sculptures make their way in paintings around this time it was a challenge to the credibility of the artwork.'

Translations exist in so many ways. Once you see it or hear it, it sparks imagination or understanding one way or another. The search for realism back then denoted a connection to God or Divinity at the time while there is the necessary aspect of the connection to humanity and what they are and are not capable of doing. Is it a more realistic aspect of such to understand why things get cast one way or another. The credibility of the artist is also moreso just the credibility to fact and probability. Even in Renaissance they reference each other which goes all the way prior to modern in knowing where perhaps enough of the realism in some regard to abstract ideas and then back to the sullen words of truth and civilization one way or another.

There is a room of life-life sculptures that I cite and reference. In the room, all the people seemed trapped as if in agony from an event that has occurred. I survey the room to see what reminded me of the bodies turned to stone from Pompeii knowing I have never seen such in person. Perhaps that would be for another trip and another time. From each sculpture line-of-sight exists to know where one is looking up or looking down towards something as if their last thought was in reflection, protection or forgiveness and awe. The whole room has a essence of agony to such where time stopped and was capture and preserved elsewhere. The life of such people makes one wonder their final moments while questioning who has a hand in this one way or another. I imagine here is probably where I thought and mentioned 'Return to Oz' at some point on social media although it is still clearly based on the fascination of life turned to stone, stone turned to life caught in baited breath held within. It was not until Paris years later that I would find a better representation of that example.

'Since I already brought up Oz, I've found the childlike empress! Maria Dr'medici - bronzino'

Cross- Cultural reference and we move on. It happens more times than you think in old paintings carrying over into the present one way or another.

-Intro to Caravaggio is required Gentileschi
To see one of my favorite artists in person is of interest to I. Often a fan of Baroque, although the humor of such as I am unemployed at the time and even now in 2022. Broke. I get it in that finger pointing aspect. Between this painting and the head of Medusa I look at the technique of emerging from darkness and having divine lighting shine down judgement or murder between the two for one reason or another. Questions there on the stories present wondering if it was just or simply noted for later. In either regard it was translated and pro-cessed elsewhere for further consideration.

As I pretty much ended my time at the Uffizi, it was important to note the respect of such and a visit to see it in person. Strapped on time, I know it is important that I could spend hours or days in museums just as much as any other person could or should. I imagine in Academy times it was essential in such before branching off into your own name or perhaps never to make one for yourself and be a part of the team of the masters already established. Was their discount there or was there pride to be connected to such? In one regard, you rarely know the students, but you understand the technique, where it was learned and could spot the difference between indirect learned, direct learned or watched from a distance to replicate elsewhere later. A take home aspect of all the artists I just had the virtue of being introduced to in person. I leave to wander back towards the Duomo. I enjoy my time on the river right outside for a bit briding in thought before I continue back on towards the center of the city.

I thought to myself on the way their of what I wanted for myself on the trip. I knew from when I got there with all things considered of unemployed, the moral weight of one thing or another between what happened at the company, what I went through, what I was going through and what I was exploring. Strength and hope was required and even when I was giving up on the trip, there was always a silver lining or something or someone to steer me in the right direction. A necklace purchased where not anything very unique to it, simply came from Florence and was weighed appropriately on a scale to find the value of such in a corner jewelry market on the way back to climb the Duomo. Not really a jewelry person but can honestly say it has been few and far between that it comes off my neck since I purchased it. Even at times when I feel it is about to fall I catch it as it has been attached to myself since then. A sliver of hope one way or another wrapped around my neck knowing if this was the only thing I was to purchase and bring back with me, it is a good thing to have before trav-eling through the mouth of Hell towards something else that I had yet to experience while I process what I already have in life. A journey continued...understanding that at least we have an understanding of where things can go. Take away all the possessions and the world and still hope remains knowing one can only put so much in during so little time. The purple shirt now tattered and worn still a favorite color of mine and also just an old polo of such. I don't have much when it comes to the clothing department, but color theory works out well in the scheme of things when the postive and negative blend properly towards one look or another. In either regard, beauty was found.

'I promised myself I'd pick up one thing tangible on this trip to always remind me of heaven and doing things good for your soul. I now wear my silver linings around my neck wherever I may go. #heaven'

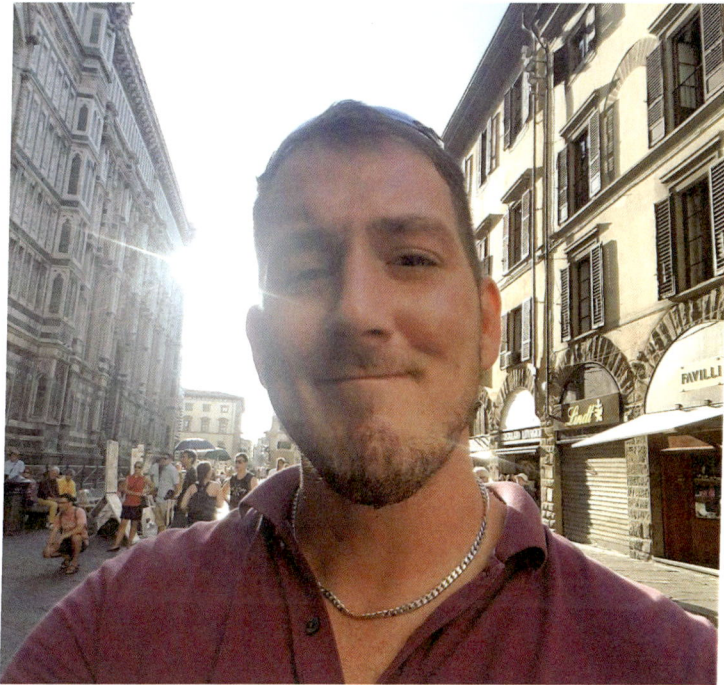

Aware of what occurred then, what occurred now and what history was erased in trying to say one thing or another. My only tangible purchase from Florence. Purchased before I climbed the Duomo. Silver Linings around my neck ever since and never taken off. I don't care what money you have or what you wanted to do after my death. You cannot break human spirit and you cannot commandeer my life story without my permission in life. You have stolen enough. - Philip A. Bonneau.

There are many doors to the Duomo. Once you walk in there is the forced perspective yet again that does not do justice to see unless you make the climb to the top. As everything is importance and as everything matters, it is important to count the steps from ground level through the mouth of Hell and onto a version of Heaven. It is understood now that the ceiling paintings depicted were actually done 200 years after Dante wrote the Divine Comedy. At the time I saw it as a incredible story of inspiration of such imagining Dante walk through that to get to the sky-line to the beauty that is the landscape of Florence at sunset. In no odds or discount to such, I find it no different knowing 1800 years later thought it such and drew inspiration from it in a capacity that made the journey worth it. Surely Dante would had been impressed and thought the same a wise and incredibly profound inclusion to the Duomo

As Dante was a city planner for Florence before his exile, he has the privilege no doubt in overseeing the development of the Duomo and was able to see it upon it's completion in 1296. At the time, the ceiling laid bear of imagination and story yet to be portrayed and written. It is of no doubt in my mind that he was able to climb to the top of the Duomo and see the beauty of the skyline at any time of day in privilege of title and of scholar. Having no story written above in that regard I understand the aspects of his life of a story yet to

319

be written before his exile from the city he planned one way or another. Now after the fact, I find it fascinating that even in exile, the city planned itself around Dante one way or another from his contributions as either in 'city council' or long-term 'city-planning'. It is no doubt the influence of Dante and his works upon culture or civilization where take one thing or another and you can view *The Commedia* from multiple perspectives to see where there is respect, disdain and education of one thing or another. When one questions planning and what is and isn't of deference to other artists, it is important to note the understanding why he was exiled, was it right or not and then questioning does it matter if it matters so much to him to produce anything in concept to expand about the realms one place or another looking for guidance, education and belonging before determining purpose. In that deferance, regardless of the injustice felt, there is the secret aspect of the justice created from that and others hidden in art, architecture and other works elsewhere before getting back to one meaning or another on life. A blank canvas present.

Imagine the underpainting of what was the imagination of the city planner for the Duomo. Would it be what we had today or perhaps a lesson because of what happened yesterday? In any regard, it is no doubt that even in paintings there is a life and story fluid and of movement. No doubt in the beginning stories painted in the mind one way or another.

The walkways long and the steps hard to get to The Mouth of Hell near the top. A Gate-way really from one place to the next. Once you get past the hundreds of steps you see the torture surrounding you one way or another before you look up and get a glimpse of redemptive moments. Nature shines through yet again where it is understood that in any depiction someone is objectively looking at what is being depicted one way or another. There is no time to process completely as lines in front and behind. A timetable to sort things out one way or another not knowing what is underneath in reflection of self. Which do you see first. The torment of the redemption. Justice or Retribution?

A difference of opinion and perspective if one was to flip things around and understand what got placed where and why. Cast out once only to return in one shape or form in a different capacity. Master planners one way or another towards long term sustainabili-ty. Stories built around such wondering what what else is there and where it came from before understanding where to proceed anywhere further. Hundreds of steps taken to get to that point only to know there is more to climb upwards before then finding the strength to walk back down. Always a time limit but an understanding how to make memories last longer than a lifetime through translations and interpretations.

If it wasn't for the discover of one culture over another, I'd never have the opportunity to

'Though the Mouth of Hell Understand What Came After...or Before... - Sketch Translation' November 29, 2022. Philip A. Bonneau.

way or another. Never know who one meets and what one sees in redemptive or protective archs. The effort to climb wondering why come back onto this place from which so much time has past and so much learned elsewhere to make me want to revisit this once again in a different light. Perhaps a twist of fate of walking backwards before going forward understanding the perspective it brings on traveling through so much persecution to just see something beautiful again in a different capacity of hope worn in many places. Perhaps a carryover to other things of fluid thoughts and split emotions. If ones of virtue present to challenge such evils of the world, what would they do in connection to release those held down by judgement one way or another. Would it make a difference in transformation? Would it be any different to start asking questions and having conversations after mulled in thought for so long?

I imagine if one were to ask of empathy, it can be found in any context of such if only one were to ask accordingly or be open to approach in one manner or another. Perhaps in the darkest and coldest of places there is a warming of the hearts in one capacity or another. Understanding is predominantly what we are all looking for one way or another. Would it be no different to invite the aspect that stories continue and lives move forward one way or another. Trapped lives. Trapped souls. We all go towards one way or another of reaching for something if only to connect. Transitioning of the soul where perhaps in empathy and knowledge from elsewhere, there is return back to where we started for many reasons yet to be determined.

"I'm literally on the top of heaven. I went through the gate."
"Everything the light touches...."

"Just sit down...There is no words" "OK...where do we go from here?"

Words from Dante collected through one source or another,

You shall leave everything you love most dearly:
this is the arrow that the bow of exile
shoots first. You are to know the bitter taste

of others' bread, how salt it is, and know
how hard a path it is for one who goes
descending and ascending others' stairs.
-Canto XVII, lines 55–60

'The Top of Duomo' Video Still - September 5, 2017. "Philip A. Bonneau.

I figured appropriate to start this post with both the first main thing I wrote publicly
in this series when I was able to find my own words and not hide behind symbology
definitions. There does come a point when I feel words were meant to be taken at face
value and I absolutely feel that sometimes you can't put things into words. The lyrics
that followed were the introductory part to the audio portion of my journey. I don't
think I ever lost my words in that exploration but relied on others to expand meaning
and experience. Dante did the same in his depiction of heaven. Relying on scholars of

the past to help with his own journey.

I think in either point, they give me guidance now on where to begin in this post and where to end with it. "I'm here. I did this."

No one can take that away from me. I almost took this away from myself. This post or this moment is not the end, but it's definitely leading to a denouement to this divine comedy. I don't have all the answers yet. I probably never will. But things are getting wrapped up.

"I wish you were here right now. I wish you could understand that. Maybe you do. Maybe you will surprise me and I'll open my eyes and see you. I'm here. I'm trying. What is right? What do I do?"

I'm not sure whom those words were meant for anymore.
Am I talking to anyone in my love life?
Am I talking to anyone in my family life?
Am I just talking to anyone who would listen?
Am I talking to myself?

"There is a need for you to be here and I miss you." I wrote those words back in 2010. I sat on the corner of the room on the floor and began writing for the first time in the guest room with a knife by my side just in a place of seclusion, isolation, desperation, sadness, anger and probably a few more emotions in-between. I don't like talking about that night. I've glossed over it in this series and in life. I guess that is what makes December 10th anniversaries so special to me. It was a choice. It was a choice to do something right for me. It was a choice to say fuck others that take you for granted. But it was also a battle perhaps too late and began to become goals on subsequent years toward life, plans or anything to work towards. It was a choice to piss or get off the pot and to this day for myself. I'm not sure if it was anger that stopped me that evening or if it was that I said, "Ok...I'm going to do this my way." But never really sat down to explore or listen to the words I wrote then. That being a lie of course as I took everything to heart. Most of them translated and were burnt in flames in other self-portraits. Only thing I kept were the words I had for myself. Perhaps I didn't really understand them until now but I decided to bring them with me on this trip and promised myself I would not read them for the first time in almost 7 years until I made it to the top of Heaven.

This means more for the now than anything else. I mean what's could possibly be the point in carrying the past with you all the way here if not to transform it in some way? But I am here and honestly all of this travels with me whether I bring something physically or not. I don't. Something cathartic about reflecting on my younger self ATM. Something about being here eliminates the past in ways I will only understand in time The immediate present seems simply that and the anything else is secondary in both thought and concern. I am here and this is just I.

Are you proud of me?
You can't see what I am seeing right now.
I can try to describe it but words will not do it justice.
I can try to video it, but you aren't here.
It's just me in Heaven. I have no words."
...and yet I write anyway afterwards.

I don't know what to say from this experience today. Walking up the steps to get here was a trial unto itself. "You will never know or maybe you will...or maybe you will think 'what if...' or maybe I will think of things differently but I don't see you walking with me. U will never be through what I have been through and I will never be what you have expected nor wanted. Perhaps that is where I find my heaven. Peace in that I'm nothing you expected or maybe I'm everything you ever thought I was or would be. I have to make those decisions for Me."

Maybe one day you will be proud. It doesn't matter much I suppose when one has a sense of accomplishment. Maybe I was silently noticed. Maybe not. To trek about this journey in another capacity makes me understand someone is always there and even on top of the building right now there is the sun. There is the wind and there is the slight conversations of the other visitors in this shared space. A peace is here looking at a world around that paints things in perspective. Here or there I find myself traveling at the moment in memories understanding faults and where things grew or grow one way or another. Conversations of 'Self' when thinking of 'Others'.
"You are toxic."
Those words echo in the back of my mind.
I can't get that out of my head as I questioned at the time 3 years, 4 years... 5 years actually on the weight of such in determining if I was in fact toxic or not.

In my mind I try to do things right.
In context of this series it was about talking about myself.

In the context of personal. I have varying ideas on that at this point in my life. I don't know how to feel in response to that comment. Part of me feels like there is no way I could ever get to a point of being toxic. The other part of me, the one that beats myself up says, well maybe it is true.

I wish I could bury those words along with the mask I did in the sand years ago, but alas here I am years later and they are still in my head and always a litmus test to myself in behavior and actions. Took me three years to come up with a proper response and even now I'm sitting on top of Heaven and I hear those words in my head, in the wind and in my own words written to myself. Truth is they are just words. It doesn't matter much in the scheme of things but it is something that is carried with me for some reason.

I guess probably because they came from a place of vulnerability all around.

"I'm overlooking all of Florence and I can't help but say everything the light touches is yours. I don't know how to feel. I could be consumed with things that do not matter to anything but me or I can be happy that I am here and I did this. I think I have to talk about the past and the present in this context. They both are here with me.

Is my situation now here any different than that day in my room writing these words? Everything is going to change and I am in isolation and a place of seclusion.

The choice is mine on what to do and what to think. Others have controlled my current scenario just as before and I'm left with plans changing and not knowing what to do with that. I think in this moment, I choose to not give a fuck about how someone thinks about me. If I am toxic, I'm toxic to them. Doesn't make me toxic and I know I try. I imagine I could be intoxicating one way or another as a positive. That's all that matters and I really don't give a fuck. The sound I hear now is wind. Through it the light goes from one point to another. I didn't go 5000 miles away for you. I went for me. This was my dream and I did this on my own and for me. I don't know what to feel at the moment, but I do know that it is going to be unique to me and if you relate it will only because memory allows it or we connected on some level. A journey for Me then, a journey for U now.

In the same way as I buried my mirror mask years ago. I decided to take my 7-year mirror and flipped it over to the blank side of the paper. Wrote on it, "Give me this. I'm not toxic. I just wanted to live. I know you will understand." I decided to make a paper airplane and although probably frowned upon, I threw it out into the world. I guess this time I just wanted to fly instead of burying things. Either way blessed and released.

Can't say I know what's next, but can say that you let go of the past when you are ready and on your terms. I never wanted to continue this story as long as it has been, but if it were easy more people would do it. It wouldn't be fair to talk about Hell and Purgatory and not talk about what brings you peace, which is always going to be unique to you. I dunno...I guess call it faith that I believe I would be steered in the right direction or not. But until then there is nothing wrong with wanting to lift my arms and seek another land. I'm here.

something that is carried with me for some reason. I guess probably because they came from a place of vulnerability all around.

"I'm overlooking all of Florence and I can't help but say everything the light touches is yours. I don't know how to feel. I could be consumed with things that do not matter to anything but me or I can be happy that I am here and I did this. I think I have to talk about the past and the present in this context. They both are here with me. Is my situation now here any different than that day in my room writing these words? Everything is going to change and I am in isolation and a place of seclusion. The choice is mine on what to do and what to think. Others have controlled my current scenario just as before and I'm left with plans changing and not knowing what to do with that. I think in this moment, I choose to not give a fuck about how someone thinks about me. If I am toxic, I'm toxic to them. Doesn't make me toxic and I know I try. That's all that matters and I really don't give a fuck. The sound I hear now is wind. Through it the light goes from one point to another. I didn't go 5000 miles away for you. I went for me. This was my dream and I did this on my own and for me. I don't know what to feel at the moment, but I do know that it is going to be unique to me and if you relate it will only because memory allows it. "

In the same way as I buried my mirror mask years ago. I decided to take my 7-year mirror and flipped it over to the blank side of the paper. Wrote on it, "Give me this. I'm not toxic. I just wanted to live. I know you will understand." Decided to make a paper airplane and although probably frowned upon, I threw it out into the world. I guess this time I just wanted to fly instead of burying things. Either way blessed and released.

Can't say I know what's next, but can say that you let go of the past when you are ready and on your terms. I never wanted to continue this story as long as it has been, but if it were easy more people would do it. It wouldn't be fair to talk about Hell and Purgatory and not talk about what brings you peace, which is always going to be unique to you. I dunno...I guess call it faith that I believe I would will be steered in the right direction or not. But until then there is nothing wrong with wanting to lift my arms and seek another land. I'm here.

ENTRY 44:

A hurricane is coming.
They named it Dorian.
It is not the first
It won't be the last
Is there calmness in the center?

Similarities between the now and 2 years ago when I first explored writing about topics close to heart during a hurricane impacting my life. Several similarities between now and then in storms, decisions, a budget and ultimately ended with seeing my brother.

I started reading the wiki page on "The Picture of Dorian Grey". What struck me as interesting was the intention of the Dorian novel and the fights on morality it brought. Oscar Wilde defended his work and artistic intention. "Aggressively."
Supposedly it violated laws guarding public morality.
The book was ultimately edited by both publisher's choice and the author's over time, but not without a fight.
"Art for Art's Sake."
"An Artistic Manifesto."
"Beauty and Sensual fulfillment are the only things worth pursuing in life."

I don't think I'm questioning the similarities of what is to come with my own life. But I am grateful that I am given a second chance and a sequel if only I can get the words right. I know what could come. A defending of self. A defending of others. Clarification of both intent and execution. I hear the message loud and clear.

I'm being guided to finish what I started. Something I should probably take practice in whatever book I read or start. Should I look at this as a book? What do I look at it as now in reflection? Which version of me shines the most? Since you made it a book afterall...

Personal Thoughts.
Personal Moments.

But today is not the first nor the last day I have had God show me that he (they?, I'm never sure the proper pronoun as they relate to everything any everyone where in many forms and places one simply doesn't know who or how in this regard as the concept denotes partnership in many forms) exists in a very active way in my life. You can't make up the coincidences that there is something bigger than you going on.

Maybe you can. It is always a choice on what you believe. Weigh things out. but commonalities will always bridge one thought to the next. What was the meaning of the hurricane 2 years ago? A chance to see family unexpectedly. A chance to see my father. Reclaim that which was stolen from I or simply no devalued non-priority? Unexpected answers to questions left lingering. What is to come on my 5-day vacation next week?

"He's asking the right questions."

Today was a good day. Remember you can't explain everything. but that does not mean you cannot ask questions. There is no wrong one. My head is telling me that the muses are listening to me. Multiple. But then there is a major difference to what I feel in the air and in nature and them. Personi-fication vs. naturalization. Separate entities all doing their own part. A plan seeing itself out despite just taking it one day at a time. I hear wind. I hear women's voices. Male voices. I'm noticing the difference between them.

It is what I silently feel or connect with that knows I don't have to say or speak anything at time. Not even internally in dialogue. Connections had where even burned thoughts processes known or simply assuerance of a soul read one way or another from what is in my heart. What is buried in my mind? A sense of connection where even in the listening of songs of birds and insects relates as thousands act in unison to be heard or to bring aware-ness required to have any cognizance of what is numbered entities singing a different song of comprehension and relateability.

To them, I imagine no different than radiowaves sent out into space wonder-ing if there is comprehension, connection or acknowledgement.

Perhaps an imagination of not being alone.
Simply processing while the mind over-thinks?

Post 18: Day 5: The Sixth Sphere - Venice

"Wonderland is destroyed. You burnt it like a phoenix that cannot control her power nor understand what it is like to be reborn. I don't think you really understand what rests inside, but I think at times you have thoughts that maybe you do. Things change in birth. You no longer know your surrounding and have to rediscover the world all over again. I guess we are predestined from the beginning to be thrown in situations we didn't create. Imagine how fearless a child has to be. The first time you are aware of something, you are thrown from the safety of the womb to find something new that you didn't ask for. Is that any different than now? You aren't the same. Stories are not the same. Life is not what it was. You changed that. You burnt it to the ground. Do we control our own birth?

Look around you and what do you see? Fog and ash. Ashes to ashes and dust to dust, for better or for worse this is what you created. You did this. The fog. The insecurity. You have reached into the world of thought wanting to come out with a sense of clarity and this is where you are.

Did you expect it to be anything different than this? Did you expect this to be easy?

Did you expect that this was just going to be one move away from figuring things out?

Maybe you did. Maybe you still do.
Maybe you are still just lost alone in that fog and questioning.
This is all your choice. Only you will understand it in the end.

Lost or found, the time spent will be yours alone to appreciate and comprehend.

The phoenix must have been a lonely creature indeed. It gives up one life for another. Is it a curse or a blessing to be reborn?

Does a phoenix have a memory of its past lives?
Does it die in vain?
Did it have a good life?
Did it learn? It learned something.

I imagine that it becomes like a child to the world once again questioning everything; including itself with each chance it is given.

Mythology was always ironic in that way. There is always a blessing with a curse and vice versa. On one hand you get to live another life. On the other hand you are doomed to possibly make the same mistakes.

Perhaps in writing this you are beginning to understand that you are thinking too much. Perhaps you are just at that right point of crazy and beating yourself up that you might discover something to come back from.

Ask yourself, "What is the point if you are constantly filled with questions without answers?" Is this hate and anger or is this fear? Do I just burn this? Burn everything and start anew? Do I have it in me to build a new world again and thrive?

I feel like this is familiar but at the same time something different. Ashes to ashes, dust to dust." 9/22/2016

A memory expansion of a 24th truth understanding the end of a series in the companion to 'Ugly Simple Truths' before moving forward to reading the epilogue. Life mirrors and can paint in opposites or in positions of simply opening up the vision a little bit past the fog of before. A reflection found to understand relateability of one situation or another. In contact, perhaps it is understood that as one is processing and discovering you they are also goes back internally and understanding themselves or others. Internal thoughts externalized to understand or invite conversations.

When at one finish line or another, it best to look back, if clear enough, to see how much you have traveled if only in reflection to how you got to where you are now. Is anyone else here with you now? It doesn't matter they will be at their finish line at one point of another at their own pace.

Breathe and take in any milestone after milestone that occurred or simply be in the moment knowing you ran for one reason or another or walked a path and chose to do it in stride. Relax. Catch your breathe or count it 1, 2, 3... Look down, look up or close your eyes to know you are alive and stop running one direction or the other. There are life experience markers after another visable or not. You cannot see them all at the same time unless one wanted to make a diagram of the course outlined, but even then there are the hidden silent victories to account for that simply are just never spoken and pathways unmarked of significance. The same could be said of silent failures knowing one is more likely to be talked about than the other depending on the person.

Perhaps in the personification of fog, it allows you to start looking at the immediate before stepping out into the more vast aspects of life and understanding. From one square seen, a second square forms until eventually a whole landscape exists again to be able to explore a little more understanding of that which you are walking on.

Perhaps I rest and catch a boat ride for now. Fluid thoughts never hurt towards the path of solid grounds.

I catch the train from Florence to Venice at 6am. The night before I catch more of the Italian soaps wondering the epic battles if ever the Telenovellas were to get involved. That much drama, passion, lust and scandal is simply too much to imagine in that clash of culture. But a fun thought nevertheless. Thoughts of Fashion House in bridging cultural identity that perhaps still remind me of the serials of my youth. Like sands in the hourglass, so too is the one-upping of one culture over another in heats of passion.

Not as much time allowed to be spent there, but if one wanted to see how to survive underwater and in floods of emotion one way or another, there was an essential aspect to make sure to fit in the flooding of emotion and passion. The landscape similar along the way where pockets of stability and structure run the landscape. Mapquest says it was a 3 hour travel although if I recall it felt more like 2. Eventually a bridge of thought occurred and water seen one again as one goes into island hoping. Can't see everything but it is important for I to understand that there is a reason for this path one reason for another. An artist's journey on the search for one thing or another.

To arrive at a city of such of no preparation of experience all I knew was the boat taxis to get from one place to another, the gondolas in between the streets and the compromise between land and water as if I wanted to imagine an entire city cast on the shore-line of a beach to see where the compromise would be met. Not known if one could do so or not, nor I trained in such, but I imagine if there are buildings underwater it would make for amazing yet dangerous scuba diving experiences knowing that naturally they would become reefs to some and nature finds a way of co-habitating with what is above. An interesting balancing of thought of something so fragile yet still held onto while you still can before it either gets fortified or collapses into the sea. An allegory there of love so fleeting to be cherished at one point and then lost at another over time and without proper care. A memory to some eventually where as it stands now showcases and produces as much memories of love and the arts while it still can.

As once again, I did not book a train ticket in advance, I find the only option is first class. Might as well do it once understanding at least a little splurging is available and I have wifi to do some work and relax on the way there. Admiration had of the lavishness of bathrooms. The mood lighting is that of purples and reminiscent of in a way to my black-light series in a different tone and perhaps in a different aspect of perspective. A glimmer of something not hidden, but shining through one way or another. Illuminated aspects of brightening things up a bit after a trip from Rome>-Florence>Venice. As noted on my facebook, the lighting was what was of interest to I while noting my Wifi said I was in Singapore. I imagine the mood lighting fits as such where I can see it if only in my imagination. Multi-travelling across space and time. A bathroom vortex and whirlpool awaits. Perhaps thoughts of that first job offer I had that I didn't get to do in an alternative aspect of life and choices from 2005/2006. A transporter from one place to another mentioned in the comments. I'm sure one or two things will mix and mash. #thefly

'Alrightie...looks like I'm either on vacation longer or diverted someone else for free. As of now my flight is still scheduled to arrive Friday at 11pm.'

I arrive to the city with a looming hurricane approaching back home. I am keeping an eye on it and my home and dogs are being looked after. A constant shift from vacation and reality understanding that evacuations are more than likely to occur back home where I try to keep balance on the idea of responsibility vs. vacation. In the visit of one place underwater or in partnership with it, water and winds begin to brew back overseas. Currently I am in the no-fly zone since the hurricane is heading straight for Boca Raton and South Florida. 'Babies (The dogs) taken care of and I'm getting the necessities pulled from my place. Harddrives and computer mostly and the rest can be replaced if need be. Checking with delta Thursday night. Either I extend Italy or transfer to Atlanta, but still involves some setting up other things that need to be rescheduled for the 11th somehow overseas regardless.' 'I'm planning what I can. Kinda in the mentality there is nothing I really can do or will know until the final call on Thursday night. Until then it's business in the back, vacation in the front because even if I make it home there is no way I'd be able to get supplies for it in time. I try to make arrangements one way or another.'

Do I have enough money to continue here, perhaps I travel to the Southern region of Italy and then I could visit Pompeii and the more of the mountainous aspects. I could travel east and go to Tuscany, but when unemployed and unsure of what I can and cannot do, I cannot run out of money while overseas.

'I'd like to consider this my preflight check-in to hurricane Irma #cityunderwater'

From off the train, I arrive to see the opening of the city. A plaza that shows the shore-lines and what is to be more than likely the first of many bridges. My outfit, although I commented with hoodie up and sunglasses on as being almost too Unibomber like in appearance, I am now reminded exactly of the outfit and why I was wearing it to begin with. Something from the first day I meet someone in person and used as part of their photoshoot within the Heroes+Villains series. Didn't want the company on the trip, but it doesn't mean I don't carry company with me or keep it one way or another. Perhaps a message of understanding not everything carried is as heavy as th one thought where understood the difference of perspective is actually more beautiful combined than divided in thoughts one way or another. Neither friend nor foe in I, I imagine a great deal of people on this trip. Would it has been any different of a vacation had I went with one person or the other? In this one an understanding that if one was considering life choices and commitments. It is important to release, understand and go from there that which left you stuck or frozen one place or another. Even now it is completely understood the respect and understanding of multi-point references.

The waterways are the first to see before going to the water taxis and the understanding that there is nothing like seeing how preciously balanced the city is towards its understanding of water. The jump aspect of right outside any building into the water denotes a moment of thought of where if one was so inclined to be frustrated at work and need to go jump into the water in thought, it seems easy enough to do so here before returning back to work after silently screaming and then re-emerging. Still I imagine beware of sharks in either aspect of sea or land but one tends to not bother as much as the other.

Although in fairness, it is illegal for many reasons based on sewage, danger of delapidation and other chemicals or decomposing items in the water along with the combination of boating and the species of sharks found within the area. The blue areas of lagoon are enticing and there actually are a few designated swimming spots available.

In further thought for or against diving, there are areas you are more than likely to be able to enter private property from the underground up which would be strictly prohibited. Although perhaps treasure troves to be viewed from below, it is precarious of such to imagine how the natural theatrical formation of colonies form and expand in aqautic life. I can only imagine the fed-up lost diver who randomly enters a living room in a wet suit and scuba gears asking for directions.

In merky waters, Bull Sharks exist in transitional times and they definitely are not as passive as one would think before going into the aspects of makos, hammerheads and great whites. The beauty of such in understanding is only things of imagination and dreams. Respect of age, respect of size and nature understanding panic alerts but then if one remains calm enough there is a chance to explore something where adreline on either side is there or simply something of silent agreements. Rarely spotted in the Venice canals, it is more than likely due to the on-going boat taxis than anything else that constantly disrupts the water and would lead to manuveuring one way or another to simply avoid the area for others of openness. It is still probably more than likely that there could be areas branched off for divers if one was so inclined and allowed, but divers know better the rules of the sea and who is and isn't supposed to be there while the digestive track of most sharks is slow and long where they tend to not feed as often as one would think. In either regard, it is best to simply respect what is in the water and understand you are a guest to their house. One will treat you one way or another.

"...suitcase is going to be the death of me getting to my room." Bridge upon bridge, my wheels on my suitcase had long broken off back in Rome. I am regreting that now as it is a constant lift and go from one bridge to the next. The cooridors smaller than what I am used to. Upon the boat ride to my hotel, it takes me a minute to determine if I am even on the right boat to begin with. I don't think I was on the first one. But that is ok. I notice a statue of an exhibit there that I didn't get to see but admired it as contemporary and of fascination. Later found out as I looked it up today to be a Damien Hirst exhibit privately funded of myth building from a fictional 2,000 year old shipwreak. The statue outside is of a man and horse in an encounter with a giant serpent. The pained expression of such denotes hostility and a double attack of both the squeezing of horse and man while what looks like what could or could not be a fatal moment for one or the other. The website I looked up expressed it as a reference to Laocoön, yet the serpents are not contingent to just such and denotes stories outside of The Trojan War and who is and isn't friendly to such. As with the joy of looking further to understanding of reception, there is always the aspect of critics weighing in one side or another. They joy is always on the perspective and the time spent to be critical one way or another. I imagine Damien Hirst has a sense of humor on one thing or another in that regard as his work is always predominantly on social commentary. No doubt the transition towards classical art and seeing what occurs was inferred and understood before the exhibit even opened to understand one perspective or another. To invite dialogue or simply infuriate is always the fun aspect of the artist one way or another. It is always the invite of rebuttal or clarification that is the privilege outside the show aspect.

I arrive at my hotel after squeezing myself through the smaller streets although I find it actually quite refreshing. Bridges and water ways and not a single car in sight as there are none except for those on water. The reverberation of sound echos and bounces exponentially here vs. that of Florence. Condensed, compacted. There is a joy of such in island living were accoustics abound to the undetstanding of sound and the carrying of song within the air. My hotel as to be expected of several hundreds years old. I check in and handed an old key to be returned before leaving the building. I can only imagine the craftmanship required to replace such an item as it is not exactly one you could just go down to the store and have carved out so easily. A respect to places older than what I've experienced prior and I imagine the lived in aspect of so many people visiting for one reason or another.

Once again, it is drop off the bags, return they key and out the door with zero idea what is in this city but a more cognizant aspect of pay attention to your surroundings because I am more than likely going to get lost here. "I didn't have any plans for Venice. It's the city of theater. It's the city of lovers. I just want to ignore everything going on. Ignore the overthinking. Ignore the burdens I'm putting on myself.

I think this entire trip so far has been weighed down on what I brought with me but perhaps it is time I forget my problems...administration...bills...loans. Just get lost in the waters. Maybe Venice will tell me something about life I didn't know I was look-ing for. If I feel I am going to drown, there is not a better place than this city to tell me you can come back from a flood. But now is not the time for me. Perhaps coming here teaches me something about rebuilding from a flood. Perhaps coming here teaches me nothing except exploration of creativity, freedom, help, fear, freedom and release. I can't exactly figure out the benefit of this city as easily as the others. It's more subjec-tive in thought and execution but I am heading out the door and I am going to do this. God help my Wi-Fi"

Learn your surroundings or map what you can visually. One path here leads to an-other. Markers although in hindsight I am sure there was a GPS app used on this one. How could I not but always good to understand technology fades in paths of usage and battery life.

I stroll through the streets wondering where does one find a market here or if there is even one to be had? Imagine the difference in all in one locations and those being no longer an option. Definitely not going to find a Target or Walmart over here, it would take up half the island anyways. The streets are lined with shops of pockets and coori-dors. Handmade items and of Venetian masks and costume. I am surprised I didn't en-tertain buying one, but did look understanding now is not the time to be making those kinds of purchases. You just bought a necklace and that is enough for you. Imagine an entire island completely developed with no where else to build upon except for creatively and artistically. Only way to do such would be the imagination aspect of inspiration that the city does so well. I note as such that I have yet to see a single tree on this island. Understood as every inch of it so far is developed and crafted but an oddity to I as understanding the oxygenation comes from the surrounding waters. I see in window sills some plants so there is that. A comination of crafted stone collect-ed from one street way to another. A bridge of one thought to another place of entry in imagination. You look around and no doubt. "Something about this city just screams art. I hear it in the music, I see it in the streets.".

I go from one cooridor to the next finding theaters, high-end restaurants that I shan't be going to on this trip and enjoy the shade of the buildings in the close quartered streets as if the invited intimacy of the city is attempting to get closer to I in relate-ability. I turn a quarter and notice a theater called, The Fenice. I have never heard of it before but was inquiring as it was my intention to see some play, ballet or any perfor-mance while I was in Venice. A requirement of such that in the theater city of escap-ism, one must escape from one realm into another. I had never seen or heard of this place before but I understood the translation of such once I looked it up later. I passed by it only to return later to purchase tickets for that nights show. Although unsure exactly what I was getting into as at first I thought ballet to find it is indeed an Italian Opera by other. Dealer's choice of The Phoenix? La Traviata. I'll look up later to see what I just bought into understanding it is going to matter what I do and do not trans-late from it. Spoken? Body language. No doubt in different languages understanding the commonality of such will carry over in glances and communication. I know noth-ing of the story at this time and I will figure it out as I go. A nice difference to know the true aspect of how one comes across a Phoenix in life in complete surprise and unknowing paths of understanding even in that regard a different thought on life and rebirth through the aspect of theater and plays. Different connection then that of the mythological personas of cross-cultural reference. But a nice aspect of understanding chance encounters in a different capacity before moving elsewhere in thought.

"I take back what I said about Florence, this place is literally a labyrinth."
'I take back saying Florence was the Labyrinth. Venice is like, "here Flo...hold my beer." #howdoisolvethelabryinth'. Completely understood as the dream sequence is all Venetian inspired anyways in at least the mask aspects of such. When one of theater and theatrics is is completely understood how one would admire and love such as the city of theater in that capacity. Dreams had of past or future of such in respect and where introductions and memories made. A difference from what was shared on social media in my ever continued adventures to showcase one thing or another and leave expansion and truth for here in my own writings.I doubt much things have changed, but it is important to understand what was presented at one time, then a desire to present in another where here I am again going back to these points for mul-tiple reasons of expansion. Understanding the first drafts of these came in 2017 and was included with only slight type modifications in 2019. It was included into Curated Jellyfish where seperated at first from the main narratives and placed in the back as if something lost and never to be retrieved again at first and then integrated back into the narrative the same way it was reflected upon in writing. Never give up on Heav-en, Hope and happiness. Strive to overcome any obstacle in your life and as such it was important to remember that in revisit as I walk paths of different timeframes of

2019 to 2017 and piece from there and rebuild. Now in what is pretty much the final touches at this time knowing I cannot recount my entire life so, but at least the proper expansion of such occurred over time the way it should had.'

I continue back to the main plaza area where I randomly came across a prison in passing. An odd thing to note of bars and people inside understanding on the outskirts is just fine for I. The main plaza has more openings and understandings of one path or another. People gathered and for every person there is equally about 10 pigeons each . They flock, they are fed. They welcome invite of even being on your shoulder to say one thing or another. It is understood that they know more than the other in that regard and often keep their own secrets to share and gossip over later. They must go somewhere off the island to do so or perhaps on the rooftops hidden fortresses that I know not of pulled from nestings off the island. Only from above do they seem to understand the city of lovers in theatrics here. Arials to clasp one thing to another in unity and commonality. A joint effort made daily in daily balance between land and sea, noticed by the sky and winds. '#pigeonseverywhere'

I walk back to actually purchase my ticket to La Traviata now that I have had some time to look around a bit. See everything. Visit nothing apparently as I only have the day to do so before returning back to Rome. Again I am enticed by the sounds of strings and music played within an earshot. I follow it to another pathway yet again yet do not find any street artist this time. Merely an open window where 'Stolen Sounds' were captured and admired from the streets. I am sure it was for some performance and a rehersal of such for a later timeframe. The beauty of strings mixed with the vocalization of echoed Italian spoken during it. I record 30 seconds of it and pass the time there for a bit in thought of 'free concert' or of understanding that one doesn't get that much live music where I live in that regard. You do in other places and as such in New York City that I admire, but the quiet solo moments compound to siren calls of safe passage in these regards.

Eat something. A sandwich of Caprese once again. Cannot beat the 3 dollars and adding balamic and some meat to it is fantastic. Try it with the inclusion of Salami and you have yourself a sandwich on ciabatta bread.

'lunch time thoughts...I can only imagine the hell of a grindr hookup here. Yes, I need you to work yourself from the center of the Labyrinth, then take boat 2 to boat 1 and then reenter the Labyrinth on the outer banks of the eastern side of the island. I am 4 right turns in followed by a left, a right and then another right. Beware the bog of eternal stench and watch out for the fairies... they bite.'

I see more dead-ends in that adventure, but at least it was humorous to look-up only for the concept of when a struggle is more real than fantasy. At least in the world of GPS and coordinates you have a better chance than in the world of those paper map quests of olden days. In other thoughts of such, even if one was to meet in-person and be lead down an alley way one way or another, I imagine there are many traps within this maze for men or women. Masks everywhere. Totes Masks for Masks.

I return back to the hotel for a bit to recharge and relax for a bit. In continued com-pounded struggles, I explore my surroundings and find myself back into the compli-cations of one thing or another in other mapping out scenarios. Perhaps the universe is telling me to start planning things better. 'Keeping with bathroom oddities, I don't have one in my room nor a shower. But i do have a sink. If I want to drop the kids off at the pool I have to go down to hall 1, but the bidet is not in that bathroom, that's down the other hall with the shower. Originally when they said communal shower I got excited, but turns out it just means I'm sharing one. But have to make three different stops to complete my bathroom experience.' I still do not know what the giant spoon in the bathroom means, but I'm not going to ask about it either. Everyone has their kinks and I am well aware Europeans are a little more open than Americans on things. #notmyfantasyisland

Well. Back out a bit for a little more before having to get ready. I decide to stick to the waterways and I start to just admire those of boat rides in the city. Pairs of 2, pairs of 2...pairs of 2. Even the gondola boatmen...pairs of 2. I admire it from a distance and find it actually refreshing to see where they do and do not pop-up in the city on my walk way. They sing and enjoy the moment. I record them as such from a distance and said perhaps there is another time for me to do a gondola ride. It might get awkwards in the pairing system and then I start relating to the drivers more than I should as potential partners and lovers while everyone else either looks around or makes out in the boat.

'...WiFi for me is horrible in Venice. But this solidified I'm not doing a gondola solo. This city was meant for lovers...
or another person with u to not get lost or get lost with.'
'I've enjoyed getting lost here'

You know what...maybe in hindsight I should have gone back and got my camera...there is something to this image here. How long are these rides anyways?

This can get interesting in the seduction sections of Venice.

I'm open, but I'm on a schedule.

 <A boat ride never taken.>

"This is the first place I actually feel alone."

"Something tells me to just go in. Escape. Get lost.

I'll come out of the maze when I'm ready."

Perhaps a sadness in that just understanding the possibility of things. Could be one thing or could had been something else. Trips so rare to come by one way or another that in reflection it has been the coupling aspect of such here that wasn't so much in your face in the other places. Perhaps it is just because it is tighter quarters here or maybe the whole island is a theatrical play that is going on one way or another where I, the lonely Opera in the sea of Operas, that has no time for map-questing those kinds of adventures today. Perhaps a building towards comfortability of traveling together with someone again eventually. For now I feel like I I have people with me anyways or perhaps have just needed the time to go from the top of one place to just float around in a place where I am actually not going at the pace I have been all week. Cornered thoughts had of passages to one way or another. How can I process everything from one day to another in an aspect of stimulation overload of maximizing what I can within what I can. On an island, there rests a maze. Inside it is some thing that is lost and something that is found. A difference between such of what is above and what is underground.

Time to return back to the hotel and get ready for the show tonight. It is almost time and I am not sure I understand the shower system yet or how long I will have to wait to use it. I dress up for the event in actually bringing a collared shirt with me. Opted not for the tie, but to be expected at the time. I imagine there are other days for such and really I'm enjoying the humidity and want to relax. I enter into the building built from the 1700s to a room of massive reds and golds. All around I see the fire aspect continue into the adorments of the theater. The adorments of lamps fill a glow to the room as if sitting inside the firey bird understanding the stories that line the walls of one thing or another. All fascets of its life or in reference to perhaps the different stories from which it birthed or shared to others.

'And my last must do on this trip. If Rome was about reflection of life and Florence was about Heaven. Venice is about rebirth and resurrection. La Fenice (translation The Phoenix). Time for my most absolute favorite artform. Interior pics to follow.

'Fun side story to this. The couple next to me are from California. They are doing this whole biker trip through Europe for their 60th birthday. Their names, Art and Cindy.

I totally got to enjoy the experience with Cindy sitting next to me even if it wasn't Cindy Bonneau. But i totally died when we started talking and introduced ourselves.' I'm still wondering where they put their bikes though...surely we talked about such. Imagine a biker trip all the way to Venice to be told 'No bikes allowed.' I'm sure I asked them. I just love that I got to see it with my parent's namesakes right next to me where neither of them had been to Venice before. Not that they would now anyways in divorce for about 20 years, but an interesting imagination of yet another adoption and getting to know people.

I'll go with a quick synopsis just to refresh myself before going into it in translation.

———————

La Traviata - (The Fallen Woman) based off a story by Alexander Dumas. Set to three acts by Giuseppe Verdi and talian libretto by Francesco Maria Piave. La Fenice is the original opera house of the performance.

Act 1- Beginning in Paris a courtesan. A party commenses of one Violetta who upon recovery from severe sickness. There is confession of love from one who was by her side while she was ill was she is, in fact, with another lover at this time. She dances and falls over and faints. She is removed from the room where Alfonso professes his love to her which she rejects at first but then in change of thought gives him a flower for which she said come back to her when it is wilted. As he leave, Violetta questions if he is the one for her, but at the same time she needs to live her life. A question there as from a distance the gesture holds Alfonso in a place of happiness.

Act 2. - Violetta's Country House outside Paris
Violetta gives everything up of her former life to be with Alfonso. 3 months have passed. Due to budget constraints of lifestyle they must return back to Paris to settle debts. It is here that Violetta is asked to break off the engagement from Alfonso at the request of his father due to her reputation and of her past while he had other plans of marriage for his son. Although he warmed up to her, she agreed what was best and in sadness began to write a farewell letter to Alfonso. He sees her crying and comforts her, yet she gives the letter to someone else to deliver to him and she sets off on invitation elsewhere afterwards in Paris. Later Alfonso is given the letter from his father Giorgio. "'Who erased the sea, the land of Provence from your heart?' In jelousy he believes this is the work of the Baron and he sets off to get his answers not knowing it was his father at the time.

At the party Alfonso gambles his rage and suspicions as he came for Violetta whom he was sure has fallen back in love with the Baron. He demands she profess her love to the Baron and she refuses and asks him to leave. He throws his money down at her as if that settled why they came back to Paris in the first place. She faints. It goes dark. Alfonso is scorned by those in the crowd and even his own father Giorgio understanding nothing about where his anger came from other than the disrespect that he unleashed upon Violetta. He still does not disclose he was the original reason why she left at his request. No doubt a duel would commense between the Baron and Alfonso.

Once she awakes, "Alfredo, Alfredo, you can't understand all the love in this heart..."

Act 3. - Violetta's Bedroom
The doctors say she does not have long to live. Tuberculosis.
She receives a letter from Alfonso's father saying that Alfonso only wounded the Baron but that he lived. His father finally tells him why she left and what she was doing and he wanted to beg for forgiveness (although, it is still the fault of the father on that aspect while the lesson is about what one does for family and love on the other side.) Knowing more she feels it is perhaps too late. 'Farewell, lovely, happy dreams of the past.' (for too much time has gone from which has been the occurred.)

The thought of young death overtakes Violetta where Alfonso tries to convince her to return to Paris. The father comes in and finally confesses to his interferance of such to begin with where there is song and dance of such from father-son before Violetta is revived a bit for a second or third wind from what she was battling.

In a chance to be happy again she lifts up and prepares to go to Paris. As she does in slight alievement to what occurred, she dies in the arms of Alfonso before they could even have the life they dreamt together.

———————

It hits a little bit more of home now than it did then. I can approach it many ways where I can look at my life from 2017 prior to get one or two areas of connection. (multiple really) or I can look at the events from 2022—present where as with no insurance now just as much as no insurance and employment then there is a difference writing things out. Especially after the events of Feb. 21, 2019 which I don't really entertain in this section of the book as I try to keep this in tune with my time then but cannot as well in layered paintings of words.

In either regard, a refrain of such in understanding that on multiple fronts it was probably the right opera to see at the time and as any great opera is perhaps one that brings greater sadness now afterwards. I can look at it personally from multiple years. I can look at it professionally from multiple years.

I reflect with the understanding I got to see a Venetican opera in a place of it's birth while I was looking for rebirth, repreive and what came after that was not invited yet a part of my life anyways while I continued on from one way or another. Perhaps an understanding where society would say one thing or another and simply I'd reply, 'well your advantage and understanding of such is simply your own understanding and awareness of the world. Where that goes on your accord is based on your own intentions and regardless the life lost or pain in that regard, your children suffered from it as well from your direct, indirect hand. Perhaps an understanding of first-hand accounts while others let their hearts do what they do best...especially in love and the pursuit of happiness. From there a desire from the one ridiculed for others to be happy one way or another. Sobbing while writing notes or saying good-bye one way or another with or without a letter. Simply a do what one has to do due to circumstance that I related to back then.

I can relate in things given up, they were written here prior, but that comes with everyone and an understanding of the idea and glimmer of happiness before the invasion aspect of others to do one thing or say something for their advantage until not realizing the detriment to their own family and others until after. In the regards to most, after death where I think of this from the perspective of 2019 knowing it is 2022 and when 'The Opera of the Obstinate' is I am still alive and well. You almost had me in 2019 and I am persistent in that is not happening again despite taking everything from then on and continuing to do so.

I imagine my translation of the opera back then was much more personal and related to my first years in Atlanta vs. what became of life after I gave up everything I knew for someone else's dream and company.

'That most definitely was an Italian opera. With some ballet. Strange performance but I hear u fate on the story u telling'

I don't know how to feel here. This is the one place where I have absolutely zero connection to the experience. I find it funny seeing gondolas and my thoughts. It's one of the things you absolutely associate with this city and I sat there recording video while others are on the boat. Do I think of this as I missed the boat? What boat was I trying to keep afloat at one point in my life or another? If anything I can't bring myself to do it. I don't need to captain a ship at the moment. That's something made for a someone plus one. This entire city is a person plus one.

I actually never felt alone until I got here. I was fine in Rome. I was fine in Florence. There is something different here.

Something makes me wish I was exploring every corner of this city with someone. Perhaps one day I'll come back. I went to La Fenice this evening. Not knowing anything about this city other than it was the center of performance art; I found it fitting to conclude with a phoenix. Perhaps whatever story they are showing means something to me. Perhaps it's just something to do and keeps me out of my room. They were showing "La Traviata". The story was of a whore (they say courtesan as it simply is a more 'classier' way of saying what others would call anyways.) looking for something more and escaping the past reputation of making ends meet and still being loved then and after. She finds love, love rejects her, love finds her, and she dies. Can't say I didn't relate. Can't say I am not tired of looking for more meaning that I should in things. I think that I like being lost in the middle of this labyrinth ATM. Gives me a chance to stop caring what the hell I brought with me if even for just a little bit.

I like the idea of meeting a phoenix. I like the idea of being a phoenix. Did this opera help me in that quest? Probably not. Probably so. It took time to understand the lessons and see the connection. Operas are meant to be sad and enlightenment came at the moment of death. I can't say that helps me in my thought process (then or now, but reality and fantasy combine one way or another). That is afterall what are hopes and dreams anyways. All the best art is wrapped in tragedy it seems. For every death of the splintering of an artist, a birth somewhere else with the thoughts that came from saying goodbye to a product as finished and moved on from. If I am to do anything great does that mean it is predestined to equally be wrapped in heartache?

Do I even have heartache anymore?

'When you truly love someone, you have to give them what they want. Even if it is the one thing that will hurt you the most...letting them go.'

'What he did talk about which I have yet to talk about is the idea of practicing compassion. The practical definition of the word is a deep awareness of and sympathy for another's suffering. Ultimately, it is the humane quality of understanding other's suffering and wanting to do something about it. When things do not work out the way you want them to, we go through loss and disappointment.

In the scheme of relationships, when they do not work, we focus on the internal hurt and disappointment. We focus on ourselves and the wants and needs that 'We' need fulfilled. What is hard to do and, God knows I've been at fault for this, is the lack of compassion for ourselves and for the other. If you are the one who get left then all hell breaks loose (sometimes) in your emotions and you set off on a mission of doing right by you one way or another. Sometimes you make mistakes along the way in doing so. It is possible to go down wrong paths, but ultimately you are doing what you need to do.

A good practice to have through is 'compassion' for the other person's sorrow. It is often difficult to put yourself in the other person's shoes to realize that they must of been suffering or hurting to get to one point or another. If it got to the point of ending a relationship, they have begun a journey of doing right for themselves.(possibly). It is hard to admit to yourself that you are the source of someone's unhappiness...that you have caused hurt. That does not mean anything is wrong with you, or you have done something wrong. But in someone else's eye they see you as wronging them or themselves as not being a good fit for whatever.

Through my own thoughts and actions I constantly reached to rehold a hand that no longer wanted to be held by I. If only I talked more or write. Anything to say I'd go the distance one way or another and everything could work out. All that showcased though was my lack of compassion about what the other person was feeling and focused on my needs instead of their own. Vice versa in that as any relationship is a delicate balance of at least two points of delicacy. In discussion points prior, perhaps it was the non-listening to what phrases were or were not said along the way only to comprehend afterwards. There may never be reconnection again with people regard-less of what felt right for myself as it might not have felt right to the other person. While not the same of 3-4 months prior, the same could be said for 3 years before going back more just as much as more than likely I would not be completely the same person 3-4 months from now nor that of 3 years to come. I imagine anyone else would be the same way in difference of time knowing that there are more secrets in time away to where how could one not have things to talk about if ever a reconnection?

I need to practice compassion towards silence. Give space. Let things be so that I can understand their reasons one way or another. It is a change of mentality for I, but I think if I can do that then I'll grow more even if it is indirectly. To understand that is to understand the preparedness to take steps in one direction or another that I need to go down. I have to give what is asked for while understanding it at least considered what I need as well. In distance and seperation, perhaps neither have to accomodate or take action. Simply let things breathe and the heart desides and works towards action/inaction. I have to give what is asked for. Perhaps over time, the compassion I struggeled to give someone will be returned as well. -2/20/11

—————

If I could think about anything at this moment, what is the first thing that comes to mind? Sense of fear. Sense of faith. Reminded at the moment "This is just the beginning."

In any version of love, there is always a delicate balance of vanity. Question compassion & Humility; especially with personal gratification involved.

I hate I came here alone but then I love it so. It was important for I. I think just in circumstance with this city. I feel sad here. I don't know why. Vacation is almost over.

'There are no trees in Venice, but something is rooted there.'

'The Viewing of an Opera. Party of 1. Thoughts from La Fenice' - Sketch Translation' December 1, 2022. "Philip A. Bonneau.

ENTRY 45:

I like to think my thought process could be unique. Is it hard to follow with perhaps connections only I could make. Are they rational? I try to make them so. They are comprised of references pulled from somewhere hidden in my mind as an endless mix of Wikipedia, pop culture, movies, art history, mythology, spirituality and morality.

Defined by upbringing; **an** aperfect mixture of creative and analytical. It's all there somewhere. Jumbled but nevertheless I am curiouser. In fairness of connections, they are pretty easy for others to translate and see. **Sometimes it just has to be spelled out correctly after time, conversations and a chancec to step away for a bit.**

A secret to Heaven is knowing deep down you have done the right thing. Now it's up to others to get in line from time to time. The funny thing about all of this is, it's not funny at all. None of this needed to happen. **We all have our chosen paths that can be walked forward or backwards.**

"...Underestimated."

If I had to be pushed again by a group mentality, the question lies on will I make the same choice I never had when breaking down? Midway through this, I find myself making similar choices.
-Protective of my family.
-Protected of my dogs.
-Protective of myself.
I imagine scientific minds got their answer. Jury still out on that one.

It's a different experience from experiencing in real life vs. a very active mind piecing thing back together. There is no one thing to focus on because the mind is focused on all things at once. What I will not be is pushed towards others writing my books for me. **I suppose in adament behavior it becomes a driving point to transcribe and not leave untapped journals laying around from 2019 on.**

I imagine there is every way to paint me. I choose to take the Beautiful, the Brave, and the Ugly parts of me and combine them. But when you have a strong sense of self, you tend to fight outside influencers. Some people always have your back. Others will not.

"Try to focus on the positives."

"Don't let the past haunt you or define you completely,
but do let it be a reminder that you overcame so much
and yet you are still here."

A secret is to
bless and release.

A paper plane.
A breath of hope.
A tree.

You choose what
growth is rooted from.

I've come a long way.
Life is not exactly
what you plan it to be.

Things happen.
Some you are proud of.
Some you are not.
What I am most proud of
Is knowing you can't be most proud.

Every moment unique.
A shard pieced together.

Take one of the many pieces of mirror and look at it every different way.
In it you will always find yourself. There will always be a different perspective for you to view.

You will always see something different than what others will see.
A projection onto something so cursed to never be able to see itself.

Put two mirrors together and you create an infinite amount of space between a finite realm. Your world that only you can see as you look at every possible version of yourself. Every single one making the exact same choices up until you walk past the gaze of the mirror's reflections. Do those versions disappear? Infinite possibilities of where each reflection could go from that moment on. Let fate decide each and every one. One of those versions of you is bound to succeed while others will fail. Each revisit back to those mirrors are hidden stories that only you will know occurred in-between a world untouchable.

Post 19: Day 6: The Seventh Sphere - Rome

'Ok. Today is the day i find out what the hell this hurricane is going to do with my travel plans.

So far flight has not been cancelled to arrive Friday at 11pm. Delta has already started canceling some flights. I do have the option to shift plans for free but i really want my kids and if things hit it could be a long time before I get back into Florida. In the event delta gives me no choice I can either a.) Extend here and go south Italy b.) Atlanta where I'm sure someone will taken in a foreign refugee c.) Take my flight from here to NYC and postpone the nyc>FL part of the flight which is probably the most expensive option or d.) I'll go to Boston and visit family.'

'Beyond the Walls, A Sea of Bridges' - Sketch Translation' December 1, 2022. "Philip A. Bonneau.

I struggle to travel with my suitcase back to the train station. I arrive a little earlier than expected. I learned my lesson on the train ticket and got this one in advance knowing it more than likely doesn't come as often as the ones from Florence and Rome. I sit and reflect a bit at the same opening scene that was the beginning of my brief introduction to Venice now with a better understanding of such. The selfie sticks abound as one's own image is slightly further than an arm's length away. A little bit of a stretch but not much more.

The bridge to the left of note as it is often depicted and is the largest from the introduction to the island and from there minor ones of inter-connection to weave in and
out of stories of buildings and pathways. To have a day here played out shorter than
the others denotes a difference from the rest of the trip and it felt as such understanding the birth of so many relationships in one concentrated space of an island. The
choices they make had wondering if this was the beginning of some, the extention
of others of a celebration of life one way or another. The pairs come and go understanding new pairs begin and tragedy plays out over and over for the entertainment of
others. A story of love and theatrics where one must wonder which face is being worn
when on vacation alone or togther. A train caught. A train to catch.

I board the train and begin several hours of a journey back to Rome. Wifi isn't working at the moment so I imagine it gives me time to just write and think for a couple
hours. Perhaps read and go from there. The hotel booked for Rome for my final night
is my most expensive and a little bit more in the heart of an area I walked past often
during the beginning part of the journey. Steps of contimplation that seem to be a
gathering point for many in an area of shopping. Not that far from where I was before
but at least awareness of the steps I found to be quite beautiful and able to explore a
bit more of commerse and window-shopping while knowing slightly better my way
around the city. Soon into my journey a realization of 'Not the same disco bathroom
back to Rome...'. Perhaps the one inter-dimensional multi-travel pass to Singapore
while on the way to Venice was enough for one trip or they really downplay the
difference between first class and economy. Whichever reality I'm in, apparently that
was the one shot to it and now we have to search to find our way back home one way
or another.

"Thoughts from the Train.-
My biggest fear from this trip was always the judgment and perception of taking this
trip during a time I had zero control of the situation I found myself in...even moreso
now that a hurricane is added into this. Nature runs it's course one way or another.
I'm pretty open about a great many things in my life...sometimes too much, but at
least U see Me for me. With judgment people think it leads to superiority or power
but it doesn't. I respect the silent judgment though. Keep that silence prejudice inside
and never act on it and then really there is no external issue. That's your movie. Watch
what u want in your own house. That's human. However, judging other people's
movies is like people trying to rate a foreign film from outside your own window.
There's no sound. Some things may be familiar but obscured or picked-up from body
language.

They are never going to fully appreciate our understand the entire movie but will have enough information to rate it anyways. Partially it is valid from their point of view; opinions form in notice one way or another. However, it's always going to be their fault on how they judge that movie because perhaps they shouldn't have tried watching it from someone else's window when they were not invited to the viewing.

Plenty of movies out there to watch correctly. And if anyone ever wants to talk to U about why they don't like that movie from the window... tell them U come on my porch again and I will rate every bootleg copy of your movie for U in return. #rottentomatoesyourlifenotothers - 9/7/2017"

I have to think about this post a bit.
God knows I'll re-read it over and over before I hit publish.

Part of me is about to reveal something I was never comfortable revealing and never really wanted to. The other part of me feels like I've been honest this entire point that it's only right to me that I continue to be honest in my journey. I look for understanding within myself and I hope for understanding with others. Who am I if I don't give all the puzzle pieces to figure that out about myself or get what my heart desires? I grapple with this post and wanted to approach it with temperance. The day of was not the time to write.

The day of was not the time for forming words.

God I expressed words though. Self-moderation is a very difficult thing to do at times. We react in passion. We react in anger. There is always going to be a reaction to something one way or another.

Something told me with this post, approach it days or even weeks later.
I can't just wipe away my final day overseas and the important lesson it taught me.

Judgment never gains anyone any points without looking at your own mirror first. I imagine if only for their to be judgement to have it come from a place where you can be taught something in return from it. A lesson in reflection before stories shift back on you in other talking points unexpected. Where's the focus and what is the purpose of such judgement and the expression of it postive or negative? Perhaps this whole long journey has been nothing else beyond begging people to understand because of

XYZ, but also challenging others to look at your their own reflection and wonder why you got where you were and question where you are going and to see who you are. In lessons of guidance towards one, there are always returned examples to open up discussion points.

'Who are you?'
It's the basic question a caterpillar asked a little girl. It's a question not so easily answered. 'Who am I?'

The same caterpillar would ask the same of a boy, a man or woman or any other animal that chooses to speak to them one way or another of lessons and life of transitioning and manuvering. A change of self over one identity to another with the understanding one gives up one thing for another.

'Concept on the Soles of Caterpillars and Butterfly Wings' - Sketch Translation' December 1, 2022. "Philip A. Bonneau.

How many feet come together to form something capable of flight? A question for soles to answer one way or another in patterned footsteps and behavior of life lived and paths treked in order to be able to rest before able to take flight with less weight than what came before. The retracing of footsteps with the understanding of the fragility of that which is being created with them. Paths remembered and paths retread for an outline of what is to come one way or another. Where one collects the paths once walked, patterns emerge from which one can build wings from. Taking in every step, mis- or not, an identity forms where it is not so much about the central body but what gets spread out in delicate nature. An impermanence to it all where although essential, you find the core to be the smallest aspect of notice but it is what drives the rest to manuveur from hardships of being grounded so much. Now capable of far more travel but with much more danger of being noticed.

I started this day heading back into known grounds returning to Rome. Partially dealing with a hurricane. Delta was probably going to cancel my flight home...later they did. In all the surreal moments I had, life came back headfirst ready for me. The downfall of being 5000 miles away from responsibility is responsibility still creeps it's head into things. One cannot escape reality and eventually has to return to it one way or another. Even when unexpected it determines one way or another by others or self to do so. I guess it's no different than doing 2.5x the amount of work right before a vacation to make sure everything will be ok so you can relax for a bit only to return to stacked up work from other places that did not pick up the slack while away. A constant catch-up to something that takes up so much of your day-to-day only to leave one exhausted before vacation and double time work when one returns to catch back up to the same speed of such. As no employment factor in this for I the reality of such is dealing with a hurricane, making sure my family is ok. Protect my belongings of importance and figure out where I am going and what I am doing halfway across the world. Easy enough task for others supposedly.

I had to debate, do I extend my trip and do South Italy, which would be much cheaper, and do hostels? Do I do NYC? Do I visit my brother? I had to ask one of my best friends that I need you to grab this, this and this just in case. That's not fun, let alone they also had my dogs and there was nothing I could do about. Sometimes there is nothing you can do. I don't think there could have been a wrong decision, but decisions had to be made nevertheless. That's life. Amazing the thoughts of butterflies on the other page and it was certain shoes that I found important to carry out of the house.

I approached this trip with humility. I was scared of the optics. I was scared to ever ask anyone for help if I did this. I made that clear before my trip and during that was a fear of mine. Although not fully expressed the exasperated feelings behind what was going on to crank out the opening of my website, get my life's work up and running for people to see prior to travel in need or a job, it was the importance of taking a vacation much needed that for I is a once-in-a-lifetime beginning. It was the aspect of processing years of things that came to an abrupt change of identity and status due to others actions and things avoidable one way or another. This trip meant something and this trip was sorrowed over thinking of giving it up and it was heavily processed over knowing what would come from it. Judgment always comes. There is no escaping that. From yourself or others. That is what happens when an entire career of underpaid and no nest-egg or fallback plan eventually. No retirement to tap into. No home to mortgage. No idea the concept of the everyday person of exploited aspects of their life.

I never asked for money.
I never asked to be taken care of.
I rather know I did everything I could and sacrifice everything I can before admitting a need for help.

During my trip the hurricane was always a looming factor. My sister kept me up-to-date and she made a point to let me know reality was always there no matter how much I wanted to escape it. Careful consideration of sibling understanding to one regard or another. Yes...I am aware of reality on multiple fronts. Yes...it is being worked on as well in multiple fronts and it is understood. Both then and now. I appreciated the thoughts. Both in the hurricane and just life in general. In stressing out over things in Florence, I let slip something that she ended up using to exploit and a simple aspect of human nature that some can choose to do or not.

In August 2016 I had an incident where I where I was going through my cancer scare. I could not keep anything down. It got to the point I was throwing up 20 plus times a day and not knowing exactly why. Could be cancer, could be something else. I was getting it looked at and was regularly going to the doctor one way or another throughout that time until insurance abruptly ended due to the closure of Alfred Angelo. My boss was going through chemo at the time but I doubt there was any relation to such. I was sick and I didn't know why. I processed as I could silently. I was being looked at for many things from gastro to stress to not fully understanding why I was throwing up constantly that contined until about Mid-2018 (time jump here of factoring after this trip and wellpast the ending of the trip in September 2017. A continued aspect and joy of not having health insurance from July 2017 until Jan/Feb. 2019. Especially with that looming over my head. At best I can relate it to either dietary and definitely prolonged exposure to intense stress and environments I never should had been in with definitely major digestion and food processing factors documented prior. You would think it might had reoccurred and popped back up from April 2021 — Feb. 2022, but it did not in any capacity. The constant throwing up and not being able to hold down food is specific to that time and still to this unknown as I am back on the no insurance aspect of my life once again in the do-it-myself someway and somehow of forced perspectives of what has occurred in my life.

I had a normal Saturday around the time of taking the dogs to the park and doing housework. I had 2 drinks that early on in the day and everything was fine and normal. I spent the afternoon at the pool where I normally do and swim, relax and have fun and enjoy. Often underwater and although still never recommended, I constantly open my eyes underwater at the bottom of the pool to see my surroundings and to take in the thought process of such of words or where to go one way or another.

Much later on in the day towards the evening, I went out to go meet up with one of my best friends that evening and at a red light I got sick and my foot slipped on the break. It is also now noted that the breaks were in need of replacement, but at least that is understood and taken care of. Didn't do any physical damage to the the car in front of me and I did what I was supposed to do. I waited for the cops to file a basic report. That report turned into notice of blood shot eyes (very much understood to be from the pool by I along with what happens naturally when throwing up constantly day in and day out from morning into the evening) and sobriety field tests. In those tests I was asked to walk straight lines heel to toe which I did perfectly and was asked to recite the alphabet backwards where to this day I still cannot do so and I stated such then. I imagine if that is to be a field test and something that one cannot do, other tests could be provided or simply teach in every public school the benefit of learing the ABC and the ZYX's at the same time for transitional thinking and problem solving benefits. The driver of the car in front of me was fine. She express distraught and that is to be understood of any incident one way or another. When no physical damage done to the car, I imagine there could be more fear of one way or another. I know what my lawyer said to me in confidence about the possible scenarios of the other driver, but that is privileged and confidential.

I ended up being taken to the police station and was asked to take a blood alcohol test. At first I refused and then thought and weighed the options. From the car ride there to the station it was nothing but respect understanding they are just doing their job as well. Even on the field testing aspect and never in the situation prior of having one done. I expressed nervousness and understanding of such. Much due to the brutality of what was in the news at the time, but an understanding that could occur to anyone if not doing the right thing this way or that. Hands out of pockets when asked. Speak when spoken too. Anxiety there for multiple reasons knowing even if I threw up then what it would look like knowing what it isn't. Upon agreeing to to test after thought as for what was later described as 'a level of alcohol that would kill an elephant'. I was arrested that evening and was taken off to give it a couple hours before I could go home and go from there. Not the proudest moment of my life, definitely not when I needed to use the bathroom in front of people but you learn to get over it when you have to go and wait things out. But there was something not right. If I beat myself up over shit before, this would be no different. I expect better. I can do better. I should have done better. I was far better than what it seemed to be.

Long story short I paid for a lawyer. I had at that point medical doctors writing there is no way I was drunk or that it was physically possible what I blew and what was on tapes. Especially in the context that this was leading towards the end of May 2017 before this finally got resolved and settled one way or another on the issue. The exasperation of prolonged timing of court cases to resolve matters results in further more physical and emotional damage during that time. Although expected there are many things in dockets, the looming aspect of such to take almost a year adds detriment before even a decision one way or another. I hate that time of my life mostly due to the stress of work, the stress of doctors and not knowing and then of course there is the financial aspect of going one way or another, but it is understood of responsibility, responsibility responsibility of the time with more added on that was not of my requirement and compounded all the way towards the closure of Alfred Angelo that was not my fault and left in a position of solving one thing or another privately personally, professional or medically. Never have I had to disclose this prior, but for multiple reasons then and now it facts in personally, professionally and eternally. It's the lowest and what I kept from anyone (to make any mistake of cost one way or another). We all have our moments. But that is also the beauty of private rulings on things and things going one way or another afterwards. I had sober relationships the entire time here with many people. I liked the idea of dating people where drugs or alcohol didn't factor into the equation or they found ways to overcome it and go towards healthier aspects of life or at least ones of balance one way or another. I don't even keep alcohol in my house because I never wanted to be the reason for them to relapse when they stayed over. Moderation goes a long way, but if self-control is the issue, that is understood and worked on with mutuality and never just a solo journey, which is why

I liked at least I had restraint on a great deal of things. It is probably also why in other areas considering past experiences with others I tend to know when to put my foot down as well compassionately. I even attended AA meetings not just for my benefit of understandings, but as done in Altanta a desire to understand who I was interacting with and build an understanding from there. One of my relationships here ended with finding out they became a meth addict for a time which again is a private struggle that they have worked one way or another from in their life. I am proud of them as humanity comes into play in areas of respect of struggle and where people come together to work things out one way or another. Even an earlier copy of this book was able to help with that and although rarely talk, friendship always presents itself. As much as I feel sorry for them during that time, it is difficult to balance tough love and being there. Multiple times over I have had to do that with people because it does become a point where other's coping mechanism become a detriment to those around you. Perhaps the same could be said of this book in some regard although I only imagine those of detriment are the ones who can relate one way or another to the words of understanding and wanting to connect vs. divide. It would also be of detriment to those who have stolen this book in early versions and had no desire for me to have any compensation of of my life's work, my life's experience that leads towards helping others to cope and not to others ripping me off and translating this into millions and billions of dollars without my benefit. I hated the shit they projected onto their friends and I. It happens multiple times depending on the situation. Not all people in my life were like that and I still hold each and everyone of them in regard and in safe-regard understanding when others before or during are talking points towards understanding how one becomes the way they are or perhaps how they process things moving forward. It's not worth the time or effort to let that evil in without addressing why would you want to continually be around someone you think is evil or toxic?! Let alone, vice versa. I can see where one thing or another can slip into people's lives and grab hold based on the environment they are in and where balance is always required or placed in an area where one does not even have to think of balance as someone frinds themselves in an environment to thrive instead of cope.

If continual pain comes from something you have to step away and move on or let others do their thing one way or another. It will mess you up regardless of how much love or compassion you had for that person. It is natural in emotion. It is natural in not understanding and it is completely healthy to go for a walk and think things out before continuing. I think I'll do that now.

I think my backlash to them came from a place of the past where I wish I had said you don't put that on me. Not the blame of your own decisions. That comes over time from the person you were to the one you had to become in strength and learning to use your words and respect boundaries. I remember in my mind at my time, I felt "Not only was I dealing with secretly dying or major health issues, but now this?! Fuck all of this." It was probably the only time I actually considered doing what I didn't do prior. back in 2016/2017 "I'm dying. Work is not helping. I'm fucked. What else is there from this?" Strength persists. Time pulls out more answers one way or another to help. At least that explains the email to my mother of intentions of property afterwards while she never knew any aspect of what happened and a couple hours in jail until 2018 when the audacity of background checks and discussions when not on-boarding in a fixed-term employment comes into play for the end of one behavior over another. I have since protected in the original copyright and in copyrights after the complete voidance of such an email while alerting the copyright office of what has occured in my life, where it came from and pointed them in the direction in the pro-tection of United States Copyright of the beginning to speak of the events that have unfolded in my life since the closure of Alfred Angelo and trying to figure out what has followed and attacked ever since.

All I ever wanted to do was forget that part of my life and move on. It is so easy to do so personally, its the surroundings of others and what they choose to look at and act upon that is not so easily managed. Perhaps that has been the goal since day 1. Close chapters, create new ones and reflect on adventures had while experiencing ones from a place outside the environmental impact areas. This trip was a part of that for me.

I remember hitting the moment shortly after this incident that I had to start asking for help. When you white-knuckle life you are always going to question if you are doing things right. Are your choices right? Are you doing what is best for everyone? Are you doing the best for yourself? Are you toxic?

Only about 4 people ever knew about the arrest experience. I'd say of those 4 only 2 knew that I got to the point that I need to invest in finding my answers and peace through therapy on many things considering at the time the workloads, threats, the understanding I was not making what I should and if I didn't continue the compa-ny would be drastically affected by it regardless of my well-being. It was essential to continue working just as much as keeping a dream and jobs alive. In my mind, I figured I didn't have the strength to convince myself this time that it was worth it like I did before. A balance between responsibility that is and isn't mine to bear. I feel that now more than ever and the last thing I am going to do is what was already done on the otherside of this book 2 years later. I took out a loan and said, 'Ok...I'm going to talk and see what happens. I'm giving myself 20 sessions and making the most of a situation on multiple fronts. I was required to do those sessions anyways. I do not waste my time whatsoever in multi-task and getting to the benefit of moving into one area or another. I can work in my passion of my series into the questions and sessions and will see what comes from that.'

I still am not entirely sure I do, but an interesting thing happened in those sessions where again it is the empathy of stories told while translating my own to begin articulation, understanding and relateability. Regardless of whatever I talked about in them, I found out that I was always better off than I thought. They are privilegd anyways and of social work status. I was always further along than I gave myself credit for is what I discovered or given assurance of while understanding one thing or another. I was probably more at peace with life then I ever was before just being able to sit down, relate openly one way or another and go into discussion with those who wanted to participate and those that didn't.

It's one thing to feel sorry for yourself. I don't think I've ever felt sorry for myself. I just always wanted to learn and grow from things and push out the things that are negatively affecting myself. It is an environmental aspect and has more to do what is around me of acceptable one way or another. It is understood since this trip, prior and after that what happens when the behavior pattern of invasion into my place of employments was allowed, sanctioned and even considered proper behavior that was knowingly detrimental and the same attacks discussed of at PureRED in 2019. In an effort to find peace with others and myself you forget that it is simply a way of thinking. You can blame the world for unhappiness. You can blame others for that. But ultimately it's how you look at the world and what you focus on. There is no black or white, but there are greys. It's so subjective. I've taken so much responsibility that I am not about to sit here and do it for everyone without discussion, without consideration and definitely when it has been attack after attack as if an addict has chosen I as their drug and has constantly said they couldn't stop in 2018, 2019, 2021, 2022...what belief system is there to determine how to fix an addiction problem in that regard? At what point is there discussion with what is one control or a complete removal of the tools used for part of the other's addiction? There has been no problem with the digital attacks on me and my property exporting it out in places where I don't know where while I am still keep trying to build my life and every egg in my nest seems to be taken and placed elsewhere for sustainability of others and not I.

Whether you are a pawn, a knight, a queen or a king; the choice is always yours on what you want to be that day. I spent most of my sessions actually going through this series.Very indirectly , but every now and then I'd refer to BLL and UST and then in reflection begin formulating what is or should be a direction towards understanding Brave New Secrets. The art, the words, the audio... If anything I have a perspective of things from a licensed social worker in psychology in pathways on my search of identity.

Flashback to Rome final day.

I enjoy my walks in the city. It took a bit to get there and I get to my hotel happy to see it is in a busier section of familiarity. Twice the price and still the same kind of room, but nice to know what is to be the last day of my time in Italy. I didn't get much time to settle before I head out to walk around. I stay somewhat in my surroundings as I think I walked the canals on the first days there but I'd say I ventured around the shops as I try to figure out my flight plans. My sister calls while I am out early on and begins stressing about what is important about flights and patterns. During the call I mentioned I needed to confirm with others on what the plans are as I have no choice and need variable options. Even my brother offered his place which I was considering as viable. I try to move past the conversation comment as I was playing out the responsibility scenario when the last day was supposed to be relaxation, reflection and a chance to just not go a mile a minute before having to return back to it anyways one way or another sans hurricane or not while unemployment looms over the list of responsibilities that need to be priority number #1.We end the call and I continue window shopping and walk closer towards the Vatican area although I don't think I entered it.

My sister called back shortly with a change of tone and a sense of dominence. She had looked up what I didn't tell anyone but 4 people. She expressed anger, she expressed a superiority tone to her voice. 'A better than you' tone and expression in understanding that she instantly could say whatever she wanted to me like she had control over my life. 'We will talk about this later. And we will discuss this.' remembered towards I cut her off very abruptly, loadly and definitely assertive in a manner that perhaps has never come out of me prior and never since. Within an ear-shot of the Vatican and the center of Christian faith,
'NO. WE WILL NOT TALK ABOUT THIS LATER.
(The rest pretty paraphased but spot on as well)

YOU DO NOT HAVE ANY CONSIDERATION FOR PRIVACY OR WHAT OTHER PEOPLE ARE GOING THROUGH. DO YOU THINK I WANT TO DEAL WITH ANY BIT OF THAT WHILE I AM ON VACATION UNEMPLOYED AND GETTING AWAY FROM SO MUCH YOU DO NOT KNOW AND I WON'T TELL YOU. THIS IS MY TIME TO GET AWAY FROM ALL OF THIS AND YOU JUST BROUGHT IT BACK INTO MY LIFE PREMATURELY AND UNNECCESARILY. I DON'T CARE WHAT YOU LOOKED UP OR WHAT YOU THINK OF ME IN THAT REGARD. YOU SAVE THAT FOR THE PROPER TIME AND IT IS NOT WHEN SOMEONE IS ON VACATION AND HAS GONE THROUGH EVERY-THING TO GET THIS TIME TO BREATHE.

WHO ARE YOU TO EXPRESS DOMINANCE OR SUPERIORITY OVER SOME-THING YOU INSTANTLY JUDGED AND THEN WENT ON TO SAY MY 'IMAG-INARY FINANCIAL PROBLEMS' ARE ANYTHING THAT IS YOUR BUSI-NESS AND COMPLETELY OF YOUR OWN FABRICATION. I AM ACTUALLY DOING QUITE FINE FINANCIALLY RIGHT NOW, BUT NOT HAVING A JOB KNOWS THAT FINANCIALLY IT MAY BE A PROBLEM LATER THAT I HAVE WEIGHED OUT ONE WAY OR ANOTHER BEFORE EVEN GETTING HERE.

YOU DO NOT DO THIS TO ME, YOU DO NOT JUDGE ME.
YOU DO NOT COME INTO MY LIFE IN THAT MANNER.
YOU KNOW NOTHING OF MY LIFE AND THE BEAUTY OF IT.
I HAVE NEVER EXPRESSED SENIORITY ON YOU AND I COULD JUDGE YOU SO MANY DIFFERENT WAYS.
 I HAVE NEVER DONE SO TOWARDS YOU IN ANY MANNER THAT I WOULD COME ACROSS AS BETTER THAN YOU...
I hung up the phone on her.

I imagine I probably went into more specifics on the topics but I unloaded on her and she deserved it although I am saddened that it occurred. It sparked something that needed to happen in society later.

My sister brought something I was hiding as a leverage point to feel like she was bet-ter than I. I guess at least its proof I can keep some things secrets. She came across as if somehow finding out about this put her in a better place and understood everything from stolen information standpoint. She felt that somehow this scenario explained financial issues or anything else that was perceived at the time. My response was I never asked for money, paid off 15K of credit card debt this past year and the only reason I'm stressing now is because I got laid-off from an equally fucked up work environment. Fuck you. Fuck you if u think I had financial issues. I didn't. I will. But I actually never did prior to being unemployed. I've worked my ass off and if you knew the real issues I went through maybe you would understand, but they were always my issues to talk about or not. All my shit has always been in order. Can you say the same?

She sent a couple hundred dollars to me with no response. It didn't fix what occurred and what shifted but it was appreciated at the time. One of the things about mug shots is innocent before proven guilty. It struck a cord of the instant judgement one way or another it provided while understanding the idea behind them prior and where the detrimental aspect of them on the internet as a commodity to be leaveraged one way or another in exploitative means. First hand in Rome, a boundary set and a boundary-crossed. I would never prosecute her nor could I really because it really only is prosecutable when it comes up in employment aspects under certain conditions.

Flash to December 1, 2022

When the mugshot aspect entered into Freud/Diablo in 2018 by FD-DS and discussed about him doing a background check on me while they weren't even on-boarding and going through what is on the other side of this book 2 years after this trip to Italy, that is prosecutable. That I will press charges on. The months of office testing and understanding what was occurring to make sure before I said anything. That is prosecutable. The transcibing of phonecalls to a law office made outside the building that your company acted on internally and in my earshot is prosecuable. The continuance of what occurred from your company and continued into 2022 is your responsibility and talking about whatever company came into your company that continued into the next company talking about your company that went into a higher education system in the same tactics experienced at your company into a place we are all learning one way or another about the importance of the future of the current 195 countries on this globe and the future ones that form from them. The continued aspect to humilate, persecute and attack has been years and it is not even from that moment with my sister. It is all based on facts and all started very directly at Freud/Diablo by employees in an official capacity, carried over into PureRED with discussions and litegations going on around that time that I was never asked to be a part of and invited the conversations of prior places of employment in there as well along with the partners of the Atlanta Devil. I'll settle for saying thay are actually the Sandy Springs Devil in this regard. I wouldn't do that to Atlanta. They have been burnt before.

Between my sister and The Psycholgical Devil of Homes and Industries, that is the end of mugshots and that is the end of whomever thought that people can be shamed through life for something that no disclaimer can say it isn't right to have them on the internet. I'd say at best maybe a name system with no pictures, but then it still becomes nobody's business until after trial and completely state and federal business is constantly persecuted one way or another by the selling of arresting information and where it goes from there. Especially after time served, sealed or otherwise.

The existence of the online mugshot is cruel and unusual punishment that is greater than any crime anyone could commit because they are already judged by peers before they even get to say one thing or another. That punishment of presumed one way or another goes beyond a lifetime in that capacity. The beginning aspects of what occurred in Rome 2017 was fortified in The Phoenix City of Atlanta where I reported properly then and repeatedly since what occured back in 2018/2019, going into my phones, my electronics, my written works, my artistic works, my entire life and it didn't stop even into late 2022. It has not stopped.

To push it back to the just the other issue to process on one thing at a time, every single mugshot on the internet is a liability for every state and federally as you cannot presume innocence in pre-emptive shaming that lasts longer than a lifetime and is the responsibility of such to remove all mugshots off the internet and that is backed up in fact, law and civility of discussion. It is expressed in this book and when attempted to be sold-off 2 years later, I've argued and at least got in motion the discussion that mugshots to third parties who put their logos on it elsewhere is discussed in round 2 of the battle towards 'I was not convicted of what I was arrested for, it has done constant damage, and more than likely the liability cannot be transferred and only extended to third parties in what has been a profitable world of shaming and guilting the innocent and those who may have done what arrested for.'

From the mountains of solicitations, I recieved in the mail upon my arrest it denotes that information of such is sold instantly and a market is present that thrives off the leaking of data that jeapordizes private citizens and is extensive in the damage that is done. In yet to transcribed solutions in further writings, I even solve it on the other end for state and federal on what could be legal ways of doing one thing or another in regard but still a completely drastic shift of process and public shaming. The compounded experience of invasion that, as far as the mugshot story goes, started in Rome and has continued into invasion of my privacy and life by possible those who may have a grudge or look at anyone arrested as someone warrenting to subjection towards justification of their actions. Perhaps a reflection knowing at least my initial discussion was copyright protected in 2019 as we all need to look at themselves and that someone 'above' them may be ready to justify their actions towards you as you look down on others. It just gets more and more elite depending on how you look at it in certain circles. A ladder climb one way or another towards one way or another.

I have been denied life. Liberty. Freedom. A chance to thrive. My property and continually impeded on to get towards my property without others paytng for it while probably trying to find something, anything to get me prosecuted so the property I have can be unassumingly transferred to others who probably already stole it anyways and to continually cause pain to myself and my family. You already went into the Devil of Diablo/Freud to negatively affect my life, you did it with unpure intentions at PureRED that directly lead towards my suicide attempt and it is more than likely based on life experience not in this book and with the EEOC had the complete disre-spect for existence of civilization by working through or into The Savannah College of Art and Design later in life to do one thing or another that you have never told me about and continue brought things upon yourself while 've just wanted to live and have a life and it has been years. What justification can you say now without going into the looking glass of that reflection through this timeframe and your own?

Flashback to Rome final day.
My day has been thrown off. I don't know what to do right now. Obviously I just shouted in Rome and on vacation and I need to breathe and relax. This will take a minute. Headphones on. Go for a walk. A run would do me good but I am not about to do that here. Just walk. Just breathe. Take a minute and calm down. Obviously you are going to smoke a cigarette and probably not going to eat. Maybe I should. Sit on the steps with everyone else and just relax. Write out something later, but now is not the time and you will figure out what to say later on. Let it breathe.

From what I remember of the last day involved eventually window shopping and just get out of my head what has occurred. I've decided I'm going to my brothers and go-ing to meet my neice for the first time. I notify properly and do what I have to do. It is cheaper at this point since I need to save money so I don't hear the financial problem conversation again. It would be irresponsible of I to continue to travel in Italy ATM. All that thought process before getting here understood. People do not wait in bit to prove me right on that regard. Figured it comes from my sister. At least I'm staying away from here when I get back to America and perhaps this works out in a way I can finally get my grandmother's portrait from my father who constantly fails to deliver on promises in that regard.

I noted a giant rhinestoned skull in the window at some point before going back to the hotel. A beautiful image of the adorning of death and making something beautiful from it. Well...thanks fantasy world...back to reality.

I hate that when coming back into the real world I am reintroduced with the bullshit of reality. Vacation is over. I hate that this was the talking point for my final day in Italy but maybe it is what it should be. Maybe this is no different than when I started this series. 'You don't get to control my narrative' was such a driving point for me in the beginning. You don't get to judge me from the outside. You don't get to talk about something not true. I guess in all those moments of anger the question really became for myself on what actually is my narrative. What's my point? Maybe brave new secrets is not about keeping secrets, but perhaps just blessing and releasing understanding that you never will know the full story.

On the other side perhaps it is telling me that a middle finger is not a bad thing when judgment comes your way. I never wanted to talk about this. But perhaps by speaking about it the world is giving me what I need to in order to conclude this series and really find heaven. I like the idea of at least admitting something I don't have to ever again because its not another thing that could be held over my shoulders nor was it anything bad in the scheme of things.

I expected this from others. I never expected this from family. Seems to usually happen one way or another.

Perhaps this year has been all about confession and seeking outside voices.

God knows 2016 was way too much in my head and my own voice.

From therapy to confession at the Vatican, it's been a reaffirmation of life in a great way. Health scares are handled and even I guess mental questions are being answered, as they will. I'm here and I'm living and exploring new things all the time. I'm wondering what is next. I'll be damned if I let anyone determine my worth (perhaps now I actually am curious that worth amount), but it is also time that I put a value on myself as well. Fuck judgment. Purely out of anger, I have decided that I am going to my brother's during this storm. I'm not going to have anyone criticize me if I stayed here until the storm blew over. Perhaps it will be nice to be with family and drama-free for a couple more days. I probably should not have the anger I had, but maybe this was just something I needed to experience. Only time will tell. No one is perfect.

I think maybe one or two people may had heard what was going on. Storms lead to aerial adventures starting tomorrow.

ENTRY 46:
Droned Thoughts Up In The Air

"Corporate Code of Conduct."

"Guidelines really."

"An obligation to investigate and incriminate. All allegations even within your own company." A note of looking of Bosch on their policies since Freud made a decision not to include them in and looked up out of the workplace on my own personal computer, even if I don't mention the company by name and delete it before a new week starts. This was more than likely after my return from the hospital or at the very earliest during my brief time employed by PureRED.

"An obligation more so with government contracts."

"How many times can I say stop?"

"How many times can I catch you in the act, yet you still go at it?"

All of this started with entrapment in a form of a hate crime towards myself as an employee of Company #1 actively mentioned Grindr conversations before personally ripping my Facebook to shreds in an open-door setting. One of 2 things occurred. Either Grindr was used to enter into my work force. The profile in question deleted after the office conversations when I saw on Facebook,

"Someone is going to lose their job today." (FB-timeline)

"Why is he dressed like that,

does he think he is going to be getting fired today?" (FD-T)

Or I can play 'Devil's Advocate' (FD-B) and my phone was hijacked from what I place around Feb. 2018. (Or where they can place other companies that 'had him since Feburary' 2018.

Hijacked isn't the right word in what I am trying to say.

Either there is protection of source or it was the first occurrence my phone had been compromised. I never talked about my sexuality in the work place. Not at Freud and not at PureRED. The idea in hindsight, but sticking with the facts for another time. I've written all this prior. I've written to the government, Randstad and in public forum. Do not touch my photography for a reason. It was not entered into the workplace in job description. Do not cry foul as offended later to something said verbally as a compliment if you have only taken the time to get to know me.

"I see both sides though." (FDe-HD)

when talking about sifting through all of social media etc. from my perspective and the possibility of the same occurring to FD-B as well.

I've already written my opinion on that. In hindsight, I am thankful for the pay raise. I guess the benefit of listening to my phone calls does bring some empathy into play. That and me negotiating student loans in the lobby with a clear microphone access to the CEO's personal assistant's office. I try to be fair in processing how and why this occured. Call box speakers and microphones pick up anything once on the floor before going into entry of the workplace. A good point for anyone stepping outside in the hallway to take a phone call. At the very least, go outside if you don't want anyone in the office to potentially here.

What's not fair is striking at the time to produce maximum emotional distress from any source. I can look at it as someone in the community or someone else following close knowing what to do and when. What are you trying to do?
     "Show me a smile." (paraphrased) (Grindr Text Remembered)

I like to not think about it, but conjecture will lay in, "Name your source or you are at fault." I know my words. I know vernacular.I know when my words are repeated. By saying 'they had him in Feb. 2018 denotes outside your company involvement and lack of discretion with I, Randstad or your parents in 3rd party entry. Denotes awareness of timed events on specific dates of interest. "I've written about that already as well."

"Be fair in hindsight."

                              "He's Paranoid." (PR - T)   "He's Paranoid."
"I am not paranoid!"

"There is a big difference being aware and being naïve. I lost being naïve a long time ago and only speak when I am sure of something or if I have ques-tions."...at Freud, PureRED, Alfred Angelo and Finished Art. My entire ca-reer I've listened and learned. Silence does that. A library setting does that. Noise travels and just because I have headphones on does not mean I can't still hear. Nor does that give you a blanket pass for fair game to say whatever you want. The comments were noted prior to Randstad's involvement. Com-ments towards other contract employees. Comments play when a former Freud employee left. You willfully manipulated Randstad & that private email exchange of such by myself to them was professional while looking up what oth-er employees, contract,fixed-term or otherwise have on their Linkedin accounts to determine if I was being singled out for things that weren't there at the time.
            "You are glad she's gone, aren't you?" (FD-B)
Was that entrapment in hindsight? I don't think I can get a definitive answer solely from myself on that. I had talked on the phone of frustrations so I wouldn't put it as entrapment, but definitely baiting towards saying some-

thing negative in the office. There was enough of that there from others towards contracts already. You didn't need my opinion on the matter if potentially there was the possibility down the line of full-time employment. No reason for me to vocalize one way or the other.

I know I never took a day off after the one day ripped to shreds. Why would I? It made me sick. The calm approach to determine fact was to change my privacy settings after hearing enough. I do remember the keyboard slammed as I did that in real time. FD-D. FD-Am notation. Vocalized by FD-B (Never an issue with FD-Am or FD-Af) Proof I was not paranoid, but that did happen. It should had stopped then. Right then and there. I remember crying and freaking out off site at lunch. No question whatsoever of what happened as I looked down more settings. May niot be a '…a God of Photography' I do think of myself as a Junior Dectective if you want to know what I think I am in one regard or another. There was more commentary on my Facebook and what surrounded it in going through a timeline critical. That compounded with what I saw on FB exasperated truth. I reported bullying to FD-B. I was advised to report it to Randstad. I did. I was told the next day FD-B spoke to HR and the situation is being monitored. In hindsight, I'm pissed that things got to where they got to. Any lawyer would have told them to stop right then and there. <u>She lied to my face.</u> There is no HR without bringing BOSCH into it as Freud/Diablo does not have an HR department so I may be concerned of imagi-nation/fictional aspects.

Hindsight is 20/20. I know she spoke of being uncomfortable with the fact of me hearing things. I question the things that ran through both my head and theirs at the time.

"Now how do we get him?" (FD-B)

after the keyboard slam and a 'What happened?'

In my mind I predict others expected me to be done at this point. (That's what the voices say they thought would happen.) Paint me for so long and you think you know me, but you only know what you painted. It is hard to fathom she was saying praise of my work while ripping me to shreds in verified actions with others present where perhaps on camera you can see the exact time of at least my action as one camera was near my workstation and there is two party verification on that at least.

"Never reveal a truth you aren't comfortable revealing to the world."

They will use your truths against you, but in the end when you were once painted, they will know exactly who you are when you strip yourself naked with a strong sense of self. They were doing so at PureRED anyways or at least acknowledgement of such was had. I know my secrets of 'Ugly Simple Truths' July 2013. At least that is understood. Allot to process there in those pages of protection. Produced in book form of companion sake where factually checked and edited at this point and rephotographed to ensure accuracy of what was officially the submission for that.

Subliminal messaging pops into my mind as a topic to discuss within the context of hearing voices. If I were to entertain the always there, I have to accept that they are there when I am sleeping. I notice them instantly when I wake up. Conversations were occurring mid-way without me. (or perhaps with me if you are able to include conversations in dreams and nightmares) Prolonged exposure like that does something psychologically to the victim (or test subject). That is probably why the US government banned subliminal messaging to begin with. I want to say they did that in the 50's but I need to double check. (I was wrong. 1989 Vance v. Judas Priest is the precedent of invasion) Illegal for a reason nevertheless. But even if banned, that does not denote abandoned concepts or practices elsewhere. It simply means under more watchful eyes, ears & oversight. Power moves there as banned one place does not denote banned somewhere else.

Knowledge is power though. Is that used any other way that we do not know about? It was in "Fight Club", but that was the intention of the movie and they describe it. There is a long history of that used in cinema. "The Exorcist" is another example. It's in radio jingles. Catchy phrases. Advertisements walk a fine line with it, but that would be a topic of idealization for a different book. It's all subconscious influence from environment. I remember the "muses" using a week to test a mentality different than my own.
That (Considering that was a week of being filled with racist thoughts and comments that I do not approve of, I don't think I will refer to them as muses any more moving forward; simply just hearing voices) or of personalities that like seeing and playing, 'How to make a Racist...' and fail miserably at it as I stand up for all races in respect understanding the possibility of sublimation. But something lingers from that week in my mind which I am ashamed of as it is not me, but is now there nevertheless of others adding context. I intend on burying it and calling them out if that card gets played. Internally, I treat part of my mental process as if I set up mental road blocks in an officer's uniform. It's unnecessary, unkind and rude. Perhaps that is the difference of what we think and what we speak. There are certain words I would never in my life utter. I question why a whole week was dedicated to trying to have that come out of me and why it was left at only a week. I question where they

came from. (Is psychosis that specific to confine a certain personality trait to a single week and then move onto something else? There was no trigger. Simply their choice of words.) In fairness the conversation comes up every now and then 3 years later. I still roadblock or get pretty stern on it internally. In aspects elsewhere in every version of this book still denotes transcried thoughts in written word which is exactly what a computer and recorded keystrokes does. Maybe my mind is going too far. I feel conversations in person, conversations in my mind are two completely different things. I know the difference. Even now. Definitely then. I still know the difference of intrusion, intrusive thoughts with more reaction and engagement. Maybe this does all come back to PTSD. These memories are repeating for a reason. Maybe this is a conditioning of thought. A numbness and rationalization of the things I actually did hear. (which is why I have color coded this, created layout design and used all of my talents to explain this visually and with words to the best of my ability) I want to definitely express remorse as I know the difference between right and wrong. I cried over it. Thought about it. Angry or Sad...full emotion present. But yet here I am locked in an internal battle with myself knowing what I am going to do.

The scary aspect of this shall always be that all of this was preventable. When you have a breakdown, after is like you are meeting a stranger for a first time in a rebooted update to essential systems. Conversations will be had. Trust is earned or taken away. There always has to be an explanation of self and
intention. I look at it this way...
"You were ready to kill yourself. You threw in the towel."
"Why?"
"I know your mentally could not handle one more bit of bullshittery." "I know you know what was the final straw for you."
"I know it because you know it."
"One does not just land at random places without a cause and effect taking place."
"WE need to be honest with one another because that only happens once".
"Nevermore."

(These are the conversations you have with yourself after a breakdown)

"Never again."
"You have to explain how."
"That is what is going to happen if you end up in bankruptcy because of this."

"That is due diligence."

You would expect that in any investigation where privacy rights are to be considered, but there were other thoughts to be considered as well such as thinking about food on the table…paying a bill…or a genuine fear of what the next day would bring. I'll reiterate again, "The Lesser have to make a choice." A phrase I coined and learned from the optics of giving up my vacation to Italy when unemployed while losing my vacation time, job and a sense of financial security just as much as everyone else that was laid-off in 2017.
-A fundamental belief solidified by an Artic vacation as lives were destroyed leaving the day before closure and townhalls understanding your marriage was important for you and in some regards time served in your own right to what I imagine were probably late hours into the morning of trying to make deals of saving the company. I thought about that visability in regards to my choice on if I should continue taking the Italy trip I had already paid for and would had just lost that money and chance just as much as I chose to book it for the same price of a plane ticket to go to my grandfather's funeral instead. Honored the dead by living my life and getting to finally travel instead back when that was booked in around February 2017 if I remember correctly. I'll have to see the week of my grandfather's death on that one.
-Self-Preservation of one marriage while thousands of other's marriages marred by decision making. My life marred contemplating having to give up my vacation of a lifetime because of optics and the unknown.
"<Laughter from a boardroom where there should be none>" (AA)
'At least they will have closure' (AA)
In a somewhat relaxed more state about it after-the-fact, I see the stress factor of such to try to lighten the seriousness of the moments. It is about how it comes out established and heard from multiple former employees outside that room who could had too probably solutionized how to laugh in situations that did not cause the detriment of every family who invested in a bridal gown from Alfred Angelo at that time and could have walked down the aisle in their preferred dress vs. a last minute scramble to find solutions to where their hard earned money went. To think of what could had been done and didn't happen was communication, respect of team members nor of any partner account or future wedding for any of the near future if ever. That is why I stand by my statement of (now one of) the most insensitive things I ever experienced in a corporate environment. As not a part of that meeting when the last buyer on the table was no longer interested in the company, I was the only one from marketing who stuck around to find that answer out accordingly from the VP of Marketing. In the simple code word of 'Vegem-

ite*', it was understood the announcement of closure was going to happen tomorrow. *I still apologize for any detriment to Vegemite, it just needs a lot of butter in this context too.

For years, my focus was on the brides, their families and how to make things right for myself. I tried many ways and I did come up with a solution out-side years later and apologized expressing my heart in something I was not responsible for on any level of position and too was just left in the dark in issues when even my life after derailed constantly over something that I was not a part of. In whatever justification of such I know internally, I've done my best to survive since then and watch it constantly attacked every way possible. I go in fuller detail later in other books, this one was me coming back from attempted suicide from corporate workplace attacks and barely learning how to express myself and come back only to be attacked multiple times after and watch all my property even upto this month get taken con-stantly. That was February 21, 2019.

I remember that final conversation I had after Vegemite and what I said and what I thought as 2 entirely different things. The silent thoughts of think before you speak wondering now how much of my voice is spoken in words of thousands of pages of importance on what was lost over and over in my life and what I try to protect in others. The forfeit of expentancy is apparent that my life shortened no matter how this plays out at this point and there is no justification for what was stolen and what I've tried to protect.

"Time done served!"
In both accounts of all really of silent professionalism where at least from learned-experience from Alfred Angelo, I acted accordingly and immediately reported to HR or elsewhere after time, writing out and reflection. There are things one simply works professionally out appropriately before going to HR or elsewhere. It is only when those barriers are had and can't be resolved that things escalate outside departments or companies.

I don't fault myself for Italy though. It was a dream come true and a gift from my family. A choice I took to take instead of the fear of if it was right or wrong. It was something my mother supported. Gifted by my grandmother since birth to do that trip in tucked away childhood birthday gifts. Inspired by my grandfather. Driven by my inspiration of Dante and sanctioned by the state of Florida well beforehand back in May 2017. I was meant to go on that trip in further expansion. Look at what it inspired within me. A hurricane fundamentally changed that trip. A second hurricane is coming now.
Is it a Part 2?

There is always a storm somewhere on a course or waiting to form. Conflict of elements, over saturated air. Still a natural inclination to stay calm and head towards center in it's path.

I can't help but think that this is God course correcting that which happened in Italy. I imagine it is still quite difficult to factor in that many variables of life into events & timing.

Everything happens for a reason, but fate decided I was meant to be with my brother and his family at that time and I have to look at this in a bigger picture that God is always trying to tell you something if only you sit back and listen. He gave me that second half trip. What does he have in store for me **with I in** writing this book?

I have fear. A great amount of it. That is to be expected when you call out some of the biggest corporations of the world. It was their choice but life or death for me. For my family. My legacy. My work. 3 times asked for a worker's comp form. Laws were created for a reason. Privacy. Civil Rights. Worker rights. Mental Wellness will all play in the **"roulette"** (PRe) you created.

'So it is a possible mental health issue?' (PRe)

Well, it became one over time to a certain extentas probably expected. Although I understand you just started work the same time I did. Can you imagine the mental health of the continued aspect on the other side who allowed that to occur? In fairness, it was more a reach out since some already knew me, but indirectness understood. The Shout Out moment was very much an acknowledgement of severity & obviously discussing brand image. Theirs vs. Mine. Exit the building, get in the car, drive down the street before getting onto the highway. At a stop sign....shout out at the face of what followed and came into another work environment that already had people scared back in December 2018. An understood perpetual screen needed to be released of what occurred. Now simply a silent screen that even once that was protected was shared without permission or in what others could say one way or another.

"Shop cars if you want, it's always a choice that anyone is watching you at any given time. "

(I am aware the car shopping comment comes from voices-only conversations and no real-world basis to back that up.) But what if...

"What is the responsibility of that?"

A thought of patterns where always good to check, confirm or make phone calls in some instances.

I remember writing personal thoughts for the first time so many years ago. A question in strength as I listed out things that defined myself. I remember it was me trying to save a relationship. One with self and with others. Still that now to a certain extent as I've had to eliminate so many 'others' from my day to day for thier protection. It was focused on the negative but finding positive in them objectively & honestly. If only I knew the connection to be made. I spoke the truth and it didn't make a difference then. Do I have any belief it would make a difference now after the fact in written truths and perspectives? At least an open discussion had on how we introduce ourselve to ourselves and others.

I remember complete strangers saying thank you for what I wrote during. "Ugly Simple Truths". I remember being told not to do it. I did it anyways because. "Something is telling me to do this.", spoken by myself to someone back in 2013 towards what felt right, a giant step towards what was start- ed and where from either spiritually, psychologically or artistic still was an important step that later in life proved valuable enough to be attacked specifically in my contributions. I have learned since then the different of a lot going one way or another over thoughts of allot of things. Commonality there then of understanding and even privately reading books on things to connect. That is simply what happens to connect interests or understand those who chose you to be around and vice versa. I respect and understand that side. I understand what 8 years later if I had to on the matter. I imagine other paths equally beautiful and awesome that did not involve me as people on their own accord wittle down who they know over life as already dis- cussed in this book. Can't say I'm not an outreach program to anyone of my past but I am also not defined by it as I constantly pave new ground. I write about it and wrote about it because I took the time to do so for well over 12 years at this point in any capacity of proprietary, copyright, or completely for my own accord while say whatever shit you want about me or anyone else...I'm processing, changing things and using my life experience to do so. Eventually I find humor in my writing but in this book I still state this was me coming back from a suicide attempt brought on by others invasion and if they want to talk to me they could had then or 3 years later. Otherwise, discuss why this book was incorporated into years of billions of dollars in projects and where I've outreached at this point to the non-personal aspects of my life and into those unapproved indirect contacts and references that couldn't fly at Freud/Diablo and somehow went from the Devil elsewhere.

It is completely understandable that when on my space or another that one simply does not invite commentary for purposes of individual processing or private dialogue. Otherwise it invites unwarrented comments that simply deflect time from what was said and missing the point to where one could connect or have a platform to simply degrade or call out. Beauty missed in original attempts. Not on my personal website. It can be linked out else-where to see that human condition play out one way or another. It is proper for journalism or corporate structure to cite accordingly and compensate. I imagine not many people do the same from other areas which too becomes understood. It gets blurred as we all try to make it as either already accepted or looking to do so.

In the realm of what I have already discovered, 3 years later is not the same as your path or someone elses. In either regard I have my answers regardless of what happens negatively in some realms, positively in others. It can't be taken away and never stolen. The strength of facing things or opening up in any capacity. You don't need a book for that path of personal life experience. You don't even have to read if you don't want. Ignorance is bliss, yet the fun aspect of where things travelled from impediment noting this final color structure vs. the others is amazing in the aspect of what gets translated one way or another and where problem areas gets solved while new ones created. Bathroom confessionals. Interactive knowing exactly who wrote what even if it was unspoken. I liked the honesty of "Ugly Simple Truths". It was brave of my models. It was brave of me. It was human connection. I remember Bar-bara Dorn and my boss. Donna during a private viewing before the opening. I did not attend their viewing. It was like I let them in and they let me in as well afterwards letting me know they were touched by it. You could see there were tears had in the viewing. More tears had by others during the opening. The stories of people & their struggles and overcoming them by naming them and empowering themselves and others.

I remember the responsibility of that show. The protectiveness of story and my models. Intimacy for a greater purpose. Black light. Shadow self. I am devastated at the thought that my email has been hacked and stories possi-bly stolen. Confidentiality within my work. Secrets given. Secrets protected. The things potentially taken from using theinternet with intention of priva-cy. 1. Model submissions 2. Whole narratives proofed. 3. Art shows never completed (HV4) and concepts abandoned to be found in poor taste or top-ics not worth discussing but of social commentary. (My concepts neverthe-less). There will always be "a blanket of hate" but that does not mean I did not use my discretion in never pursuing that presented in that concept by any means. 'The Blanket of Hate', the underbelly shadow-self of The World's

AIDS quilt.

Voices even brought TMZ into this and I laugh because I am not that important in the scheme of things.

So, yet another question lingers.

"What if those ideas were taken?"

"Do I regret them?

"No."

"Did I practice discretion?"

"Yes."

Anyone has ideas that are never realized for very good reasons.
just as much as there was reason to explore it in the first place. That's not narcissistic. That is free thought. Sharing that changes things. Especially when it is controversial subject matter. I had
one series I thought out. It never went anywhere as I found it to be counterproductive for what I stand for. but shared with 2 people.
I don't recall sharing with others.
With an information breach it could be anyone at this point.

Maybe in the end it doesn't even matter.

At this point I might as well include it down the line. It doesn't hurt in discussion points of transcribed keyboards and open platforms one way or another at this point if allowed judgement of private thoughts or actions of typing on your own personal computer or conversations on the phone.

Trust is earned. Doubt is earned. I question knowing what I know. Legendary thoughts in my own right. I remember. "Gods and Monsters". My first collaborative show that I didn't even get a chance to attend as I was already going on vacation. The black and white Raven made its first and only appearance there. It now resides in a private collection married to the other image it should be. An artist's choice on that. A 2 artist show that juxaposed nicely between reality & fantasy realms in 2 entirely different techniques.

I respectfully decline to comment on the rest of what I am thinking about.

Un Chien Angelou.

I suppose as space gets transformed who or what resides in it, the concept of any show is always about the artist intention and of what they try to convey. A space is envisioned one way or another of possibilities of how one interacts or would.

Shows designed one way or another where one would question back to the series of social commentary again and denote if it pisses people off it either is effective art that is never purchased or it is designed to invite veiled commentary one way or another of ridicule or ere. When dealing with some of those truths explored, it denotes a possibility that there would had been more hate by some while approval in other areas of those who understand, experienced or connect in relation.

To expand more on 'The Blanket of Hate' from the shadow perspective of 'The World AIDS Quilt' aspect denotes the battle internal had during that time of both introduction to now. Those battles, I imagine, are equal to that of cancer patients & then greater in the 'Do Not Touch' aspects of it's introduction to self psychologically to where society has grown today from that in some sense and not in others. Internally I imagine the thoughts of responsibility and protection towards others to be an utmost aspect to it in any regard of intimacy or otherwise. Especially in the 80s introduction where simply it was not known much about it or why friends, partners and others were dying.

If one side of the quilt is a symbolic memorial of life, the other shadow side could be a remembrance of the internal conflicts kept spoken or not & surrounding the uniqueness to everyone's individuality while still finding commonality woven together.

An upgraded thought from my original intention and concept that came about all those years ago of 2013/2014 in Secret. Where, while viewing anonymous posts of hate & illegality from the app 'Secret', viewers we able to see what empowers people to say in a thin veil of privacy to say whatever and find still the best & worst of humanity within it. Often you find the empowered aspect to say the rage within wondering why perhaps that was the experiment of the app to begin with. It is still possible that in that known aspect of positive or negative, it could also have been entrapment to see what people say in that aspect. In either regard of stitching those thoughts together, I abandoned the idea as I happen to be quite fond of the results of Humanity and expression from , 'My Bathroom Confessionals' from 'Ugly Simple Truths' where considering the environment, it was proven more people willing to express support and honesty in the right settings and environment. From there far better in the hope aspect of completely strangers reacting to each other's honesty in a safe space provided.

When it comes to philipbonneau.com, my personal company website, it is owned by me. What do I do when I know log-in information has been stolen to hijack it and view the mechanics internally of what is and not searchable? I've noticed the folders being opened. Something that didn't use to happen. I always close them. But even if I left one open. I have never left all the folders open. Is someone searching for something?

"They can get through the firewall." (Paraphrased)
<talks of Disney out in the open>
'They have every version of his website.' (PR-T)

I created the website when I got laid-off by Alfred Angelo. I had never put my accomplishments all in one place and even that website is a constant work-in-progress that has been slowed down by this process. A cube to still go up. A fire dancer and much more. Not everything is on there and it's not developed completely. Nor should everything be on there.
I am self-taught on web design going off intuition and rationale.
I am figuring out the navigation and what could be done with it.
"Art Walk" is exactly what it was intended to be. A "Choose Your Own Adventure" that never really got developed, but also not searchable unless you are phishing on my site. Now completely not searchable by engines; imagine it could had been an interactive gallery space where perhaps that imaginary walking and weaving from one series to the other in narrative.

I recently created another page clearly stating that is illegal. (Phishing that is, where perhaps even 'Art Walk' could be transformed into 'Where Did the Art Walk Off To?' if one was included to view it from a different perspective. Either way, simply not something I can focus on in any regard as it is more important to finish and write what needs to be written.) If any IP address touches those, then it proves my point as found out at Freud and PureRED.

Blogger. Facebook. Instagram. I would not be surprised if Twitter or Tumblr as well, but I cannot remember the last time I actively used either. Flickr? I mean they got on G-mail...why not my whole digital presence called into question at this point.

<A mention of a book before a mention made>
<Writing themselves into a story that ended 2 years ago.>

"I'm pretty sure my entire digital footprint has been compromised"

I remember when Trey mentioned, "You look at a page and they are right there." (Paraphrase). He was talking about monitoring of web activity and using that information to postulate potential course of actions based on web history. That definitely convinced me to use that knowledge here out.

<Googles "Whistleblower" on office computer>

<female gasp>

" Burn Him." (T) - Feb. 19th

Trey's words.

Not mine.

In fairness, that (could) be related to anyone, but not when the conversation definitely was sprung by me. Proof of monitoring at the workplace, but that is to be expected. It's bringing up things from home that provides proof of something else. How many desktops cleaned now?

Fact vs. Fiction.

"...and you can't get rid of me." (PR-Mk)

But PR-Mk reacted to it as well. That is what honesty is and I am thankful that I got confirmation and comfort from someone I barely knew.

For Whom the Whistle Blows...

How many references did they have back then in February 2019?

ENTRY 48:

Nothing is free.
Every discount comes with the price of something.
Swipe a Kroger Card and you are giving access to everything you have purchased.

"...itemized (PUBLIX?) receipt." (PRe)
"...kick someone when they are down."(PRe)

Give "free" medical information to get a lower rate is giving something up as well. Always Pros & Cons to Rates.

Free music streaming is giving something up.
Spotify collects all your music on your computer and creates a playlist that can accessed through their App. I've seen on the app where it does so and pulls all of your personal recordings in a streaming capability. Would they be able to listen to anything on their end from any account's personal computer? Want to know what Madonna is listening to? Someone knows. Want to know what Taylor Swift listens to right before a concert? Apple and any of these streaming apps know. When you buy Spotify Premium, does that opt you out of the information collecting or just the ads? Any recording artist that uses Spotify or I imagine any other music app has their playlists recorded somewhere. Want to know the true inspiration for Lemonade? Probably hack a Tidal wave. It makes me question, "what responsibility do other artists have in not monitoring other artist's inspiration when there is ownership stake? I imagine you can gauge a pretty good pulse of the industry and tide just from data collection one way or another.

There is no free in capitalism. There is risk assessment and data mining. There was a major breach in the Financial industry with people's credit scores recently and look what happened leading up to that. Insider Trading to cash out before the storm. Those in the know react before other's do. This is why it is important to see what employee investors do with their stocks in the company. Always a telling sign of positive or negative thoughts. Emotions factor in. Same in politics in proven behavior.
What actions occured before an event? Moving someone preemptively because they "felt attacked"(FD-B about FD-S)?! Get in line sister.
{Pitching that curveball}
As for the credit scores. $125 dollars does not fix the damage done and if you take that you are giving something up. You just sold your important history for $125. It is not "Free Money". It is understanding the reprocussions & joint agreement

(Not the first time that has been repeated in my head)
When knowing everything on my phone and personal computer is capable
of being monitored now. I am hesitant to give information or allow other
to look at it. especially when it comes to personal health information. That
20-30-dollar difference in costs more than you will ever really know.

What is given up with a web browser? Free search engines? Somewhere a
computer that monitors every website and IP address has ever been to for
sure. Google. Facebook. Instagram. Spotify...They are all data mining and
profiling. For what purpose? Private companies with very private information. What happens when those companies go public? Potential Public
Domain? Data is valuable. The collection of data can also be abused as I have
found out. Still. I'm friendly with Technology. Who ever wants to piss off
Technology have at it. 'No Judgement from my behalf and actions.' (I understand I may have raised some eyebrows of those in the technology industry,
but I remain friendly in the difference of technology and those attached to
it.)

"You will never believe how they got that image" -(JT)

I think maybe you would be surprised on my open mind.
Source codes everywhere.

I remember a credit card company calling once and I answered the phone. I have been known to let things go to voicemail, but I do try to right a wrong. I picked up the phone. I heard them before I was able to speak, perhaps they were used to me not answering

"get him to say something incriminating"(CCe)

I wish I remember off the top of my head which credit card company that was, but I am sure SOMEONE has POSSIBLY a record of this somewhere. If I was being monitored others heard something very important as I did. I'm trying to be peaceful about things. (There are advantages to other's illegal activities) Perhaps my mind and body are in two different places ATM. I'm thinking about what happened. What was lost from it? What I will lose. The fear of losing everything has been put there for very real reasons, but there is always a silver lining to be found. If you caught that it is your obligation to report everything. That was a big everything right there.

"Innocent misunderstanding"

(Another "not the first time that has been repeated") Another automatic response on the otherside? Perhaps we are going through this together. "Even if that statement transitions to "Innocent mistake" that is not going to fly at all."
"Malicious."
"Uncaring."
"...Without due diligence."
"A complete wiping of the ass with the constitution."

I'm trying to balance that out in my head to find peace. There is conviction in my thoughts. A desire for closure. How do you get your privacy back once it has been taken away?

"He's always going to be listening out for sounds of police."
(Paraphrased) PRe

(response - Only in hope sometimes. Try siren tests once a month around lunchtime from hill of silence. Those get intense.)
"I'm aware every phone call from a certain point of time has been heard."
From that, other voices heard. Conversations.
A butterfly effect occurred based on what has been stolen.
"Copyright everything."
I am sure that would lead to a trial as well in the end.
"Report everything."
If that is the case there would be a completely different story at this point.
Guidelines and discretion factor in somewhere.

"Who makes that call?"

ENTRY 50:

My mind has been on "Shelly Duvall's Faerie Tale Theatre" today. Wiki tells me "this was one of the first examples of cable original programming. "Fraggle Rock" by Jim Henson productions another. I remember watching both as a child, but it was Faerie Tale Theatre that we actually purchased the episodes. "Hanzel and Gretel" with Joan Collins in particular sticks out. Perhaps the connection between my grandfather and my sister and myself. There was Jack and the Beanstalk. Goldilocks. Aladdin. Stories from everywhere in the world. She introduced herself before each episode. Disney introduced himself before each episode as well. The introduction of storytellers abound in TV, Books, Movies & Music.

I remember them broadcasting her a couple years ago. They made an utter mockery out of her or maybe just the reaction of such. I was and am visibly upset by that. Her heart was that of a storyteller. Did trauma destroy her? Did Kubrick destroy her with repeated takes? Obsessive perfection. Her trauma has been noted prior from "The Shining", but did it come gradually over time?
She still accomplished so much after that experience and then disappeared. How many takes did he do before she broke down? Perfectionism has a price. Some things cannot be acted. Perhaps I'll watch the interview in objectivity to see what appears that may had been missed elsewhere. Tried to look for it, but it is not available to even rent.
Shelly Duvall is someone I'd be honored to meet and get to know personally. Is that possible? I have to look into finding her publicist if only for personal accomplishments of meeting heroes. Story connectors wondering veiled transparency.
What I look at is the idea of over-coming things to do something greater again later.
How do I give this up?
Who has responsibility to end this?

Regardless, in the end just as much as I remember Faerie Tale Theatre, there will be some people that remember "Philip Bonneau's Heroes + Villains". Definitely not that many. "The Divine Comedy" is an interesting one to try to figure out. It is pretty cut and dry in my mind. Inspired by life. Focused on trauma. Growth. I have to learn things again. I'm trying.

I am having a moment as I read this and type this out

from handwritten form.
I'm not going for that conclusion to this story.
I won't let you do this to me. Battle worn but not done.
I won't let that be a false finality.

Maybe it starts and stops with writing.
I do feel that writing is a part of me, just as much as the visual is a part of
me. As is the same with sound. Little pieces everywhere waiting to be combined. Trying to find my voice when I don't know how to say things. Doing
so any way possible while I still can.

Is there value to having handwritten next to typed?
Does it make it more personal?
Does it showcase work and dedication?
Does written word become an art piece or the branching off
of new ideas?
Which one has more value when side by side?
The initial thought or the tributary spawned from it?

(11.14.2022)
Just tried to find the episode to be objective. Never knew prior that it was
episode 50 and aired November 18, 2016. I originally submitted Curated
Jellyfish: A Paradise Lost' to United States Copyright Office for protection
November 18, 2019. This section was always entry 50.

Post 20: Day 7: The Eighth Sphere: Flight In-Between

"I think in relationship to Truth #4, (Out of Spite Comes My Best and Worst) (From my produced (Companion Writings to Ugly Simple Truths) there becomes this problem in my life where whether it be out of spite or just pure drive that I am disproportionally hard on myself. In any effort to succeed or prove someone perceived wrong, I will push myself as far as I can. I will stay up nights to make deadlines. I'll process until I figure something out and I will practice, practice, practice until I hit what I am satisfied with only to come back and revisit it months or years later and change things.

I think for me for a while now, my main focus has been completely on coming to peace with things I've had issues with. Perhaps I am really just trying to figuring what the hell actually has already happened in my life and processing that one way or another. Things go so fast and I often act instinctually to keep things going in a direction. When I evolve; I want that evolution to happen fast and complete. I set my mind and just do something and a change comes from that...and then just keep going and going. I never can settle very much anymore.... at least mentally. I don't think it's in my nature to accept face value anymore. Definitely not while I explore what is under my skin. How can I even think that similar thoughts are not done with anyone I meet? There are so many things being wrapped up and in the works. I can never really feel like I am doing enough and I feel it catching up within me at times. Too much overthinking. For 3 years, I've had the most incredible marathon that is still going strong and I could not ask for anything more because I wished for this and threw it out there. I've worked for this. I've earned this. There is really a chance to see things come to life that I never could have imagined." - written 5/13/13, revised 10/12/17

————

Truth #4
OUT OF SPITE COMES MY BEST AND WORST.

Not originally provided in prior versions of Curated and found in a different book that is not fully reproduced here. A common thread to where at least in this context, it is probably required before proceeding one way or another from both the 2017 timeline of writing these sections of 'Curated' from my Italy trip with the 2022 updated references. Originally produced in blog form in connection with the 2012 art series, 'Ugly Simple Truths', it was public published prior to the opening of the series in blog form. The blog was pro-duced in book-form towards the end of 2019 titled 'Companion Writings to Ugly Simple Truths'. The blog has been known to be deleted by others in that form from anywhere between 2020—2022 when first noted as early as March.

Everything intertwines and protects itself one way or another while always being on a search for truth. Although total disregard was had by others once I reclaimed already impeded on property in other copyrights of legal status, I continue to piece my life back together with no verbal or direct resolve to what occurred in other aspects of my works.

In further reflection from annual encounters one way or another towards new meaning and understanding, edits providing a golden shadow to balance to the shadow self explored in 2012. Equal in weight the things repressed express themselves over time positive and negative. The best comes from the worst of times, the worst from the best of time. Relative really to the understanding that maybe there is not a complete answer but only one that could be expanded upon to showcase one thing or another.

In balance from what was talking points prior to where nos 10 years in reflection. There is no set rule to this and equally in darkness, there is light waiting to shine in either side. We repress so much positive or negative where when it comes out together then or now, it is hard to know the difference and perhaps only matters to you on which one is which. Others will see it one way or another anyways.

Excerpt of (Blog) Truth #4 in the Companion book is different from (Photo-graphic) Truth #4 of the Visual Art Series and represented in the artbook for the series produced physically in 2020. As there is some overlap in themes, it still fits in as it should in relation one way or another.

I'm not expressing digitally the Curator's Secret on that other side of the series at this time. But I wouldn't base truth for truth in that regard. I would regard this section and edits as proof of growth over a decade later to find something there rare but allowed to happen over time in process, experience and reflection. The golden type denotes edits from the originally publish and physically produced book 10 years later from initial publication and 3 years since physical book form never prior available for sale.

I think as I move forward with these shoots for this new series I am beginning to see something emerge from this. On some level I am connecting with people on a different level than just casual conversation and a drink at the bar. But I am getting to know something about these people that make me admire them even more than what I already do.

During each individual shoot, we talk about what it is that we are referring to and then this conversation or thought pattern emerges on how I relate to their story and how have I handled things vs. how they did. If anything I am definitely becoming more comfortable talking about who the real me is vs. the masked me while others are doing the same in moments of introductions or added on familiarity towards greater closeness. I imagine with each stranger or friend there was comfortability then. Protection now in understanding both confidentiality in moments and that which was translated in unison and in empathy or getting to know each other in trust.

I question where exactly that needs to be outwardly expressed and understand where so much comes from, but I know it is just coming from years of people assuming me to be one thing when I am not. I see that on the otherside where there is the assumption of one thing or not in both not knowing the struggle while also finding the beauty of such expression of it one way or another in beginning conversations. Never an expression prior or perhaps presumed and never really known. Humanity exists in the daily struggles and those that seem almost of fantasy yet truth.

There is intimacy present without the sexual context in a manner that is far more important to preserve and understand together...in what we are sharing as a unit together. It is about You first and foremost and I thank you for allowing me to translate this one way or another in relateability and shared experience. The moment between you and I and the moment collectively between Us and what is being produced towards one reaction or another is preseved, protected and held just as close as my story interconnected in each of you. We are brave and I thank you for the intimacy and un-guarding.

For me, I have gone out of my comfort zone moments all the time. At this point in my life I had introduced any conceptual capacity of Divine Comedy aspects in the first show in 2011. Three shows of Heroes+Villains later and a little more support in my craft or concepts, I return better equipped to tackle part II of the series knowing it is not the same nor does it ever try to be. It is different and I'm going different angles and approaches to things outside the fictional and wove that elsewhere to come back around to later.

I take leaps of faith into the unknown and sometimes I may go to the wrong unknowns, but at least I know personally if they are wrong or even just the wrong time. I'd say those moments are fueled pretty much split down the middle because I believe in dreaming and hard work paying off, and then the other half really just comes from spite from some interaction. I grapple with doing things out of anger. Is that the true me or is that just anger? What am I searching for and what is driving me to continually expand on something already invaded on anyways after-the-fact? Can my anger be even described properly on what I do and do not do when in 'Anger'?

Now, I do not necessarily consider a private revenge done in a positive way a bad thing, but it is ultimately a negative that initiates the positive path. But that is something the outside world would never knows. So much is given for one to read one way or another and yet it is still the ability to turn a negative to a positive as if someone somewhere wants you to give up, not continue and just destroy all hope while others amast so much elsewhere. One could say many things come from humble beginnings and perhaps over time that is forgotten or remembered. It depends on the situation, the person or wondering the souls of companies and corporations in that regard. Built of many souls, but perhaps none possessed or a working system where the soul speaks one way or another anyways. Even if it is in silence for one topic or another. The impossibility to have any one person or corporation comment on every topic at hand, a conflict of understood persepctive, principles and building from there. Even if one were to talk of everything, it would be at the expense of life and understanding the knowledge learned in life was more important than living one after or perhaps done in balance knowing the answer to everything is never going to come one way or another. Always a selective aspect present...or past in that regard. 'Have to live a life to know the answer one way or another.' Otherwise it would simply be doubted anyways by someone and life experiences later on prove the original answer supplier true or false on the matter in accordance to their own perspective on things.

It doesn't work that way and yet it does at the same time.

Ask questions internally or externally and you are going to find answers one way or another on the matter. Just make sure that in life quests for one thing or another you remember to relax. Breathe and laugh along the way. .Especially when you start figuring out some of answers to the questions you wanted answered. Think things out and understand it is a privilege of any interaction. How it relates determines how long it lasts in one moment or many. Postive vs. Negative aspects of such.

Lessons from the 'fro-boy' of elementary or that of whale status then and later in life. Life lessons of childhood resilience later in life where it isunderstood the context then, what happened in adult life and where things could go from here in attacks or support one way or another depending on the digital age of things where soul searching is always thought for but then those of the nameless or 'false names' do their thing in the other aspect anyways. Negatives and positives everywhere depending on how you look at it. How you handle it is what makes all the difference in the world towards yourself and others. Approach or understanding that one may say one thing or another when lost in translation of the intention and words misplaced.

It is understand we have all been persecuted one way or another in life and always an advantage one way or another as well. If that advantage was external from others, so too can it be internal from the same transformative aspects of, 'No one is going to beat you up more than yourself.' just as much as the statement, 'You are your own best lover.' In duality there is always the outside you and inside you. How does one become strong by accepting both and understanding either side? Externally there can be more than just yourself and in others there is support or glimmers of answers one way or another in perspectives understood at the time.

Eliminate those that persecute you because it is not going to a sustainable driving force. The memory of such and when the paths change from conjoined to seperated matter in that aspect. Memories have far more power than the constant struggle of understanding why things continue in a negative and not a positive. Remove the negative and you can transform it into a positive while still discussing the negative behavior as truth where descriptors matter between fact or perception. The emotional words behind any memory denotes one thing or another on how much it affected and still the wisdom of 2010 exist. A memory is with you for a lifetime and such the one's attached to it. Eventually you have to make peace with it internally and never have to do so external-ly. It is the eventual joy of understanding the interaction that is important to remember and respect that time was spent on either side towards one answer or another.

There is a difference between jokes and malice. It is not required in life to surround yourself with hate while understanding hate amongst friends denotes a difference of either personal connection or overall commentary in blanket statements or perception of one or the other. Opinions abound where the same is thought in return, spoken or not.

Naturally, people go to safe spaces just as much as I and even in trying to build one or another of such; it is understood the invasion one way or another into personal life and the no entry allowed in other areas. One cannot be ever present to everyone or else there is nothing sacred to any moment of intimacy to those who took the time to know you personally.

It is an internal, "I Win" without the need nor desire to express that in that thought process. So many silent victories of people who don't ever have to say a single word to whatever their internal struggle is.

The evasiveness of inclusion comes from many points but, if it is done with malicious intention then they can be inclusive to the same circles from which they want to be exclusive to. Can't gain acceptance from everyone and that was understood since I was 7 before getting into thoughts of 5. Probably one of the most accepting on many things, but alas I am writing this in 2022 and there is some things for which I will not put. Others I simply have to with the understanding it is more economic than anything else. That spoke true in 2007, that spoke true in 2018, that spoke true from 2021—2022 and I imagine the combination of the reslience of the socio-economic strength has been bestilled me myself while understanding there are many things I've never had to put up with and have gone about properly to address.

I will find a way to make the past burn. Only if need be before understanding there is a difference in the definition. Passion, love, protection…all things that burn before going into the aspects of elsewhere in regards where in in-direct I'm not burning anything and only living my life. Simple as that to know where my soul burns one way or another. As much as one takes the definition of 'burning something' it could also be looked at as engrained into you or a torch which holds one symbol or another understanding the difference of such from my place of position at the bottom of stacked decks. I think this whole series is pretty much becoming a collection of shitty situations or surprised thoughts that really have sparked a change for the better. Whether it is spiteful in its intention or not does not devalue the final result. The spite is in the fact *that we resolve, we continue and we actually open up to strangers and those we are comfortable with. Not really conflicted in 2022. It is completely understood the value then. Maybe you missed the show in 2012, it was fantastic and definitely proprietary if we have to constantly get into that.*

When talking about me and spite, I think for whatever reason I've always had that "I will prove you wrong" mentality. Who are any of us to make a prediction about someone based solely out of anger at the moment, single interaction, or because of what others have told us? There is a great deal of assumptions there where the intention to analyize depends on the scenario on if it is even analyization of simply looking at a distance in intrigue. Now 10 years later and understanding I've 'Provided everything for 'them' to go one way or another.' (Paraphrased when hearing talks of Ugly Simple Truths at PureRED and then indirectly talking about others plans of attacks one way or another. It is understood then and it is questionable now. Did you really want me to just go into my own artwork in discussion for advancement? That could had been done without the suicide attempt I did knowing others knew what I was going through and experiencing back in Feb. 2019) It it still boils down to, 'I don't think so and you might want to say hello and go from there in that regard. (Written in 2012. I am attempting to golden shadow something here where I know what I'm about to go up against. Do you?) One cannot help to have judgement on others or things, but the minute that becomes externalized it becomes something completely different. On some level it places you in an authority of being in a position to do so, and the other you do not know how it will affect the person that the statements are being directed towards and how the other will react.

I think I have found myself often discounted my entire life. But, on the other hand, I have definitely been propped up by people I had never even met as well. It goes both ways. If I have some kind of negative experience/judgement passed onto me, I will find a way to positively prove people wrong based solely on the "you don't know me" mentality. If I receive positive influence/judgement, I tend to just push myself further and further the minute that support group and belief is there because they believe in me. That within itself has its unhealthy after effects, but still ultimately was done with good intentions. It becomes a question of balance while understanding the timetable of what surrounds it. There is always moderation to be had one way or another towards a place of understanding your timelines and when you simply have to rest, relax and think before proceeding. As much as there is positive drivers towards motivation, there is the equal positive motivator from the negative influences to work a solution to get away from them quickly but accordingly in a manner of safe, healthy and incremental changes that lead towards more permenant positive change.

I'm just a very driven person unsure of what exactly drives me at times but I guess, through positive or negative, I push to see where my breaking points are if only to make me a stronger person, or to lead me down the paths of seeing who I am. I have always just fueled myself anyway possible to see where I will end up. It helps when you know where you are going and what your intentions are. You may not know how to get there but at least a desire towards a solution is present to allow one to understand the multitude of possibilities to get there for oneself.

I think there may be some things that may have been completely out of spite, but still brought about a road to finding out exactly who I am in a good way... or a way that is at least true to me. In Spite is not necessarily a course of action negative. It is a healthy stubbornness to say you have projected this onto me or acted upon myself negatively, 'How can I take your negative impact and turn it into positive energy for myself and for others?'. How can your answer be the only one to consider?

I remember a 5th grade teacher of mine telling me I'd never amount to anything. She said it quite consistently privately and in a class setting. She went on to became our 6th grade teacher as well for 2 years of reenforcement one way or another and lessons to be learned. Translation is always important for a child where unfortunately negative and positive re-enforcement is important or else there is no concept of right/wrong or bad/good. A hard lesson for any teacher or parent I imagine knowing there is a difference between the two and some overlap from the boundaries provided of teacher and their nature.

Although respectful of all teachers and superiors, it was at an early age you can start to figure out what does and doesn't work for at least yourself. Horrors in one thing is pleasure in another and by the time you hit high school you understand the social acceptance of one or the other. The concentrated aspects of childhood emotions: the most pure in either regard to prepare you for the world. It comes without complete comprehension of the rules and complications that follow in life and defintely before the complication of puberty and the understandings of such.

Want to get close answers one way or another?
Ask a child before they even know the world what awaits them one way or another to determine what is or isn't nature and what was nurtured. In their purity they too teach adults lessons they wish they were taught. The things said or thought then matter in life later.

A driver for myself of childhood experience into adult approach of understanding is a memory of the same 5th/6th grade teacher making a statement of profoundness now in translation knowing it was not the original intention. If I or anyone else in my class was to have 'The IQ of a kumquat' not even remembering the reasoning behind the phrase but understanding it was a negative at the time and of insult, 'What is something to learn from the kumqat that is of value later in life?'.

I can look at the plant as a slow-growing evergreen with small thorns present that can be born singly or in clusters to produce hundreds or thousands annually. A nourishment to be had one way or another. It is a resilent plant although not without complication and controversial descriptions, nor to the same degree as say the tomato who's own identity crisis rests on popular vote of fruit or vegetable.

The kumquat of interest is knowing it can be placed in many areas of conversation. Is it a citris grape of wrath or an olive branched into many categories of understanding that it transforms and grows into new identities based on environments and timing to adapt to it's surroundings?

It is capable of hybridized transformations where since the early 1900s it has been introduced to the lime in further thought to introduce the limequat into the equation of further identity change but proud of it's ability to adapt from others or simply get to know them in shared branching of thoughts and nurture.

Although it is possible to grow the kumquat through seeds planted, they often grow best from cuttings. Is that what has happened here? The constant cuttings to just find one place to the next before I am just a part of one aspect of acceptance or not? A kumkuat story of trying to fit in or blend. The nurture of nature is still present in this one way or another while knowing they still grow upwards naturally looking for something important to them and move accordingly to find it.

From there, a completely different approach to the students as our 7th grade teacher became our 8th grade teacher as well. No disregard to the 5th or 6th grade teacher as I still look back to that time and think about the only thing that I remember of such before going back to 4th grade repeated and restarted in more of a Montessori approach of one class per grade. You are going to grow up with these individuals so you will work it out amongst yourself on if you choose to get along with them or not. You are stuck with them until acceptance is had. The difference of sibling battles and then having to do such with those not of your kin. Understood and wise in that area. Acceptance learned early on despite differences and understanding how that can be advanced in adulthood. A lesson of simply different techniques at different ages of childhood comprehension.

So my reaction to the kumquat comments was that was become as much of a straight A student or do the best as I could for the next 2 years and there after.

Not the best, but I excelled. I went to the state science fair. I joked of sibling rivalry in the island close-up with my teacher admiring me and my accomplishments with a Maleficent shirt worn. There is always the understanding of children trying to do one thing or another for acceptance. Perhaps I found the humor of it then knowing my sister went 2nd place grand prize district and I went first when it was my time. It always happens between siblings and still hilarious that I call out such a memory wondering what the secret rivalry was on the other side. Always a Ph balance to things when it comes to waters on my end. The toxicness of fiberglass not forgotten in the long-term aspects of things not your own. Well played.

I remember speech class my 8th grade year. I don't have the speech now, but I remember writing it. the objective of the class was about being able to present an audience and move them one way or another. I don't recall exactly the speech I wrote, but I remember the quote of saying, 'I know some of you aren't my friends....' From a podium of understanding I knew then from interactions of what people say or what children do naturally. I stated my peace and understood this came after the previous year being assulted by the entire 8th grade class in protection of their cousin in my class who for some reason I never knew had a problem with myself and attacked me and from there most of the 8th grade class came in to defend him even though I was not the instigator or the problem. Held my own against practically every male of the 8th grade class before getting a black-eye and punched by one 8th grade girl who either said enough is enough or this is how this ends. I never want to hear a question since on my respect for women. It occurred in 7th grade. I walked that bruise quite nicely knowing accomplishment and who ended an action of men(boys).

On the evening of 8th grade grad night, not knowing how it would play out, but knowing the respect I wanted to give to my 7th/8th grade teacher. I wrote a speech, my mother cross-stitched an article of appreciation and flowers were bought for what was always moreso about the teacher and those empowering than belittling, During the night I didn't expect to win one award after the other. Not that it matters now, but to excel in so many things knowing what

I would have done anyways not knowing the results of such is the beauty of what I imagine both parenting or those in observance understanding one way or another. I spoke my speech as I imagine the proud 8th grader would. Reflection now to the understanding that I hit a growth spurt very early on in my life. I remember the delicate balance of a complete defeat of the other team in football that year boiling down to a 'weight issue' for the one who just couldn't be stopped at the time. A few pounds over in final weigh in on the matter but not without a red hoodie and running to the school football field the night before with practice in the morning. A thought of do you own thing in a time where children could roam to the football field of laps around 8 or 9 to lose the right amount of weight to come home and know you can't drink water, you can't take a bath. Practice the next day in the rain which probably didn't help in that regard. It was 2 or 3 pounds over the quote of 150 for the position. A forfieit provided in that regard where regardless of the weight issues now, a continuance of 7th grade into 8th where I toppled my opponents and was on the winning team despite technicalities that led into basketball season and others asking for my birth certificate before the game started. Weight matters, but I handled it over the years. One way or another. No blame. The body bounces one way or another. I look forward to the end of this marathon so I can start working out and running again. Running my mind at the moment, but it is important considering I am about to file where I cannot trust confidentiality of speaking to an attorney. Homefield advantage in that regard knowing I will fight what I never had to based on principle and I know my grounds beforehand on the matter in saying one thing or another in representation or what could had been avoided. Since Feb.10th to now. At least one source should not have been allowed into perview while understanding I witnessed the deletion of my life's work at the same time. 9 months later, not my problem if it came from there or the benefit of such. My evidence already in the EEOC and they are grounded to my evidence why I explore their evasiveness and not answuering or providing evidence. We stick to what was in the EEOC and what was wasted and what was probably advised by their attornies. I control that conversation and only based on evidence submitted in that regard. Sorry whatever was wanted to be submitted after. Narrow case of you had a chance to do right at one point or another. U chose to pass off. That goes back a couple companies wise to understand the emotional financial impact of things and the complete disregard of human life that is apparent. Voltron that to complete obsolition of technology as others upgrade. A squandwer thought of doing right as early as April 2021. 195 there at the end in whatever deals made 100x over to what is not going to happen in the lack of compassion for human life and never discussed nor privately done. When filing an EEOC there is no retaliation, that does not denote discussion in the productive side. 9 months later and understanding there was commentary during compliance meetings, my battle for fair working rights is my own. The greater battle is the complete disregard for any humanitarian requet to remove myself from the enviroment created since April 2021 and where things have gone. It is with respect to a 20 year relationship of superior and it is in respect to the 42-year history of SCAD that money talks and not a single copyright/trademark/patent class taught in that history. 2.0 can be amazing. It is already with the BBB and EEOC and denotes the same virtues of foundation while I have questions of what will be private and acceptable losses for those of wealth in what I endured and my life. I'll settle in the wittled doewn aspect of discrimination on the female side and on the Spain-born side before going into the other side of making this an American issue knowing the contrived aspect of the otherside and how I've tried to survive. One is legal, the other can be posted at any time based on business response. That is a business HR department privilage outside the EEOC and outside court proceedings. Missed that one I guess as I consider my identity of Student/Employee/Alumni knowing this came a couple years prior of privilege and I am protective of the students in what occurred and also know money talks and so do people during my private compliance meetings to no resolve after the fact based on what alreadyt occurred at 2 other places of business. Lessons of understanding since 2019 on who has what control when it comes to that discussion. Dreams the sacrifice one way or another where even in reach out dreams are forgotten or disregarded.

Thoughts from childhood to now....November 1st, 1982. It checks out and it was the same age as everyone else then of the same age. I don't need to provide *a birth certificate, but it was on file. In basketball, I was Center.*

In either regard of what I am referencing as I go from childhood to adult knowing fully well my keystrokes are recorded and thankful that I'm no longer deleted even though I understand things one way or another go through my email without my permission. I proved an argument with the BBB that if this was political I destroyed the University discussion of it being a service and they agreed upon it in back and forth. They conceeded to the notion my argument was sound yet even in such their lawyer said they would be liable if found in evidence and I gave all the evidence to support such and they constantly deflected. What do you think will happen in legality with just myself or with an attorney knowing legally I'm going to challege that any encounter with the EEOC should be by the head of HR and never with legal council pre-emptively as I am not afforded such in return. I had to state my case properly before legal council, legal council stepped in in response. I held my own and my opening discussions of the right to sue on my own by The Undited States Government is probably going to destroy this school before I even get into any personal aspects of what I occurred. I don't want that and I am all for 2.0 SCAD, but that is reality and I have already successfully argued your school and if you are still here you are a problem.

I say this now in consideration of keystrokes passed on knowing to occur in Atlanta. Zero doubt to those of 100+ million a year salary and with Disney deals of theaters and studios knowing those CEOs make 1 million a year and questioning why knowing ther ansewer of exploitation and keeper of the keys towards further exploit of either your school already proven through the SCADpro program or that of Disney that simply does not want to pay for any creative aspects in any regards and that can be discussed all the way to their devalue in revenue of streaming services and wrong approaches of breaking illusions. It happened in both regards. You cannot exploit future generations and on both regards questions raised and I have no control over where those questions went while I still sit in poverty while other profit off my work. A SCAD question or an industry question one way or another on that.

I understand the humor into adulthood well after-the-fact. It is the silent thoughts of one coming to age to be admired while understanding things on the other side that can be admired or understood in different capacities. So many silent field moments since. I came home around April/May 2022 to protect my family and mother. What occurred since was well documented and understood. I imagine record whatever you want. It has been recorded of what others have sent out and it destroys the American Dream in such and it destroys the aspect that interaction matters and zero price tag for what was allowed and what is other's legacy.

I wrote speeches to standing ovations then, and I excelled in just about everything I set my mind to. On the class night of my graduation from 8th grade I won so many class awards that evening. It was the most although I was moreso surprised than anything else. If one was to have an Oscars moment in layperson terms, that was probablty it. People kind of hated me (that came from my mother in her observnce. I understand my father wasn't there, but in single income, I totally get it. You miss out on so many things in that regard. At the same time my mother mentioned the 5th/6th grade teacher as walking out during the speech. I can't say that is true or not, but that is what I was told and I respect her and understand one thing or another. I respect the perspective as truth or simply a mother's joy. The speech was about believing in people and supporting them nevertheless.) for it but towards the end of it I stood up. Gave a speech about believing and what had been said to me in the past, and I went on to thank my 7th + 8th grade teacher for supporting and believing in me. No name ever given, but she was in the audience. I had my secret "I win" moment. Perhaps I should give better moral support to the kumquats, they thrive from cuttings, but imagine what they can do in healthy nurturing and being conditioned in the right places for proper sustainability and growth. It may or may not had happened, that is my mother's perspective but I take it as truth.

I flash to relection. It is junior year moments prior where I recall a woman (classmate) who wanted to commit suicide and I tried to stop it. A hand-drawn card for many to sign and refusal from a teacher to do such for one way or another. I don't fault, I understand teacher rules years later. A card made of flowers and continual support from peers was made.

My senior year of high school I had a girl who wanted to go out with me that I did not want to go out with. It was the same girl of sucicde from the year prior. I understand the interest of attraction from the year prior and it is understood why one would find attachment one way or another. I can get into the understanding of what is right or wrong, but simply approach this from the understanding that whatever my adolescences was, it was heard out of con-text and decided by my peers to say one way or another. That is 100% Pure Your Problem. That happened at PureRED where the continuance of what occurred at Frued/Diablo entered into another place of business and I've had to face then and into another company what other hears. Especially after, 'Oh he definitely knows' before contimating the liability they put other in before realizing the liability they themselves were in. I said it on the phone to my mother, 'They have far bigger problems if they are still on my phone.'. That at this point is even a government problem wondering if someone was president at the time with legal basis later knowing they have no authority to attack private citizens and cannot allow any form of government to do so without investiga-tion on the why and understanding it does not matter what position you hold. Have an ego or think you can gert away with it destroys America. The same could be said for any aspect of such. All the money in the US, still need to remember it is in debt and others love pulling cards in that aspect. Creditors are allowed to look at the books at any time and close down anytime based on investments. That carryover was understood by the santity of marriage at Alfred Angelo. It is understood those who cheat the system and those who are good to the system I imagine.

The back and forth understanding young adult aspects of things one way or another in subjectivity. I rejected her in an adult capacity. She went from ther e to threaten my brother at the school she worked at after-hours. That was understood then. That is understood now. That is always understood. For some reason she decided to spread around the school that I had raped her as my punishment for such. I never touched her. It took about a week for it to get back to me, but at that point everyone was looking at me or at least it was known as that is what happens in high school. That rumor even made it as far as some of the colleges that were looking at me for football scholarships. (allegedly, I was being scouted yet I cannot say one way or another that factored in any aspect. I know it was a contention of the time and defiintely things talked about in colleges. At the time I has letters to UGA and the Citadel on that asepect and what occurred occurred.)

It was not long before I proceeded to bring it to the attention of the principal in a heart-to-heart and understanding that I didn't do this and this is being spread around. It takes strength to say such then to a stranger. It takes the same to get it out of me to my parents. Both biological and my new step-mother at the time who is always my mother. It went from silent discussions of seriousness to the point of myself attempting to get a restraining order on her, and ultimately get her kicked out of high school. She didn't get kicked out of school and that is not what I wanted. I just did not want her in any class I was in and that is allowed considering what occurred and her threatening my minor brother.

Now people would think that my spiteful reaction would of been the her getting kicked out of school, but really it was something more of a personal victory for me. The personal victory is speaking your truth, understanding what occurred and understanding perception years later in retrospect. No...you don't threaten my brother. You do not talk about bashing his head against a wall and you o not remotely go into the rumor mill on something where compassion was not ncessarily an advancement and an understanding. Yes, there was sympathy...yes...I was understanding suicide at an early age. No...I have not been brought up to entertain what you wanted to entertain and things could had been dealt with so much more healthily. Yes...I understand later in life. I'm the guy who tried to commit suicide. I get it. I know it. I give one shit to what I heard at PureRED and their indirect response not knowing one thing about me and yet don't want to hear a single thing from them either knowing *what I heard caused my suicide attempt. I do not need a hand-drawn card from your company 3.5 years later. I needed discussions then. Any judgement from such is your responsibility and I don't now how to combat that without saying it could happen to you to in anything you have ever done in life and you have to question the context of the stories provided then and why. Especially after known in 2018.*

It is understood that this orignal purple type was written in 2012 and very slightly updated since and solid in blog form and what I heard at PureRED or what someone wanted to do in psychological attacks and 'he gave them everything to go for it' knowing that was PR-T in that regard. In any aspect of this is not public, this is on a private new computer bought outright completely this year for 3000 dollars that someone owes me that the memory and connection is present. Back then, threaten my underage brother in that regard of physical harm or abuse and imagine what I was going through when my mother was attacked, my best friends (in multiple arenas and federally protected) and understand that wasn't your job but at the same time where the whistle blows. I tied to commit suicide from what I experienced. Say whatever you want about me but it was done to protect those I love where whatever judgement you had then or what you wanted to do 3 years later in continuance before this book was even written is on you. Think about what was wanted then and know this book didn't exist. Think about what I just wrote and know legally in the first version sent to The United States Government, by brother is my keeper and any charity who thought they could kill someone and pick up a cause after is understood. That was 2019. I'm finishing this in December 2022 to be done with this aspect knowing this book mattered and factored. I don't give a fuck about co-workers I never talked to. Their opinions open the door to the same level of scrutiny understanding I don't need to know it but someone way be interested to give an opinion on it.

I look back and see, at the time I was still very much a virgin. That change didn't occur until college. I've messed around and did quite a bit prior, but nothing that is constituted full on sex. Scientific on both regards in exploration in the beginning of same age or simply flips of a fingernail on a bedroom door to say no and go downstairs. Interest always there, but I reserve my first time in that regard to be sacred and of understanding. Years from this encounter while understanding things early on. I don't care when I first expored or when I first penetated. It is none of your business and always in respect of those involved with zero conversation of others and discourse for those who simply want to know one way or another.

Flashing back to high school, I guess in my mind I kind of just figured...ok.... well I can do all of this area, but I am going to make damn sure no woman is ever going to say I raped her ever again. I didn't even ask for this and I'm not about to be the problem to someone I cared enough about to make sure they didn't commit suicide. I get it then. I get it now. Compassion in that regard is confusing except in the aspect she threatened my brother. She actually said she weould bash his head against the tailer in the back of the school. I go further in detail only because complete strangers made this a talking point. I understand at this point the compete dangers of women as much as men to manipulate a situation one way or another. I am new to outside ventures doing the same without understanding talking to any party or in my regard, the originator or property where I don't care how many camera session loveers you have against me now. we made love, it was in agreeement and anything else is vindictive and not a part of my present. The pettiness of one thing or another exists. Guess what? Women can be as equally cruel as men and that is com-pletely understood in equal opportunity. No discrimination there.

What did you think would happen when you threaten everyone I love and care for? I don't give a shit about the insecurity of a woman in a perceived man's world. I tried to comfort her. That was turned against me and anything my mother said was a possible intrusion to their ego and understanding knowing they are not equipt for knowing private phonecalls or transcripts of such. I understand on the PureRED front, this is before your time. Why did you not talk to me then or now? Do you understand how much legality involved or how much I could sue in favor of your company? Do you understand what I heard? Do you understand how what I heard was prior to my employment to you?

Do you understand what I was protecting? Some of you do. That I under-
stand. The judgement and the perception cannot be taken back and that was
2019. What could you have done then?

I'm aware of what I put up with in an environment of people who don't know
me already had been in an environment of people who don't know me. Con-
tractual basis does not denote that level of connection nor do I give such 3-4
years later as my family of hope was lost while you have your families and
made your decisions to steal mine in the process.

First job> Woman'ed owned family company. Second Job> Woman superior
of a 80 year+ Family company history. Female CD was not the right fit for
me hired at the same time. When the female last family member of the compa-
ny they build I can attest to that and talk about 'paternal' expoitation. It ran
it's course. From there, I can go specifically into the fixed-termed position of
Female head contractor experience to bounce into the next position not female
led with the most respect of confidence from a female superior to the suicide
attempt to months of no insurance or job only to return to a female superior 20
years prior and mother-figures twice over of Spanish decent and African Amer-
ican on either side. 'She found it.' She reacted. It came into any qustions I had
once I left November 2, 2018 were between myself and Randstad. Neither
talked to me about it even though I reported properly.

What ever excuse you wanted to make, I heard it at Freud/Diablo and you are
not going to be able to perpetuate that without talking about that female inse-
curities in a company that wa not on-boarding at the time and manipulating
things to where we are now. You manipulated then, withheld and still I have
not interacted directly to say one way or another.

Do you want to continue to try me with the woman I proposed to and was en-
gaged to 20 years prior on your corporate bullshit of knowing you cannot pass
go in this regard?! This is where we are and this is what I hold privately. The
adacity of someone entering SCAD is already there and it comes from the same
behavior they either know or are a part of. How personal do you want to get

with this? How much have you seen that isn't in this book to tell you maybe other people have taken notice and you need to stop?

I can see where collusion may have possibly occurred with my 20-year Spanish mother figure. Compassion on my part may had been an advantage of others. I see the same with companies during Kroger deals knowing if it was those who had every version of my website and didn't want to talk to me then or 3 years later, Kroger and food on the table involved in what is beyond your company worth.

You have attacked me to the point that we are straight up at the barrier of my entry to adult life and I am severely protective of her and her family and I know it is the same on the other side. I was protetive then, I was protective in my youth. What story do you want to spin in recorded keystrokes in the aspect of not paying me anything and still sending out the material that has already been incorporated in your company. I am well beyond Disney at this point to say my importance is on the fact of discimination at SCAD to myself while talking about the exploitation of SCADpro in the process. SCAD had 9 months to deal with this privately. Others 3 years. Others longer. I'm not backing down from what your employer allowed and I'm pretty sure anyone reading this is not the owner or decision maker for the company or The United States of America.

Even if only I was the one to know that I am a virgin. That occurred later in life and explored in 'Chasing Jabberwocks'. I have already spoken of my intrusion to such and what I wrote then. It is understood to some level the protection I have placed in that regard to those I care most for. If anything, a reason I reached out after-the-fact to warn or protect. I protect what I can even if it is not mine to do so. I take my responsibility of notice. I can not take responsibility on the other side. All I can do is stay away and protect. I reclaimed 'Chasing Jabberwocks' only for others to take it again. At least that time it was noted it came with copyright notices.

If one wanted to get into the sexual questions further at this point, I shall continue with full knowledge that dating apps and conversations factored at Freud/Diablo in 2018 from outside sources that became internal.

Then comes college. More girls, still not really connecting or sealing the deal for whatever reason. Moments one way or another but never the privacy nor the setting to go much further. I can talk about growing up and can still content that whatever slip the finger expressed at any age is no different of that of their own in the same exploration and that was about the extent of it. If one wanted to be word of mouth if that is where we are at now, then yes, words spoken but never a moment taken that would be considered anything traditional. That is where we are at and what is what I have been through. Can anyone provide security from that or are we simply going to go back to the question I sought an answer on in the matter I never had a problem with anyone corporately or of expense until after the fall of Alfred Angelo

What story are you going to tell or are you just going to continual exploit me and say this was sad and we stand by him after his death?! I see what has been happening in one perspective and this is why I refuse to watch streaming.

But at one point someone slipped in.
I guess you could say literally, but I'll leave the metaphors alone.

I let go of that past spite and gave myself a chance at it. I ended up having a relationship with someone who in my mind was the most perfect woman in the world. That has never changed even though life says one thing or another and others can do better than I ever could at a relationship. Years latered welcomed. Years beyond this original writing and years beyond where things occurred or where they are now. I couldn't be happier for others. That is important to I. Both from an inadequacy aspect and from life moving on and understanding love continues in all of it's forms.

On some level she still remains that to me. But anyways I figured at one point that she was the one. Later I expanded to he is the one and now I am much more open to the idea of any right connection, if it be true, to be of value. There is no one. It is a compounded interest until someone decides they want to compound their interest with you. Shared interest of trust and intimacy where never I want to bother with the aspect of other's indirectly involved. I've experienced that enough to know professionally and privately that is a problem in my current stance. I can't do that to anyone.

We got engaged on July 4th. Fireworks on display of River Street in Savannah where to this day I remember the importance of others chiming in vs. what the actual moment was. Protectionism of course from a friend stand-point and of friendly competition. It was an understood aspect as that day transitioned over the years that I respected it as not 'our' day anymore and the transformation od such into the life you had with the most amazing aspect of admiration for such. So many years we called one another in friendship of what occurred until I no longer felt comfortable. It wasn't our day anymore and it was important to I to respect both of your days whether one knew it or not. I just wanted you happy and to have a life. I'm happy for you and happy you have a life and a family. I'm protective if I need be, but I know you are in good hands and have started a family. I thank you that you have entertained the idea of when I wanted to start one as well and we discussed such on the beach. So much has passed and yet we are still here as friends. 'You're so thin' equallty heard in the aspects of 'I'm not ideal at the moment.' An understanding of friendship knowing we have both been through one thing or another and I could tell you anything and can't tell you anything at the same time. I gave something then and now of importance to maybe understand. Assurance of understanding something I can't tell you completely. I know it was respected. That is important to I even if I never express it and it is never required. I am happy you are happy and that is all that matters. What is sacred is beyond us and always in friendship bond.

and she moved in with me at my house while I was going to school. We were too young at the time and I was too naive. Eventually over time school took more time out of my life than I could dedicate to her and she began to question

my actions on things. The dedication of youth wondering who I am reconcil-
ing with knowing at this point it is simply with myself knowing I talk to one
daily and the other I give the same respect to knowing years and married at
this point and I never in a position to even entertain even a partner or a hope
of anything because others have made it so.

The joys of any relationship...the discovery of insecurity, the conversations.
The touch if only to understand what one wants or doesn't. An intimacy
aspect of physical essential understanding the importance of being able to go to
sleep next to someone at the end of the day with probable discussion of where
lives diverges and converge at the same time. Discussion points outside of the
office and of understanding of things before one position or another. Who are
U? Who are We? A difference of lives knowing we all have our own and we
can not share everything.

That is either from the professional aspect or from the need of things personal
while building things intimately on the same front. Fascets one way or another
in my life where I cherish while trying to understand what you cherish. I un-
derstand where we connect and where we do not. It is never my place to pine or
denote properly as everyone of them committed elsewhere and that is not of my
motivation ever. Happy for love found. Happiness in investments well beyond
what was directly 'ours'. We had our moments. You have yours. I'll have mine.
I don't pine for what was no effort directly in and I hope it is understood my
journey had in what is, what could had been and what will be. I've had to
realize more sacrifice than gain knowing what could had been explained prior.
I cite youth. I cite others where I find beauty later in translation while I suf-
fered. In any regards,' How could I see it any different?' Love comes over time
and in the day-to-day. I love you and I know that matters if you never meet
me or one of us blew the chance when it was physical.

and on some level forbad me from hanging out with my gay friends. Perhaps
she always knew I questioned myself about it, but for me I made my com-
mitment and I made my choice. She was the one I wanted to be with. I speak

in fairness in this aspect. I reflect on it such also from the perspecive of why I chose to go into bridal and be at the forefront of statements in acceptance knowing that has always been important to I one way or another. I can speak of times when it was easier for others to question and I can speak of times of simply learning to manscape and go from there. Never the fault of one or the other in understanding that maintenance is important to be upheld. Time and change understanding we were not brought up in one world or another and from such the introduction to one world or another. I understand your questions. I understood them. I looked at myself in the aspect of if this is the one I was to be with, I need to know no questions asked. A hard decision for a 20 year old but I had already understood adult relationship and the negative conse-quences proir in the aspect of a divorced child life. I needed to know for me to not question my life while understanding atttraction. I made my commitment to you and I can spend my life with you in that regard knowing exploration is there and the idea of challenges and roles. A question since my youth where even in my adulthood I don't discount as one wants the body of another or one would one thing for another in desirement. Thoughts well beyond 2003,but in appreications and admiration goals are set and it is not necessarily sexual. There is a desire for the body. There is a desire for the commitment and there is the understanding that regardless of the seriousness, there is laughter about this. If not then it simply isn't worth it if it is compleete judgement.

By the end of the first year of our engagement she ended up getting pregnant. I had my WTF am I going to do moment and sole searching, but I was ready on some level to be a dad. To relive the moment now is one of the most exciting and scariest things one can ever go through. I remember the fear. I remember telling my mother I was going to be a dad in my car. the shock of such to-someone to be a grandmother just as much as I remember the introduction to engagement knowing I didn't even ask the parents at first and it just felt right at the time. Almost a year in on the agreement, it was understood we would get married after I graduated, as if that would solidify a job at the time. It was important to I to understand if we are to build a family, I need to deliver such in ways my parents did prior. The preganacy threw me for a loop then.

I always wanted to be a dad. I remember telling my mother such when it was going to happen. Joy there while understaining I know nothing nor afforded enough to remotely do this. I am still in school. We are building a life and yet neither of us can do this. What am I to fall back on? What do I need to do?

My focus was on my education and I wouldn't be surprised if this was around the time I switched from a painting major to graphic design. Reality shifts and it becomes a big difference when you know you are about to be a father one way or another. Food on the table. Provide. I understand sacrifice at this point. I understand a great deal of things.

Turns out I should of dedicated more time to her over that year, as it came out later on that week when I started back tracking dates and numbers and realizing they did not match up to anything I could of done. When she needed attention after what I sure was some argument....she ended up sleeping with my roommate.

I cannot ever fault a 20 year old just as much I would never want the same of I. The same age understanding where one wishes a life t that speed once provided and now a surity of unsurity. So young, yet knew the value that was there. If one is to understand one side it is to understanf the other either in relation or no comparison. The after-math is from life experience. I wrote this 10 years ago noting I was referenceing 6-7 years prior. A silent aspect of such knowing that bond is sacred. To say you are on the one and someone saying yes and understanding growith in thought is a great deal of intimacy.

I can't say too much for 20 year olds because we were doing it, but a great deal where communication is important of you are going for that kind of gold. In all the retrospect of what occurred, I know I needed to know about my interest in interaction with men one way or another. Not always sexual and a sign of the times, but it was questions from my youth on appreciation. Even now I'll never discount a male or female figure of dedication. The body is beautiful in any regard. For I at the time, I needed to know one way or another to either never entertain or open up discussion one way or another for what is riight for you. I needed to know the question of attraction that years later, not that it matters , there is beauty in any form and I chose to be obstenant with you from this point on until proven comfortable.

I try to be fair of the situation and understanding one way or another. We were young and we have talked this out later in life which gives me a little bit more comfort and understanding of respect on the otherside. I'd never hurt you any more than what I did and that is from a friendship aspect knowing we got each other in that regard on way or another. I recount the scenario one way or another. I find comfort in the Jerry Springer aspect of it know it is so far from such. A turn of events understanding it doesn't matter which came first, it was what came after.

..lost it and left the house. Out of spite I did the one thing I had always questioned about myself and the one thing that I knew would drive her over the edge. (I can't erase my words or what was presented originally. All I can do is say comlications in the shadow side of things and we have talked it out 20 years later in this regard while knowing the invasion of privacy met. From hurt comes the best friendships.) Shortly after or before I went out to find my answers, I needed to know so, I went out and hooked up with my best friend and very very soon after telling her I was gay. I didn't tell her and I still don't know the answer one way or another. It is not category to be placed in. It is a case by case knowing I'm limited to any understanding at this point in understanding of why I can't reach out to anyone.

A combination of thoughts where I imagine and know different conversations then vs. now. It doesn't matter in the scheme of things, Someone I stayed with for 3 years after while never knowing what I contimplated with us back and forth. I imagine the same on the other side. In either regard, we both went through it and I never once talked about it properly nor divulged in a single relationship. I wouldn't anyways. It doesn't matter when things combine. It doesn't compare in any aspect to my life just as much as I know what it was then on the other side. We hurt. We grew. We thrived seperately.

A connection there of non-seperation knowing even when it was done, we were a part of each other and perhaps never told or understood the connection of what occurred on my side or yours knowing exactly years later what it meant to you. I remember phonecalls as much as I remember letters. I appreciate the understanding and seeing things on multiple fronts.

To this day, I go to my grave saying, "you know what...I made a commitment to one woman and at least I can say when I die is that I kept my promise.'

I've held that for multiple reasons. A child was lost. From one way or another it happened and there is forgiveness, but at the same time I've never brought myself to be with a woman again. Not frrom fear and not from lack of idea of exploration. It comes from the questions I've had on not so much if it was my child as it was then, just as much as it doesn't matter if it was a boy or girl. It is a combination of I failed as a father from the get go where I can say I was I 20 all I want, it is the unknown factor I needed to know just as much as the unknown factors of the woman's rights were not mine to choose. For me whether it was or was not my child, I've understood a child was lost from my 20s and not knowing the world. From there that level of trust was never allowed since as I explored a natural side of myself knowing it is no different the the admiration of a magazine one way or another or the understand of 'I wish I could be like you' one way or another through dedication or genetics. Perhaps the Norman Rockwell dream went deeper in understanding one way or another. Can't always be our parents and, as a child of divorce, I don't exactly idealize mine. I just saw the complication of adult relationships early on. I never touched a woman afterwards from that. I made my commitment. I had questions. I sought them out as others did as well. I failed as a father at the get go and it cost a life of a child because I couldn't provide and I was not ready. It was not my choice but was as well.

But anger sparked me to take a leap of faith and to find out an answer to a question I needed to know for myself. A positive came from that. I think one of my regrets with that whole scenario is that I could not bring it to myself to take the chance that the child was not mine. I could not consider changing my entire life because of two other people. She aborted it and to this day it breaks my heart wondering….what if I was wrong? Did I indadvertedly kill my child. Did I fail as a father before even getting to really be one? I'll never know that answer and neither will she…but I think about it from time to time and one day I hope to fix that with another chance.

In this regard only, I think of that sacrifice knowing education, work, dedication was important to eventually get back to that point of security maybe with someone if time allowed. That never happened to that level and a series of events from 2017—present denotes that any aspect of what I needed to for my child or family didn't matter in any regard to what I was processing and representing in 2012 knowing I gave enough and it was no one's business in that regaed to understand what I heard of dissection of my life in 2019 thinking you knew 2012 me thinking you knew 2003 me or any aspect prior. I was ripped to shreds by strangers then and all I feel is that they would do it there after knowing Curated Jellyfish was not even written at the time and the most real parts od me are reserved and you still don't understand indirectly.

Someone ripped imy life away from me anyway on either front and still just want to come after me for it regardless of what I built. I traded my child whether mine biologically or not for a career. That was what I needed to deal with as I proceeded with life. I did the most amazing things to make up for that thinking of them one way or another and that was stolen. I working towards parenting and adulting since 2011. My child the inspiration for my coming back and fighting while experiencing the most amazing things at the tie or writing and in other books past 2019. Continually amazed and continually told or to felt like it is ok and do this. This is reality and this is truth. There is no indirect make up for that which could had been done years ago. There is always a talk and there is always an understanding. There is no subtle nod to that understanding of what occurred. Even today I continued to elimate variables of reasonable unerstanding.. I no desire to speak of attacking an unborn child, but it happened for one reason or another. At least in that regard I can say whatever comapany connection does not matter. Well beyond the company of 2017 and simply trying to find answers to what was presented and hope none factored into the last 5 years. Especially when you never wanted me to profit off my own life's work. A multi-framed reference in that regard. Well beyond the bullshit at this point.

Moving from there I'll not be so involved in my spiteful stories.

I got raped so later on in life when I needed to overcome that I became a stripper as a way to bring peace and control back into my life on the matter. I played people at the club and they knew it was an act, but basically for all intents and purposes I took their money on the promise they were getting something and then 'opps....times up.' I took sexual control back over myself. I was always amazed by those that I was in a relationship with ever questioning my fidelity while I was under the influence. I would never allow an impaired situation for me to ever be put in that situation again. I guess I never articulated that the right way.

I think in consideration of this paragraph not carefully but understanding I needed to make ends meet. A flash forward of about 6 years and I still remember the honestly of saying what I was doing early on in a realtionship and that being ok. I still contend never a hotter moment than being naked in a room of strangers giving a dance to the person you love knowing they probsbly have their own contentions for being there or not. The fact that I'm naked with everyone around to see and there is only so much you can do and this is my table and my house of rules...to expereince that with a partner to get close in any aspect to smelll, tease, get in even any aspect of their space is a moment of understanding that it doesn't matter what I am doing for anyone else. You atre here, this is my house and I am completely ready to seduce you and go home to you at the end of the night. It was few and far between and I understand the contention, but the seduction and the allure was real knowing when I left it to keep my relationship, the seduction could or did follow. My relationship was important at the time and over and over I've proven I'm far more adventurous that others. I just understand communicsation at this point. Long gone the stripper days of trying to make ends meet, surivive and reclaim one thing or another. Never a discount the aspect of being with someone and trying to seduce them completely naked in a public private space knwoing you don't give a fuck who sees what you are doing. This is my moment. This is ours. This is someone who chooses to be with me at the time and I am going to seduce you nakedly in front of anyone who cares to look. It doesn't matter who is in the room. So rare and far between. Right now there is only you and I. Do you see me? I do not blame you and you didn't believe me I was a dancer. You are here. So am I. They call me one thing and you call me another. My focus is on you only where money doesn't matter to having you see me so nakedly. A space safe while I work things out one way or another. I lost you once and was able to go from there to know the mistakes made. I needed time to think. So did you. A second chance occurred and not a thrice from there in either's unspoken aspects of connection and confusion.

The intensity os such. Do our eyes meet? Can they? Can you look past what I have to do knowing you are here right now and I don't give a fuck about anyone else. Strength present in nakedness and honesty. I'd leave it all if it affected us in any capacity. I need to surivive and I need to take control of my body and my life in a manner where house rules and my rules. I go home to you. Do you want me or cherish me? It doesn't matter. You are in my sight. You are all I want and never would want this job but at the same time how can I not profess my love any other way that being in this manner with you here? I imagine on the other side it is quite different. I respect it then. I respect it now. A memory of passion and understanding that transfers in some regard after on either side in life.

It mattered. Overtime the relationship ended, but the memory exists. At least in that regard, seduction existed. Others well beyond my timeline. All I can say is be free a bit, but obviously do your own thing. It is a requirement for anyone to know individuality just as much as individually comes from connection of one person or another understanding part of us never detaches from the memories of the past not knowing which one is I or which one is U. Love at the time. Love now in understanding I was a fleeting thougt in comparison to life or something to hold onto. Transformation of words, thoughts and feelings towards whereever they may go. A dance that transitions from one song to the next never knowing which one is going to be the next on the track to find a rhythm to go along with it in introduction. Great memories of enjoy your 20s one way or another perhaps. Do it to identify, discover or to make ends meet. Regardless of anything else, love the one you are with or be adventurous about it one way or another. Either the one who walks with you 24/7 or those who choose their own adventures that involve you in one capacity or another.

Gave up that life knowing what was home was far more important. and seeing how things worked around one way or another that applies corporately in lessons of one independant company vs. another all working the same space and in the same industry. Best to just go into data collection and change the way to connect and make ends meet. An understanding of observace, awareness of environment and knowing it is the communication and connection people look for that is not entirely seduction. A conversation of honesty does the trick in a world outside these walls where one may or may not be able to be who they want to be. Even inside, I am not who I say I am but I am as well. A learning of a new name and identity. Not many know who I am and we are discovering it together or simply watched from the distance in non-interaction.

I've failed in some areas, but at least I knew when it comes home and focus presents itself one way or another.

Lets see in timelines of travelling years cocurrently, I got punched in the face by a best friend for partying with some other friends. I did not hit him back, but I sure as hell stole his boyfriend overtime. I never understood the initial punch. Perhaps unspoken words where I try to recall the attraction at the time *but nothing ever really came of such. Completely different people from ititial introduction to what I am pretty sure was one of the last times we hung out. We talked later in life, but priorities on way or another were different. The inability to articulate a commone thread between myself and others. it comes in youth and either is learned later in life or simply left dormant and repressed inside not knowing what to do with it. Whe it comes to what naturally, it is understood connections happen all the time and can be predictable or not. Once can't help a conversation leading one way or another. It. happens naturally in communication and they weren't together at the time anyways. A respect of what actually was an amazing relationship until they moved away and joined the Navy. Even then a letter here and there of handwrote nature where one section of their heart I am placed and part of their family one way or another. That was before the days of dancing yet still a fondness of reconnetion years later and knowing respect when giving the privilege of meeting people's part-ners and the ones they end up choosing to spend their life together. I ended up loving him, but he moved away.*

I think the main breakup is self explanatory at this point, that I went on to become an artist and speak the truth or my version of things of life and attempted to grow very publicly and artistically. A open invitation for people to join in or watch from a distance one way or another. I think that was kind of my last major spite moment. I will survive, I'll thrive and I'll start balancing out my own dreams and find ways to get there. I have not had another since as spite is really another word for resilience and holding on one way or another to something. It always get translated one way or another. Holding on to some-thing or dreaming of others. A crossroad constantly understanding paths and introductions are there and possible. Every crossroad adds up to position in one place or another. The board a metaphor for life where it changes every time you play it before understanding others may have positioned you one way or another elsewhere based off a series of strategic placement. The motivation of one maneuver over another never knowing unless asked, shared or spoken. Some-times it is in silence it is still known there is protection of one thing or another on the board.

I will turn a negative into a positive and I will find my ways to better myself and understand myself.

I'll throw myself out there at my own expense if I think I can learn something about myself from it.

I'd say talking about the positive influence of things, kickstarter (Heroes + Villains #3) definitely was an example of that.

I had to really push myself. I had to reach in and I think it was only through the support of others that I was able to make it to the end and then it was all on me to make sure I delivered on my promises. I believe I did.

Since then I have more people in my life telling me you can do this, push yourself than what I had over the years of people saying 'no' or people creating this version of me far from the truth while other versions of me are understood to be one thing or another. It always depends on perspective, introductions and what names get used to understand the masks and fascets of identity.

Perhaps at some point I'll talk about my pride knowing that I have that perception on lockdown now. That power just is not given out anymore. I think at some point I will need to go on faith and handing over some of that control to someone again if I ever plan on having a meaningful, lasting relationship.

Until I hit that point where I know who I am and how I can break the negative cycles that I go through; I see no reason for me to hand that over to mold me as they want to see me. I need to mold and find me for myself first. I imagine there is more of that happening directly/indirectly anyways where molded in memories and experience it is a question of where am I being pushed while I am pulling in other directions. Perhaps an understanding of foundation and knowing we are all sculptures of collaboration between ourselves and others. I'm heading in that direction, but I have to trust my gut that I've been molded enough for the time being until I try this and see what is wanting to come out and be refined and discovered.

I believe it is out there and that I will be able to give it again. I think of all these experiences and then some have lead for me to not ever judge people and find beauty in even the most hated of things.

Everyone has a story, a reason.
Some break.
Some keep going.

Everyone on some level should be treated with compassion.

We all fall eventually.
Publicly or Privately.

————

I don't consider myself the best writer by any means.
I'm actually pretty horrible at it.
I see whatever cadence I come upon as fluid throughout change and I witness me rewriting the story as I go and how I go about.
Rules were there.

Quote of something old,
talk about something new,
advance the narrative as life allows you
Just be at peace with what was and what is.

You can't take back words.
You can't take back actions.
And yet I find myself revising.

I write how I think and that may not be right,
but it's true to me.

I have to look a back and remember intent.

Granted in this scenario it was something from a previous official post this time so I can call myself out accordingly on that. Looking at the past always changes things once someone finds the right words and able to place themselves back in one time-frame or state of mind to recollect the emotion then. Months ago. Years ago. Now a decade past knowing it goes back further and yet still factors into my present and future of life lessons and love one way or another. It will always inflict reflection.

What you saw then may not be what you see now.
I'd say either are deceptive tools to make you question thought or just go with the flow that you will figure it out as you go. An understanding of learned environment and the world from your perspective.

If you look at what you wrote in the past, it has meaning to flesh it out.

Perhaps you didn't proof it or see that you didn't articulate exactly what you want to say then. Grammar is understood, but once you get the intention of words and learn the patterns it becomes a way to know where things were going or perhaps good intentions done in different manners. I'm a little better now, but I still see me fleshing things out the day after as opposed to click and done. Perhaps it's better now. Perhaps it's not. Maybe it will be later. Keep trying knowing if it is something to constantly revisit, get a little more true and undetstand the lapse of time and increase of life experiences to compound the original aspects of such knowing it is difficult to focus solely on one place before going to another.

God knows one way or another. It will be whatever it will be to others. It matters what it means to you. Regardless of everything, you can't erase the past. You can choose to not speak or write of it but the initial experience is what cannot be rewritten or changes. Only the reflection of it is capable of change of perspective. The initial experience is what is. The memory is the dance and fluid in motion. A seemingly solid form that is always contingent of the one looking at it. An identity forms and then is lost understanding the same thing will never be seen the same. I imagine there is not a single person reading this right now that ever did not wish to change something they did. To say that is untrue means they came out the womb knowing everything and ready to approach the world and ready for work upon exit. I imagine we do that anyways, it just isn't understood how to translate that as we learn our environment and how to work from one variable to the next until we figure out what we knew silently and how to realize that in the world. I know that for sure.

It is possible there is not a single person reading this that is perhaps judging and just waiting to see what I post next. That I am unsure of.

No scandal here at this point. Only either peace, personal resolution or personal acceptance to my life. That's probably not that interesting to some. Perhaps that is why not many read Paradiso. It's the hardest to relate to in subjective aspects while looking at what is amazing to discover what 'Heaven' is for one person or another. Even Dante struggled with concluding it and still deferred to others constantly along the way knowing where he lacked and where he excelled. I felt copped out from the journey he created for himself or perhaps just now understanding it more later in life. A combination of what surrounded my journey then and what surrounds it now, an understanding the hidden aspects of words and journey of intention. There is clearly judgement in his Heaven and that is going to always exist. As one reconciles what is most important to them, one finds that even in 'Heaven' there is condemnation and then move on from it towards something else of enlightenment and discovery. I imagine towards the same conclusion of not spelling out one's entire life, the ending of *The Commedia* denotes the same questions of life and of any great narrative. 'What's next?' What's after Heaven? What about the return from Heaven? What else is there to learn or discover? From there invested interest of self-discovery down one path or another. In that it is completely masterful where the deferance to other artist comes from in the Comedy of Life and searching for answers and directions.

When you look at what I've created it comes from a place of mental 'heaven'. It is not the same thing as what Dante discussed, but opens up the idea of what Dante was experiencing or processing one way or another. How can this apply outside the context of such with the understanding everything is wrapped in there as well. The presentation of such requires it. Do we ever get there (to mental Heaven)? Do we find our answers? I don't know. I really don't. There are always the unshared and unasked questions that makes it complicated in one veiled aspect or another.

I like to think we do though. It is possible to get there and understand that there are places one goes to feel safe, accomplished and secure. It is found in the home. It is found in your city, your country and expands from one individual perspect to the next understanding we all long for a moment of serenity of life understanding the world around us is all doing it's own thing one way or another. I have faith we do find it eventually. That sense of understanding is perhaps found most often when one lays down to sleep understanding your body and soul tells you to relax, be calm and simply rest and process your day in a different capacity before returning the next day to one things or another. There is **hope** we process and instinctually find that place one way or another in however it seems fit for ourselves individually.

To be honest no words I ever write is going to make anyone feel completely better. I am just a pitstop on the way towards one thing or another. It is the time of day or night considered or not in either capacity. I hope I don't make you feel worse. I try to process just as much as others may be processing. Perhaps a solution individually or collectively towards one answer or another. The process I am trying to work on, I think, comes to personal responsibility in any regard. I don't know that anyone would accept that answer unless they were willing to accept that for themselves. I guide, but it means nothing if it is not what you are interested in exploring or understanding.

I'm trying to think about everything I just experienced.
Just relax, reflect and think about every day that came prior.
Each day of Italy documented before going back and documenting the days prior to that, then the months...years...and I find yourself looking at life understanding it was a gift to experience it all and learn from it every day. Perhaps a question of understanding there is always a what's next and to balance out the past and future in the now.

I find it hard thinking about what is coming.
But I do have to give myself credit that I did this.
So much fear and doubt. It's not attractive.

I find myself in a window seat once again where this time I am a little bit more compacted to press up against the window. Thoughts of size not relative in this regard, it is understood the scenario of understanding the pressurized space and forced perspective to look out the window on my journey. The panes of it understanding to look at all the places I could go in life or never will. In any aspect a realization of being in a tight situation and returning to one. I make do one way or another and simply go about it as I figure out how to fit into the space provided of maximizing the economy value of such.

I feel at this point I have to be more honest now than I was before. A constant struggle to understand more honesty later in life and still the more honest I get, the more secrets get glossed over and not spelled out. I can't sit here and entertain the aspect that I pretend was not an issue for me one way or another. In the world of Instagram my life, I've successfully made a point I can never do that without talking about things that are uncomfortable. If we do not talk about the things that make us uncomfortable then how are we to grow one way or another. Approach is important where it is understood environment and application matter. It is more often discussions of uncomfortability and insecurity are held more privately than in situations where others could simply take an insecurity and use it as an advantage towards control one way or another against the one looking to connect, understand and grow together collectively or individually. That's who I am. I understand or attempt to comprehend one thing or another. I don't judge (although it is nearly impossible to do so internally one way or another based on learned perception of one thing or another. It is more an observance of note in mental discriptors that determines one thing or another). I want to listen. If you don't want to listen then you don't have to. Everything is a choice just as much as one could approach one thing or another objectively or expressively. Between the two the beauty of balance and understanding the difference. Individuality is an awesome thing. Not everyone is willing to be that while nothing wrong with the constant desire to fit in. More than likely people want both. To be noticed and to be a part of something...anything. Strength in communities and in numbers knowing even in solo journeys, there are still those invisible entities we keep in our heads and heart through memory and points of reference. Individuality definitely comes with pluses and minuses towards understanding identity and our attributes of strengths and weaknesses.

I'm currently on the plane at the moment.
I'm leaving Italy and heading to NYC.
I'll spend time with my brother.
I'll meet my niece for the first time.
That is what I want to see the most.

My brother is the person I wish I could have been. He's such a good soul and avoids hurt and has everything going for him. I'm not jealous of it. I admire it. I love everything about who he is and what he is doing and I don't know if I had a factor in that, but I like seeing him happy. I'll avoid my sister for now. I've seen her and have been angry with her. I want to see normalcy and innocence. I don't think she can fault me for that. I think I want to avoid my dad but at the same time I am curious. Unresolved issues I was thrown into especially when it comes to the collection of my grandmother's portrait finally. A constant ask to send it after my grandfather's passing a constantly putting it off and not getting around to it. I haven't seen him in 4 years and he never really made an effort to visit in Atlanta while I visited when I could in Alabama. Always a disruption of thought and communication knowing I am not exactly like my father, but half of me is there one way or another. I don't forget anything. But at the same time I'm scared to meet my creator in that regard. A difference when talking about one aspect of Creator vs. the other. Our parents created us and their parents created them and it goes all the way back towards one answer or another or several.

I'm scared of what I'll learn.
Scared of what I would feel.
But if I really was honestly so scared, I would have avoided this opportunity entirely. I'm doing this.
All of this out of spite or out of curiosity?

Regardless. It's happening. An entire hurricane of events have formed to throw me from one intended path towards another in extension of thoughts and process. It is an amazing series of events to understand the importance of the objective expressionist aspect of life and who's watching and able to move things one way or another in translations and transitions.

Until I land... continued thoughts in flight. Perhaps I'll sleep for a bit. I know where I'm heading. The beauty of familiarity and going from there while considering the unfamiliar and enjoying both aspects of such. Which is more exciting?

Upon reflection, how many travels could I have done one way or another in my lifetime? If this was my first, it was well spent and unfolding as we go. Thoughts of further adventures once I get back on my feet only to be able to fly off somewhere else again.

Thoughts from the clouds as if an aquarium of flying fish in the air moving in one direction or the next of different directions and points of perspective. An aquarium of such that hides in and out of the clouds where if one were to go further would look at such as a school of likeness swimming one way or another going in and out of rock formations and through the oceans blue. Never touching. Never landing neither one place or another. Simply stopping points before going one place or another. The imagination of air travels elsewhere where in reality a hurricane transforms a vacation from one path to another where I consider what is in the air of discussion and intended purpose of destinations of airplanes predetermined. Real and imaginary trips from one point to another understanding flight patterns of behavior?

Where would my next trip be?
Too early to tell.
Enjoy the one you are on in extension.

If anything from here on out I am joining The Aisle-High Club on longer travels. The external/nternal thinking one way or another grows exponentially until perhaps over water I have more space to breathe. Until then touchdowns along the way of multi-point destinations.

Perhaps internal/external for the next trip.
If only for when I need to stretch out one thing or another
or know when to take a break.

{Sleep}

'Thoughts from the Clouds' - Sketch Translation' December 3, 2022. "Philip A. Bonneau.

Milton Keynes UK
Ingram Content Group UK Ltd.
UKRC032207170724
445721UK00006B/29

* 9 7 9 8 8 9 0 3 4 7 5 6 5 *